RACE IN YOUNG ADULT SPECULATIVE FICTION

Children's Literature Association Series

RACE IN YOUNG ADULT SPECULATIVE FICTION

EDITED BY
MEGHAN GILBERT-HICKEY AND
MIRANDA A. GREEN-BARTEET

University Press of Mississippi | Jackson

The University Press of Mississippi is the scholarly publishing agency of the Mississippi Institutions of Higher Learning: Alcorn State University, Delta State University, Jackson State University, Mississippi State University, Mississippi University for Women, Mississippi Valley State University, University of Mississippi, and University of Southern Mississippi.

www.upress.state.ms.us

The University Press of Mississippi is a member of the Association of University Presses.

Elizabeth Ho's chapter previously appeared in *The Victorian Era in Twenty-First Century Children's and Adolescent Literature and Culture*, edited by Sonya Sawyer Fritz and Sara K. Day © 2018. Reproduced by permission of Taylor and Francis Group, LLC, a division of Informa plc.

Copyright © 2021 by University Press of Mississippi
All rights reserved

First printing 2021
∞

Library of Congress Control Number: 2021934630
Hardback ISBN 978-1-4968-3381-5
Trade paperback ISBN 978-1-4968-3382-2
Epub single ISBN 978-1-4968-3383-9
Epub institutional ISBN 978-1-4968-3384-6
PDF single ISBN 978-1-4968-3385-3
PDF institutional ISBN 978-1-4968-3386-0

British Library Cataloging-in-Publication Data available

To our children, who remind us to look
at the world through young eyes

Contents

Acknowledgments xi

Introduction 3
Miranda A. Green-Barteet

I. Defining Diversity

Blood Rules: Racial Passing and the Commodification
of Difference in Victoria Aveyard's *The Red Queen* 15
Sarah Olutola

The Fairy Race: *Artemis Fowl*, Gender, and Racial Hierarchies 35
Kathryn Strong Hansen

Enchanting the Masses: Allegorical Diversity
in Fairy-Tale Dystopias 54
Jill Coste

II. Erasing Race

Neoliberalism's Erasure of Race in Young Adult Fiction:
Sherri L. Smith's *Orleans* as Counterexample 75
Sean P. Connors and Roberta Seelinger Trites

(De)Stabilizing the Boundaries between "Us" and "Them":
Racial Oppression and Racism in Two YA Dystopias
Available in Swedish 93
Malin Alkestrand

Postracial Futures and Colorblind Ideology: The Cyborg as
Racialized Metaphor in Marissa Meyer's Lunar Chronicles Series 111
Sierra Hale

III. Lineages of Whiteness

"'I've Connected with Them": Racial Stereotyping and White
Appropriation in the Chaos Walking Trilogy 131
Meghan Gilbert-Hickey

Asian Masculinity, Eurasian Identity, and Whiteness
in Cassandra Clare's Infernal Devices Trilogy 147
Elizabeth Ho

Eugenics and the "Purity" of Memory Erasure:
The Racial Coding of Dis/ability in the *Divergent* Series 165
Alex Polish

IV. Racialized Identities

"Vine Head," "Snake Lady," "Swamp Witch": Racialized Othering
in Nnedi Okorafor's *Zahrah the Windseeker* 187
Joshua Yu Burnett

Between "Castoff" and "Half-Man": Pressuring Mixed-Race
Identity in *The Drowned Cities* 204
Susan Tan

Black Girl Magic: Bioethics and the Reinvention of the Trope
of the Mad Scientist in Black YA Speculative Fiction 222
Esther L. Jones

Fore-fronting Race and Law: Ambelin Kwaymullina's
The Interrogation of Ashala Wolf and Challenging the
Expectations for Idealized Young Adult Heroines 237
Zara Rix

Contributors 257

Index 261

Acknowledgments

Any volume of this sort exists due to the input and work of many people. First and foremost, we are thankful to our contributors, whose work has stretched our thinking and given this project shape and whose patience and continued excellence has made this collection possible. We appreciate your insights, your patience, and your commitment to making this collection what it is. We are immensely proud of these essays and look forward to seeing how these works contribute to on-going and new conversations regarding race and representation in young adult speculative fiction.

We owe additional gratitude to the Children's Literature Association Publication Committee and to Jackie Horne, in particular, whose detailed and insightful feedback throughout this process was invaluable. We also appreciate the thoughtful input of the editing staff at University Press of Mississippi—Katie Keene in particular—as well as the guidance of the community of Children's and Young Adult literature scholars, many of whom have given us advice or offered suggestions throughout this project. We especially want to thank Katharine Capshaw, Michelle H. Martin, Ebony Elizabeth Thomas, and Sara K. Day for their guidance.

We each thank our departments and universities. Thank you to the Faculty of Liberal Arts and Sciences and the Office of Academic Affairs at Stella and Charles Guttman Community College, a part of the City University of New York, for providing both professional and financial support for this project. Thank you to the Faculty of Arts and Humanities, the Department of Gender, Sexuality, and Women's Studies, and the Department of English and Writing Studies at the University of Western Ontario. Miranda also thanks Jeremy Fairall and Jeremy Johnston for research assistance.

We would like to thank the colleagues and friends who read early drafts of this work. Our utmost appreciation goes to Nicholas Lawrence, Jeremiah

Hickey, and especially Cody Barteet, who read and commented on various drafts, often at a moment's notice.

Meghan would like to thank Dohra Ahmad, Shanté Paradigm Smalls, and Jennifer Travis for their guidance and support, as well as her family for their patience and love. She is forever grateful to Miranda, as well, for her calm tenacity during this process.

Miranda thanks Sara Day for her constant support and willingness to brainstorm at all hours. She also thanks Kimberly Brown, Wendy Pearson, and Anne Phillips for their suggestions and encouragement. Miranda also wants to thank her children, who are always patient and try to recognize that their mother's work matters. Miranda also thanks Meghan for agreeing to coedit this project. She is eternally thankful for Meghan's persistence, patience, and dedication.

Finally, we acknowledge our partners, Cody Barteet and Jeremiah Hickey. Thank you for the willing ears and ready support, especially during those nights away and long chats. You both often put our work ahead of your own, and you each repeatedly told us to keep going because this work is important. Without you, this would not have been possible.

RACE IN YOUNG ADULT SPECULATIVE FICTION

"Real change, enduring change, happens one step at a time."
Ruth Bader Ginsburg

Introduction
Miranda A. Green-Barteet

On August 31, 2015, Dawn Abron, a teen library worker, published a blog post entitled "Diversity YA Life: Diverse Science Fiction, Fantasy, and Horror" on *The Hub*, a blog run by the Young Adult Library Services Association. In the post, Abron explained that many of the teens she works with "like to escape into fantasy and science fiction" when they find life difficult. These teen readers also "like to see themselves" in young adult speculative fiction (YASF). Abron argued that "if people of color can survive slavery and oppression and poverty, they can also survive zombies and maniacal kings and dragons. So," Abron asked, "where are the black Hermiones?" Abron is far from the only person working with children and adolescents who is asking this question. Numerous other blogs devoted to young adult (YA) literature, including *Diversity in YA*, *We Need Diverse Books*, and *Crazy QuiltEdi*, among many others, asserted the "critical importance of brown [and Black] girls [and boys] being seen in worlds of light and fantasy" (Campbell, *Crazy Quiltedi*). Critic Ebony Elizabeth Thomas echoes these calls, arguing that the lack of characters of color in children's and YA literature generally and in children's and YASF specifically amounts to "an imagination gap." This gap, Thomas explained first in her blog and later in her book, both titled *The Dark Fantastic*,[1] is not due "to any failure in the imaginations of young people. Those are humming right along as always, as kids and teens all over the world are now using new media to inscribe themselves into existence . . . Our young people have not failed us." However, many adults, Thomas contends, have, and they have done so by failing to imagine that young people would want to read books about diverse characters, by failing to consider how diverse characters living in diverse worlds could inspire readers from a variety of backgrounds, and by failing to study and/or teach books that do feature diverse characters, written by diverse authors. This collection was inspired, at least in part, by these bloggers and by their calls both for increased representation of characters of color in children's and YA literature and for increased awareness of texts written by diverse authors. Like Abron and Thomas, we are specifically interested in YASF. This is, after all, a genre known for imagined worlds in which fairies are leaders, people can travel through time, and vampires and werewolves can be friends. Why then, Abron and Thomas, along with countless other scholars, critics, bloggers, authors, editors, and—perhaps most importantly—readers, ask, are young people of color so underrepresented in these imagined worlds?

Race in Young Adult Speculative Fiction began as a way to consider this question. Our initial conversations on the lack of characters of color in YASF led us to ask other questions: How are racially diverse characters included in YASF? Why are characters of color so often relegated to secondary roles? Are authors of YASF attempting to create fantastic worlds in which race is no longer a salient issue? What is the effect of creating postracial speculative worlds for YA readers, especially for YA readers of color? Do white adolescent readers notice the lack of diversity in the speculative fiction they read? Do they care? How might educators, librarians, and authors make them care, and is it their responsibility? Gradually, as our primary fields of interest are literature and literary scholarship, our conversations shifted to focus on literature and criticism, and we began asking other questions: What are critics of YA literature saying about racial diversity in YASF? How are racially diverse characters represented in the genre? Are authors of YASF creating fully developed characters of color? Are authors recreating contemporary or historic systems of oppression in their imagined worlds? Do characters of color experience forms of oppression that can be seen as similar to racism? If racialized characters exist in the imagined worlds of YASF, is race openly discussed? In considering these questions, along with many others, we worked to bring together other scholars interested in examining race and representation in YASF through a sustained and cogent analysis of the genre.

The purpose of this collection, then, is to consider how characters of color are represented in YASF, how they contribute to and participate in speculative worlds, how race affects or influences the structures of speculative worlds, and how, in the words of critic Mary J. Couzelis, "ideologies about race are present" in YASF (131). This collection also examines how race and racism are discussed in YASF or if, indeed, race and racism are discussed at all.

In our conversations about this project, with fellow readers, critics, scholars, and educators, we have been repeatedly offered an explanation for why race, racism, and racial hierarchies may not be discussed in many YASF texts:

these texts feature imagined worlds in futuristic or fantastical locations. Thus, perhaps authors of such texts imagine worlds in which race is no longer a marker of difference, in which race is no longer used as a justification to "other" individuals or groups. We recognize this is a valid response. YASF does rely on imagined worlds; authors can, and often do, create worlds in which race neither signifies nor is used to justify systemic and structural oppression. In some ways, then, many YASF texts recognize that race is now understood "to be a socially constructed category" (Newton-Francis and Hamilton 384). As sociologists Michelle Newton-Francis and Steve Hamilton posit, racial categories "are superficially imposed to categorize, differentiate, and construct certain social groups as 'others'" (384). Further, "racial groups are often ... singled out for differential treatments compared to their White counterparts" (384). Historian Nell Irvin Painter similarly defines race as "a powerful social construct" that allows "whites [to] think of themselves first and foremost as individual" (388). In other words, race was constructed to enable those in power (and, historically, in the United States, those of European descent and, thus, white) to claim, maintain, and codify their power. In writing speculative fiction texts for young adults in which race is not a prominent feature, some authors may be imagining worlds in which race, while present, is no longer used as a way to create and maintain hierarchies of power.

While some texts may create worlds in which race or racialized difference is no longer used as a means to "other" groups or as a way to establish and maintain power structures, some YASF texts do "reinscribe current social and racial hierarchies" (Couzelis 113). Some novels draw on such hierarchies, as Couzelis points out, through their character descriptions, and others reference historical events, such as the enslavement of Africans and African Americans, race riots in the United States, residential school systems, and eugenics policies, to inform their imagined worlds, as Alex Polish argues in their essay in this collection. Few YASF texts that include racialized characters or refer to past racist polices or practices in their world building, however, discuss race or racism directly—or at all. This elision of race and racism implies to readers not only that race and racism, along with racism's very real consequences, are irrelevant to the imagined worlds of YASF, but also that race and racism have little impact on the contemporary world or on the lives of YA readers.

YASF featuring characters of color and drawing on past or current systems of racial oppression to inspire their own imagined worlds operate within what political scientist Sherrow O. Pinder calls a colorblind framework. Colorblindness "reject[s] the significance of race in determining social outcomes" and enables individuals to believe that we are now living in a "postracial society" (3). Colorblindness and postraciality assert that "race no longer matters and racism is disappearing" (3). Critic Tanya Ann Kennedy argues that postracialism can be seen as "an attempt to engineer a past of injustice so that [past injustice] is incorporated back into a national narrative of progress" (9). If we accept that the West generally and the United States specifically have achieved postracialism, we can use it to reinforce the ideal that the United States is a progressive nation that can now look beyond racial identity. The effects of postracialism and colorblindness are not, however, as many white people seem to believe, an end to racism but, rather, a suggestion that racial discrimination and inequality are no longer issues that can—must—be confronted directly.

One purpose of this collection is to consider the effect of colorblind ideology and postracialism on YASF, a genre that is often seen as progressive in its representation of adolescent protagonists.[2] Thomas argues that the "trouble with colorblind ideologies in text and culture is that by not noticing race, writers and other creatives do the work of encoding it as taboo" (59). Simply put, colorblindness silences those who believe—and whose experiences demonstrate—that race and racism do continue to matter. In examining how some YASF texts normalize many of our "existing social hierarchies—including hierarchies of race" (Thomas 59)—this collection examines how race and racism are represented in the genre and considers how hierarchies of race are reinscribed in some texts and transgressed in others.

It is important to note that speculative fiction has a long, evolving, and continually contested set of parameters. In his 1947 essay "On the Writing of Speculative Fiction," Robert A. Heinlein contributed to the term's widespread use with his decision to replace "science" with "speculative" to describe the fields with which science fiction is engaged. Since then, the term has evolved into an umbrella category for what Marek Oziewicz calls "genres that deliberately depart from imitating 'consensus reality' of every day experience." Therefore, "speculative" is a broad term encompassing fantasy, dystopian, and science fictions, the genres upon which this collection primarily focuses, along with others, including gothic, steam punk, and superhero. R. B. Gill argues that "because the creation of alternative worlds is at basis an assertion of values, world views turn out to be an especially helpful approach to classifying speculative fiction" (78). Thus, the essays in this collection examine the worldviews inherent in the fantasy, dystopian, and science fiction texts—the speculative fiction—that are discussed herein. In some books, racial markers are displaced by categories of otherness: extraterrestrials, cyborgs, telekinetic and intellectual powers, and technological adaptations, for example. In others, racial differences disappear altogether under the guise of a postracial society. Many of these mainstream series feature characters who are depicted as uniformly white. The lineage of normalized whiteness they uphold allows these books to present readers with a view of the world in which race is no longer significant. By reading YASF through the lenses of critical race theory, whiteness studies, and colorblind discourse, readers and critics alike can challenge postracialism and colorblind ideology and consider why race and other types of socially constructed forms of otherness can be implied but not explicitly discussed. Further, these theoretical frames assert that race does matter, even—and, perhaps, particularly—in these genres of YA fiction.

Exploring how race and racialized otherness have been presented and overlooked in recent speculative YA literature comprises the foundation of this collection. The essays in this collection are concerned with how the portrayal of race and other forms of difference both reflect and perpetuate contemporary discourses of otherness. While most of the fictional works analyzed here focus on Western culture, works such as Paolo Bacigalupi's *Drowned Cities* and Marissa Meyer's Lunar Chronicles series draw on Asian settings, Nnedi Okorafor's *Zahra the Windseeker* is influenced by African culture, and Ambelin Kwaymulina's *The Interrogation of Ashala Wolf* employs Indigenous Futurism to examine the systems of the Palyku of Western Australia. Further, the essays scrutinize how the genres of YASF seemingly value diversity while they simultaneously reify existing Western hegemonic structures. Thus, many contributors draw on critical race theory, gender theory, whiteness studies, and posthumanist theory to frame their analyses of these texts.

Each section has been organized with a unifying theme in mind, although we believe the contributors' essays speak in concert with one another, to the broader purpose of the collection. The first section, "Defining Diversity," considers novels that feature characters of color but that do not directly confront the ways in which race affects characters' lived experiences. In "Blood Rules: Racial Passing and the Commodification of Difference in Victoria Aveyard's *The Red Queen*," Sarah Olutola considers how the novel, a combination of fantasy and dystopia, invokes familiar discourses of racial otherness. The novel, Olutola argues, reflects an uneasiness regarding the inclusion of racial minorities into American society and political structures. Similarly taking up the concept of otherness, Kathryn Strong Hansen's essay, "The Fairy Race: *Artemis Fowl*, Gender, and Racial Hierarchies," asserts that the *Artemis Fowl* series fails to consider race and gender directly, while it simultaneously offers readers essentialist readings of race and gender. Thus, this series, which has the potential for creating characters with intersectional identities, reinforces current hegemonic structures of race and gender, ultimately eliding race and racialized differences. Finally, Jill Coste's "Enchanting the Masses: Allegorical Diversity in Fairy-Tale Dystopias" analyzes Stacey Jay's *Of Beast and Beauty* and Marissa Meyer's Lunar Chronicles series, arguing that these works use allegory to present diversity but in fact "deracialize" diversity while still representing marginalization.

The essays in the second section, "Erasing Race," consider how race and the lived experiences of racialized characters are elided under the guise of colorblind ideology and through the creation of postracial worlds. In "Neoliberalism's Erasure of Race in Young Adult Fiction: Sherri L. Smith's *Orleans* as Counterexample," Sean P. Connors and Roberta Seelinger Trites argue that "neoliberalism has influenced the erasure of race" in contemporary YA dystopian fiction. They devise a framework for determining if a YA novel critiques or condones neoliberalism and, thus, "whether it is reproducing, complicating, or resisting" neoliberal ideologies. To demonstrate how YA dystopian novels reproduce neoliberalism as a means to privilege the individual and erase race and racist power structure, Connors and Trites consider Sherri L. Smith's *Orleans* as a counterexample, arguing that Smith's novel "employs neoliberalism" to challenge "the erasure of race." Malin Alkestrand's essay, "(De)Stabilizing the Boundaries between 'Us' and 'Them': Racial Oppression and Racism in Two YA Dystopias Available in Swedish," analyzes Swedish author Mats Wahl's *Blodregnsserie* (the *Blood Rain* series; 2014–2017) and Austrian author Ursula Poznanski's *Die Eleria* Trilogie (the Eleria trilogy; Swedish translation 2014–2016), originally published in German between 2012 and 2014. She considers how the texts speak to racism and ethnocentrism in a contemporary Swedish context, using recent immigration history and tribalism in Sweden and Europe at large. The final essay in this section, Sierra Hale's "Postracial Futures and Colorblind Ideology: The Cyborg as Racialized Metaphor in Marissa Meyer's Lunar Chronicles Series," considers the series' use of colorblind ideology, arguing that the use of literary colorblindness and technology as a metaphor for race perpetuates racist discourse. Hale specifically demonstrates how "the use of postracial spaces that espouse a colorblind ideology" elides experiences of difference in a genre that purports to deal with difference directly.

"Lineages of Whiteness," the collection's third section, considers the ways in which whiteness is privileged and normalized even in texts that seemingly confront representations of racialized otherness directly. Meghan Gilbert-Hickey interrogates Patrick Ness's *Chaos Walking* in "'I've Connected with Them': Racial Stereotyping and White Appropriation in the *Chaos Walking* Trilogy." Ness's trilogy seemingly "problematizes the normalized heteropatriarchal family" while also critiquing "the settler colonial mindset" that supports this structure. Gilbert-Hickey argues, however, that despite Ness's sympathetic portrayal of Indigenous characters and characters of color, the trilogy "replicates both settler colonialism and Western racism," thereby reifying whiteness and erasing the experiences of Indigenous characters. The second essay in this section, Elizabeth Ho's "Asian Masculinity, Eurasian Identity, and Whiteness in Cassandra Clare's Infernal Devices Trilogy" considers how whiteness, masculinity, and Eurasian identity inform each other in Cassandra Clare's Infernal Devices trilogy. Ho argues that, because it does not provide a thoughtful "ethics of appropriation" of past and present systems of oppression, the series ultimately reinscribes Victorian racist structures within the text and beyond. Finally, Alex Polish examines how disability is constructed as a form of racialized otherness in "Eugenics and the 'Purity' of Memory Erasure: The Racial Coding of Dis/ability in the *Divergent* Series." They contend that the series creates a colorblind world, which they define as an ableist term and a privileged world, enabling characters to believe that race no longer exists.

The collection's final section, "Racialized Identities," examines texts that feature racially othered characters, simultaneously unpacking an insistence on racialized discourse and looking toward works that include characters with intersectional identities. Joshua Yu Burnett's "'Vine Head,' 'Snake Lady,' and 'Swamp Witch': Racialized Othering in Nnedi Okorafor's *Zahrah the Windseeker*" demonstrates that Okorafor simultaneously critiques speculative fiction for its one-dimensional depictions of race and works within the confines of the genre to advocate for fluid, multifaceted intersectionality. "Between 'Castoff' and 'Half-man': Pressuring Mixed-Race Identity in *The Drowned Cities*" by Susan Tan examines the complexities of race and racialized otherness in Paolo Bacigalupi's novel. Tan contends that the novel offers exciting possibilities for including racial identity in YA speculative fiction. The third essay in this section, Esther L. Jones's "Black Girl Magic: Bioethics and the Reinvention of the Trope of the Mad Scientist in Black YA Speculative Fiction," understands the texts she analyzes—all written by Black women authors—as challenging and rewriting social scripts of mental health and disability, particularly as they relate to young Black women. Her work, and the works she examines, forces us to interrogate our own complicity within these cultural narratives and challenges us to work through and beyond it. In the collection's final essay, "Forefronting Race and Law: Ambelin Kwaymullina's *The Interrogation of Ashala Wolf* and Challenging the Expectations for Idealized Young Adult Heroines," Zara Rix argues that Kwaymullina, an Indigenous Australian author, imagines a dystopian Australia as a way to teach readers about Australia's "history with its indigenous peoples." The Indigenous Futurism Kwaymullina employs allows her, according to Rix, to envision a path forward for Australia—one that respects and honors Indigenous tradition while also leaning on Indigenous notions of law to move the nation toward a more ethical social order.

In closing, we want to note that putting together a collection of this nature takes time, and since beginning this project, YASF's seeming hesitancy to discuss race directly has changed. As of 2018, the number of authors of color, specifically Black women, publishing in YASF and writing texts that feature characters of color has increased significantly. In her recent essay for *LitHub*, critic Stephanie Tolliver describes this shift in YASF as "an earthquake." With the publication of Tomi Adeymie's *Children of Blood and Bone*, Justina Ireland's *Dread Nation* and its sequel *Deathless Divide*, Dhonielle Clayton's *The Belles*, and L. L. McKinney's Nightmare-Verse series, among many others, "YASF written by Black women authors and prominently featuring Black girls pushed through the small publishing fissure that has limited the telling of these stories" (Tolliver). Other writers of color similarly broke through this fissure, with their YASF texts featuring protagonists of color, including Rin Chupeco's *The Bone Witch* series, Andromeda Romano-Lax's *Plum Rains*, Cherie Dimaline's *The Marrow Thieves*, and Samira Ahmed's *Internment*, among others. These books prove that young people of color can, as Tolliver asserts, be "the hero, the zombie slayer, or the magic wielder." These texts also prove that "the long-entrenched lack of diversity" should cease to characterize YASF (Thomas 4). "The imaginative landscapes" of the genre can—and should—include all readers, and "the speculative hopescapes for the next generation ... are more promising" (Tolliver).

The essays in this collection point toward the potential of YASF to both address and interrogate racial inequities in the contemporary West and beyond. They critique the texts that fall short of this possibility, and they articulate ways in which readers and critics alike might locate diversity within the narratives nonetheless. This is a collection troubled by the lingering emphasis on colorblindness in YASF, but it is also the work of scholars who love the genre they critique, who celebrate its progress toward inclusivity, and who see in it an enduring future for intersectional identity.

Notes

1. Thomas's blog, which she began writing in 2014, is titled *The Dark Fantastic: Race & the Imagination in Children's & YA Books, Media, and Fan Culture*. Her book, published in 2019, is titled *The Dark Fantastic: Race and the Imagination from Harry Potter to the Hunger Games*.

2. Contemporary YASF, specifically dystopian and science fiction texts are often described as progressive in their representation of gender. See Day, Green-Barteet, and Montz, and also see Hintz and Ostry. We want to emphasize that many YASF novels, despite their seeming progressiveness, focus primarily on white, cisgendered, heteronormative, able-bodied protagonists.

Works Cited

Abron, Dawn. "Diversity YA Life: Diverse Science Fiction, Fantasy, and Horror." *The Hub: Your Connection to Teen Collections*, 31 Aug. 2015, http://www.yalsa.ala.org/thehub/2015/08/31/diversity-ya-diverse-science-fiction-fantasy/, Accessed 18 Sept. 2019.

Campbell, Edith. "Black Speculative Fiction: The Hunger Imagining." *Crazy QuiltEdi*, 21 Oct. 2014, https://crazyquiltedi.blog/2014/10/21/black-speculative-fiction-the-hunger-of-imagining/, Accessed 15 Sept. 2019.

Couzelis, Mary J. "The Future Is Pale: Race in Contemporary Young Adult Dystopian Novels." *Contemporary Dystopian Fiction for Young Adults: Brave New Teenagers*, edited by Balaka Basu, Katherine R. Broad, and Carrie Hintz. Routledge, 2013, pp. 131–44.

Day, Sara K., Miranda A. Green-Barteet, and Amy L. Montz. "Introduction." *Female Rebellion in Young Adult Dystopian Fiction*, edited by Sara K. Day, Miranda A. Green-Barteet, and Amy L. Montz. Ashgate, 2014, pp. 1–16.

Gill, R. B. "The Uses of Genre and the Classification of Speculative Fiction." *Mosaic: A Journal for the Interdisciplinary Study of Literature* 46, no. 2, 2013, pp. 71–85.

Heinlein, Robert A. "On the Writing of Speculative Fiction." *The Nonfiction of Robert Heinlein: Volume 1*. The Virginia Edition, 2011. pp. 219–28.

Hintz, Carrie, and Elaine Ostry. "Introduction." *Utopian and Dystopian Writing for Children and Young Adults*, edited by Carrie Hintz and Elaine Ostry. Routledge, 2003, pp.1–20.

Kennedy, Tonya A. *Historicizing Post-Discourses: Postfeminism and Postracialism in United States Culture*. SUNY Press, 2017.

Newton-Francis, Michelle, and Steve Hamilton. "Deviance and Race." *Encyclopedia of Race, Ethnicity, and Society*, edited by Richard T. Schaefer. Sage Publishing, 2008, pp. 384–87.

Painter, Nell Irvin. *The History of White People*. Norton, 2010.

Pinder, Sherrow O. *Colorblindness, Post-Raciality, and Whiteness in the United States*. Palgrave MacMillan, 2015.

Oziewicz, Marek. "Speculative Fiction." *Oxford Research Encyclopedia of Literature*. March 29, 2017. Oxford University Press, http://literature.oxfordre.com/view/10.1093/acrefore/9780190201098.001.0001/acrefore-9780190201098-e-78. Accessed 13 Sept. 2018.

Thomas, Ebony Elizabeth. *The Dark Fantastic: Race and the Imagination from Harry Potter to the Hunger Games*. New York University Press, 2019.

Thomas, Ebony Elizabeth. "The Imagination Gap in #Kidlit and #YALit: An Introduction to the Dark Fantastic." *The Dark Fantastic: Race and the Imagination in Children's and YA Books, Media, and Fan Cultures*, 10 June 2014, http://thedarkfantastic.blogspot.com/2014/, Accessed 15 Aug. 2019.

Toliver, Stephanie. "On the History (and Future) of YA Speculative Fiction by Black Women." *LitHub*, 8 Aug. 2019, https://lithub.com/on-the-history-and-future-of-ya-and-speculative-fiction-by-black-women/, Accessed 10 Aug. 2019.

I
DEFINING DIVERSITY

Blood Rules
Racial Passing and the Commodification of Difference in Victoria Aveyard's *The Red Queen*

Sarah Olutola

In the post–*Hunger Games* YA market for dystopian tales, the YA dystopian genre has seen a proliferation of novels with similar storylines: an all-powerful totalitarian government inflicts an oppressive social order upon its inhabitants, and the often-female protagonist, a member of the oppressed class, must lead the revolution against it.

Victoria Aveyard's *The Red Queen* primarily fits this mold. Although *The Red Queen* takes place in a secondary fantasy world, its narrative plot and world building align it with dystopian YA. Like much of the dystopian teen fiction preceding it, the book follows a teenaged, female protagonist who, as a member of a marginalized class, lacks socioeconomic and political power and eventually joins a revolution against the oppressive ruling class. Here, the distinguishable difference hierarchizing society is blood. The novel's protagonist, seventeen-year-old Mare, is a Red, and her red blood seemingly dooms her to a life in the destitute district known as the Stilts. Her life changes, however, once she finds employment in the Silver Palace, the domain of the Silvers whose silver blood gives them supernatural abilities. The Silvers act as the novel's ruling class: with their startling supernatural abilities, they hoard social, political, and economic power, which allow them to maintain dominance over the Reds. Once Mare enters the royal palace, she is in an ideal position to disintegrate the dominant social order from the inside.

The market push behind dystopian narratives of teen rebellion lies in the appeal of the genre's tropes to its target audience. Assessing the massive popularity of YA literature, Michael Cart and Christine A. Jenkins estimate that it is the supposed privileging of marginalized positionality that speaks to YA's target readers, explaining that "[i]n this quintessential literature of the outsider who is too often rendered invisible by society, there is also the need to see one's face reflected in the pages of a book and thus to find the corollary comfort that derives from the knowledge that one is not alone in a vast universe, that there are others 'like me'" (1). The pleasure of consuming dystopian fiction for its young target audience stems in part from the layered marginalization of the main character as a teenager, a young woman, and a member of the oppressed underclass, yet the predominance of white protagonists in YA dystopian fiction (and YA fiction in general)[1] adds another dimension to this framework. As teen readers devour these stories of systemic oppression, as they identify with the plight of the protagonists, what narratives are they really consuming, and whose ideological aims do the books truly serve?

The very nature of the dystopian genre offers the possibility of dismantling hegemony. Indeed, the apocalypse, conceptually, is about both endings and beginnings: "the myth," according to Lois Parkinson Zamora, "comprehends both cataclysm *and* millennium, tribulation *and* triumph, chaos *and* order" (4). Thus, the apocalypse is an imagining not only of the end but of possible new beginnings, new ways of inhabiting the world. As such, dystopian YA fiction, in its preoccupation with the world after the apocalypse and the world after apocalyptic rebellion, can offer readers different, and potentially productive, models of power, structure, and society that can serve as a counter to real-world dominant hegemonic structures. Instead, the predominant privileging of white characters in these texts, as well as the mass production of narratives of oppression written largely by white authors for a primarily US mainstream audience, necessitates that we examine the hegemonic imperatives that may underlie these texts, contradicting the genre's potential. As the YA dystopian protagonists rebel against repressive structures that would neutralize, silence, and erase them, the North American mainstream YA dystopian genre, with its repetition and mass production of narratives of antiwhite oppression and rebellion, risks reaffirming for its young audience dominant relations of power.

It is within this problematic that I locate *The Red Queen* as a cultural text. Through blending fantasy and dystopian elements, it enables readers to examine the contradictions of repression and rebellion characteristic of the genre and perhaps YA literature generally. In particular, by invoking familiar discourses of racial otherness, the novel allows readers to engage more explicitly with the racial politics already saturating the cultural space within which the novel was produced. As expressed in the novel, these racial politics are centered on socioeconomic structures of Western and, particularly, US late-capitalist modernity. Indeed, the implicit politics of the narrative reveal the book as reflecting an uneasiness surrounding the incorporation of racial minorities into the US body politic. Upon entering the Silver Palace, Mare discovers she possesses Silverlike supernatural abilities, despite being of Red blood. The ambiguous nature of her blood thus enables her to pass as a Silver. While this positions her as a Trojan Horse for the Red resistance group, the Scarlet Guard, it also allows her to experience the romance and upper-class glamor of privileged wealthy court life.

The juxtaposition of racial ambiguity, racial oppression, and upward mobility positions this text as a window into the complex meaning of race in the United States. *The Red Queen*, perhaps more explicitly because of its direct engagement with racial discourses, inevitably forms part of the racial disciplinary power structure of late-capitalist US society. By working with the concept of race through colonial discourses and the language of neoliberal global capitalist modernity, the book exposes the anxieties and tensions of historical and contemporary debates surrounding racial equality while offering a narrative of racial inclusion that ultimately runs counter to the notions of rebellion characteristic of the genre. I address this quandary by first placing *The Red Queen* within a larger framework that connects colonial discourses to the pedagogical dimensions of speculative literature. I then read the novel in terms of its semiotic representations of race, connecting the different modes of passing Mare demonstrates in the Silver Place. I also examine Mare's ambivalent feelings towards the Silvers' patriarchal socioeconomic power. As Mare navigates a society divided by racial privilege, her simultaneous attraction to and hatred of the Silvers' power compounds the novel's racial and neoliberal thematic undertones to present a story of racial oppression that is ultimately apprehensive of the possibility of racial rebellion.

Colonialism, Race, and the Novel

In an interview with *Publisher's Weekly*, Victoria Aveyard named the Roman Empire as her inspiration for the novel's setting. However, given the novel's preoccupation with blood as a racial determinant, contemporary US racial politics is more applicable. As a novel produced within a US contemporary cultural space characterized by violent histories and ongoing negotiations of power, we can analyze the book through North American white supremacy. Indeed, by reading the book as a product of a larger colonial history of knowledge production—a history in which both the novel as a cultural form and speculative fiction are deeply embedded—we can unravel the implications of its explicit politics and implicit anxieties.

Edward Said has argued that the novel as a narrative form has its origins in reinforcing colonial frameworks, reaffirming for white, middle-class Western consumers their perception of non-Western geographies and peoples.[2] This function becomes important when considering speculative novels, including dystopian fiction. As John Reider argues in *Colonialism and the Emergence of Science Fiction*, the science fiction genre arose out of the nineteenth century during the height of imperialism. Consequently, many of the tropes currently uniting the genre's vast narrative reservoir engage in that period's ideological anxieties, desires, and contradictions. He writes:

> Evolutionary theory and anthropology, both profoundly intertwined with colonial ideology and history, are especially important to early science fiction from the mid-nineteenth century on.... The complex mixture of ideas about competition, adaptation, race, and destiny that was in part generated by evolutionary theory, and was in part an attempt to come to grips with—or to negate—its implications, forms a major part of the thematic material of early science fiction. (2)

As white Europeans came into contact with non-Europeans and "scrutinized, analyzed, theorized, catalogued, and displayed" their perceived differences, they developed and confirmed their conceptions of humanity, evolution through the paradigm of race, which dystopian narratives ultimately project into imaginings of the future (4). In his essay in this collection, Joshua Yu Burnett examines the cognitive dissonance inherent in this colonialist writing tradition in "'Vine Head,' 'Snake Lady,' 'Swamp Witch': Racialized Othering in Nnedi Okorafor's *Zahrah the Windseeker*." Framing his analysis of Okorafor's racially subversive *Zahrah* alongside her criticism of the "magical negro" trope, Burnett notes that the other-ing of racialized bodies has often been masked by the speculative author's utopian colorblind aims. Just as the "magical negro" trope presents itself as an empowering representation of Black figures (who are wise and powerful, but must only use their assets to benefit white protagonists), much of speculative fiction from the nineteenth century onwards has endeavored to produce fantasies of futures supposedly unencumbered by racial politics. Yet, the racial coding in these narratives suggests that the specter of colonial racial politics exists nonetheless, insidiously reaffirming European constructions of the racialized body.

If speculative fiction, true to the origins of the novel as a cultural form, has largely functioned since the colonial period to produce knowledge about racialized bodies in service of hegemonic frameworks, then we must consider the survival of these narrative traditions in contemporary offerings like *The Red Queen*—and this is especially important considering the power of novels to align readers' interests around those of the dominant class, "block[ing] other narratives from forming and emerging" and limiting possibilities for imagining other ways of relating to others (Said xiii). Much like H. G. Wells's *War of the Worlds*, which imagines the (neo)colonial oppression of the (white, European) human race by the advanced Martians, *The Red Queen*'s dystopian setting invokes the perceived relationship between whites and nonwhites entrenched during the colonial era to frame its races.

In the first chapter, though Mare refers to the Silvers as "gods" because of their advanced supernatural abilities, she ambivalently positions them as mortal by placing them on the same continuum of humanity as the Reds; however, her articulation of the differences between them explains how the book relates the two. While watching Silvers battle in the Arena, a periodic event meant to reaffirm the Silvers' power over the Reds, Mare muses to herself, "We are not their equals, though you wouldn't know it from looking at us. The only thing that serves to distinguish us, outwardly at least, is that Silvers stand tall. Our backs are bent by work and unanswered hope and the inevitable disappointment with our lot in life" (5).

Mare's imagery parallels Western representations of humanity at different stages of evolution, most commonly depicted by Rudolph Franz Zallinger's 1965 scientific illustration, *The Road to Homo Sapiens*, or, as it is commonly called, *The March of Progress*. In the illustration shown in figure 1, humanity, represented by a white European male, stands tall and walks forward with the ape far behind him, slouching.[3]

The writings of colonial European travelers and missionaries, who attempted to assess, justify, and categorize perceived bodily differences, corroborated scientific discourses connecting the ape, the beast, and the savage to the racial other.[4] The metonymic slippage in Mare's words between the oppressed Red and not-yet-evolved ape is further structured by economic relations of production. The Reds' backs are bent by work, highlighting their status as part of the laboring underclass upon whose work the privileged benefit. As Mimi Sheller suggests, the European "logic" that framed the colonized body as an exploitable economic resource normalized these relations of power, framing labor as a feature of their very bodies (157).[5] This logic becomes "proof" of their subhumanity. Such logic normalizes—and *naturalizes*—oppression and always assumes the place of racialized bodies within the economic order. Indeed, the semiotic correlation between the colonized body, the unevolved subhuman, and the impoverished working body is so powerful that it survives in the contemporary era.

The seamless alignment of Mare's description of the Reds with colonial discourses is significant because *The Red Queen* appropriates experiences of

DRYOPITHECUS	OREOPITHECUS	RAMAPITHECUS
Though its skeleton is tantalizingly incomplete, *Dryopithecus* can be fairly described from a few jaws and teeth. First of the fossil great apes to be discovered, it was widely distributed; remains have been unearthed throughout Europe, in North India and China.	A likely side branch on man's family tree, *Oreopithecus* is believed to have stood around four feet tall and weighed about 80 pounds. Its teeth and pelvis led scientists to wonder if it could be ancestral to man, but it is now better known, and was clearly an aberrant ape.	The earliest manlike primate found so far, *Ramapithecus* is now thought by some experts to be the oldest of man's ancestors in a direct line. This hominid status is predicated upon a few teeth, some fragments of jaw and a palate unmistakably human in shape.

Fig. 1. An abbreviated version of "The Road to Homo Sapiens" from *Early Man* (1965).

racialized oppression to tell its white heroine's story while reinforcing the language that has contributed to the oppression of racialized peoples. Indeed, the book further demonstrates its framing of the connection between Reds and Silvers as Mare remembers her father's frustrated assessment of their lives: "Long ago he called us ants, Red ants burning in the light of a Silver sun. Destroyed by the greatness of others, losing the battle for our right to exist because we are not special. We did not evolve like them, with powers and strengths beyond our limited imaginations. We stayed the same, stagnant in our own bodies. *The world changed around us and we stayed the same*" (Aveyard 48). It is possible, of course,

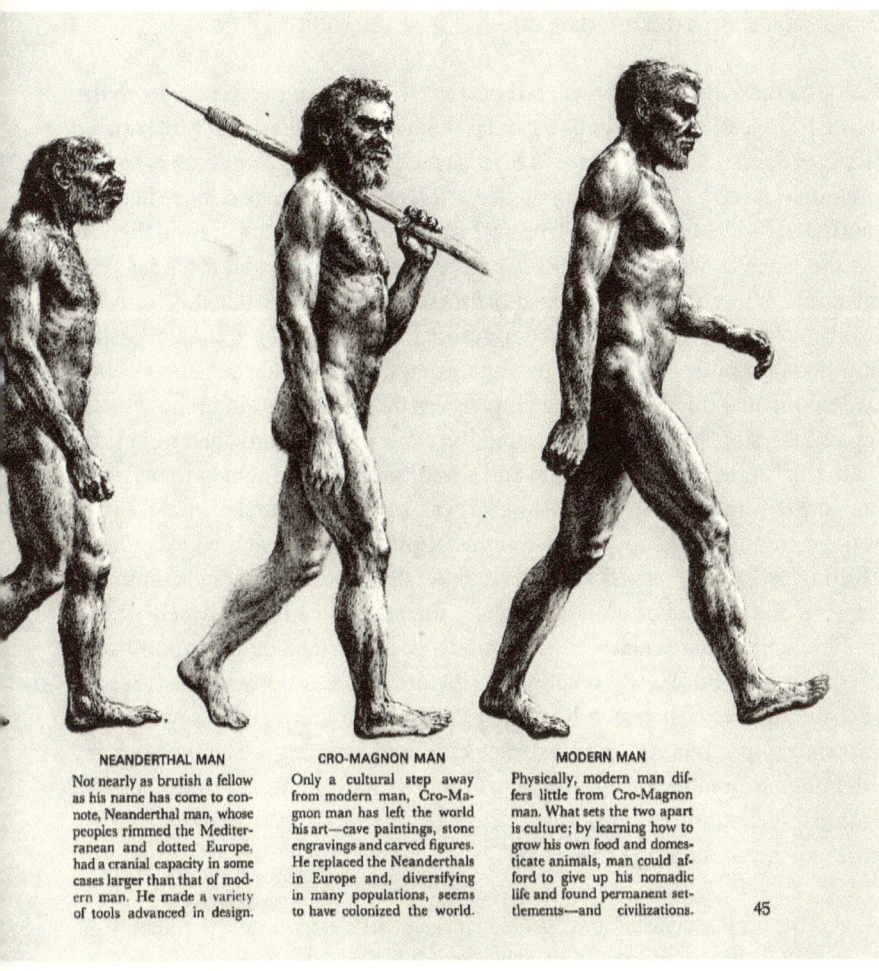

NEANDERTHAL MAN
Not nearly as brutish a fellow as his name has come to connote, Neanderthal man, whose peoples rimmed the Mediterranean and dotted Europe, had a cranial capacity in some cases larger than that of modern man. He made a variety of tools advanced in design.

CRO-MAGNON MAN
Only a cultural step away from modern man, Cro-Magnon man has left the world his art—cave paintings, stone engravings and carved figures. He replaced the Neanderthals in Europe and, diversifying in many populations, seems to have colonized the world.

MODERN MAN
Physically, modern man differs little from Cro-Magnon man. What sets the two apart is culture; by learning how to grow his own food and domesticate animals, man could afford to give up his nomadic life and found permanent settlements—and civilizations.

45

that Mare and her father's positioning of the Reds as developmentally behind the Silvers on the evolutionary timeline of progress specifically references their feelings of insecurity, hopelessness, and powerlessness in the face of the Silvers' overwhelming sovereign power. However, the mobilization of Eurocentric, racial discourses persists throughout the book, emphasizing its embeddedness within particular racial histories. Specifically, the book articulates Mare's story of oppression through the racial legal language powerfully cultivated in the Southern United States. Thus, her narrative ultimately reveals lingering anxieties over the presence and place of the racial other in the social order.

Blood Rules, American Terror, and the Science Fiction of Race

Colonial racial discourses regarded perceived biological differences from the white European as proof of both racial difference and the other's inferiority. In *Black Space: Imagining Race in Science Fiction,* Adilifu Nama refers to this discourse as the "science fiction of race." "Race is the ultimate science fiction," he argues, "and America has a lengthy history of promulgating how biological features such as skin pigmentation, hair texture, eye color, and facial features are used not just to classify people into different racial groups but also, unfortunately, to justify preconceived notions of each race's behavioral characteristics and mental abilities" (43). Through analyzing numerous science fiction films to demonstrate this point, Nama emphasizes the manifestation of these racial logics in dystopian narratives through the trope of blood and contamination.

In the United States, as cultural and scientific discourses sought to perpetuate and naturalize notions of white superiority, the hierarchal social order wanted to maintain supposed white racial purity. The imagined exceptionalism of whiteness served to justify the Western world's genocidal colonial venture and slave economies; however, the sexual contact between whites and nonwhites, particularly within slavery, posed an ideological conundrum: if whiteness is pure and exceptional, if whiteness and nonwhiteness represent the difference between humanity and subhumanity, then how can one explain the production of mixed-race children? Policing sexual boundaries attempted to resolve the anxieties surrounding these contradictions, and the antimiscegenation laws that "turned sex acts into race acts" had blood at their core (Koshy 1). As Nama states,

> Nowhere is this concept [of eugenic management] clearer in practice than in the colloquially defined "one-drop rule," which asserts that "one drop" of "black blood" compromises white racial purity. Despite the spurious and pseudoscientific nature of the "rule," blood is not categorized by race but by types: A+, A-, AB+, 0+, and so on. Nevertheless, this racial convention is an integral part of the cultural politics of race in American society in which "black blood" is viewed as not only a potent pollutant but also a fundamental element in assembling an essentialized racial identity for both whites and blacks. (44)

It is important to note, however, that the use of blood rules in an attempt to establish and fix essentialized racial identities varied according to the needs of settler society. The one-drop rule ensured that children born from the rape of enslaved women would not jeopardize the enslaver's patrilineal control over his property through inheritance (Koshy 5). Simultaneously, state laws, such as Virginia's "The Pocahontas Exception," enabled state governments to reclassify Indigenous children as white, particularly in the cases of white fathers and Indigenous mothers; during earlier periods of colonial history, such exceptions worked to legitimatize white patrilineal claim over Indigenous lands (4–5). Such laws demonstrate that blood rules are arbitrary, constructed specifically to serve the perpetuation of white patriarchal capitalist supremacy. More specifically, the anxieties surrounding miscegenation involved not only the strict management of racial categories of difference but also the terms of the inclusion of racial minorities into dominant society.

We can place *The Red Queen*'s fantasy setting within this fraught history. Indeed, the segregated society of Silvers and Reds reflects these racial logics in ways that normalize the ideological frameworks from which they emerged. At the narrative's beginning, Mare fixates on the blood lost by the Silvers battling in the arena. As her friend Kilorn cheers wildly at the violence, Mare instead notes, "[h]e honestly wants to see blood, silver blood—*silverblood*—stain the arena. It doesn't matter that the blood is everything we aren't, everything we can't be, everything we want. He just needs to see it and trick himself into thinking ... that they can be hurt and defeated. But I know better" (9). Here the concept of the gaze comes into play.[6] Arena battling, as Mare explains, is designed as a disciplinary measure. Reds are forced to watch Silvers, who are using their supernatural powers, battle each other to reaffirm to the Reds the Silvers' superiority and, thus, the Reds' own inferiority. Mare states, "Only Silvers can fight in the arenas because only a Silver can *survive* the arena. They fight to show us their strength and power" (6). As I explained earlier, the ability to perceive and ascertain racial difference was a power mobilized throughout colonialism. This was done to ascribe qualitative differences to white and nonwhite beings that would then justify the latters' oppression. However, in the case of categorizing nonwhite blood as inferior, there is no scientific evidence to support the idea that blood confers certain behavioral "inferior" racial traits. As Nama explains, blood rules are pseudoscientific, sutured together through arbitrary and unstable racial discourses (44).

Through the differences between Reds and Silvers, *The Red Queen* explicitly connects blood—most specifically the color of blood that can be viewed and assessed once it is outside of the body—to the supernatural ability that confers magical and socioeconomic power. In doing so, the novel seems to provide that missing, biological link between notions of blood, race, and difference. As Mare goes on to state while watching the battle unfold in the arena, "their blood is a threat, a warning, a promise. *We are not the same and never will be* . . . This is the true division between Silvers and Reds: the color of our blood. This simple difference somehow makes them stronger, smarter, *better* than us" (9).

Because the book's central conflict between the Silvers and Reds serves as a metaphor that can be easily mapped onto the contemporary racial politics and discourses already legible to a US audience, the handling of this metaphor as it plays out through the narrative is crucial. That Mare has Red blood but Silver abilities, which give her a way to pass as Silver, explicitly evokes white anxieties surrounding miscegenation. As Hee-Jung Joo explains, in the decades during and after slavery, white anxieties surrounding the ability of mixed race individuals to pass as white concerned the value of whiteness: "The value of white skin ... lies not only in its claims to citizenship, but also to its correlate, the potential for upward socioeconomic mobility that was denied to African Americans after emancipation" (172). The anxiety that "they" could be walking among "us" and sneakily participating equally as full citizens is voiced through Mare's infiltration plot. Although Mare's passing is facilitated by the members of the Silver royal court, who force her to pretend to be a Silver, the manifestation of Mare's power while working at an exclusive and privileged Silver event is what forces them to disguise her to justify her existence, giving them time to study her blood.

Her passing reaffirms the legibility of contemporary racial discourses; however, Mare's existence also proves that supernatural ability may not be completely tied to the silver color of blood. If Mare believes that supernatural superiority is tied to the color of one's blood, then her ability to conjure lightning despite having red blood negates this belief. Thus, it is possible that Mare's abilities deconstruct the white supremacist eugenic rules of racial purity. The problem arises in the way Mare's inclusion into the privileged space of the Silver court is narrated. Mare, as the book's white protagonist, occupies dual subject positions for the reader. Within the narrative, she represents the oppressed racial minority. Outside of the narrative, in the white bourgeois mainstream within which and for which this novel was produced, Mare is empowered. As I argue later, Mare's affiliation with oppression and privilege, along with her ambivalent perceptions of dominant racial order, directs the narrative away from its radical deconstructive potential. It instead reaffirms the racial discourses that not only tie blood to ability and power but also celebrate and normalize the socioeconomic order that produces them.

Cinderellas, Rebellions, and the Neutralization of Racial Anxiety

Here, I return to Zamora's analysis of the apocalypse narrative in fiction. Dystopian narratives can project the interests, desires, and anxieties of the socioeconomic context within which they are written. However, as Zamora suggests, society's "fascination with endings often manifests itself in elaborate strategies for their subversion" (5). That is, imaginings of the end of civilization can be constrained by those social anxieties that the narrative then resolves. Nama reads dystopian films focused on the politics of African American blood and racial contamination along these lines, noting that these films operate "on a broader ideological level" to neutralize the threat passing poses (45). He suggests that "despite African Americans holding unprecedented, respected, and even admired social positions in [contemporary] U. S. society," "a palpable uneasiness with the struggle for and consequences of full social integration of blacks (and other nonwhites)" still exists (45).

In *The Red Queen*, the uneasiness surrounding the inclusion of racial minorities into dominant society clashes with the book's narrative of teen rebellion against oppression, producing ideological tensions. The novel very clearly acknowledges the systemic, institutional nature of Silver rule. Mare describes the state's repressive apparatus, represented by their kings, who once "burn[ed] dissenters with nothing more than a flaming touch" (Aveyard 60). In the same passage, she connects this repressive disciplinary apparatus to the ideological apparatus of schooling.[7] After noting that their current king "might not burn Reds anymore, but he still kills [them] with war and ruin" (60), she explains that her schooling was instrumental in shaping her understanding of their monarchy as their rulers. The narrative further elaborates that the dehumanization and perceived disposability of racial minorities is a consequence of power structures; in one early scene, a Red is drowned by a *nymph* (a water-manipulating Silver) enraged over a televised broadcast of the Scarlet Guard declaring war upon the state (37).

Despite the novel's frankness in describing oppression, its appropriation of racial discourses and real-world experiences of racial oppression creates a problem for its Eurocentric framework. The book acknowledges oppression, but Mare's ability to gain access to the Silver court through passing and her eventual joining of the Scarlet Guard reflect an implicit uneasiness surrounding the potential for racial inclusion to overthrow the social order. These ideological tensions most powerfully manifest through Mare's multifaceted perception of the Silvers and their power.

Before she enters the Silver Palace, Mare's descriptions of the Silvers reflect a kind of ambivalence towards their oppressive power. When Mare, while still living her life of hopeless poverty, describes the Silvers as "monsters dressed as lords," she suggests a connection between their otherworldliness and socioeconomic position (43). However, underlying Mare's thoughts is a subtle confusion as to whether to view Silver power as worthy of loathing or awe. In another passage, Mare describes the Silvers as "beautiful, cruel creatures calling themselves humans" (57), suggesting a dichotomy between cruelty and beauty, monstrosity and godhood. In both phrases, Mare represents the Silvers as being more than human, but is this "superiority" to be reviled or worshipped?

We can embed this problematic within the larger framework of the novel's depiction of racial resistance. A debate runs throughout the narrative: Is resistance necessary? If so, what forms of resistance? Is resistance ever worth the potential costs? Mare's ambivalence towards the Silvers is echoed in her conflicting feelings over whether to rebel against them. Her hesitation is not necessarily simply out of fear of Silver retribution but out of fear of the loss of life rebellion could cause. Interestingly, it is Silvers who explicitly present the conundrum of rebellion to Mare and to the reader—namely Julian Jacos, brother to the late first queen and Mare's personal tutor in the palace, and Prince Cal, son of the first queen and heir to the king's throne. While in the palace, Mare learns that Prince Cal wishes to uphold the status quo between Silvers and Reds, but only to avoid death. As he explains to Mare, if their province moved towards equality between the races, "the rest of the continent would not let it last. We would be invaded, divided, torn apart. More war, more death" (152). Likewise, once Julian hears of Mare's involvement in the Scarlet Guard, he warns her. He does so not to maintain Silver oppressive rule for, as he tells her in an earlier scene, "oppressing you, trapping you in an endless cycle of poverty and death, just because we think you are *different* from us? That is not *right*. And as any student of history can tell you, it will end poorly" (131). He warns her because he is concerned for her and, presumably, those who might suffer the consequences of her actions. After telling her that the court killed his sister, the late queen, and, thus, is capable of killing Mare, he asserts that change "takes time, planning, and too much luck to count on . . . I don't want you getting in over your head" (183).

Through both arguments, the book attempts to present a broader picture of rebellion and oppression. However, it is important to note that Silvers, especially royal Silver men, seem to be the primary vehicle, along with Mare, through which the novel can voice these tempered considerations. In contrast, the narrative presents the Scarlet Guard as rash, violent, and largely cold to what the book considers to be the costs of revolution. When Prince Maven, son of the second queen and younger brother to Prince Cal, tells Farley, the Red resistance's leader, that her "violent methods aren't winning [her] any friends," she laughs, saying, "We've spent the last few centuries under a Silver boot, and we're not going to get out by being *nice*" (189). Of course, it is possible the reader will identify with Farley and the Scarlet Guard's position, but the book's storytelling and representational choices seemingly work against this, for example, in the aforementioned scene in which a Silver murdered a Red in a spur of the moment display of rage over the Scarlet Guard's declaration of war. Though the scene ends with Mare's horror over the Reds being drowned, the narrative makes clear that the tragedy is a direct result of the Scarlet Guard's actions as much as the murderous Silver's. Mare witnesses the broadcast in a bar filled with Silvers. Though she had been wearing a red band that signifies her race, she'd been able to pass by Silvers unnoticed because, as she writes, "[f]ortunately, no one pays attention to another Red servant, another insect wandering past the feet of gods" (33). However, directly after the Scarlet Guard's broadcast, she feels the immediate danger of being surrounded by Silvers: "They scream about Farley, calling her a terrorist, a murderer, a Red devil. Before their eyes can fall on me, I back out into the street" (37). Though in a racially oppressive state, racial minorities are already vulnerable, the Reds' exposure to potentially fatal peril is here depicted as a direct result of the Scarlet Guard's tactics. The narrative emphasizes its framing of the Scarlet Guard's actions as reckless and dangerous once Mare inevitably joins the group herself. Towards the end of the scene, Mare is asked to give a decisive answer as to whether she will join their side. In that exact moment, she remembers Cal saying to her, "More war, more death" (164). She joins anyway, believing in the importance of change. How the narrative describes the group in the wake of this decision is telling. After one member utters their mantra, "Red as the Dawn," Mare notes, "In the flickering candlelight, our shadows look like monsters against the walls" (164).

The term "monster" places the Scarlet Guard and the oppressive Silvers on the same subtextual continuum. This placement suggests that although the book is concerned with the injustice of racial oppression, it distrusts racial minority resistance, which reinforce its anxieties over the management of racialized bodies. Tellingly, the narrative associates minority rebellion with death and destruction (presenting a limited framework of resistance), and while the book is concerned with the potential costs of Red lives, the consequences of rebellion most powerfully manifest in the Silvers massacre in the Silver Palace. Using her privileged position as a "Red" inside the Silver Palace, Mare helps the Scarlet Guard attack the Parting Ball, but the resultant Silver deaths traumatize her. As she observes the dead bodies, Mare's guilt is clear: "And beyond the wounded are the bodies of the dead, laid out before the king's throne. Belicos Lerolan's twin sons lie next to him, with their weeping mother holding vigil over the bodies... *I never wanted this*" (255).

If the Silvers, within the narrative's racial dimensions, represent the dominant class, then their deaths are symbolic of the underlying anxiety over the death of the social order brought about by the mismanaged inclusion of racial minorities and the transgression of society's blood rules. While Mare's ambivalence towards Silvers and the ongoing debate about resistance represents the narrative's attempt to discern how racial minorities should feel towards power and behave in light of oppression, the deployment of popular fiction tropes aimed at young (female) readers provides a strategy for managing the ideological tensions resulting from the plot's politics. In particular, the book's use of the Cinderella narrative to frame Mare's infiltration into the Silver world acts as a sort of safety valve that redirects the political imperatives of the novel towards the ideological investments of dominant Western social order—a resolution palatable to the narrative's Eurocentric framework.

I borrow the term "safety valve" from Laura Mulvey's analysis of the 1950s Hollywood melodrama genre. In *Notes on Sirk and Melodrama*, Mulvey argues that while the melodrama exposes the sinister underside of the nuclear family as a hegemonic institution by presenting its ideological tensions, the melodrama ultimately neatly resolves these tensions through its narrative and aesthetics. As she writes, melodrama becomes a "safety valve for ideological contradictions centered on sex and family" and thus an outlet for "probing pent-up emotion, bitterness and disillusion well known to women" (53–54). Likewise, Mare's Cinderella arc, despite its movements towards subversion, allows for a similar reading.

Critic Amanda K. Allen refers to the Cinderella narrative as the underlying framework of the "commodity tale" genre, which emerged in the US post–World War II economy (282). These tales, which she dubs "the American fairy tales of the late capitalist period," were considered part of the YA literature of the postwar/Cold War period (284). Aimed "specifically at white, American teenage girl readers," they served a pedagogical function: to teach them to "become women" (284). Like the *Bildungsroman* narrative, which demonstrates proper modes of entrance into the dominant social order for child readers, the Cinderella narrative, with its emphasis on downtrodden heroines transformed by balls and gowns, ultimately presents a fantasy through which a young woman gains "recognition and eventual acceptance by the dominant society" (286).

The Cinderella fantasy resonates with some racial narratives. For US racial minorities in today's era of global capitalism, their inclusion into the social body has always been conditional upon the "eventual acceptance" of dominant society and its ideals. As Prudence Carter notes, "cultural gatekeepers use dominant linguistic and dress codes as signals of intelligence and respectability," codes that would align them with middle-class ideals; thus, for racial minorities, following these codes offers a way into the realm of social citizenship (138). More specifically, the "cultural legitimacy" of racial minorities largely depends upon their assimilation into the nation as proper participants in late-capitalist society. This is another disciplinary technology of power, a way for structures of power to control and mitigate the worrisome inclusion of racialized bodies into dominant society.

Mare, as a Red in the Silver Palace and, eventually, a member of the Scarlet Guard, threatens dominant society. Yet the narrative's covert messages tell a different story. Once the Silver court, upon the manifestation of her powers, decides to pass her off as a Silver, Mare experiences the spoils of wealth and privilege. There are moments, of course, in which it seems as though the narrative deconstructs this trope. In one scene, as Mare is painted in silver makeup to hide the red flushes of her skin, she narrates her transformation with dismay: "With a gasp, I realize it's supposed to hide my natural flush, the red bloom in my skin, the red blood.... I look cold, cruel, a living razor. I look Silver. I look beautiful. I hate it" (Aveyard 88–89). Indeed, when Mare, wearing a gown, describes herself as "a corpse being dressed for her funeral" (89), the text seems to explicitly reject the ideals underlying the Cinderella plot.

The subversion is betrayed, however, by the book's detail of the excess Mare can now access. The novel's description focuses on the opulent surroundings, the beautiful dresses, the numerous feasts. Following her description of her transformation into a Silver, Mare describes her new room as "finer than anything [she's] ever seen—marble and glass, silk and feathers" and light that shifts "to the orange color of dusk" (91). While going to a feast, she describes the upper levels of the palace: "Like the Spiral Garden, the architecture is all curves of stone, glass, and metal, slowly turning downward. Diamondglass is around every corner, showing breathtaking views of the marketplace, the river valley, and the woods beyond. From this height, I can see hills I didn't know existed rising in the distance, silhouetted against the setting sun" (93). Although she "suffers through the feast," there is "more food than [she's] ever seen" (103). And indeed, the excess of food is built into her daily schedules; the timetable she is given allots more time to leisure and eating than classes (116).

Perhaps the clearest contradiction to the supposed subversion of Mare-as-Cinderella is her relationship with Prince Cal. Although Mare states that she despises her Silver appearance, her opinion changes once Prince Cal sees her: "I whirl around to see the maids stooped in identical bows. And standing over them: Cal. Suddenly, I'm very glad that makeup covers the blush spreading over me" (89–90). The sight of him shakes her, and when she speaks to him, she "[forces] as much disdain into [her] voice as [she] can," whereas earlier the disdain flowed naturally (90). The romance that blooms between them is forbidden for she is betrothed to his younger brother, Maven. Their relationship proceeds nonetheless, reaching a crucial point when, the night before the Parting Ball, they kiss as he teaches her to dance: "His lips are on mine, hard and warm and pressing. The touch is electrifying...As much as I want to pull away, I just can't do it. Cal is a cliff, and I throw myself over the edge, not bothering to think of what it could do to us both" (228).

Interestingly, Mare's romantic, Cinderellaesque dance with Cal happens before the ball, where she goes on to share intimate moments with her other love interest, Prince Maven, before helping the Scarlet Guard launch a rebel attack against the Silvers. The tug of war between her impulse toward her rebellion and the dominant order, which forms part of the explicit narrative, and conformity operates implicitly within the text. Though the rebellious heroine is crucial for the YA dystopian novel, the young, white, middle-class female readers would likely derive some pleasure from the novel's Cinderella story.[8] The attraction to the Cinderella narrative could stem from its alignment with the changeling trope popular in children's fiction such as the *Harry Potter* series: that a child, who is disempowered at worse and ordinary at best, actually belongs to another community, one that is glamorous and magical (Gunn 146). Mare is oppressed, but like Cinderella and Harry, she is also special and perhaps must be special for her tale to resonate with readers. In being special, she can access a world of wealth and privilege; while she doesn't fully enjoy it, the readers do. This enjoyment seems to implicitly narrate the ways in which the oppressed can experience their oppression without feeling too bad.

Indeed, part of her positioning as special also derives from being treated especially well by both Prince Cal and Prince Maven, despite their membership in the oppressive ruling class—and it is important to note here that she ties her attraction to them, particularly to Cal, semiotically to their imperial strength. As prince and general of the Silver Army, Cal is a soldier—a point Mare reiterates throughout the novel. Despite his affiliation with the military complex that oppresses and kills Reds, the narrative curiously sexualizes his status as a soldier and a ruler, interpreting his physical strength and status through the lens of desire and admiration: "Cal and Maven are deadly creatures, soldiers," she muses, invoking the supposed enticing danger of male power (Aveyard 119). "My eyes linger on Cal, currently doing push-ups in perfect form," she says later, allowing readers to imagine, almost voyeuristically, his military-honed physical prowess, which the text later flaunts when she states, "*He's a warrior, a solider. Five on one might even be fair for him*" (362). In a subtly admiring tone, she describes Cal as a "soldier born and bred" who "could burn [a] whole village down if he really wanted to" (163), but despite moments of distrust and fear of him, she falls for him.

It is important to make clear that Mare's humanization and admiration of Cal, Maven, and even Julian, all imperial Silvers, don't necessarily extend to the Silver women in the palace. Underlying the Cinderella paradigm is a neoliberal framework that valorizes socioeconomic competition; only one girl can win the prince. Indeed, when Mare first enters the court as a servant, she witnesses young women showcasing their beauty and supernatural abilities as they compete for Prince Cal's hand in marriage. After she is reintroduced to the court as a Silver, Mare notes that the other young women regard her with distrust: "*They think I'm taking Cal away from them. They think I'm their competition*" (99). Ironically, both accounts are true; from the moment she witnesses the magical pageant as a servant, she becomes a participant. This is seen first through her immediate negative perception of the competing girls. In one instance, as she dismisses and belittles one of the contestants: "Her gaze lands on Cal—I mean the prince—trying to entice him with her doe eyes or the occasional flip of honey-blond hair. In short, she looks foolish" (66). Indeed, Mare frames the women of the court as frivolous throughout the book. However, the most poignant example of Mare's competitiveness towards the other girls is her immediate dislike of future nemesis, Evangeline. Interestingly, the novel similarly frames Evangeline as possessing warlike imperial strength. However, unlike Cal, Maven, and Julian, Evangeline is demonized almost immediately. Upon first seeing her, Mare notes that Evangeline "rises in an outfit of black leather. Jacket, pants, boots, all studded with hard silver. No, not silver. Iron. Silver is not so dull or hard" (68). However, in contrast to her assessment of Cal's military prowess, after watching Evangeline fight, Mare concludes, "*She doesn't look magnificent to me*" (69). It is only after Evangeline's display that Mare's own supernatural power to produce lightning erupts, which forces the king and queen to pass her off as Silver. Mare's power erupting during the pageant only further reinforces Mare as a subtextual participant.

Considering Mare's narrative arc within the palace, and her differential and often contradictory perception of the Silvers, the novel seemingly suggests that not all members of the ruling class are deserving targets of anger. In fact, by presenting examples of bad (largely female) Silver rulers[9] and good (largely male) Silver rulers, the text implies a solution to oppression that seemingly undermines its earlier engagement with oppression as systemic and institutional. Before warning Mare of the dangers of the Scarlet Guard's plans, Julian implies that a positive change could occur simply by raising a royal Silver who would be a kinder king. Referring to his sister, the former queen, he tells Mare, "She was kind, compassionate, a mother who could raise Cal to be the king this country needed to unite us all" (182). This is corroborated once Maven betrays both Mare and Cal at the novel's climax. Although at the end of the novel, Mare resolves to continue to fight with the Scarlet Guard, her aim is not to overhaul the social order but to exact revenge against Maven, exemplified by the book's final line: "*I will kill him*" (383).

The book, then, seems only partially committed to its theme of antioppression, at times denouncing and at others romanticizing the white, patriarchal imperial structures that oppress nonwhites; indeed, in a particularly telling scene, the book seems to almost excuse and erase these unequal structures by drawing a false equivalency between Mare's hatred of the Silvers and the Silvers' murder and domination of her people. Despite admitting that the Silver oppression of the Reds is "wrong to the very deepest levels of humanity," Julian also tells Mare that "[t]hinking all Silvers are evil is just as wrong as thinking all Reds are inferior" (131). Through this contradictory statement, the novel presents a bourgeois, white, middle-class framework of equality mired in respectability politics. Although Mare's rebellion against the opulence and power around her informs her performance as a racially oppressed individual, the narrative itself aligns uneasily with the psychic space of bourgeois whiteness that derives pleasure from that same opulence and power. Taken together, then, Mare's narrative of rebellion subconsciously offers a bourgeois model of how racial minorities could—or perhaps should—exist within dominant power structures.

Conclusion

To craft a story of a white heroine fighting against racial oppression, *The Red Queen* borrows, without fully subverting, Western capitalist frameworks of race that continuously repress, define, and control nonwhite peoples. Examining the novel in regards to how it may inadvertently promote white patriarchal economic logic provides an avenue through which to critique many other dystopian YA novels. The countless stories of reverse oppression and their privileging of ideals of whiteness beg the question: to what extent are the stories of rebellion crafted within and for the cultural space of middle-class whiteness truly rebellious? If the books present an experience of oppression that, through perpetuating problematic discourses, ultimately fails to dismantle those power structures that oppress real members of the underclass, then we can conclude that such stories are offering readers a commodified racial experience. Thus, although examinations of race in YA literature within the publishing world call for more racial diversity, we must also discuss the numerous ways these narratives reflect dominant racial ideologies. Indeed, as *The Red Queen* shows, narratives uncritically immersed within the white Western episteme can limit and control the terms of race in YA narratives in ways that ultimately reaffirm oppressive systems of power.

Notes

1. In 2015, the Cooperative Children's Book Center assessed diversity in children's books published in 2014. During 2014, the number of children's books by and about people of color and First/Native Nations was around 14 percent. Although, as publisher Lee and Low note, this is a 4 percent increase from 2013, the statistics show that books and creators of color are still heavily underrepresented.

2. Said identifies one of the first English novels as *Robinson Crusoe*, a tale of colonial domination in which the "protagonist is the founder of a new world, which he rules and reclaims for Christianity and England" (70). Indeed, the economic prosperity of bourgeois society was the "goal . . . of the market place," which was fueled by exploiting peoples across the world (David and Hall, qtd. in O'Malley 10). This places novel reading and publishing within colonial relations of power.

3. Since the illustration first appeared in the Time-Life book *Early Man*, the image has become iconic, globally symbolizing evolutionary biology (Shelley 85).

4. For more on Western philosophical frameworks of evolution as they pertain to white and specifically African peoples, see Mbembe 2–18, Mudimbe chapter 1.

5. In an 1888 account, William Agnew Paton describes the laboring Black bodies of slaves, focusing on their "muscular limbs" and sweat-drenched skin, which Paton describes as "a sugary glaze, that . . . looked . . . like a life-sized animated chocolate figure" (qtd. in Sheller 157). The rhetoric used to describe the enslaved ties them to the socioeconomic laboring sphere while simultaneously dehumanizing them, rendering them a product.

6. I refer to Focault's use of the "gaze," a concept he demonstrates in *The History of Sexuality* (141).

7 . With the terms "ideological" and "repressive" state apparatus, I rely on Althusser's theorization, in which he considers the state's biopolitical structures. As he explains, schools, religions, family, and media are ideological state apparatuses, whereas the police and military form the repressive. Each play key roles in maintaining hegemony (132–45).

8. The narrative seemingly uses the Cinderella narrative for the reader's enjoyment.

9. Queen Elara, Cal and Maven's mother, is the story's main villain. Although later Maven betrays the Silver Court and Mare when he and the queen force Cal to kill the king, Mare primarily blames Queen Elara's machinations (338).

Works Cited

Allen, Amanda. K. "The Cinderella-Makers: Postwar Adolescent Girl Fiction as Commodity Tales." *The Lion and the Unicorn*, vol. 33, 2009, pp. 282–99.

Althusser, Louis. "Ideology and Ideological State Apparatuses." *Lenin and Philosophy, and Other Essays*, translated by Ben Brewster, New Left Books, 2001.

Aveyard, Victoria. *The Red Queen*. Harper Teen, 2015.

Cart, Michael and Christine A. Jenkins. *The Heart Has Its Reasons: Young Adult Literature with Gay/Lesbian/Queer Content, 1969–2004*. Scarecrow Press, 2006.

Carter, Prudence. "Black Cultural Capital, Status Positioning, and the Conflict of Schooling for Low-Income African American Youth." *Social Problems*, vol. 50, 2003, pp. 136–55.

Ehrlich, Hannah. "The Diversity Gap in Children's Publishing, 2015." *Lee and Low Books*. 5 March 2015. http://blog.leeandlow.com/2017/03/30/the-diversity-gap-in-childrens-book-publishing-2017/. Accessed 4 January 2015.

Feder. E. K. "The Dangerous Individual('s) Mother: Biopower, Family, and the Production of Race." *Hypatia*, vol. 22, no. 2, 2007, pp. 60–78.
Foucault, Michel. *The History of Sexuality: Vol 1. An Introduction*. Vintage Books, 1990.
Gunn, James. "Harry Potter as Schooldays Novel." *Mapping the World of Harry Potter: Science Fiction and Fantasy Writers Explore the Best Selling Fantasy Series of All Time*, edited by Mercedes Lackey and Leah Wilson, BenBella Books, 2006, pp. 145–56.
Howell, F. Clark. *Early Man*, New York: Time-Life Books Inc., 1965.
Joo, Hee-Jun Serenity. "Miscegenation, Assimilation, and Consumption: Racial Passing in George Schuyler's 'Black No More' and Eric Liu's 'The Accidental Asian.'" *MELUS*, vol. 33, 2008, pp. 169–90.
Koshy, Susan. *Sexual Naturalization: Asian Americans and Miscegenation*. Stanford University Press, 2004.
Mbembe, Achille. "Necropolitics." *Public Culture*, vol. 15, 2003.
Mudimbe, V. Y. *The Invention of Africa: Gnosis, Philosophy, and the Order of Knowledge*. Indiana University Press, 1988.
Mulvey, Laura. *Notes on Sirk and Melodrama*. Palgrave Macmillan UK, 1989.
Nama, Adilifu. *Black Space: Imagining Race in Science Fiction Film*. University of Texas Press, 2008.
O'Malley, Andrew. *The Making of the Modern Child: Children's Literature in the Late Eighteenth Century*. Routledge, 2004.
Reider, John. *Colonialism and the Emergence of Science Fiction*. Wesleyan University Press, 2008.
Said, Edward. *Culture and Imperialism*. Vintage Books, 1993.
Sheller, Mimi. *Consuming the Caribbean: From Arawaks to Zombies*. Routledge, 2003.
Zamora, Lois Parkinson. *Writing the Apocalypse: Historical Vision in Contemporary U. S. and Latin American Fiction*. Cambridge University Press, 1989.

The Fairy Race
Artemis Fowl, Gender, and Racial Hierarchies
Kathryn Strong Hansen

Holly Short in Eoin Colfer's *Artemis Fowl* series (2001–2012) is truly astounding. Holly is the first female officer in the elite Recon division of the Lower Elements Police (LEP), the law enforcement agency for underground-dwelling fairies, and the first woman considered for the rank of major in the LEP. As a pilot, "She was a natural. First in the academy" (Colfer, *Artemis Fowl* 49). Holly seems ideally placed to challenge stereotypes in YASF because she demonstrates that female characters can be active and dominant. The pervasiveness of stereotypes is overtly referenced in Colfer's series when a dwarf notes that humans "could find a reason to distrust almost anyone. Height, weight, skin color, religion. It was almost safer to be different in some way" (Colfer, *Eternity Code* 114). This statement appears to celebrate difference by presenting heterogeneity's perniciousness. While the *Artemis Fowl* books might initially seem to celebrate diversity, a minority character is not the protagonist of the books. Instead, the wealthy white male Artemis Fowl upstages Holly even while relying on her capabilities to further his goals and save his life. Troublingly, Holly repeatedly follows Artemis, replicating gender dynamics that YA literature of previous eras employed.

Yet it is not only Holly's gender that makes her sidekick status disappointing; her race does, too. While Artemis is human, Holly is an elf. Although in the *Artemis Fowl* series "race" usually delineates the human race from fairy races, Artemis's superiority is inescapably linked to his ethnic race: repeatedly, the narration emphasizes Artemis's extreme literal whiteness, both as a sign of his ethnicity and evidence of his gender nonnormativity. His skin color relates to his dislike of typical outdoor boyishness, and because the text ties his indoor pursuits to his incredible intellectual skills, his extreme whiteness also indicates his exceptionality. The series' narration reinforces Artemis's superiority to fairies and other humans and also demonstrates a hierarchy among the fantasy races. Trolls rank lowest, with elves and centaurs at the top. The books position Artemis at the pinnacle of all rankings, an all-too-common spot for a wealthy white man. Despite Holly's street smarts and combat skills, she acquiesces to the hierarchy that grants Artemis authority over her.

Such insistence upon hierarchies is all the more disappointing because this series initially appears to challenge normative gender assumptions through its distribution of skills to characters with nonnormative gender performances. Holly defies traditional femininity in her abilities and interests, and Artemis and demon № 1 do not display stereotypical hegemonic masculinity. In fact, Artemis, Holly, and № 1 possess few stereotypically gendered traits. This could have allowed these books to endorse nonstereotypical gender performance. Yet Artemis's development into sexual awareness reclaims him into heteronormativity, and the books ultimately endorse hegemonic masculinity as a necessary characteristic of superiority. In their nonnormative performances of gender, Artemis, Holly, and № 1 occupy liminal spaces that help to reify the centrality of heterosexuality. In this essay, I argue that, despite initially seeming to resist traditional ideas, the *Artemis Fowl* books construct a fantasy world that reinforces hidebound notions of gender and sexuality as well as of race, all of which these books interconnect. To do so, I first outline the conditions that raise the possibility that the *Artemis Fowl* series might celebrate gender queerness, and I explain how the books ultimately reinscribe cisgendered maleness as a precondition for excellence. I then discuss how the issue of race—both in the sense of the fairy and human races as well in the sense of ethnic races—celebrates racial and gender hierarchies. The essay concludes with a discussion of how the books affect readers through their insistence upon the heroism of heteronormative whiteness.

Atypically Gendered Exceptionality

Initially, Holly's excellent police skills seem to indicate that the *Artemis Fowl* series depicts gender as unimportant in a character's abilities. The fact that Holly is the first female in the Recon division is an often-referenced reminder of her exceptionality. Conrasting Holly is Corporal Lili Frond. Holly loathes Lili, a descendant of the first elf king, calling her "a bimbo. An airhead" (*Artemis Fowl* 37). Lili is "the bimbo face of the LEP. Sexism was alive and well … It was rumored that Frond's LEP scores had been bumped up because she was a descendant of the elfin king"

(Colfer, *Arctic Incident* 51–52). The narration hints at Lili's ancestry, not her sex, as the reason for her preferential treatment, but it also indicates that she has her position because of sexism, not nepotism. Conventional gender characteristics are her only explicitly discussed traits, reducing her to a stand-in for women who do not defy cultural expectations of gender. Lili is depicted "tossing blond tresses over her shoulder" (*The Arctic Incident* 52) with "inch-long manicured nails that were absolutely no use in the field" (Colfer, *Opal Deception* 79), and labeled "the glamorous face of the LEP" (Colfer, *Atlantis Complex* 100). Reduced to appearance-based traits, Lili is all surface and no substance. Because Lili is not depicted as engaging in any behavior other than performing femininity or adequately executing the tasks of her office, the narrative's derision of her contrasts with the ways Holly's excellence is idealized. In other words, for Holly to be exceptional, other women must be typical, and the references to Lili suggest that male fairies do not value typical fairy women. In the fairy realm as in the real world, social institutions are structured by and for men's power, and Anupa Batra has explained women's three options for their presentation of gender in her discussion of feminism in the works of Gilles Deleuze:

> One, the adoption of the traits that are constituted as feminine in and through the relation to the standard, man. ... In other words, women who have these traits to a high degree are viewed as being "real" women. Two, women can also be "male." This is in the sense of having traits that have been indexed onto the masculine. However, since these traits are coded as masculine, an individual woman with these traits will either fall short in comparison with a man or the expression of the trait will appear as a kind of perversion of masculinity. Third is the path that will lead to the transformation of gendered subjectivity. (Batra 6)

Lili takes the first option, reinforcing the binary structure that informs widespread understanding of gender. Holly takes the second option, exhibiting traits usually coded as masculine, such as engaging in combat and training with weapons. But this option ensures that women will fall short of men by departing from the expectations created by gender dualism.

Holly's excellence can only exist if she does *not* display traditional femininity. Unlike Lili's traditional gendering, Holly's gendering is complex. However, rather than her complexity being a hallmark of individual gender identity, indicative of the kind of transformation Batra sees as a third choice for women, Holly's abilities are coded as masculine:

> Holly was undeniably ten times the pilot [Artemis] would ever be, and also several times more macho than he was. Artemis had once seen Holly get into a

fistfight with another elf who said her hair looked pretty, because she thought he was being sarcastic, as she was sporting a fresh crew cut on that particular day. Holly didn't go on many dates. (Colfer, *Last Guardian* 273)

Holly's skills are overtly constructed as masculine via the descriptor "macho." Further, the fact that Holly seldom dates simultaneously casts her "machoness" as the reason that she is unable to secure the many dates that the narration establishes as a suitable metric with which to measure women.

Holly's performance of traits commonly gendered masculine creates her as a foil for Artemis's nonperformance of traditional masculinity. Because the books present Holly as falling short of excellence due to her lack of traditional femininity, they undercut her achievements. However, the books consistently present Artemis as remarkable specifically because he does not display stereotypical masculinity. For instance, when evading attacking trolls, Holly and Artemis jump into a river: "Holly dived in, gracefully arcing through the air before entering the water with barely a splash" (*Opal Deception* 185). In contrast, "Artemis stumbled after her. All this running for one's life was not what he was built for. His brain was big, but his limbs were slight" (*Opal Deception* 185). This reminder of Artemis's intellectual capacity deflects attention from Artemis's inabilities toward his exceptionality. In this way, transgressing gender stereotypes is presented as laudable for young men. However, despite the notion that femininity "is less rigidly codified, precisely because it is not the center," the possibility for Holly to be admirable is denied because of the series' insistence that Holly exemplify heteronormative femininity (Batra 7).

The name "Artemis" associates the main character with the virginal Greek goddess of the hunt, helping Artemis Fowl differ from stereotypical YA male heroes in ways that complicate gender. Among other responsibilities, the goddess Artemis "was recognized as necessary to the ritual process that formed the male community. ... Artemis inspired the intense emotion male citizens needed to transform themselves into the soldiers war compelled them to become" (Cole 188). The goddess performed gender atypicality by inspiring soldiers, but typical ancient Greek women "were generally denied a public voice" (Blundell 10). While she was not the only gender-atypical goddess—Athena was goddess of war strategy, for instance—such gender performance was allowed only because of her deity status. She models powerful gender-role atypicality, since she was explicitly described as a *parthenos*, or virgin. The goddess Artemis "had to remain permanently a *parthenos* and biologically a girl, for she could protect girls, brides, and adult women from the dangers of reproduction only if she herself was immune to its disabilities" (Cole 209). This explanation, conflating pregnancy with disability, shows the belief that motherhood renders women imperfect. Because Artemis was a goddess, she was exempt from the social expectation of motherhood and could choose to be a virgin, and therefore not "disabled." However, because motherhood is considered central to heteronormative, if "disabled," femininity, the women she protected were seen as committing "a rebellion against [their] essential role[s]" (Roberts 100). Ancient Greek society expected women to be mothers, and only the divinity of a goddess provides an exemption for Artemis. Artemis Fowl's atypicality elevates him in part because his masculine body makes him never at risk for the "disability" of motherhood.

Further, just as the Greek goddess's "bold heart" (Hesiod 453) and hunting ability establish her as not conventionally feminine, Artemis Fowl's critical thinking and logic skills establish him as nonconventionally masculine. For instance, just as the goddess inspired Greek soldiers, other characters take inspiration from the boy Artemis's brilliant plans and therefore can fight their enemies zealously. Artemis Fowl's name is inextricably tied to his exceptionality through its femininity, as he explains to another character: "About my name, *Artemis*. You were right ... it is generally a female name. After the Greek goddess of archery. But every now and then a male comes along with such a talent for hunting that he earns the right to use the name. I am that male" (*Eternity Code* 267). Artemis emphasizes his status as male even as he highlights his difference from most men. It is because of his biological maleness that Artemis's name hints at his exceptionality, appropriating femininity as a prize for his talents; but here, biological maleness is a necessity for superiority. While Artemis can appropriate gender fluidity in ways that emphasize his excellence, Holly does not share that privilege because different expectations attach to biologically female bodies.

Artemis's Queerness in the Service of Heteronormativity

The difference of cultural expectation for men and women contributes to the sense that, in these books, feminine power is only acceptable in a male body. The series demonstrates the importance of the male body through its updated invocation of the goddess Artemis. Artemis's male body is not subject to the same cultural demands as the goddess's body. His indeterminate sexuality allows him to serve as an example of both feminized masculinity and of asexuality before the series establishes his heterosexuality. At one point, Artemis tries to forestall his puberty, behaving atypically for a teenager. As Judith Butler points out, "only the feminine gender is marked ... the universal person and the masculine gender are conflated, thereby defining women in terms of their sex and extolling men as bearers of a body-transcendent universal personhood" (14). Because men's bodies encode universal personhood, and because culture encodes power as a male trait, male bodies enjoy greater leeway than female bodies as to what is deemed acceptable.

Artemis's decision not to act on his sexual feelings obliquely aligns him with his namesake, whose ability to exempt herself from procreating required divine status. He is exempt from culturally prescribed notions of sexuality not because he is divine but because he lives in a culture that valorizes male heteronormativity. He can choose to exempt himself from sexual choices simply because he is male, which makes his sexuality difficult to define throughout most of the series. Before finishing the books, Colfer explained his plan to spare his protagonist romantic entanglements. In 2003, Colfer said, "I don't want [Artemis] to get much older. I don't really want to get into girlfriends and romance" (Colfer and McDonald 10). When romantic attraction does enter the novels, Artemis expresses unease when he asks his bodyguard Butler, "Is it normal, during puberty, to feel these blasted feelings of attraction at stressful times?" (Colfer, *Lost Colony* 265). Tison Pugh discusses how Artemis's "reluctance to pursue his likely future as a heterosexual" allows the novels to "question the desirability of heterosexuality while endorsing it as normal" (Pugh 120). This endorsement forecloses the gender diversity that the books initially seemed to offer. The series constructs the sexual awakening that puberty brings as threatening to intellectual prowess. Artemis is strengthened when he ignores his maturation and tries to stay asexual, suggesting that nonheteronormativity is an important component of Artemis's superiority.

However, the eventual revelation of Artemis's attraction to girls establishes heterosexuality as the books' norm. The series therefore creates an alternative third category, or what anthropologists have labeled a third gender: "The 'third gender' concept is by nature flawed because it subsumes all non-Western, nonbinary identities, practices, terminologies, and histories. Thus, it becomes a junk drawer into which a great non-Western gender miscellany is carelessly dumped" (Towle and Morgan 676). Rather than tease out the specifics of what might constitute an alternative to binary concepts of gender, the *Artemis Fowl* series places Artemis's sexuality temporarily in this metaphorical drawer only until Artemis chooses to accept his heterosexuality. This renders that third gender category a stepping stone to heterosexuality, which has the effect of telling young readers that nonheterosexuality is merely a way station to heterosexuality, relegating gender queerness to a temporary and diminished state. The series therefore tells genderqueer or homosexual readers that they depart from the norm if they continue to experience nonheterosexual desire. The series' narrative reinforces a return to heteronormativity by allowing Artemis to follow a feminine version of the hero's journey. In setting his sexuality into abeyance temporarily, his story follows that of the heroine taking a "green world" lover, or embracing nature through a bond with, say, a horse (Pratt and White 17–19). Artemis's version sees him embracing the fairy realm as a component of nature, particularly through his close association with the fairy Holly. Yet the archetypal heroine must leave behind her "green world" lover and her independence to be reclaimed by heteronormativity, maturity, and civilization (Pratt and White 36–37). In Artemis's analogous journey, he leaves behind his genderqueer time in the fairy realm to progress into heteronormativity and adulthood, yet in marked contrast to heroines, his maleness allows him to remain independent.

Artemis's heterosexuality grants him privilege that allows him to experiment with nonheteronormativity, highlighted through Orion, Artemis's "alter ego" (*Atlantis Complex* 263). Orion, gallant and brave in a traditionally masculine manner, cannot formulate complex intellectual plans as does Artemis. It would be easy to interpret Orion as a critique of traditional masculinity writ large, but Orion instead specifically critiques masculine traits that are not assumed by a sufficiently masculine body. Orion focuses on chivalry, fighting, and poetry, fulfilling long-outdated requirements for masculinity. Orion's personality also occasions humor that highlights his ineptitude. This can be seen in the contrast between idea and delivery when he longs to start a fight: "'I live for aggressive action!' thundered Orion squeakily, which was unusual" (*The Atlantis Complex* 183). Spending time with Orion makes Holly miss Artemis's brilliance, casting Artemis as superior to Orion. "I wish we had Artemis now … He would know what to do," Holly says while facing danger with Orion (*The Atlantis Complex* 185). Orion's inabilities allow readers to value Artemis's abilities as facets of his nonnormative gender identity rather than see Artemis as lessened by his atypical performance of masculinity. Again, Colfer draws on essentialized notions of gender: Artemis is unusual, but what is usual—Orion's desire for "aggressive action"—is a facile gender stereotype. By extension, readers understand that traditional masculinity requires the kind of strong body that the bodyguard Butler possesses, not Artemis's weak body. Orion's bodily failures—which are, of course, Artemis's as well—demand an atypical gender identity to allow a state of excellence.

№ 1 and Failed Sexual Nonnormativity

The warlock № 1 also demonstrates that a body's failure to meet cultural ideals of gender requires gender atypicality for that entity to be exceptional. Because his inability to transform from imp to demon is characterized as an inability to display suitably masculine traits for his race, the books present essentialized ideas of gender as normal. Gender binarism is assumed to be the natural order in demon culture, which readers will recognize from their own culture's gender rules: males are strong and do not show emotion; females tend the young and serve the males. The books introduce № 1 as unable to fit into this order and therefore portray him as gender atypical. Usual demon evolution is that they are born as imps, adorable creatures who undergo a vicious, viscous adolescent "warping" into violent demons. Sticky "warp muck" less than subtly suggests adolescent boys' semen production, the necessary precondition of their adulthood. № 1 is initially disappointed in his own disinterest in becoming a human-killing demon and, simultaneously, a sexually aware adolescent. The spelling of his name reflects his culture's dim view of him. In one reading of his name, he is always first in line to warp, constantly surpassed by younger imps. The way that his name is written, "№ 1" rather than "Number One" or "#1," also means that his name can register as "no one." Without a clearly defined sexual identity, he is "no one" within demon culture.

However, № 1 is superior to all other imps and demons, and, like Artemis, his superiority relates to nonnormative gender status. This initially appears as № 1's prolonged childhood, and teachers also construct him as insufficiently aligned with pre-existing gender taxonomies. When № 1 laments, "I'm not like the others," his instructor Rawley constructs № 1's emotions as unmanly: "'Are you going to cry?' asked Rawley, his eyes bugging. 'This is too much ... He's going to cry now, just like a female'" (*Lost Colony* 77). Demon culture constructs stereotypical femininity as weaker than masculinity, and masculinity is essentialized and monolithic. Rawley berates the imps, all of whom are male, by calling them "girls" or "ladies," and describes dishonor as "grub hunting with the females" (*Lost Colony* 62). The use of feminine epithets to denigrate male characters indicates a gender hierarchy, and for readers to understand the denigrating nature of these remarks, they must recognize essentialized ideas about proper behavior for beings of different sexes. In that act of recognition, readers help reify gender stereotypes.

The clearest markers that № 1 differs from his classmates are his inability to warp into adulthood and his gentle, cultured personality. As with Artemis, the books associate № 1's cultural and intellectual pursuits more with femininity than with masculinity. Artemis and № 1's feminine traits occur in bodies sexed male, which are allowed to display excellence, while the bodies of cisgendered women in the series, like Lili Frond, are not. In both demon and human culture, stereotypical masculinity is associated with bodily strength as well as a lack of interest in artistic or intellectual pursuits. № 1's interest in vocabulary is one indication of his cultured mind, and he revels in the new words of nondemon languages. When he learns the word "pink," he explains, "We don't have a word for that color in the demon commonspeak. Pink is considered undemonlike, so we ignore it. It's such a relief to be able to say pink!" (*Lost Colony* 175). The strong extradiegetic associations of the color pink with femininity suggest that if "pink" is undemonlike, then demon traits are stereotypically masculine. № 1's gender nonnormativity is, like Artemis's, difficult to label: "№ 1 is not conclusively depicted as a homosexual, but the differences marking him as unique among demons undermine constructions of normatively gendered identity in his culture" (Pugh 136). № 1's gender distinctiveness, however, is clearly related to his powerful capabilities.

What the demons view as unacceptable gender nonnormativity—№ 1's prolonged adolescence—is actually an indicator of his status as a powerful warlock. Among the demons, only warlocks do not warp, and warlocks are the only demons that can harness magical power. № 1's difference from other demons is at least partially a difference of species, so he is revealed to be not a nonnormative demon but a normative warlock. He recognizes the power of this distinction when he decides to keep the name № 1 rather than take a traditional warlock name. "I am № 1. The name used to mark me out as different, now it makes me unique," he asserts (*Lost Colony* 377). The change in his self-view from shameful difference to exceptional uniqueness mirrors how his seeming gender nonnormativity shifts into normativity for his species.

Unlike Holly, whose atypical gender expressions cause her to be less than feminine, Artemis's and № 1's departures from gender stereotype cause them to be more than merely hegemonically masculine. Unlike Artemis, № 1's warlock status means that he cannot participate in heteronormativity as the culture in which he was raised defines it. Artemis is therefore distinct from both Holly and № 1, and this difference establishes that certain bodies are restricted in the ways they can perform gender. While both Holly and № 1 are uniquely skilled, their nonnormative gender performances make them outcasts or, at least, the butt of jokes. This diminishes their power, but № 1 can no longer be seen as nonnormative once his identity as a warlock is confirmed. His reveal as a normal male warlock rescues him from disrespect, but Holly's feminine body is never rescued from ridicule. In contrast, the series depicts Artemis as so exceptional that his feminine name is overlooked, as are his gender nonconforming behaviors. As Artemis emphasized when defending his name, maleness makes nonnormativity his right (*Eternity Code* 267). Just as Artemis insists on the importance of maleness to justify his appropriation of whatever he likes, the books insist upon biological maleness as required to excuse the blurring of gender lines; Artemis can challenge gender expectations precisely because he is male.

Despite gender queerness marking some characters as powerful, the *Artemis Fowl* series ultimately demonstrates that normative heterosexuality is an essential component of a hero. Gender queerness is a capacious term, roughly analogous to nonconformity with culturally constructed gender expectations. Kate Bornstein describes gender nonconformity as "a crossing, mixing, and blending of gender specific signals all at once" (Bornstein 19). The exceptional capabilities of nonnormatively gendered characters are depicted as departures from traditional gendering, upholding the heteronormative/nonheteronormative binary with its insistence on the preservation of cultural norms. However, the books shift Artemis's sexual identity away from gender queerness over time, as he begins experiencing adolescent impulses of sexual attraction. The objects of his affection—Holly Short, Juliette Butler, Maria the limousine driver, and Minerva Paradizo—are all heteronormatively female. So, while the series initially casts Artemis's nonheteronormative sexuality as a strength, heterosexuality becomes more clearly a part of Artemis's personality as he develops into adulthood.

Ethnic Race, Fairy Race

In these books, gender is not the only identity category presented in retrograde fashion. Race is an explicit topic, with fairies, pixies, and other imaginary races populating the books. This is a function of the series' genre hybridity, with the books drawing on conventions of spy novels, science fiction, and fairy tales, among others. While science fiction "is readymade for voices traditionally deemed marginal" and displays a "penchant for racial play, for making new races or species" (Kilgore 17, 21), Colfer's books do not capitalize on this potential for giving voice to the marginalized. The series borrows from science fiction (via advanced technologies and futuristic medicines, for example), creating expectations that the books will capitalize on speculative fiction's "ability to ask relevant questions about our society in a way that would prove provocative in more mainstream forms" (Wyatt, qtd. in Jackson 128). This includes the expectation that the books might question racial hierarchies, given science fiction's history of such questioning. Yet while science fiction has the potential to critique racial hierarchies, it often instead reinscribes them. Novelist Samuel R. Delany argues that "racism is as much about accustoming people to becoming used to certain racial configurations so that they are specifically not used to others, as it is about anything else," so when books present alien races as hierarchically taxonomized, they influence readers to believe in the inherent truth of those hierarchies (Delany). Further, Isiah Lavender describes how science fiction "has mirrored rather than defied racial stereotypes throughout much of its history" and actually transmits "assumptions of racism even in stories that are ostensibly envisioning a future where race has become irrelevant" (Lavender 12, 20). These critics demonstrate that even well-intentioned attempts at inclusivity fail when they reify racial hierarchies, and Colfer's series does just that.

The series essentializes race in its reinscription of hierarchies, presenting members of different races more as stereotypes than as individuals. Often, a character's racialized skills become essential to the success of Artemis's team. For instance, the dwarf Mulch Diggums proves repeatedly helpful by virtue of his tunneling skills, described as unique to dwarves. Foaly the centaur is also important because of his centaur-specific advanced technology engineering. The series presents these characters' traits as racially, not individually, specific, perpetuating an essentialist view of race. Race also appears in the books in a different sense of the word, with Artemis's Irishness frequently mentioned. Historically, Irishness has been often invoked as analogous to nonwhite Commonwealth identities (Peatling), so Colfer's emphasis on Artemis's Irishness and his extreme whiteness implicitly argues that the Irish are indeed white. But by elevating whiteness through its association with Artemis, the series recapitulates Irishness as "a force that was turned inward, preoccupied overwhelmingly with 'Ourselves,' expressing little, if any, interest in parallel movements for emancipation in other parts of the world" (Nelson 11). Moreover, the books do not offer any model of race as constructed and instead portray racial characteristics as simply genetic.

Artemis's whiteness marks him as distinct from other characters as much as his nonhegemonic masculinity does. Butler, his bodyguard, is Eurasian and serves Artemis seemingly more by tradition rather than choice because "[t]he Butlers had been serving the Fowls for centuries" (*Artemis Fowl* 15). Butler's Asian background reinforces Artemis's sexual and racial superiority by invoking a feminized Asian man stereotype: in the early twentieth century, miscegenation was discouraged by popular culture depictions of Asian men as effeminate. Further, their "employment opportunities were also limited in scope, consisting primarily of 'feminine' work such as laundry, housekeeping, and cooking, which translated into restaurant work" (Shek 381). These stereotypes have become so entrenched that any depiction of Asian house employees is not entirely free from them. The longstanding history of his family's servitude to the Fowls, combined with Butler's overdetermined name indicate an entrenched power differential despite Butler's remarkable bodyguarding and weaponry skills. In contrast, Artemis is proudly Irish, reinforcing historical hierarchies of white Europeans exerting power over people of color. Artemis's position of racial authority over Holly is similarly troubling. Holly has a "coffee-colored complexion" (*Eternity Code* 83), which is evidence of her elvish race because in the "Spotter's Guide" to fairy races, in addition to having red hair and pointed ears, elves are described as having "brown skin" (Colfer, *Artemis Fowl Files* 78). Because Holly, despite her own exceptionality, chooses to serve Artemis, their relationship is similar to Artemis's relationship with Butler in that both reinforce the prevailing racial hierarchy: white men who "rightfully" maintain power over members of other ethnic groups.

The "Spotter's Guide" also demonstrates the hierarchy that exists within the fairy races. Its entries for centaur and pixie have the descriptor "extremely intelligent," elves and dwarves are labeled "intelligent," and sprites are described as having "average intelligence" (*Artemis Fowl Files* 78, 79, 82). Goblins, however, are "not clever, but cunning," and trolls are "very, very stupid—trolls have tiny brains" (*Artemis Fowl Files* 80, 81). That these categories reference prejudiced real-world racial views is suggested by one of the characteristics of trolls: "hairy, with dreadlocks" (*Artemis Fowl Files* 80). Critic Dianne Johnson has cautioned that Black hair has "historically been the focus of racist interpretive strategies," and the association of dreadlocks with trolls, the least intelligent of all the fairy peoples, suggests just such a racist interpretation (Johnson 341). This reference to an ethnically specific hairstyle as a troll trait suggests that the fairy races in some sense map onto human races. Other subtle associations between fictional races and real-world minorities appear in the series. For example, the narration mentions a "goblin ghetto" (*Lost Colony* 21). Since the term "ghetto" carries racist overtones, an unflattering association is implicitly made between the goblins—described as "evolution's little joke … the dumbest creatures on the planet" (*Eternity Code* 28) and as the only one of the fairy races "inclined toward the criminal life" (*Atlantis Complex* 201)—and real-world disadvantaged minority races. The descriptions of these characteristics function similarly to descriptions of orcs in fantasy literature. As Helen Young explains, descriptions of orcs "resonate with anti-Black racist stereotypes which developed particularly in the eighteenth and nineteenth centuries to justify colonisation and slavery" (Young 93). Orcs are further racialized through "their black plaited or dreadlocked hair, heavily muscled hyper masculine bodies, and the iconography of their armour and weapons which codes them as savage, tribal, and not-White" (Young 93). That trolls may be of a different fairy race than orcs is less the point than is the fact that both "lowly" creatures not only appear as lowest in the hierarchies of their respective fictional worlds but also possess characteristics unmistakably similar to racist stereotypes of extradiegetic Black people. Historically, such taxonomies were constructed to disenfranchise people of African heritage and to privilege individuals of European descent, seen at least as early as *The*

Inequality of Human Races (1853–55) by Joseph Arthur, Comte de Gobineau, and traceable to the racist taxonomies of humans set forth by Carl Linneaus in the eighteenth century. So, while Colfer's books might initially seem to represent a beneficial spectrum of fairy race—intelligent green-skinned sprites and resilient brown-skinned elves—the explicit ranking of those fairy peoples destroys any potential advantage of such representation.

Instead, Artemis's extreme whiteness is depicted as a rationale for his superiority, perpetuating the books' emphasis on hierarchies that replicate extradiegetic racist taxonomies. The narrator links Artemis's paleness with his nonhegemonic masculinity by connecting his whiteness to his disinterest in boyish, outdoor play: "Sun did not suit Artemis. He did not look well in it. Long hours indoors in front of a computer screen had bleached the glow from his skin" (*Artemis Fowl* 3). If whiteness is constructed as the antithesis of color, "white discourse implacably reduces the non-white subject to being a function of the white subject, not allowing her/him space or autonomy, permitting neither the recognition of similarities nor the acceptance of differences except as a means for knowing the white self" (Dyer 544). Artemis's whiteness functions this way, constructing other fairies and humans as foils for Artemis, and readers therefore understand those characters as less important than Artemis. Constructing Artemis's whiteness as absence of color only reinforces the privilege that his whiteness bestows upon him.

While the narration uses grammatical negatives ("did *not* suit," "did *not* look well") to describe Artemis's paleness, it does so to elevate Artemis. By emphasizing the "long hours" that Artemis devotes to researching his brilliant schemes rather than playing outdoors, the narration establishes Artemis's dedication and drive, and by repeatedly reinforcing his whiteness, the books solidify it as an important signifier of his mastermind status. For instance, when a waitress notes that Artemis seems vampiric, she mentally connects the whiteness of his skin and his impressively mature speaking style: "The waitress scurried to the kitchen, relieved to escape from the pale youth at table six. She'd seen a vampire movie once. The undead creature had had the very same hypnotic stare. Maybe the kid spoke like a grown-up because he was actually five hundred years old" (*Eternity Code* 7). The waitress immediately associates Artemis's whiteness with his elevated intelligence, which reinforces the association of Artemis's paleness with exceptional abilities.

The waitress's description of Artemis as a vampire is not unique, since Artemis's whiteness is frequently described as vampiric. The figure of the vampire "has always threatened binaries, such as dead/alive, animal/human, male/female, heterosexual/homosexual, and has often functioned as a destabiliser of the category of race" (Frohreich 33). Artemis's vampiric appearance destabilizes the human/nonhuman divide because it announces quasi-supernatural abilities. The blurring of boundaries between human and fairy could have been structured to highlight beneficial cooperation between races or to find common ground between heretofore opposed factions, but the narration uses Artemis's vampiric qualities to reinforce his superiority.

Artemis's vampiric characterization also points to the ways his race and gender intersect, indicating how his nonnormative gender identity works with his race to make him distinctive. In other words, Artemis is unusual because his whiteness highlights his gender identity. That the series insists upon establishing a hierarchy among the different races suggests that the books are more interested in preserving Artemis's exceptionality than in descrying inequalities. Thus, Artemis's nonnormativity highlights his superiority rather than the multiple ways he has been oppressed. Indeed, his wealth enables Artemis to indulge his intellectual pursuits, which keep him tied him to a computer, spending the time indoors that renders him preternaturally white-skinned. Further, the Fowls secure and build upon their wealth in part because race-based hierarchies, like those that ensure that the Eurasian Butlers continually serve the Irish Fowls, exist. Artemis's race and gender intersect in a vector of rarified privilege, which the books present as a natural outgrowth of that intersection.

With the descriptions of Artemis as a vampire, his whiteness marks him as superhuman. Yet vampires are figures of more than just whiteness, since their gender queerness has, at least since Anne Rice's *Vampire Chronicles* novels began in 1976, been essential to their identity. The methods of recruiting vampires, while never depicted as being employed by Artemis, emphasize non-heterosexuality in their focus on bodily fluids rather than the gender of bodies. After all, "[v]ampires reproduce themselves through the sharing of their blood, through the spilling of the gooey, messy fluids that course through our bodies ... Transferring immortality through fluids, this bizarre reproduction without sex takes us out of that sacred metaphysics of solids that is so dear to this western, white straight male symbolic" (Winnubst 12). Artemis need not engage in such vampiric reproduction to be associated with its symbolism, and the mere suggestion of Artemis as vampiric invokes these cultural associations with queerness. What's more, Artemis's vampiric traits seem to indicate that nonnormative sexuality correlates with mastermind-level genius. As noted, his personal traits—physical inability, tidy appearance, love of pop culture—connote nonnormative masculinity. As Judith Butler argues, "There is no gender identity behind the expressions of gender; that identity is performatively constituted by the very 'expressions' that are said to be its results" (Butler 33). Artemis's expressions of gender at first seem to make him a symbol of nonhegemonic masculine power, admirable in part because of his deviations from traditional male stereotypes.

Artemis's Hierarchical Whiteness

Artemis's initial difference from normative masculinity is allowed by his whiteness, which is encoded in the books' vampire references. Artemis is also vampiric when it comes to fairy magic since he is willing to take magic from fairies in any way he can. Artemis's many appropriations of magic reify his white privilege. For instance, Artemis lies to Holly and № 1 about why his mother has become ill (it is his fault, but he convinces them it is theirs), and he uses their magic to travel backwards in time to effect a cure. In the process, he magically switches one of his eyes with one of Holly's and soon realizes her eye has magical powers. Though the switch happens outside of his control, he lies about the eye's powers so that he can retain those powers: he "had more magic left than he had pretended" (*Lost Colony* 384). So, while he might not have intended to vampirize Holly, he nonetheless takes an element of her body into his and benefits from that transfer. Artemis's superiority, conferred by his extreme whiteness, allows him impunity in taking from Holly what he wants to further his superior status. In contrast, when Holly in that same switch receives one of Artemis's eyes, she receives no benefit.

Since both Holly and Artemis have demonstrated nonnormativity in their gender displays, Artemis's partaking of fairy magic without fully becoming a fairy employs the cultural association of the term "fairy" with homosexuality to establish Artemis as queer but not homosexual. Through his vampirization of Holly's eye, he appropriates the power of fairies, in all senses of the term, without becoming one. Though functionally little different from parasites, vampires enjoy a substantially different image. While vampires connote power, sex appeal, and superhuman qualities, the categorization of someone as a "parasite or a leech is not a neutral statement but expresses disapproval and derision, it functions as an accusation and/or denunciation" (Musolff 219). Moreover, "On account of their derogatory connotations, the terms *leech* and *parasite* are considered to be instances of discriminatory hate speech when used as references to human beings" (Musolff 220). When someone from a marginalized group takes something without the giver's permission, the metaphor is likely to be that of the leech/parasite, as with "the infamous case of the genocidal Nazi propaganda against Jewish people and other minorities as parasites on the German people's body" (Musolff 220). The *Artemis Fowl* books valorize Artemis's borrowings from Holly's body and from queer culture. Those borrowings are as parasitic as they are vampiric, but Artemis's whiteness provides him with more power and prestige than other characters. In contrast, Mulch Diggums steals, but he is labeled a thief rather than depicted as a vampire. Mulch's heteronormative masculinity and dwarfish race disbar him from the same kind of vampiric depiction used to characterize and elevate Artemis's thefts.

Conclusion

The potential for a positive message about the malleability of gender roles in the *Artemis Fowl* series is usurped by the books' insistence on racial hierarchies, perpetuating intolerance throughout the books. Celia Keenan points to this insensitivity in a discussion of the first three *Artemis Fowl* novels. They may have action-packed plots, she admits, but

> [a]t times ... there is a lack of sensitivity that jars. An example occurs in the first volume, where the use of the phrase "Cripples and beggars huddled on rice-mat islands" ... shows a surprising lack of awareness that his young readers may not all be able-bodied people and that some might be upset by this usage. The phrase has a slightly archaic flavour, placing it in the world of pre-1950s travel and adventure writing. (Keenan 262–63)

This retrograde feeling creates a tension with the progressive notions suggested by the presence of protagonists who seemingly defy gender-based stereotypes. After all, the main characters in Colfer's series initially present the possibility that gender queerness grants exceptionality. That the term "fairy" has the dual meanings of "magical entity" and "gay" and that Artemis's eventual display of heterosexual desire suggest that Artemis's difference from and superiority to magical beings shut any doors to celebrating queerness that the series might have opened. Moreover, despite the presence of fairies in a children's book calling to mind the fairy-tale genre, the *Artemis Fowl* series displays regressive attitudes toward race more like those employed in older examples of the fantasy genre. As Helen Young has discussed, "twenty-first-century Fantasy genre-culture developed its habits of Whiteness early in the previous century," largely because of the popularity of J. R. R. Tolkien and Robert E. Howard; their fantasy realms of Middle-earth and Hyboria "became the default setting for Fantasy, making race the conventional framework around which difference is built into the genre" (34). While difference might be celebrated, the fantasy genre has historically been more likely to use difference to divide for the purpose of elevating whiteness. As a result, nonwhite and nonheteronormative readers are left with the message that they are inherently lesser than Artemis and that his superiority is as much about race and gender as it is about skill.

Ultimately, Artemis is a fairy in no sense of the term. Not being of the magical fairy race and not being homosexual, the justification for Artemis's superiority comes from the series' essentialized presentation of whiteness as hierarchically superior to other races. Artemis's extreme whiteness allows him the safety of racial privilege that makes his gender experimentation culturally safe. Artemis's social position stands in marked contrast to that of minority subjects, people whose "identities are formed in response to the cultural logics of heteronormativity, white supremacy, and misogyny—cultural logics that ... work to undergird state power" (Muñoz 5). While there are many "ways in which identity is enacted by minority subjects who must work with/resist the conditions of (im)possibility that dominant culture generates," Artemis operates within a rarefied realm of identity possibility (Muñoz 6). The power that accrues to his maleness, wealth, and whiteness protects him when he vampirizes queer culture. Artemis ultimately transforms into a young man who is clearly heterosexual, but his ability to foray into the fairy world, in the term's magical sense, excuses Artemis's appropriation of "fairy" traits in the gendered sense. The series thus establishes queerness an element of the fairy realm, not the readers' real world, though racial hierarchies are part of both realms' cultures.

In 2015, *Kirkus Reviews* began noting the race of central characters in YA and children's books. An editor later explained the rationale behind this move, asserting that "naming race and identity is one of the duties of a reviewer. Parents and caregivers of children of color want books that reflect their children, as do librarians and teachers serving children of color" (Smith). While calling attention to and fighting whiteness as a perceived default for characters unless race is otherwise specified is an important goal, the *Artemis Fowl* books demonstrate that including characters of a minority race is simply not enough to qualify a text as diverse. Colfer's fairy stories privilege their well-to-do white male protagonist at the expense of the members of other races so socioculturally depressed that they literally live underground. Though the series raises the possibility of disrupting the status quo through suggesting Artemis's potential queerness and including characters of many races, the *Artemis Fowl* books deny the need for changes to traditional heteronormativity and regressive ideas about race, encouraging young readers to preserve the status quo.

Works Cited

Batra, Anupa. "Women and Becoming-Women: Deleuze and Feminism." *Academia.edu*.1–8. Accessed 6 April 2016.
Blundell, Sue. *Women in Ancient Greece*. Harvard University Press, 1995.
Bornstein, Kate. *My Gender Workbook*. Routledge, 1998.
Butler, Judith. *Gender Trouble: Feminism and the Subversion of Identity*. Routledge, 1999.
Cole, Susan Guettel. *Landscapes, Gender, and Ritual Space: The Ancient Greek Experience*. University of California Press, 2004.
Colfer, Eoin. *Artemis Fowl*. Disney Hyperion Books, 2001.
Colfer, Eoin. *Artemis Fowl: The Arctic Incident*. Scholastic, 2002.

Colfer, Eoin. *Artemis Fowl: The Atlantis Complex*. Disney Hyperion Books, 2010.
Colfer, Eoin. *Artemis Fowl: The Eternity Code*. Scholastic, 2003.
Colfer, Eoin. *The Artemis Fowl Files: The Ultimate Guide to the Best-Selling Series*. Miramax Books, 2004.
Colfer, Eoin. *Artemis Fowl: The Last Guardian*. Disney Hyperion Books, 2012.
Colfer, Eoin. *Artemis Fowl: The Lost Colony*. Disney Hyperion Books, 2006.
Colfer, Eoin. *Artemis Fowl: The Opal Deception*. Scholastic, 2005.
Colfer, Eoin, and Craig M. McDonald. "Eoin Colfer: An Exclusive Interview." *Art of the Word* (2003). Rpt. in *Children's Literature Review*, edited by Tom Burns. Gale, 2006, pp. 6–11.
Delany, Samuel R. "Racism and Science Fiction." *The New York Review of Science Fiction* no. 120 (1998). http://www.nyrsf.com/racism-and-science-fiction-.html.
Dyer, Richard. "The Matter of Whiteness." *Theories of Race and Racism*, edited by Les Back and John Solomos, Routledge, 1999. pp. 539–48.
Frohreich, Kimberly A. "Sullied Blood, Semen and Skin Vampires and the Spectre of Miscegenation." *Gothic Studies*, vol. 15, no. 1, May 2013, pp. 33–43. EBSCO, DOI 10.7227/GS.15.1.4. Accessed 7 May 2015.
Hesiod. *The Homeric Hymns and Homerica*. Translated by Hugh G. Evelyn-White. Harvard University Press, 1936.
Jackson, Sandra, and Julie Moody-Freeman. "The Genre of Science Fiction and the Black Imagination." *African Identities*, vol. 7, no. 2, 2009, pp. 127–32. DOI: 10.1080/14725840902808736. Accessed 1 Jan. 2017.
Johnson, Dianne. "Hairitage: Women Writing Race in Children's Literature." *Tulsa Studies in Women's Literature*, vol. 28, no. 2, Fall 2009, pp. 337–55. JSTOR, www.jstor.org. citadel.idm.oclc.org/stable/40783423. Accessed 15 June 2015.
Keenan, Celia. "Who's Afraid of the Bad Little Fowl?" *Children's Literature in Education*, vol. 35, no. 3, 2004, pp. 257–70. Academic Search Complete, http://search.ebscohost.com/login.aspx?direct=true&db=a9h&AN=14426260&site=ehost-live. Accessed 4 May 2015.
Kilgore, De Witt Douglas. "Difference Engine: Aliens, Robots, and Other Racial Matters in the History of Science Fiction." *Science Fiction Studies*, vol. 37, no. 1, March 2010, pp. 16–22. JSTOR. http://www.jstor.org.citadel.idm.oclc.org/stable/ 40649582. Accessed 1 January 2017.
Lavender III, Isiah. *Race in American Science Fiction*. Indiana University Press, 2011.
Muñoz, José Esteban. *Disidentifications: Queers of Color and the Performance of Politics*. University of Minnesota Press, 1999.
Musolff, Andreas. "Metaphorical Parasites and 'Parasitic' Metaphors." *Journal of Language and Politics*, vol. 13, no. 2, 2014, pp. 218–33. DOI 10.1075/jlp.13.2.02mus. Accessed 11 April 16.
Nelson, Bruce. *Irish Nationalists and the Making of the Irish Race*. Princeton University Press, 2012.
Peatling, G. K. "The Whiteness of Ireland under and after the Union." *Journal of British Studies*, vol. 44, no. 1, 2005, pp. 115–33. DOI 10.1086/424982. Accessed 31 July 2019.
Pratt, Annis, with Barbara White. "The Novel of Development." In *Archetypal Patterns in Women's Fiction*, edited by Annis Pratt. Harvester, 1982.
Pugh, Tison. *Innocence, Heterosexuality, and the Queerness of Children's Literature*. Routledge, 2011.
Roberts, Dorothy. "Motherhood and Crime." *Social Text*, vol. 42, Spring 1995, pp. 99–123. JSTOR, www.jstor.org.citadel.idm.oclc.org/stable/466666. Accessed 29 March 2016.

Shek, Yen Ling. "Asian American Masculinity: A Review of the Literature." *The Journal of Men's Studies*, vol. 14, no. 3, Fall 2006, pp. 379–91.

Smith, Vicky. "Unmaking the White Default: Writing about Race." *Kirkus Reviews*. 4 May 2016. https://www.kirkusreviews.com/features/unmaking-white-default/. Accessed 12 Jan. 17.

Towle, Evan B., and Lynn M. Morgan. "Romancing the Transgender Native: Rethinking the Use of the 'Third Gender' Concept." *The Transgender Study Reader,* edited by Susan Stryker and Stephen Whittle. Routledge, 2006. pp. 666–84.

Winnubst, Shannon. "Vampires, Anxieties, and Dreams: Race and Sex in the Contemporary United States." *Hypatia*, vol. 18, no. 3, 1 October 2003, pp. 1–20. *Project MUSE*, muse.jhu.edu/article/46067. Accessed 7 May 2015.

Young, Helen. *Race and Popular Fantasy Literature: Habits of Whiteness*. Routledge, 2016.

Enchanting the Masses
Allegorical Diversity in Fairy-Tale Dystopias
Jill Coste

In the spate of dystopian YA literature published in the last decade, a new hybrid has appeared: the fairy-tale dystopia. Marissa Meyer's Lunar Chronicles series and Stacey Jay's *Of Beast and Beauty* are notable direct fairy-tale retellings, and several others, including Julianna Baggott's *Pure* and Lauren DeStefano's *Wither*, borrow heavily from the fairy-tale format. The pairing makes sense; both genres offer moral lessons, transmit cultural fears and values, and—in YA publications—provide some sort of triumph for the protagonist.

These genres also have a common problem: neither is noted for its diversity. YA dystopias frequently feature white, heterosexual female leads who, despite their subversion of stereotypical femininity, reinforce hegemonic power structures. Similarly, fairy-tale retellings also try to subvert patriarchal norms, but they often reify whiteness. Furthermore, fairy tales are laden with a white, European history, one that the occasional diverse Disney princess, such as Jasmine of *Aladdin* or Tiana of *The Princess and the Frog,* cannot overcome. Thus, dystopian fairy tales, with their spirited female leads, nestle comfortably in the canon of novels with strong, subversive heroines that, unfortunately, circumvent the topic of race.

However, these fairy-tale dystopias provide readers with a compelling way to investigate representations of diversity in YA literature. The success of these particular dystopias lies in their very fairy-tale heritage, which grounds readers in familiar territory and offers protagonists who step beyond Disney and fit into an increasingly futuristic—and diverse—twenty-first century. Moreover, because of their mutability, fairy tales easily facilitate complex conversations about race. Tellingly, fairy tales fit where they are needed. In her book *Fairy Tales Transformed?: Twenty-First-Century Adaptations and the Politics of Wonder*, Cristina Bacchilega emphasizes the adaptability of fairy tales, explaining that they "come in many versions and are in turn interpreted in varied ways that speak to specific social concerns, struggles, and dreams" (3). Because fairy tales evolve to reflect contemporary issues, they are an ideal site for engaging with the call for more diversity in literature for teens and young adults.

Paired with dystopias, fairy-tale revisions offer a course for change: they reach masses of readers and present diversity through fantasy, exploring the complications of heterogeneity by offering fantastic renderings of diverse characters. The fairy-tale-dystopia hybrid may not be a solution to the dearth of diversity in popular YA literature, but the allegory of difference at work in many of them offers a clear starting point for racial critique.

Two recent works in particular serve as new depictions of diversity in dystopian novels, providing allegories that open space for discussions of difference. Stacey Jay's *Of Beast and Beauty* follows the vein of feminist fairy tales by subverting the female role, but it also uses the dystopian touchstones of political strife and class hierarchy to allegorize contemporary race relations. The Smooth Skins—the ruling majority who are also called "whole" citizens—have privilege and power, being safely ensconced in a domed city on a ruined planet. The Monstrous, relegated to the wilderness outside the dome, battle the Smooth Skins over limited resources. The ultimate solution to their constant conflict is miscegenation. Similarly, Marissa Meyer's Lunar Chronicles tetralogy uses well-known fairy tales to explore a science-fiction future conflict between the residents of Earth and those who dwell on the moon. As in *Of Beast and Beauty*, the potential remedy for racial hostility seems to be the merging—in both platonic and romantic ways—of different ethnicities or species. Both *Of Beast and Beauty* and the Lunar Chronicles explore difference through allegory to present a fictional world where diversity is key to survival and success.

In these texts, "diversity" means a coming together of characters of different backgrounds, skin colors, and classes. There is certainly a utopian element to the characters' cooperation, but it is mitigated by the overt allegorical connections to familiar race and class complications and by the characters' harnessing of their own marginalization to push for social change. The protagonists in Jay's and Meyer's texts embody a version of what Patricia Hill Collins dubs the "outsider within." Collins uses the term "to describe social locations or border spaces occupied by groups of unequal power" and notes that "[i]ndividuals gain or lose identities as 'outsiders within' by their placement in these social locations" (5). The characters' narrative arcs send them through numerous social locations, forcing them to reconsider their identities and, in some cases, to push for political recategorization of those identities. "Diversity" in these novels represents marginalization, and it allows characters to do what Collins pushes for in her examination of racialized diversity: "to reclaim marginal locations as places of potential intellectual, political, and ethical strength" (5).

The allegorical difference as an impetus for reclamation and social change is enhanced by the genres of these novels. The dual genres of fairy tale and dystopia offer a distinct, productive space for exploring social change. While racial allegory in fiction is nothing new, the surge in fairy-tale–dystopia pairings for YA readers and the way allegory is situated within those works *are* new. Dystopias are quite clearly political allegory, but within the influx of dystopian texts for young adults, such books also encourage youth activism and agency. Fairy tales, in contrast, may seem at odds with the overt political work in dystopias. Indeed, fairy tales have a history of serving as moral instruction, originally urging young readers to behave in accordance with social norms. But fairy-tale retellings have increasingly allowed for subversion, for flouting expectations instead of capitulating to them. Whereas well-known nineteenth-century fairy-tale heroines were unendingly patient and amiable, today's are imbued with wit and intensity, genuinely irritated about the restrictive societies they must navigate and the categories that are thrust upon them.

The fairy-tale genre can also diminish the bitterness of postapocalyptic worst-case scenarios in YA dystopias. In their book *New World Orders in Contemporary Children's Literature: Utopian Transformations*, authors Clare Bradford, Kerry Mallan, John Stephens, and Robyn McCallum claim that dystopian fiction for young adults "present[ed] for the first time bleak analyses of human society without promise of the euphoric ending which is usually expected in [children's literature]" (29). They also assert that this bleakness is "a major impediment for authors aspiring to engage with new world orders by envisaging more utopian outcomes, so strategies need to be found to enable such a perspective" (29). Fairy tales are one such strategy. With the inherent "happy ending" associated with the average reader's knowledge of how a fairy tale unfolds, these familiar stories make dystopian worlds accessible and make the differences therein accessible as well.

Ideally, this accessibility will lead to a greater empathy in the reader and a greater desire to understand one's own agency. In the introduction to their book *Contemporary Dystopian Fiction for Young Adults: Brave New Teenagers*, editors Balaka Basu, Katherine R. Broad, and Carrie Hintz point out that in reading dystopias, "adolescents can at once fit themselves to better meet society's demands *and* shape society to better reflect their own desires and goals, creating the world they need, the world they want, and the world that they deserve" (6).¹ Furthermore, they note that "[d]idacticism and escape have a role to play in the reception and impact of the YA dystopian genre" (6). They argue dystopias for young adults are more than just diversionary adventures. They are moral tales that can teach activism. Here, the link between fairy tales and dystopias is clear—fairy tales have a long history of didacticism, and they are surprisingly complex in their history of activism. Jack Zipes states that, at the turn of the eighteenth century, "the fairy tale showed allegorically the way toward self-realization, or, in other words, the alternative path history could take if human beings actually took charge of their destiny" (105). Fairy tales have long offered readers a lesson in possibility.

The twenty-first-century combination of fairy tales and dystopias in YA literature offers new possibilities: it has the potential to encourage young readers to understand the urgency of social activism, to push for inclusion, and to stress the importance of diversity. As Bacchilega points out, fairy tales "historically scripted a wide range of desires" and "at least some versions are also produced and/or received as inspirations to undo privilege and prejudice" (4). These stories have always reflected human desires, and new fairy tales have a place in the realm of social change, speaking as they do to contemporary cultural need. Indeed, I argue that dystopian YA fairy tales use depictions of fantastic difference to reach readers and invite consideration of political change. The way that fairy tales change to reflect cultural concerns opens a space of analysis for white readers who either may be reluctant to engage in examination of race or have simply not been exposed to sufficiently nuanced examinations of how race functions in contemporary culture. For readers of color, these political fairy tales offer the possibility of a world where the status quo is not only questioned, but upended.

Readers also benefit from looking at dystopian fairy tales critically. In her article "Critical Conversations on Whiteness in Young Adult Literature," Melissa Schieble argues that critical literacy benefits from acknowledging whiteness as a construct and examining how that construct is reinforced or challenged in YA literature. Since dystopian fairy tales often privilege the systems of power associated with whiteness, they can reinforce whiteness as a construct. But because the characters fight for social justice and recognize the instability of the hierarchies that inform their respective lives, their stories illustrate the possible futures for which speculative fiction is known. Indeed, these texts invite a "dream of justice" (Oziewicz 4). As Marek Oziewicz claims, "[f]airy stories... are narratives not about the actual, but about the desirable" (12), which allows readers to envision the kind of world that could be. Moreover, fairy-tale heroines represent the way a person in a position of privilege must confront their culture's complicity in perpetuating prejudice. The allegories at work in

Of Beast and Beauty and the Lunar Chronicles invite a critique of privilege, as the protagonists learn to question their own biases. Along with the characters in the texts, readers see that "[s]tories show how as individuals we can both reproduce and resist racism as we interact with historical, cultural and institutional patterns and practices" (Bell et al. 9). As stories, fairy-tale allegories can serve as "an accessible and concrete way for youth to engage with abstract ideas such as racism" (Cann 98), and they can encourage readers to critically assess hegemonic power structures.

Since literary fairy tales have a long history of folding normalization into their storylines, they inherently demonstrate these power structures. Indeed, the literary fairy tale, with its European roots, cannot help but carry colonialist notions with it. As Ebony Elizabeth Thomas notes in her book *The Dark Fantastic: Race and the Imagination from Harry Potter to the Hunger Games*, "colonialist ideas are inscribed in the generic conventions of the fantastic" (29). The ideas appear in the way that fairy tales can perpetuate a bourgeois ideology—for example, in Mme. Le Prince de Beaumont's "Beauty and the Beast," Beauty's steadfast patience and virtue result in her ultimately gaining rewards, riches, and a transformed prince, which highlights the way such tales normalize wealth and power. Furthermore, the well-known stories about learning to love someone different from oneself—"Beauty and the Beast" and "The Frog Prince," for example—often advance an unconscious lesson that difference is either dangerous or must be "fixed" in some manner, civilized into hegemonic conventions.

At the same time, fairy tales also invite varying interpretations that challenge normalization. Narratives of difference can become messages for progressive behavior. Cinderella must tussle with and overcome her enforced marginalization. Little Red Riding Hood navigates her encounter with "The Other" (who turns out to be legitimately dangerous—but contemporary retellings envision more of a kinship between the wolf and the girl, as in Marissa Meyer's *Scarlet*, or a sexual awakening, as in Angela Carter's "The Company of Wolves"). Hans Christian Andersen's Little Mermaid eschews her own heritage to such an extent that she ends up with nothing, providing a lesson on the importance of accepting oneself. All of these characters envision or encounter life outside their own and learn from it.

YA fairy-tale dystopias extend that narrative of progressive behavior into the political realm. Today's lessons reveal that "what's inside" a different outside is a person with whom to have kinship and that such respect for diversity is the route to political change. When paired with contemporary dystopia, the fairy tale shows how that change can take a political form. Jay's and Meyer's novels demonstrate the political nature of change by highlighting different issues. Jay's *Of Beast and Beauty* foregrounds kinship and stresses the significance of human connection, while also creating characters who push against hegemonic and patriarchal values in order to forge a better world. Meyer's Lunar Chronicles series focuses more closely on the protagonist Cinder's journey to self-acceptance, which is bolstered by the various fairy-tale characters Cinder encounters, ultimately emphasizing the importance of community. Meyer's characters do not come together by choice, but they gradually accept each other's differences and work together. Additionally, the natural evolution of their friendships—they are all working to save the planet—reflects the natural evolution of progress in their world. Through accepting each other, these characters cannot help but forge a better world. Without a conspicuous didactic message, Meyer's series advances its allegory more effectively than Jay's novel.

"She Is My Monster, and I Am Hers": When the Beauty and the Beast Save Each Other

The path to diversity in *Of Beast and Beauty* relies on love and acceptance as its main guideposts, and it uses the allegorical monster en route. Hearkening to its fairy-tale forbears, the novel offers a lesson of acceptance, and in true YA dystopian form, it emphasizes standing up to political might as integral to coming of age. In this novel, acceptance of difference breeds change in myriad ways, from individual to societal. In alternating points of view, *Of Beast and Beauty* follows Isra, a young queen bound by duty to her domed city of Yuan, and Gem, an imposing member of the Desert People, a race of evolved, hearty humans living in the harsh conditions outside the dome.

Jay's *Of Beast and Beauty* begins with an omnipotent narrator who laments the destruction of a distant Earth: "The ships ... came belching smoke and fire, stinking of space and beings living and breathing, loving and hating" (4). Immediately, the narration sets up a dichotomy: love and hate will beget clashing cultures, and the harsh climate of the world will cause some to adapt and some to retreat. This narrative device lays the groundwork for Isra and Gem to save the planet. Isra herself is tasked with being the one to remember the past, to realize that the destruction of her world can indeed subside if she can learn to love someone different from herself, in this case, Gem. It is the classic fairy-tale love story, with the raised stakes of a dystopia: Isra won't only save Gem like Beauty saves the Beast. Instead, Gem and Isra will liberate each other—and the whole world.

Isra begins the novel literally blind—the result of a childhood accident, so she believes—and her blindness is a metaphor for her ignorance. Isra's view of Desert People, whom her culture calls "The Monstrous," is naïve and crude.

With a description that denotes stereotyping and prejudice, Isra explains, "The Monstrous are bigger, stronger, with poison seeping from their claws, and skin as thick and hard as armor…They are brutal beasts determined to destroy humanity and take our cities for themselves" (19). Gem's view of the Smooth Skins is equally derogatory, but shrewder. Gem describes Smooth Skins as "softness like uncooked dough, empty eyes sunk in privilege-rotted flesh" (25). While Gem is more aware than Isra of the unjust differences between them, he is similarly hard-headed in his beliefs. Their oppositional views situate them as the quintessential beauty and beast—weak versus strong, soft versus hard.

Isra, however, also views herself as beastly, as "tainted," the word her people use to refer to Monstrous physicality (38). In her blindness, she cannot see herself, and because of her dry, peeling skin (the mundane affliction of eczema), she believes she will grow scales, a Monstrous trait. Her physicality is significant because it allows her to function at times as the "Beast" character and underscores the similarity between her and Gem, the ostensible "Beast" character. Jay extends the blurred boundary between the beauty and the beast, flipping the familiar narrative so that Gem is the one who has to leave Isra to care for his family, returning to profess his love and save Isra from death.

This interplay is not unusual for the Beauty and the Beast tale, and many feminist revisions recognize that monstrosity is not exclusive to men. However, instead of making monstrosity a lesson, these revisions make it part of the female character's journey of identity, which helps reinforce the idea that "normal" and "different" are not binaries. In his article "Monster Culture (Seven Theses)," Jeffrey Jerome Cohen notes that "the monster stands at the gates of difference. To conquer the monster, then, in whatever format, is to enter the realm of difference" (7). Thus, for the beauty to conquer her monster is to accept his difference—and not only to accept it but also to immerse herself in it. Cohen also notes that "the monstrous lurks somewhere in that ambiguous, primal space between fear and attraction" (19), a description that is suitable not only when the beauty encounters the beast but also when the beauty is a beast herself. For a female character to realize her own beastliness is for her to realize her own agency, which in turn empowers her to seek political change.

Isra's "beastliness" may be in her head, but she is physically different from the people of Yuan, who are "almost invariably small of stature and petite of bone, with nut-brown skin and straight black hair" (Jay 35). Isra has "light olive skin" (221), which allows her to straddle a line between light and dark and emphasizes her liminality. In fact, Isra's looks come from her mother, who was brought to Yuan from another domed city as part of a marriage alliance. Thus, Isra's lighter skin and tall build mark her as an outsider. But because she cannot see herself, Isra is certain she's part Monstrous.

That feeling of difference enables Isra to relate to Gem. Isra is drawn to Gem and wonders "Is it the tainted part of me that makes me ache for a Monstrous boy?" (Jay 146). Jerry Griswold, in his examination of various critical responses to "Beauty and the Beast," notes that psychoanalytical scholars, particularly Jungian critics, "see the Beast as Beauty's animus—as a part of her personality that she has denied and excluded, a part that is animal-like and sexual" (54). This is especially notable in *Of Beast and Beauty*, wherein Gem serves as a sexual foil to Isra. As a member of the matriarchal desert culture, Gem, at age nineteen, is much more sexually experienced than seventeen-year-old Isra. Indeed, Gem has an infant son and accepts that the mother of his child has chosen a different mate. In Gem's society, it's not unusual for women to have multiple sex partners, and the ultimate choice for how she would like to raise her family is hers. Isra, in contrast, was raised to sacrifice herself, both in body and in marriage, as she is meant to forfeit her life when the city demands it, and she is expected to acquiesce to an arranged marriage. Her society is starkly different from Gem's: Isra's domed city clings to staid patriarchal standards and an authoritarian government—reminiscent, perhaps, of where our own society has come from and a reminder of how far we have to go—while Gem's wild desert offers an almost utopian vision of a society where men and women live in equality. In this allegory, one must accept the wild to truly be civilized.

And Isra's journey is one that accepts the wild. If, from a psychoanalytical perspective, the Beast is Beauty's wild side, Isra encounters and embraces it when she and Gem venture out to the desert together. *Of Beast and Beauty* reveals sexual sensation to be worthy of awe: "I don't care what he is, who I am, what's wrong or right. There is no shame or fear, only the driving need to get closer, kiss deeper, consume and be consumed, to lose myself so completely that I will never be found" (Jay 162). That Isra imagines losing herself in sex reflects the Jungian idea that the Beast represents a heretofore repressed part of her, something that is essential to her nature yet so foreign she cannot imagine herself comprehending it as she is. Furthermore, the fact that Isra notes how Gem "know[s] exactly how to untangle" her sexual desire reveals the allegorical emphasis on embracing difference (163).

Embracing difference yields immediate agency for Isra. After her first sexual encounter with Gem, she requires no coaxing to assert her feminine empowerment, which in turn has political implications. When she returns to her castle after her desert trek with Gem, Isra rebukes her potential suitor, Bo, who is irate that she has gone without his permission: "We aren't even *betrothed*," she scoffs, cutting Bo off when he claims that eventual marriage was an understanding between them (205). Isra declares that such an understanding is meaningless, telling Bo, "You never even asked permission to court me. You certainly haven't earned the right to act like a jealous husband … I've done nothing to deserve this, and *even if I had*, it isn't your place to speak to your queen like a woman you bought for the night!" (205; emphasis mine).

In reminding Bo that he has not asked if she wanted to be courted, Isra implies that he has to first receive her permission to pursue her romantically. Furthermore, she claims that even if she has had sex with someone else, Bo has no business speaking to her like she's his property, showing that her choices belong to her alone. In comparing Bo's treatment of her with his likely treatment of a prostitute, Isra also cunningly reveals her knowledge of both Bo's extracurricular activities and the plight of women in her society. Through her encounter with difference, Isra comes into her own, and as a result, she changes.

Isra's change into a more assertive ruler has implications for the hierarchy of Yuan and provides thought-provoking fodder for critiquing ingrained social strata. The most overt hierarchical divide is between the Smooth Skins in Yuan and the Desert People in the harsh land outside. Blessed with ample food and water due to a blood sacrifice that the women of the ruling class make each generation, Yuan is a land of plenty. Conversely, the Desert People are starving and dying off. Their only hope, they believe, is to infiltrate the dome and steal the magic-giving roses—the plants that soak up the blood sacrificed by Yuan's queens. Gem notes, though, that "blood magic is dark magic" (194), emphasizing the unnaturalness of Yuan's vitality and thus reinforcing an allegory that privilege at the expense of others is evil.

Yuan also experiences class-related strife. The city is divided among nobility, otherwise known as "whole" citizens; the "tainted," people who have shown monstrous traits (a scaled neck or an errant claw, for example); and the Banished, who are proverbial lepers, the city's lowest class, composed of people who are missing limbs and other body parts. When Isra regains her sight (she finds out that she was being poisoned in order to remain an ignorant and willing sacrifice for the greater good of Yuan), she insists on seeing the Banished encampments and is horrified to learn that her people live in squalor. Throughout the novel, Isra is presented as an empathetic queen who is concerned for others, but her relationship with Gem enriches this empathy and makes her aware of unjust suffering. Furthermore, it allows her to reckon with her own monstrosity and complicity in maintaining Yuan's hierarchy of privilege.

Indeed, all change in this dystopian world stems from Isra and Gem desiring each other, in an allegory of learning to accept difference. Isra moves from offering patronizing speeches to Gem, explaining that "[w]e're raised to believe The Monstrous are worse than animals, that they are savages who kill for pleasure, and that their ugliness is a sign of the corruption of their souls"

(168), to determining that she and Gem "are both human in the same way" (213). Wonderingly, Isra asks herself, "How could I have ever thought differently? How could I have thought him a monster, even for a moment?" (213). The resolution in *Of Beast and Beauty* emphasizes that a genuine meeting of the minds is more important than what one is raised to believe. Furthermore, that meeting of the minds gives the characters the fortitude to actively work against the prejudicial nature of their societies. What works particularly well for fairy-tale dystopias is the promise of the better future that will come when a character has the courage to change. While this certainly applies to Isra's and Gem's initial opinions of one another, it also applies to Isra's maturing as a queen. She doesn't *have* to sacrifice her blood to the roses. She doesn't *have* to acquiesce to tradition. She can be an agent of change for her society.

At the resolution of the novel, "change" means dismantling the existing world completely. Because Isra and Gem love each other, Yuan's enchantment ends, demolishing the dome and healing the desert. While this is ostensibly the happy ending associated with the fairy tale, it actually complicates Isra and Gem's journey of accepting difference. When they leave the city and enter the desert, Isra dies in Gem's arms, having been crushed by falling debris in the disintegrating dome. She is, however, revived by the desert's magic and Gem's declaration of love. Moreover, she is transformed: "Ribbons of flame whip out to tease at her chest, her arms, all the way down to her knees and bare toes. Her legs grow longer, her hips and shoulders wider ... orange and gold scales unfold like cloth laid across her skin" (381). While Isra takes on some of the physicality of the Desert People, Gem loses some of his: "My teeth grow smaller and slicker against my tongue, my tongue creeps farther back into my throat, and ... my jaw ... firms up again in a different, more delicate shape than it had before. My shoulders and arms grow looser and lighter" (382). Isra and Gem both become hybrids of Smooth Skin and Monstrous. After a journey of accepting each other for who they are, they end up muffling that difference by becoming alike.

That said, what this new "likeness" does is underscore the notion that only in fully letting go of prejudice can our protagonists forge a better world. Thanks to fairy-tale transformation, Isra and Gem both become the other they despised at the beginning of the novel. Furthermore, their matched appearance can symbolize that they understand each other. As Gem notes in his final line, the woman he loves is "the loveliest person in the world, no matter what skin she wears" (Jay 386). While a bit moralizing, Gem's declaration also emphasizes the importance of acceptance and provides a genuine takeaway for the reader: embracing difference can change the world.

"I'm Going to Stop Hiding": A Girl Full of Wires and a Revolution

Marissa Meyer's Lunar Chronicles series also considers whether difference can save the world. Composed of four fairy-tale retellings, one per book, the first three novels of the series set the stage for the Cinderella character to instigate a political paradigm shift, with the fourth novel seeing that shift put into action. While each book features a different fairy-tale heroine with her own story of progress, it's the title character from the first novel, *Cinder*, who ties each story together, serves as an allegorical other, and pushes a dystopian world toward revolution.

Of all the famous fairy tales, "Cinderella" might be the one that most immediately evokes the blonde, blue-eyed heroine. Disney, of course, introduced the world to the iconic pretty princess in her blue dress, a princess who remained equally Aryan in the 2015 live action version of the film. Thanks to Disney (and Charles Perrault, who wrote the fairy godmother, pumpkin coach, and glass slippers into canon), Cinderella is firmly entrenched in people's minds as a European tale. However, like most fairy tales, the Cinderella story exists in nearly every culture. Indeed, the earliest known version, "Rhodopis," hails from Egypt and was recorded in in the first century BCE, and the Chinese "Ye Xian" was recorded in approximately 860 CE during the Tang Dynasty (Heiner). These locations are both significant to Meyer's series, which is set in a futuristic China and has a global scope. Simply by setting her Cinderella story on the other side of the world, Meyer destabilizes the American notion of who Cinderella is.[2]

In fact, Meyer's Cinderella doesn't conform to any mold. Cinder is a cyborg mechanic, a girl without description that readers have now created in their own image. She is, as Jennifer Mitchell explains, "an icon of hope for the disenfranchised groups with which she identifies and belongs" (57). Cinder is a new diverse heroine for contemporary readers. In her article "A Girl, A Machine, A Freak: A Consideration of Contemporary Queer Composites," Mitchell argues that "Cinder ... can and should be read as queer. Such a reading acknowledges the importance of non-normative narratives in terms of their bodies, selves, romances, and, ultimately, activisms" (54). Cinder is an ideal character to read as queer, since she's cyborg—physically queer—and of ambiguous ethnic heritage. Her diverse world is peppered with various cultural references, but humans' virulent hatred for the Lunar culture—former earthlings who now live on the moon—as well as their disdain for cyborgs serve as allegorical renderings of racial strife. *Cinder* doesn't overtly address race as we know it, but the message is clear: the "other" exists and is treated poorly.

Initially, the Earthen society in the Lunar Chronicles universe seems to have achieved postracial utopia. The novels eschew whiteness in favor of multiculturalism—it's unremarkable for characters to be of variable ethnic descent and skin color. The male love interests all have vastly different appearances—from Asian to Lunar to Caucasian—as do the female heroines. However, this multiculturalism still stands in for normalization, as "otherness" takes different forms. In Meyer's world, the two major marginalized groups—cyborgs and Lunars—are disenfranchised largely due to fear and a questioning of their "humanity." As in *Of Beast and Beauty*, the marginalized characters in the Lunar Chronicles are perceived as monstrous. They evoke Cohen's claim that monsters refuse "to participate in the classificatory 'order of things,'" which makes them "disturbing hybrids whose externally incoherent bodies resist attempts to include them in any systematic structuration" (6). Both cyborgs and Lunars can be seen as hybrids since both are enhanced in some way. As Meyer explains, cyborgs have some percentage of metal and wiring in their physical makeup that allows them to circumvent what would otherwise have been a physical disability; for example, Cinder has a mechanical foot and hand as well as a computer in her brain that operates her prostheses. Similarly, Lunars, who were born and raised on the moon, have the supernatural ability to manipulate bioelectricty. Because of their difference, both groups are feared and controlled. In the series' first book, Cinder discovers she is both cyborg and Lunar, a double-marginalization that simultaneously sends her into an identity tailspin and highlights "normal" culture's distaste for both. Cinder's distress at learning her Lunar identity is clear: "To be cyborg *and* Lunar. One was enough to make her a mutant, an outcast, but to be *both*?" (Meyer, *Cinder* 178).

Before learning of her heritage, Cinder also subscribed to stereotypical notions about Lunars. Her commentary echoes Isra's ignorant statements about the horrors of the Monstrous: "Lunars were a society that had evolved from an Earthen moon colony centuries ago, but they weren't human anymore... Their unnatural power had made them a greedy and violent race" (*Cinder* 48). Cinder overtly believes that Lunars are inhuman, despite her own experience with being called inhuman due to her cyborg body. Even when Cinder learns of her own link to the Lunar race, she still clings to her stereotypes: "Lunars were a cruel, savage people. They murdered their [ungifted] children. They lied and scammed and brainwashed each other because they *could*. They didn't care who they hurt, so long as it benefitted themselves. She was not one of them" (*Cinder* 178). Her immediate reaction is not to consider what humanity might actually exist among the Lunars but to reject the truth.

In this regard, one can read Cinder as relatable—she feels marginalized but also marginalizes others, so she is simply a flawed human. However, there's a deeper meaning at work here, for in marginalizing others, Cinder participates in a hierarchy that Richard Dyer notes is inevitable when defining privilege.

While in Dyer's study (and our reality) it is whiteness that confers privilege, in Cinder's universe, being Earthen is allegorical to whiteness. Just as, in Dyer's words, "the concepts of race and the white race that developed during the late eighteenth and through the nineteenth century ... shored up the sense of a category worth getting into if you could" (20), the concepts of humanity and being Earthen in the futuristic society of the Lunar Chronicles prove tantalizing. Rejecting Lunars as inhuman allows Cinder to "shore up" her own humanity, which is already in question due to her cyborg body.

Cinder then begins to learn of other Lunar refugees who are also passing as Earthen, evincing the privilege of Earth-bound humanity. These refugees, though, remind Cinder of her own connection to the Lunar race. Accepting the truth of her heritage also means accepting her destiny as the rightful heir to the Lunar throne, currently occupied by a tyrant bent on oppressing Earth. Learning that her own people are refugees complicates Cinder's understanding of her multimarginalized status and pushes her to embark on social change.

Cinder's growing political awareness mirrors that of the reader, and she is written in such a way that allows the reader to identify and grow along with her. In the first book, a descriptive emphasis placed only on Cinder's cyborg body highlights the physical aspect of her marginalization, setting her up to be an othered character to whom readers relate. In fact, descriptions of her face and coloring are scant in *Cinder*, and it's not until the second and third books of the series that Cinder's looks are even described. The fact that descriptions of Cinder's looks are omitted in the first book—the one in which she has the greatest number of point-of-view chapters and thus is the character readers are meant to identify with—reinforces her ethnic ambiguity and works to establish her as a character onto which readers can project themselves. Her location in the Chinese Commonwealth might evoke an Asian image, but her unknown (at first) heritage leaves room for other interpretations. Even the descriptions in the next two novels are somewhat vague, with Cinder's cyborg features still the main focus of her physical descriptions when she is a fugitive and her description is plastered all over the world. This is particularly notable since, with the right clothing, Cinder can easily "pass" as a noncyborg human. That the narration places so much emphasis on her cyborg body reveals a fixation with difference, both on the part of Cinder herself and as an allegory for racism.

Indeed, that allegory is particularly apparent in the laws that have been enacted regarding cyborgs in the Chinese Commonwealth. Cinder and her fellow cyborgs are governed by the Cyborg Protection Act, which evokes the Jim Crow–era laws that segregated Black people under the premise of separate-but-equal and legalized the marginalization of Black bodies from Reconstruction through the mid-twentieth century.[3] As with the justification of Jim Crow,

Cinder's Cyborg Protection Act purports to be about the safety of marginalized groups: the act "protects" cyborgs under the guise of making them the property of legal guardians. The protection's meaninglessness is evident when contrasted with the cyborg draft, which requires cyborgs to essentially donate themselves to scientific research for the so-called greater good. A plague called letumosis threatens everyone on Earth, and in the Chinese Commonwealth, scientists inject cyborgs with the plague in an ostensible effort to find a cure. Since there is no clear cure, the cyborg draft is actually a death sentence and an egregious violation of human rights. Furthermore, there is no limitation to what kind of cyborg is drafted; whether one has 6 percent mechanical properties or 36 percent, they are considered cyborg, evoking the one-drop rule that has categorized African American identity for centuries.

When Prince-turned-Emperor Kai, Cinder's potential love interest, eradicates the draft in the third book, he calls it "an antiquated practice that was neither necessary nor justifiable. We are a society that values human life—*all* human life ... Our country was built on a foundation of equality and togetherness, not prejudice and hatred" (Meyer, *Cress* 312). His political decision outright acknowledges the injustice of marginalization and underlines the allegory of diversity at work in the series. Thanks to their connection with Cinder, readers already know that cyborgs are human and deserve equal rights; through Cinder's story, they've seen the political implications of prejudice, and now they are seeing the implications of political change.

Kai is tasked with leading the Chinese Commonwealth, a role that allows him to ruminate on his country's many prejudiced laws. In fact, it's through Kai that readers understand the injustice of the Cyborg Protection Act, and the way Kai works through his complicated feelings about Cinder echoes how Isra in *Of Beast and Beauty* also struggled with her learned beliefs. Kai notes that "he'd been convinced, as his grandfather before him had been, that [the laws] were so obviously *right*. Cyborgs required special laws and provisions, for the safety of everyone. Didn't they?" (*Cress* 306). Kai's affection for Cinder is what drives him to change what laws he can, and because he is a voice of reason in a chaotic dystopian world, his behavior is important. That he changes his own mind and, subsequently, laws suggest that others can also change if they are willing to think through their own biases.

While Kai reconsiders his stance on outdated laws, Cinder still judges herself for being cyborg, showing that individual progress is as significant as social progress. The other characters with whom Cinder travels and fights in books 2, 3, and 4, however, are less fixated on cyborgs. While Cinder's cyborg nature is still a major point of her identity and political action throughout the series, her cyborg difference is muted somewhat by the introduction of the other fairy-tale stories. The heroines of those tales all have their own point-of-view chapters, with their own character journeys and concerns. What's more, descriptors like "golden" (*Cress* 88), "olive" (*Scarlet* 13, *Cress* 232), "warm brown" (*Cress* 270, 516), "pale" (*Cress* 73), and "dark" (*Winter* 776) evince multiple shades of skin color and foster an understanding that these characters are not homogenous. The involvement of the other characters makes the series more diverse and subtly offers an allegory of accepting difference and working toward a common goal. To the other characters who populate Cinder's world (and will help her save it), her cyborg otherness is unremarkable. This inattention to what, in Cinder's view, makes her "a freak" (*Cinder* 126) helps Cinder see that not everyone she meets will be fixated on her otherness. As the characters collaborate, each bringing their own unique skills to their quest to dethrone the evil Lunar queen, Cinder begins to rethink her own prejudices against herself.

As an allegorical other and the primary protagonist, Cinder invites readers to understand her marginalization and to root for the camaraderie she develops with her diverse crew of fairy-tale figures. As Cinder grows from a prejudiced Earthen into the leader of a revolution, readers are privy to her progression, her self-doubt, and her steadfast sense of what's right. She remains distressed about her marginalization throughout the second book, her outcast status compounded by her being a fugitive, wanted for defying the evil Lunar queen's orders. During one of Cinder's musings on her situation in *Scarlet*, the text layout shifts from paragraphs to a single word per line, five in a row, creating a checklist of marginalized identities: "Lunar. Cyborg. Fugitive. Outlaw. Outcast" (Meyer 333). Nowhere in Cinder's list are two other truths of who she is, "Princess" or "Heroine," revealing that her identity continues to be shaped by her feelings of otherness. However, the second book ends with her glamoring her cyborg hand—that is, using her Lunar gift of manipulating what people see in order to pretend that she has skin instead of metal—and then decisively dropping the glamor. Resolute, she declares, "I'm going to stop hiding" (*Scarlet* 452).

Thus, the first two books in the Lunar Chronicles retell two different fairy tales while tracing a marginalized character's journey to self-acceptance. The third book details Cinder's testing out her leadership abilities while she and her group of co-conspirators learn to coalesce. The fourth book follows suit, bringing into the mix a Black fairy-tale heroine in an inversion of Snow White.[4] Because Cinder is clearly set up as the primary heroine and struggles with her liminal identity in the first two books, readers learn to empathize, relate to, and champion both Cinder and her multiethnic world. In doing so, they also root for those who rally around Cinder and fight for change, internalizing the allegorical diversity at work in the Lunar Chronicles.

Progress and Problems

While Stacey Jay's *Of Beast and Beauty* and Marissa Meyer's the Lunar Chronicles never discuss diversity and racial tension outright, their use of allegory is clear. These novels imagine worlds where heterogeneity is a given, but people are still intolerant, thereby raising questions about human nature. The "other" is categorized by the ruling class, but members of that ruling class also exhibit their own characteristics of "otherness." Due to the complexity of the cast of characters, these novels manage to avoid being patronizing. While *Of Beast and Beauty* is a little heavy-handed in its concluding moral that all Isra and Gem needed was love, the novel offers a nuanced exploration of political strife and racial hierarchy. Similarly, Meyer's novels do not shy away from the consequences of political upheaval, and each character ends up either physically or emotionally affected by their efforts. In these novels, readers can identify with characters of all colors, and readers of color will not see their heritage tokenized by white characters.

Still, these are not perfect novels that hearken a new era of utopian harmony. The authors themselves are white, and Jay's descriptions of Gem's tribal culture occasionally veer into troubling stereotypes of Native Americans. Additionally, these novels lack any LGBTQ diversity; both Jay and Meyer's novels adhere to the fairy tale's typically heteronormative pairings. That said, these books are still broaching the topics of prejudice and hatred and the damaging consequences therein, and, in the case of Meyer's work, they are reaching widely diverse audiences in huge numbers.

The popularity of these fairy-tale retellings proves that readers are eager for these stories. Using fairy tales in a dystopian setting allows authors to harness the fairy-tale associations of romance, journeys, and transformations in order to present different forms of progress. And as Bacchilega notes in her examination of contemporary fairy-tale adaptations, "reflecting on [these retellings]—both their production and reception—illuminates and affects how we construct human relations in the present and how we map out our options for the future" (7). In spite of their typically Anglo-European heritage, literary fairy tales ultimately benefit the field of dystopian YA, provoking a discussion on what constitutes diversity and positing new narratives that push for inclusivity and social change.

Notes

1. All italics in quotes are original unless otherwise noted.
2. This is not to suggest that Meyer does so intentionally. Meyer's website reveals a rather simplistic view of the implications of a Chinese Cinderella, as the author merely notes that she

was paying homage to Cinderella source texts and that "it seemed more interesting than setting another story in America" (Meyer, "FAQ").

3. The metaphorical presence of Jim Crow in the Lunar Chronicles is especially relevant, considering how many Jim Crow–era justifications still perpetuate racism in the United States today. As Michelle Alexander argues, mass incarceration reveals the same discrimination that Jim Crow did, "marginaliz[ing] large segments of the African American community…[and] authoriz[ing] discrimination against them in voting, employment, housing, education, public benefits, and jury service" (17).

4. Beyond the scope of this particular essay is a more thorough examination of the character of Winter, who is depicted as mad due to her suppression of her Lunar gift. I question Meyer's choice to make her only Black POV character mentally unstable. Additionally, Winter has the least happy ending, ultimately struggling with posttraumatic stress disorder.

Works Cited

Alexander, Michelle. *The New Jim Crow: Mass Incarceration in the Age of Colorblindness*. The New Press, 2010.

Bacchilega, Cristina. *Fairy Tales Transformed?: Twenty-First-Century Adaptations and the Politics of Wonder*. Wayne State University Press, 2013.

Basu, Balaka, Katherine R. Broad, and Carrie Hintz. "Introduction." *Contemporary Dystopian Fiction for Young Adults: Brave New Teenagers*, edited by Basu, Broad, and Hintz, Children's Literature and Culture series, Routledge, 2013, pp. 1–15.

Bell, Lee Anne, Rosemarie A. Roberts, Kayhan Irani, and Brett Murphy. *The Storytelling Project Curriculum: Learning about Race and Racism through Storytelling and the Arts*. Barnard College, 2008. PDF file.

Bradford, Clare et. al. *New World Orders in Contemporary Children's Literature: Utopian Transformations*. Palgrave Macmillan, 2008.

Cann, Colette N. "A Reboot of Derrick Bell's 'The Space Traders': Using Racial Hypos to Teach White Pre-Service Teachers about Race and Racism." *Whiteness and Education*, vol. 1, no. 2, 2016, pp. 94–108.

Cohen, Jeffrey Jerome. "Monster Culture (Seven Theses)." *Monster Theory: Reading Culture*, edited by Jeffrey Jerome Cohen, University of Minnesota Press, 1996, pp. 3–25.

Collins, Patricia Hill. *Fighting Words: Black Women and the Search for Justice*, Contradictions of Modernity 7, University of Minnesota Press, 1998.

Dyer, Richard. *White*. Routledge, 1997.

Griswold, Jerry. *The Meanings of "Beauty and the Beast."* Broadview, 2004.

Heiner, Heidi Anne. "History of Cinderella." SurLaLune Fairy Tales, SurLaLune Fairy Tales, http://www.surlalunefairytales.com/cinderella/history.html. Accessed 2 Oct. 2015.

Jay, Stacey. *Of Beast and Beauty*. Delacorte, 2013.

Meyer, Marissa. *Cinder*. Feiwel-Macmillan, 2012.

Meyer, Marissa. *Cress*. Feiwel-Macmillan, 2014.

Meyer, Marissa. "FAQ." Marissameyer.com, http://www.marissameyer.com/faq. Accessed 15 Dec. 2015.

Meyer, Marissa. *Scarlet*. Feiwel-Macmillan, 2013.

Meyer, Marissa. *Winter*. Feiwel-Macmillan, 2015.

Mitchell, Jennifer. "A Girl, a Machine, a Freak: A Consideration of Contemporary Queer Composites." *Bookbird: A Journal of International Children's Literature*, vol. 52, no. 1, 2014, pp. 51–62.

Oziewicz, Marek. *Justice in Young Adult Speculative Fiction: A Cognitive Reading*. Routledge, 2015.

Schieble, Melissa. "Critical Conversations on Whiteness in Young Adult Literature." *Journal of Adolescent and Adult Literacy*, vol. 56, no. 3, 2012, pp. 212–21.

Thomas, Ebony Elizabeth. *The Dark Fantastic: Race and the Imagination from Harry Potter to the Hunger Games*. New York University Press, 2019.

Zipes, Jack. *Breaking the Magic Spell: Radical Theories of Folk & Fairy Tales*, revised and expanded edition, Kentucky University Press, 2002.

11
ERASING RACE

Neoliberalism's Erasure of Race in Young Adult Fiction
Sherri L. Smith's *Orleans* as Counterexample
Sean P. Connors and Roberta Seelinger Trites

Many political theorists define *neoliberalism* as an ideology that advocates for the maximal deregulation of the free market. We acknowledge that the term is demonstrably contested, especially when it is used with the term *globalization*, which can be defined as the process by which neoliberal economic forces have spread internationally. In this chapter, we propose that neoliberalism has influenced the erasure of race in recent YA dystopias. To demonstrate how this is the case, we build our argument on four pillars: first, we examine the deregulated, free-market economies depicted in recent YA dystopias: specifically, Marissa Meyer's *Cinder* (2012), Suzanne Collins's *The Hunger Games* (2008), and Marie Lu's *Legend* (2013). In doing so, we argue that these novels depict talented individuals for whom social constructs such as race and ethnicity pose few obstacles. Next, we interrogate these books' deployment of biopolitics; third, we analyze their presentation of social structures (such as race and ethnicity); and finally, we critique the commodification of knowledge production in YA dystopias, attending closely to how YA dystopias can turn knowledge into a commodity to replicate racial privilege. Collectively, we argue that these four pillars help lay a frame for readers to examine whether a YA novel is critiquing or condoning neoliberalism and, by extension, whether it is reproducing, complicating, or resisting ideologies associated with the latter.

To better appreciate how these recent YA dystopias reproduce neoliberal ideologies in ways that erase race, as a counterexample, we also apply our four-part framework to Sherri L. Smith's *Orleans,* a postapocalyptic novel that we suggest employs neoliberalism specifically to critique the erasure of race. In doing so, we argue that *Orleans* demonstrates how individualism is affected in a deregulated free-market economy, shows how biopolitics can be used to replicate social stratification, acknowledges the erasure of race and the elision of the local and global as problematic, and approaches epistemological issues, such as knowledge production, as a direct antidote to racist neoliberal thinking. To conclude our chapter, we argue that erasing race is a racist gesture that serves the privileged entrepreneurs of the neoliberal economy far better than it does members of underprivileged groups.

Individualism and the Free Market

David Harvey's widely used definition of neoliberalism proposes that this political ideology was triggered largely by neoliberal economic policies that emerged out of Reaganomics in the United States and Margaret Thatcher's economic vision for the United Kingdom. Harvey defines neoliberalism as "a theory of political economic practices that proposes that human well-being can best be advanced by liberating individual entrepreneurial freedoms and skills within an institutional framework characterized by strong private property rights, free markets, and free trade" (*Brief* 2). We emphasize Harvey's point that neoliberalism is an economic doctrine that assumes that "individual entrepreneurial freedoms and skills" thrive when they are unfettered. Neoliberalism privileges the economic power of the individual over the economic power of collective forces, such as governments, in order to position individual entrepreneurship as the economic engine of the world. Implicit in this worldview is an assumption that individuals are not disadvantaged by social constructs such as race and ethnicity but gain advantage in the marketplace by exercising their unique talents.

Shauna Pomerantz and Rebecca Raby extend a critique of neoliberalism's influence on YA fiction by assessing how one specific type of entrepreneurial individual—the "smart supergirl" (291), which they refer to alternatively as the "post-nerd smart girl" (287)—has become prominent in popular culture as a result of neoliberalism. Relying on Rosalind Gill and Christina Scharff's work and on Angela McRobbie's ideas, Pomerantz and Raby argue, "[M]odern-day girlhood is now defined by individualism, consumerism, hypersexuality, and the belief that girls can do, be, and have anything they want without fear of structural inequalities such as sexism, racism, or homophobia interfering with their individual efforts to achieve success. As a consequence, such structural inequities have now come to be seen as individual rather than social problems"

(288). In Pomerantz and Raby's analysis, characters such as Gabriella Montez from *High School Musical* are supersmart, beautiful, strong girls who succeed within their social contexts because of their own individual talents—and without ever giving credit to those social structures or cultural traditions that have enabled them to succeed, such as their schools, their middle-class status, or their families' ethnicities (296–97). They cite Deirdre M. Kelly and Shauna Pomerantz to present an even more damaging effect of neoliberalism: these girls think they are succeeding because of their own individual merits, but they are incapable of critiquing the social structures that oppress them, such as racism in Gabriella's case and gender in the case of all supersmart nerd girls. As a result, the focus on individual talent flattens or erases altogether the effects of institutionalized social constructs, such as racism, a point we return to later in this chapter. These ideologies hold girls (as well as minorities and other people who are socially and economically marginalized because of inequitable social systems) complicit in their own oppression. Thus, our first term for examining how neoliberalism contributes to erasing race in YA dystopias involves the depiction of individualism in light of larger market forces.

For example, in Marissa Meyer's *Cinder*, a popular retelling of the Cinderella story, the eponymous protagonist is ashamed of the very feature of her embodiment that gives her an edge in the marketplace: her cyborg body. She is a human rebuilt with computer parts that enable her to be the "best mechanic in the city" because of the robotics implanted in her brain (10). Cinder lives in New Beijing, the capital of the Eastern Commonwealth, a country that is allied with the five other Earthen countries predicated on their mutual recognition of how bad war has been for past economies: "Millions had died in World War IV; whole cultures had been devastated, dozens of cities reduced to rubble—including the original Beijing. Not to mention the countless natural resources that had been destroyed through nuclear and chemical warfare" (267). In this neoliberal world, the greatest threats to the populace are wars and a plague (letumosis) that threatens the Earth's entire economy. The inhabitants of the moon—Lunars, who are a different race than Earthens—pose the greatest threat of all to Earthen citizens. Thus, Meyer erases the multicultural population of the Earth in favor of an "us-versus-them" racial divide between the citizens of Earth and the moon. Although the presence of cyborg bodies creates another layer of social stratification, the way that "humans" treat technosentient beings serves as a better metaphor for racism in this book than the way Earthen populations are depicted. Even then, as we demonstrate, Cinder's status as a cyborg poses relatively few insurmountable obstacles for her.

Cinder embodies Pomerantz and Raby's concept of the "post-nerd smart girl" insofar as she is "defined by individualism, consumerism" (287). Following the fairy-tale conceit on which the novel is based, Cinder pulls herself out of an inferior social status as a cyborg and becomes royalty by dint of her ancestry and her ability to trade on her individual talents and genetics. In this way, Cinder's talents and bloodline combine to mark her as capable of rising above her social and material conditions and rescuing the rest of a population that submits to its conformity. The novel thus implies that problems such as racism are individual, rather than systemic, matters.

Cinder is hardly the only supersmart nerd girl thriving economically in a dystopic world; this trope is also discernible in popular YA dystopian novels such as Suzanne Collins's *The Hunger Games* and Marie Lu's *Legend*. In both of these books, female protagonists, by dint of their hard work, intelligence, and ability, manipulate free-market aspects of the economy and confront corrupt governments. Katniss Everdeen, the heroine of *The Hunger Games*, has honed her survival skills building her own black-market business. She also trades on her status as the "Girl on Fire," a figure who is perceived as different from other competitors, to earn the support of wealthy sponsors in the Capitol and, hence, to survive in the arena. June Iparis, the female protagonist in *Legend,* is a prodigy who attributes her rise to a position of prominence in her country's military to her own intellectual and athletic superiority. Rather than acknowledge how her privileged background as a member of her society's elite class has worked as an advantage to her, June insists that her intellectual and physical attributes are innate, a result of "what the Republic considers *good* genes" (13).

In contrast to YA dystopias that validate the role of the supersmart individual entrepreneur within a free-market economy, Smith's *Orleans,* which features an African American protagonist, portrays a new world order in which the ideologies of neoliberalism have been followed to their logical and most destructive extreme. In the world of Orleans, blood, rather than race, provides a logic for social hierarchization. In the novel, a series of hurricanes, each more powerful than the last, has ravaged the city formerly known as New Orleans, unleashing a plaguelike epidemic—Delta Fever—that has decimated the population. Unable to discover a cure for the blood-borne contagion, and unwilling to shoulder the financial burden of continually rebuilding the hurricane-ravaged city, the US government, to protect its economic interests and workforce, abandons the people of the Gulf Coast, literally segregating them from the rest of the population by constructing a concrete wall patrolled by armed soldiers and blood-sniffing drones. The people trapped behind the wall have learned how to survive in tribes based on their blood type, and the book repeatedly maintains that no one can survive without a tribe. In *Orleans*, individualism matters far less than group identity. Nevertheless, because some blood types are less susceptible to Delta Fever than others, individuals with those blood types assume greater economic value, and every person must become her or his own self-serving blood entrepreneur. The result is a terrifying free-market system that, in the absence of government regulation, reduces everybody to the status of a commodity.

The subsequent blood warfare that results from an unfettered economy structured solely around survival is brutal. The text thus communicates an ideological critique of economies predicated on maintaining a rigid system of haves and have-nots, as when the protagonist, a teenage girl named Fen, wonders, "Ain't it be like that everywhere? Either you got it or somebody else do?" (Smith 167). In contrast, the small-scale economies that do succeed in Orleans involve some type of regulation. For example, each blood tribe provides security at the Market, which "be right at the edge of the Mississippi, with her back up against the Old French Quarter" (18). In this way, the blood tribes, having filled a vacuum created in the absence of government intervention, serve as the collective force regulating the Market, so that each group can trade.

Orleans imagines a world in which the logic of neoliberalism has prevailed: social and political institutions that once safeguarded people's interests are broken, with the result that individuals compete against one another to survive. Fen's tribe has been dispersed because of a massacre led by another tribe; the leader of Fen's tribe, Lydia, dies immediately after the massacre while giving birth to a child: Baby Girl. Despite the fact that churches have long been considered safe zones in the Delta, Fen learns that even they have become corrupting centers of commerce. When Fen and Baby Girl, whom Fen vows to deliver safely over the wall before the infant can contract Delta Fever, a process that typically occurs within a week after birth, seek sanctuary in a Christian church they happen upon, Fen thinks to herself that it "ain't seen God in a long time," an observation that proves prophetic later when she learns that a voodoo priestess named Mama Gentille co-opted the structure to lure the unsuspecting children of freesteaders—people who try to live independent of a tribe—with the goal of selling them into bondage in the blood trade (76). When Fen confronts Mama Gentille with this knowledge, the latter states, "God a business, just like any other" (102). Thus, Fen, as narrator, critiques neoliberalism: Mama Gentille is corrupt because she places her own individual economic interests ahead of others, exemplifying how neoliberalism conceptualizes people as a resource (or in neoliberal terms, human capital) to be used and discarded.

Throughout *Orleans*, Fen demonstrates an understanding that her survival is threatened if she cannot function within a group: indeed, in her world, unchecked individualism is a liability. In contrast, Cinder—like Katniss and June—values her individualism and her entrepreneurship above all other skills, and at no point in any of these novels is capitalism depicted as anything other than the most logical and efficient way to maintain social order. Viewed through the lens of individualism and its role within free-market economies, these other novels exemplify YA dystopias that mitigate the impact of race as a social factor.

Biopolitics and Social Stratification

Our framework for understanding neoliberalism's erasure of race includes examining both the econo-politics of the individual entrepreneur and recognizing how neoliberalism encourages business enterprises to expand economic production by moving into new territories, which necessarily creates environmental tensions (Pellizzoni and Ylönen 4). These tensions, in turn, have an effect that demonstrates the interface between humans and other biological systems. In children's and adolescent literature, environmental critiques frequently rely on the genre of the dystopian novel, in which the landscape has been laid bare by neoliberalism's rapacious relationship to the land. The overcultivation of the environment has ramifications that are biopolitical, in the sense of the term Michel Foucault employs "biopolitics"; indeed, Foucault insists that the study of biopolitics is integral to the neoliberal state. In a neoliberal economy, the market comes to regulate all biological phenomena—people, animals, the environment—but the term *biopolitics* indicates that a relationship exists between biological forces and government control.

Christopher Breu extends Foucault's work on biopolitics, arguing that the latter "suggests that a relationship between biopolitics and neoliberalism can be adduced in relationship to the neoliberal concept of 'human capital' as the means by which human life and biology are regulated under neoliberalism" (15). Moreover, in a neoliberal economy, "immaterial production" begins to replace material production as the core of the economy, so that cities that once depended on "a largely industrial, shipping, and manufacturing base" become "organized around the [globalized] electronic, service, and financial sectors of the economy" (21, 134). In other words, neoliberalism prioritizes the production of any individual (including immaterial production) as a cog in the economy, such that even the individual's biologically situated body is regulated through economic forces. In this context, people are viewed as "human capital" fit for consumption by corporations.

Examining neoliberal biotechnologies in fiction for young people, Naarah Sawers argues that their advent "makes problematic any definitive understanding of the self or subjectivity," explaining that "[a]gency is crucial to understanding how humanity is enacted as performativity in posthuman narratives for children and young adults" (171, 173). Likewise, Stephanie Guerra suggests that "the possibility of creating or altering subjects to accommodate corporate interests . . . echo[es] through fiction [with] questions at the very heart of bioethics about what it means to create, design, and alter human life, and the potential of such staggering capabilities in the hands of profit-seeking corporations" (290). Thus, Sawers (170) and Guerra (288)—like Clare Bradford, et al. (16)—understand that children's and YA literature focuses on agency and subjectivity, whether the novel at hand is a celebratory tale about the potentiality of technoscience or a cautionary tale about dystopic forces of globalization at work in a dark future. With this in mind, here, we examine how YA dystopias employ biopolitics in ways that can either reproduce or resist social stratification. Although we focus specifically on social class and tribes, we extend this argument in the next section to interrogate race and racism.

In *Cinder*, the titular character has a booth in the city's bustling marketplace where she is regarded as "the best mechanic in New Beijing" (Meyer 10). Although merchants in the marketplace sell local material goods, such as baked items and silk, Cinder sells her specialized knowledge and services— "immaterial goods"—as a mechanic. Meanwhile, Queen Levana, Cinder's nemesis on the moon, has relied on biopolitics to create two weapons of war: a mutant army and the letumosis plague. Emperor Kai describes the latter crisis in the language of neoliberalism: "My father was fighting a war against letumosis, the pestilence that has ravaged our planet for over a dozen years. . . . The good people of the Commonwealth, and all our Earthen siblings, have lost friends, family, loved ones, neighbors. And with these losses, *we face loss of trade and commerce, a downturn of economy, worsened living conditions*" (311; emphasis added). Biopolitics—here, taking the form of biowarfare—is problematic not only because of the loss of human life but also, and more importantly, because the plague is bad for business.

Biopolitics also creates this novel's social stratification. While Cinder, as a cyborg, is considered "36.28 percent not human," her best friend, Iko, a robot, occupies the lowest caste of all, that of the android, which is 100 percent not human (82). Cyborgs are Earthen culture's pinnacle achievement of the free market, although government decree defines them as second-class citizens. Presumably, this second-class citizenship guarantees "fully human" citizens a competitive advantage in the marketplace, which results in social stratification and explains why Cinder tries to hide her cyborg status from others. The text thus positions cyborgs as "other" compared to humans, resulting in a distinct form of biopolitical social stratification.

In Collins's *The Hunger Games*, the workers in District 11 provide material production to the neoliberal economy in the form of coal, but the workers of

District 3 provide immaterial production in the form of the knowledge production that leads them to create new technologies, the result of which curries them favor with the Capitol. Similarly, in *Legend,* a government edict requires that all ten-year-olds take a standardized exam, known as the Trial, which assesses their potential to contribute to the work of the regime and determines their fate in life. Although the test is ostensibly used to identify talented individuals, the government also uses it to reproduce the status quo and preserve its power. Thus, whereas June, whose upper-class background allowed her to attend elite schools, earns a perfect score on the exam and is rewarded with a comfortable military position focused on information (as immaterial production), young people from working-class backgrounds generally perform less well on the exam and are consigned to work dangerous, less desirable jobs associated with material production. In this way, in YA dystopias such as *Cinder, The Hunger Games,* and *Legend,* a person's social status is tied to her ability to participate in the neoliberal economy via immaterial production: those who contribute to its material production, in contrast, are portrayed as having less social capital and hence less agency.

In *Orleans,* however, social stratification depends on blood type, as well as on whether a person lives in a tribe or as a freesteader. Based on a logic of biopolitics, people band together in tribes according to blood type. Life is precarious in Orleans, however, as biopolitics also provide the city's citizens with a rationale for social stratification: because those with type O blood carry the disease but are not adversely affected by it, they are considered economically more valuable in their society (137); as a result, they are preyed on by Blood Hunters, who traffic in the sale of blood, and other tribes that, due to their biological susceptibility to Delta Fever, must sustain themselves through transfusions. Due to their complete independence, freesteaders face the most risk. Reproducing the social knowledge available to her, Fen hierarchizes the above castes when she explains, "In Orleans, you either a tribe, a religion, a hunter, or a freesteader. Better a tribe than a religion, but freesteader be as good as freedeader" (82). The level of a person's vulnerability thus depends on biopolitics.

Yet another layer of biosocial stratification exists in *Orleans*: people who are not infected with Delta Fever (those in the Outer States) are considered more valuable to the free-market economy than those who carry the disease. As explained, the US government, to protect its workforce, erected a concrete wall to segregate the people of Orleans from those in the Outer States. Later, the government claimed Louisiana as a base for strategic military operations, assembling its forces there en masse and summarily killing anyone caught crossing the wall. Daniel, a military scientist who engineered a virus he hoped would destroy Delta Fever, but which in fact threatens to kill anyone on the

Delta who has the Fever's pathogens in their blood, understands the lengths to which the government would go to protect its economic interests. He worries that the government, upon learning that "the Delta could be recovered, stripped of Delta Fever and harvested for its natural resources—timber, oil, shipping lanes, and more ... might very well use it. Genocide in the name of money" (47). His suspicion is not far off, as the text implies that the government is arming the blood tribes with weapons to facilitate their self-annihilation so that the Outer States can capitalize on the Delta's resources. Delta Fever thus offers the federal government a rationale for "managing" the population via genocide.

Race, Exploitation, and the Elision of the Global and Local

Bradford and her colleagues express concern that "subjectivities in the new global order are both dispersed and integrated," and they identify a problem "associated with the widespread use of the term 'globalisation': as an all-encompassing signifier it evades charges of ethno-euro-anglocentrism" (42, 41). They also rely on Harvey's recognition that "globalization is about the socio-spatial relations between billions and individuals" to argue that "globalising processes reconfigure social space" in a "universalising process" that can lead to erasures of specificity, such as racial and ethnic identity (42). Harvey directly connects race to neoliberalism via the mechanism of social class and the exploitation of workers: "Employers have historically used differentiations within the labour pool to divide and rule. Segmented labour markets then arise and distinctions of race, ethnicity, gender, and religion are frequently used, blatantly or covertly, in ways that redound to the employers' advantage" (*Brief* 168). Harvey argues that the "mobility of global capitalism" allows it to move into markets where laborers can be exploited; race and ethnicity are often implicated in the exploitation that globalized capitalism affords (*Brief* 168–69).

Roland Robertson, however, critiques uses of the term *globalization* that rely on a simple global/local binary and ignore how much of "what is called local is in large degree constructed on a trans- or super-local basis" (26). He believes the term *glocalization* better "describes the interactions of the global and the local" as it more precisely captures the interplay between local forces and the global economy (26). Additionally, Robertson argues that the concept of glocalization helps us to avoid what he recognizes as a tendency to confuse "globalization" with "homogenization" (31). He acknowledges that people are capable of evading or resisting homogenizing forces, noting that corporations "increasingly tailor their products to a differentiated global market" (46). Thus, to cater to international markets, McDonald's sells products such as rice McWraps in China, the McLobster Roll in New England, and India's McPaneer Royale. In every case, McDonald's profits off of local flavors that are often sold to exploited laborers confined to work in the country of their birth because of immigration policy and/or their lack of personal capital.

Young adult dystopias such as *Cinder* and *Legend* demonstrate the erasure of racial and ethnic identities, as well as the elision of the global and the local. In *Cinder*, Meyer privileges class distinctions in ways that erase race and racism. She depicts characters that are largely lacking in defining racial features, an exception being the Asian prince (later emperor) of the Eastern Commonwealth, Prince Kai, who has "Black hair" and copper-brown eyes (6). Reflecting Bradford et al.'s concern that globalization tends "to erase cultural difference and locality" (41), Meyer also places little emphasis on local culture. All Earthen countries, for example, speak Standard (American) English, and no mention is made of why any one language has become the dominant universal language. Well-off people in New Beijing sometimes wear Asian silk, but with the exception of a reference to dumplings (83), the novel's characters seem to experience little in the way of ethnic or racial specificity; the novel is thus more globalized than glocalized in its approach to ethnicity and race.

Collins's *The Hunger Games* and Lu's *Legend* also tend to erase race or racial identity. In the former, Katniss is described as having "olive skin" and "straight black hair" (Collins 8), and Rue is said to have "dark brown skin and eyes" (45). Beyond this, however, few references are made to characters' racial identities. So too, in *Legend*, Day, June's fellow protagonist, is said to have "some Asian blood" (Lu 180), and June describes him as "a mix of Anglo and Asian" (125), yet his primary defining features are his blonde hair and blue eyes. Likewise, while June is described as being "a little paler than other girls . . . in the sector," with "large dark eyes that shine with flecks of gold," her race is otherwise ambiguous. As Day states, "I can't tell *what* she is, which isn't unusual around here—Native, maybe, or Caucasian. Or something" (112). Beyond this, few, if any, other references are made to the race of characters in the novel, and as is the case in *The Hunger Games,* race does not appear to present any significant social barriers for characters.

Meyer's, Collins's, and Lu's novels show how interdependent neoliberalism is on biopolitics—and how racialized biopolitics are. One of the inherent contradictions in neoliberalism is the paradox by which the free market is sustained by infinitely complex biopolitical regulations. For example, enforced segregation in the southern United States could not have existed without the biopolitical dynamics between (false and essentialized) biological concepts of race and legal statutes, such as Jim Crow laws. Similarly, Cinder's status as a cyborg advantages her in the marketplace, while offering her society a rationale for treating her like a second-class citizen.

Sarah Trimble connects stories about contagion and disease—such as letumosis in *Cinder*, the plague in *Legend*, or blood fever in *Orleans*—to anxieties about how "transformations of the state under neoliberalism (re)shape the national response to disease" (298). Specifically, Trimble links "the dis/ease generated by neoliberalism and the new proximities wrought by globalization" to "a patriarchal survivalist fantasy that articulates among whiteness, rage, and (corporeal) fortification" (298). Although *Orleans* is predicated on a narrative of dis/ease, it rejects many narratives of neoliberalism and problematizes what Trimble calls "white rage" (303). In *Orleans*, contagion is not a metaphor for white, middle-class fears that the world is becoming corrupt; rather, the social construction of race itself is problematized as the original source of contagion.

The official narrative surrounding the creation of the Institute for Post-Separation Studies in *Orleans* is that a team of doctors, psychologists, researchers, and graduate students, "willing to dedicate their lives to the cause," stayed behind in the city after the government abdicated its responsibilities there to study whether constructs such as race and gender would matter once people stratified along medical lines (74). Racial divide, then, proves to be the most powerful metaphor for corruption in the novel. Had scientists not wished to have a project in which they could study a "postracial" cultural system, the text implies that a cure for Delta Fever might have been more strenuously sought.

When Fen leads Daniel, a military scientist, to the Institute in a trade by which he promises to help her get Baby Girl over the wall, he is horrified to learn how callous its leaders have been in the name of science. Instead of developing a cure for Delta Fever, these scientists selfishly allowed people to perish so they could pursue their research agenda, prompting Daniel to compare this abuse of institutional power to the real-life Tuskegee syphilis experiment, where researchers knowingly left African American men infected with the disease in rural Alabama to die so they could study its natural progression. Fen tells him that "studying tribes" has been the Institute's "pet project" because the lead scientist "ain't interested in the Fever" (207). Daniel replies, "Ending racism.... For the most part the rules of blood make race irrelevant. Blood types cross all ethnicities." Fen agrees, stating, "If folks stop hating each other 'cause of skin color, the only difference be blood type" (207). Her observation leads Daniel to conclude, "A new form of racism.... It's like Tuskegee all over again. They never wanted a cure" (207). Revealing her distrust of social and political institutions that have consistently failed her, Fen thinks to herself, "I don't know nothing about Tuskegee, but if it mean folks with power always gonna abuse it, then I got to agree" (207).

Although rules of blood have shifted rules of class and race, Smith does not erase the latter as a concept from *Orleans*. Fen refers to one character's "ruddy brown" skin (35) and another's "mahogany face" (249). One woman has skin "too dark for blond hair" (123); a smuggler is described as "white, whiter than you see in Orleans anymore, with yellow-blond hair stuck to his forehead with sweat" (77–78); Fen also refers to the way the people of the region have become "mixed up" (78). Indeed, one of the only people in the novel described as "pink" is a corrupt priest who hopes to commodify Baby Girl to give himself a blood transfusion (297). Another exception to the creolization of races is Asian Americans, who are largely immune to Delta Fever and who have developed their own shanty town along the river—although it is a culture among which mixes "Koreans and Japanese, Chinese and Vietnamese and Filipino. But nothing else. Folks in Orleans all be mutts except for the Asians" (144). Smith's depiction of this tribe reinforces how inescapable racial stratification still is in US constructions of social groups, even when an author such as Smith is committed to exposing racism as a function of neoliberalism.

Knowledge Production, Epistemology, and Narrative Levels

Living with self-awareness about race is an epistemological issue, as W. E. B. Du Bois first noted in 1903 when he referred to "this double-consciousness, this sense of always looking at one's self through the eyes of others . . . One ever feels his twoness—an American, a Negro; two souls, two thoughts" (5). White privilege, then, is its opposite: the ability to live un-self-aware as to how whiteness provides economic, social, and political advantage. Indeed, what is privilege if not the very ability to be confident that one's epistemological position is secure and unthreatened and does not bear examination? Much of the impetus for the globalized neoliberal economy has come from corporations that have the privilege of ignoring race as an epistemological experience. This elision of race is further enabled by the role of immaterial production in the neoliberal economy. When knowledge is commodified, it is often depicted as deracialized, as if knowledge knows no race (or racism). Interrogating how knowledge production occurs in YA dystopias can expose racial privilege and racism. For example, characters immersed in social stratification created by immaterial production have the privilege of ignoring race, as do Cinder, Katniss, and June; Fen, on the other hand, does not have this privilege.

Texts communicate about knowledge production in at least two ways that can guide readers to confront neoliberalism's racist privileging of knowledge (as immaterial production): first, through individual characters' epistemological insights, including how they trade on what they know, and second, through the way that texts communicate information to the reader. These two mechanisms—particularly the narrator's insights—have the potential to demonstrate the "resistant logics" by which texts can respond to the hegemonic forces of neoliberalism (Crary 134). We thus examine the narrators' relationships to knowledge structures in *Cinder* and *Orleans*. In doing so, we demonstrate how textual positioning of the narrator's knowledge production can be connected to neoliberal racism.

Within a globalized neoliberal economy, knowledge production itself becomes a prized form of immaterial production. *Cinder* depicts learning almost entirely in terms of knowledge-as-content, as though it were a commodity to be traded on. This commodification of knowledge occurs when characters use their own knowledge to barter for material gain. Moreover, several characters in *Cinder* are prized because of what they know or what they learn. Prince Kai's android, for example, becomes a contested commodity because she has been researching the identity of the missing Lunar princess. Since there is a market for this information, what the android discovers is valuable knowledge. After Kai learns that Queen Levana has planted a communication chip in the same android, he understands the value of this knowledge as a commodity: now the Queen "knows everything that android knows, everything she'd been researching," including information about the identity of the missing Lunar princess (322).

Cinder withstands a confrontation with Queen Levana because the girl's bioelectrical knowledge is finally unlocked, giving her the intellectual energy to weather Levana's attack. Once Cinder realizes that she is the missing princess—and that she is of the Lunar "race," and not Earthen—she has a "thought" that "both sickened and frightened her" (387): she can transform the material through her knowledge. It is worth noting that her knowledge of her own race forces her out of the privilege of ignoring race; she now has a double consciousness, even though she does not acknowledge that fact. Nevertheless, because of her epistemological power, she will be the superheroic individual who transcends the rest of her community and its vague notions of race. She will save her neoliberal world, but without having the self-awareness to critique the social stratification that results from its market forces. In this way, a novel that treats knowledge production as a commodity also erases race.

While reading *Cinder*, readers themselves are restricted in the process of knowledge production: they usually know only what Cinder knows. *Orleans*, however, employs three shifting narrative levels, the result of which enables the reader to view events in the story from multiple perspectives that help to create what Crary calls "resistant logics"—in this case, resistance to neoliberalism and its related forces, especially those that privilege individualism and generate racism (134). Resistant logics and multiple ways of knowing are necessary for those who are not insulated by white privilege; the narrative structure of *Orleans* thus demonstrates the importance of multiple ways of knowing. For example, on one level, the text relies on a third-person limited narrator to describe the events that Daniel, the military scientist who travels to Orleans in search of a cure for Delta Fever, experiences. These chapters initially reflect a privileged, patriarchal faith in neoliberal-technoscience, although this bias gradually erodes as the story unfolds. On a second level, a teenaged Fen narrates events in a patois variant of African American Vernacular English as she experiences them in the first person and in the present tense. These chapters indicate an epistemology that focuses more on knowledge as an embodied and collective process than as a commodity. Finally, on a third level, Fen recounts events from her childhood in the first person and in the past tense. These chapters take the form of flashbacks and are distinguished by Fen's use of Standard (American) English, a register that she acquired growing up in a family of academics.

In this story world organized according to ideologies associated with abuses of free enterprise and technoscience, Smith uses the three narrative levels described above to examine competing perspectives on neoliberalism, tribalism, and privilege. Throughout much of the story, Daniel—whose status as a white, male, college-educated scientist working for the US military places him in a socially empowered position—is confident in his ability "to save the world" (109). His perspective is that of the neoliberal who values individual ingenuity and whose faith in rationality and technology assures him that there are no problems too great to solve through their careful application. Smith uses an objective third-person narrator to mediate Daniel's experiences, thereby permitting the reader to perceive shortcomings in his character and individualistic worldview that he is not cognizant of himself.

For example, like Cinder, Daniel is oblivious to the role that social systems play in advantaging him. He is financially secure, as evidenced by the fact that he has the personal means to fund an expensive research expedition to Orleans. He also naively assumes that his access to high-end technology will give him the epistemological power to navigate Orleans safely without ever considering the possibility that the technology might fail him, which it does repeatedly. He is dependent on outdated maps, with the result that he often gets lost; he loses access to his datalink when its battery dies; he uses scientific methods to retarget the Delta Fever virus but inadvertently creates an "even deadlier strain of the disease" that puts everyone in Orleans at risk (46). When he reaches the Institute for Post-Separation Studies, where he expects to find data he can use to transmute the virus he created into a cure for Delta Fever, Daniel entertains the possibility that he might "signal the States for help, call in the cavalry" (197). Because he is presumably a white, male American citizen, he trusts that he has access to a military that will respond if he beckons. Never acknowledging the extent to which his social positioning and privilege empower him, Daniel, like Cinder, effectively assumes the role of the neoliberal "hero" with "a world to save" (197, 200). Cut off from the institutions that privilege his race and empower his knowledge production, however, he is ultimately forced to concede that though he had expected to "save this unsalvageable place … he had failed" (243).

In contrast, Fen—who is socially marginalized following the dispersal of her tribe and who lacks access to institutional and structural resources she can draw on for support—is decidedly more clear-eyed about what she is (and is not) capable of accomplishing in her world. Her knowledge is often the embodied knowledge that has come from living within the Delta region: she knows, for example, how to navigate the area without maps and where she can safely find refuge. As a result of lived experience, she is capable of navigating urban as well as rural terrains without calling attention to herself. As a nonwhite person, she is cognizant of how racism privileges some people over others, informing Daniel that in the eyes of those with power, she and other residents of Orleans "ain't people, we rats" (206). Unlike Daniel, who aspires to rescue humanity, Fen merely hopes to survive in the context of a tribe. She is fiercely loyal, having learned through experience that "tribe is life" (192). She insists that there can be "[n]o more 'every man for himself,'" rationalizing, "If Orleans gonna have a better future, we in this together now" (207). Problematizing the myth of the neoliberal hero, the ambiguity of the novel's ending implies that Fen may be a strong and resourceful individual, but that she may nevertheless have failed even her one goal of survival precisely because of threats to her existence by social forces structured around individualism.

Fen embraces an epistemology that emphasizes the collective knowledge of the group as an antidote to neoliberal individualism. For example, she foregrounds the role that the Ursuline Sisters—a group of Catholic nuns who embrace the motto "*Serviam*, I will serve" (111)—play in caring for the people of Orleans after the church and other patriarchal institutions abandoned the Gulf Coast. Fen is also inspired by Lydia, the leader of her blood tribe, whose goal of "bringing together not just the Os, but all the tribes" is motivated by an ideological commitment to inclusiveness and community. Fen also shares her knowledge with Daniel, especially once she realizes that if they work together, the prospects of their saving Baby Girl's life will improve dramatically.

Fen most clearly articulates the ideological divide between knowledge as a process of collective sharing and neoliberalism's emphasis on knowledge as an individually owned commodity that can be traded on for profit tied to racial exploitation. Acting as narrator, she distinguishes between the competing moral codes that guide the Ursuline Sisters and the researchers at the Institute for Post-Separation Studies: "Everyone is supposed to help everyone. That's what Sister Mary Margaret says. It's called the Golden Rule. It's not the same as Dr. Warren's Rules of Blood. Those are different. Those say everyone has to stay apart from everyone else" (187). Later, when she and Daniel are preparing to leave the Institute, Daniel wonders whether they ought to help Dr. Warren and his colleagues, who, in the absence of a vaccine for Delta Fever, are dependent on computers and machinery to keep them alive. "They ain't tribe," Fen responds, leading Daniel to exclaim, "That's insane" (207). In a remark that is notable for its condemnation of neoliberalism's destructiveness, Fen insightfully replies, "That the world they made" (207). Worlds that cannot respect racial difference and in which ethnic tribes cannot learn from others are doomed to fail.

Conclusion

Examined through the four-part framework for reading neoliberalism in YA fiction that we have begun to develop in this chapter, dystopias such as *Cinder*, *The Hunger Games*, and *Legend* are found to reproduce neoliberal values insofar as they celebrate free markets and individualism, elide race and ethnicity to minimize the destructive impact of racial discrimination, and represent knowledge as a commodity to be traded on. In contrast, we interpret *Orleans* as offering a counternarrative to neoliberalism and the value that it places on liberating both markets and people from all regulatory constraints. Rather than celebrating "the one shining soul" or the exceptional individual who trades on her unique abilities to overcome adversity, Smith's novel acknowledges that race and class serve gatekeeping functions. In Fen's world, hope for the survival of humankind depends not on unchecked individualism but on its opposite: people's willingness to set aside their self-interest and work for the betterment of the social collective. The text argues that our future as individuals is implicated in our relationships with the environment, in our valuing the knowledge of people from varying racial and ethnic groups, and, ultimately, in the well-being of the social collective. As Fen states, "we in this together" (207).

The underrepresentation of racially and ethnically diverse protagonists in YA fiction is well documented, as indicated by this volume. For example, at the 2017 ALAN Workshop, which took place in Saint Louis, Missouri, YA authors Cindy Pon and Dhonielle Clayton suggested that of the many genres of YA fiction, dystopia and fantasy have been particularly slow in responding to calls for greater representation of diverse characters. Instead, many authors of YA dystopias opt for a "color-blind" approach to race, erasing issues of racial tension and racism. By focusing on the exceptional individual who trades on her talents to overcome oppressive governments and institutions, these books ultimately imply that problems such as racism are individual, rather than systemic, problems. Because of this tendency, they impede the potential for real progress to be made in terms of readers' critiquing unjust systems.

YA fiction can potentially mask the detrimental effects of neoliberalism and reify its championing of rugged individualism when it depicts talented individuals who seemingly rise above their social conditions purely as a result of their exceptionalism, regardless of race and/or ethnicity. Nevertheless, novels that permit readers to confront neoliberalist ideologies and values, as *Orleans* does, can help teenage readers connect fictive worlds to a social critique of the world in which they live. Through its refusal to celebrate individual exceptionalism, its insistence on acknowledging local practices and ethnic traditions, and its conceptualizing knowledge as collectively produced and shared, *Orleans* demythologizes neoliberalism's racist erasure of race.

Works Cited

Bradford, Clare, Kerry Mallan, John Stephens, and Robyn McCallum. *New World Orders in Contemporary Children's Literature: Utopian Transformations*. Palgrave Macmillan, 2008.

Breu, Christopher. *Insistence of the Material: Literature in the Age of Biopolitics*. University of Minnesota Press, 2014.

Collins, Suzanne. *The Hunger Games*. Scholastic, 2008.

Crary, Alice. "What Do Feminists Want in an Epistemology?" *Feminist Interpretations of Ludwig Wittgenstein*, edited by Naomi Scheman and Peg O'Connor, Pennsylvania State University Press, 2002, pp. 97–118.

Du Bois, W. E. B., *The Souls of Black Folk*. 1903. Millennium, 2014.

Foucault, Michel. *The Birth of Biopolitics*, edited by Michel Senellart. Translated by Graham Burchell. 2004. Palgrave, 2008.

Foucault, Michel. *Discipline and Punish: The Birth of the Prison*. Translated by Alan Sheridan. 1977. Pantheon, 1978.

Foucault, Michel. *History of Sexuality, Vol. 1*. Translated by Robert Hurley. 1978. Vintage Books, 1990.

Gill, Rosalind, and Christina Scharff. Introduction. *New Femininities: Postfeminism, Neoliberalism, and Subjectivity*, edited by Gill and Scharff, Palgrave, 2011, pp. 1–20.

Guerra, Stephanie. "Colonizing Bodies: Corporate Power and Biotechnology in Young Adult Science Fiction." *Children's Literature in Education* 40, no. 4, 2009, pp. 275–95.

Harvey, David A. *A Brief History of Neoliberalism*. Oxford University Press, 2005.

Harvey, David A. *Spaces of Hope*. University of California Press, 2000.
Kelly, Deirdre M., and Shauna Pomerantz. "Mean, Wild, and Alienated: Girls and the State of Feminism in Popular Culture." *Girlhood Studies: An Interdisciplinary Journal* 2, no. 1, 2009, pp. 1–17.
Lu, Marie. *Legend*. Speak, 2013.
McRobbie, Angela. *The Aftermath of Culture: Gender, Culture, and Social Change*. Sage, 2009.
Meyer, Marissa. *Cinder: The Lunar Chronicles*. Square Fish, 2012.
Pellizzoni, Luigi, and Marja Ylönen. *Neoliberalism and Technoscience*. Ashgate, 2012.
Pomerantz, Shauna, and Rebecca Raby. "Reading Smart Girls: Post-Nerds in Post-Feminist Popular Culture." *Girls, Texts, Cultures*, edited by Mavis Reimer and Claire Bradford, Wilfred Laurier University Press, 2015, pp. 287–311.
Robertson, Roland. "Glocalization: Time-Space and Homogeneity-Heterogeneity." *Global Modernities*, edited by Scott Lash, Roland Robertson, and Mike Featherstone, Sage, 1995, pp. 25–44.
Sawers, Naarah. "Capitalism's New Handmaiden: The Biotechnical World Negotiated Through Children's Fiction." *Children's Literature in Education* 40, no. 3, 2009, pp. 169–79.
Smith, Sherri L. *Orleans*. New York: Penguin, 2013.
Trimble, Sarah. "(White) Rage: Affect, Neoliberalism, and the Family in *28 Days Later* and *28 Weeks Later*." *The Review of Education/Pedagogy/Cultural Studies* 32, no. 3, 2010, pp. 295–322.
Wald, Priscilla. *Contagious: Cultures, Carriers, and the Outbreak Narrative*. Duke University Press, 2008.

(De)Stabilizing the Boundaries between "Us" and "Them"
Racial Oppression and Racism in Two YA Dystopias Available in Swedish
Malin Alkestrand

Within YA dystopias,[1] young protagonists recurrently stand up against oppression in their dystopian societies; they become saviors when their rebellions change the status quo. The numerous rebellious young female protagonists highlight intersections between the power categories of age and gender (cf. Day 3–4). Many of the rebellions are *righteous rebellions*, a narrative that is common in fantasy and science fiction (Alkestrand, "Righteous" 110). For example, Katniss Everdeen's rebellion against two corrupt leaders in the *Hunger Games* trilogy (2008–10), Jonas's rebellion against his dystopian society and its willingness to kill children that do not fit into society's mold in Lois Lowry's *The Giver* (1993), and Tally Youngblood's rebellion against the manipulation of people's minds and free will in Scott Westerfeld's *Uglies* series (2005–07) are righteous rebellions for two reasons: they are motivated by righteous motives, such as creating a world where adolescents are not severely abused, and they lead to a change in the status quo of the power distribution (cf. Alkestrand, "Righteous" 110, 114–15). A righteous rebellion is thus more subversive than the rebellions Roberta Seelinger Trites identifies in predominantly realist adolescent literature, in which adolescents rebel against parents, norms, and institutions but soon adjust to the social order in order to mature into adults (xii).

While age and gender are generally explored in Anglophone YA dystopias, Mary J. Couzelis argues that "racial tensions [...] are often not addressed in futuristic novels" (131). Therefore, YA dystopias risk preserving "hegemonic cultural relations" (132). She illustrates how white privilege, "a subtle form of racism in that white people receive benefits and power just because of their skin color," is reinforced in Collins's, Lowry's, and Westerfeld's texts (132). I define racism as "a racial project that combines essentialist representations of race (stereotyping, xenophobia, aversion, etc.) with patterns of domination (violence, hierarchy, super-exploitation, etc.)" (Omi and Winant 963). Racism has real and felt consequences because it affects people's interactions with each other and the distribution of privileges (Omi and Winant 963). The nature of racism is context dependent (Collins, *Black* 286). Therefore, an analysis of racial oppression and racism in YA dystopias from non-Anglophone cultural contexts can provide insights into how racial oppression, racism, and white privilege influence these texts, as well as how racism is defined in different cultural contexts.

In this chapter, I analyze two YA dystopias available in Swedish in which assumptions about different ethnicities—not skin color—are the predominant basis for racism: Swedish author Mats Wahl's *Blodregnsserie* (the *Blood Rain* series; 2014–17) and Austrian author Ursula Poznanski's *Die Eleria Trilogie* (the Eleria trilogy; Swedish translation 2014–16), originally published in German between 2012 and 2014.[2] I thereby highlight crucial differences from the depiction of racism in Anglophone YA dystopias. The primary texts address racial oppression and racism in distinctly different ways: the former reinforces the distinction between "us" and "them," while the latter transgresses and challenges it. Currently, research about racial oppression or racism in non-Anglophone YA dystopias available in Swedish does not exist.

In contemporary Sweden, the word *race* is taboo, and differences between "us" and "them" are usually based on ethnicity instead of race (Hübinette and Lundström 426). That is not to say that whiteness is not afforded privilege in a Swedish context. "Contrary to the general attitude in Sweden which refuses to talk about any other 'ethnic' binary than that between 'Swedes' and 'immigrants,' and in opposition to the antiracist condemnation in Sweden of speaking about race [...] whiteness is a pivotal analytical category for understanding" contemporary Swedish racism (Hübinette and Lundström 426). In the *Blood Rain* series and the *Eleria* trilogy, ethnic stereotypes are incorporated into racist discourses, thereby positioning all people from a certain cultural background as inferior.

The *Blood Rain* series reinforces Swedish hegemonic whiteness and stabilizes the intradiegetic hegemonic culture's perception of immigrants as different from Swedes. It portrays a white protagonist, Elin Holme, who faces discrimination due to her gender, age, class, and educational background but who never has to deal with racism on a personal level because of her white privilege.³ The series addresses illegal immigration and racism as threats to the society as a whole—threats with which Elin must grapple during her political career. However, all major characters are coded as white. This leads to a distanced, detached portrayal of racial segregation. Elin neither questions nor rebels against the view of immigrants as different from Swedes, and the final book does not incorporate the hope for the creation of a new and better future that is common within the genre (cf. Day 3).

The *Eleria* trilogy, in contrast, explicitly discusses the construction and transgression of racism through the protagonist's righteous rebellion against a racist society. The *Eleria* trilogy foregrounds intercultural knowledge and acceptance as a prerequisite for a righteous rebellion that prevents genocide in a future Central Europe, depicting antihegemonic knowledge about the crimes of the dominant culture as the most important asset in a righteous rebellion against a dystopian state and in the creation of a new world order, in which the rigorous boundaries between "us" and "them" are destabilized in an effort to create an all-encompassing "us."

Using Patricia Hill Collins's matrix of domination and Edward W. Said's *Orientalism* (1978), I clarify how racist discourses about people with a different cultural background legitimize an uneven distribution of privileges in the primary texts and how the distinction between "us" and "them" is used by the dominant culture to justify racist actions and discourses. I apply a constitutive intersectional approach to racial oppression and racism throughout this chapter. Yuval-Davis defines constitutive intersectionality as "the differential ways in which different social divisions are concretely enmeshed and constructed by each other" (205). The term intersectionality was first coined by Kimberle Crenshaw, who clarifies how racism and sexism intertwine and multiply to create a specific form of discrimination against Black women ("Demarginalizing"). My analysis mainly focuses on intersections between racial imagery, ethnicity, and class.

Stabilizing the Distinction between "Us" and "Them" in the *Blood Rain* Series

Throughout the five books in the *Blood Rain* series, adolescent protagonist Elin Holme is trying to survive and protect her family in a dystopian future Sweden, where the destroyed environment causes storms, floods and migration waves (*Krigarna* 63, 73, 217; *Lagstiftarna* 433). At first, Sweden is ruled by a government that uses strict surveillance and violence to control the population (*Ryttarna* 22). Elin's aunt, the rebel leader, offers her a political career in the rebel-backed regime (*Krigarna* 395–96). Elin is elected to the parliament in the fourth book (*De levande* 431), and she has a long political career that culminates with her attaining the role of prime minister (*De älskande* 264–65), the most powerful political position in Sweden.

Elin's intersectional subject position is not that privileged at the beginning of the series: she is young, female, has neither class privileges nor a lot of capital, and has been home schooled because of her parents' disagreement with a rule that forces all pupils to take calming drugs (*Ryttarna* 129); this educational background makes people question her in the role of a politician (*De levande* 321–22). All these intersections are problematized and highlighted throughout the series.[4] However, Elin is privileged in the sense that she is white. Hübinette and Lundström apply the concept of hegemonic whiteness to a Swedish context: "In contemporary Sweden, hegemonic whiteness is [...] upheld through a colour-blindness that constantly reinscribes whiteness as the normative, yet unmarked, position that, for example, effectively forecloses, silences and excludes experiences of everyday racism among non-white Swedes" (426).[5] I argue that Elin is indeed hegemonically white, since she is defined as ethnically Swedish, and that the series' depiction of racism is strongly affected by the protagonist's privileged position, which is based on both her skin color and her ethnicity. Elin never has to deal with racism on a personal or institutional level, nor does anyone close to her. In addition, she has the option to stay silent when faced with a racist worldview since she herself is not directly affected by it. Further, her white privilege is neither problematized nor critically highlighted in the series.

Systemic racism theory highlights "social structures, material conditions, knowledge and everyday practices and experiences of racial oppression," as well as the discourses that organize and legitimize race hierarchies (Feagin, and Elias 944). Patricia Collins's matrix of domination explains how these different aspects are related to each other. As Christopher Owen argues, the matrix of domination can be applied to literary fiction in order to clarify how a specific text depicts systemic oppression, for example racism (Owen 10–11). Collins defines power "not as something that groups possess, but as an intangible entity that circulates within a particular matrix of domination and to which individuals stand in varying relationships" (274). The matrix consists of four different domains. The *structural domain* organizes the interlocking of social institutions, for example the institutions of law and housing, in order to enforce the subordination of the oppressed through policies (Collins 277). Within this domain, discrimination can lead to exclusion from high-level work or political opportunities (Collins 277). The *disciplinary domain* manages domination through bureaucratic hierarchies and surveillance, enforcing rules that are oppressive in order to control the population (Collins 280–81). The *hegemonic domain* justifies oppression through consciousness, culture, and ideologies, for example in the form of school curricula and mass media (Collins 276, 284). The *interpersonal domain* refers to how social interaction is influenced by the privileges and disadvantages that affect each individual due to different systems of oppression and their intersections (Collins 287). In the *Blood Rain* series, racism is a structural issue that Elin fails to address in her role as a politician, both in terms of the structural domain's citizenship rights, and in terms of the disciplinary domain's way of managing and disciplining immigrants.

Throughout the series, discursive distinctions are made between groups of "us" and "them"; this, in turn, legitimizes privileges and disadvantages for the respective groups. According to Collins, the hegemonic domain ties the rest of the domains together, by functioning "as a link between social institutions (structural domain), their organizational practices (disciplinary domain), and the level of everyday social interaction (interpersonal domain)" (Collins 284). Said explores the raced discursive construction of "us" in opposition to "them," arguing that the Orient is "one of its [Europe's] deepest and most recurring images of the other" (9) and that the conception of the Orient "helped to define Europe (or the West) as its contrasting image, idea, personality, experience" (9–10). The discursive process of defining a culture in relation to its perceived opposite leads to the establishment of clear discursive boundaries between the two groups (Said 13). A hierarchical opposition between Europe/the West and the Orient, "a relationship of power, of domination, of varying degrees of a complex hegemony" (Said 13), was established from the eighteenth century onwards, in which European culture was hegemonic (Said 15). Said emphasizes how the hegemonic domain established boundaries between the two cultures, which in turn legitimized domination and led to racial discrimination.

In the *Blood Rain* series, the hegemonic domain's construction of "the other" underpins a racist worldview that affects the structural, disciplinary, and interpersonal domains. A hierarchy is established between "us" and "them": immigrants are excluded from full citizenship in Swedish society, and their rights and protections are limited. The immigrants have fled from starvation in the Balkan countries—the same countries that the majority of contemporary Swedish immigrants came from during the 1990s—and have become settlers in a part of the country that has been contaminated by nuclear waste and sealed off (*Krigarna* 217). Immigration and immigrants are described pejoratively by several different people throughout the series and, rather than challenging this discursive strategy, Elin continually remains silent.

For example, a man she is attracted to expresses concern that it will be hard to find a solution to "the *problem* [italics mine] with people from the Balkan countries who have started settling down there" (*Lagstiftarna* 64),⁶ and he asks how Swedish society should deal with immigrants who get leukemia from living there: "Are humans who settle down in areas where they are not allowed to live and who are not Swedish citizens entitled to qualified medical healthcare after they have broken the law?" (*Lagstiftarna* 64–65). While the ethnicity of the immigrants is clarified in this quote, not their skin color, they are defined as a non-Swedish group, and a clear distinction between Swedes and immigrants is established, in which Swedes are citizens and immigrants are criminals. This worldview groups together all immigrants to one entity defined by one negative trait, thereby establishing a discourse about how the immigrants should not be entitled to the same privileges as the Swedes. Elin does not answer the man's question (*Lagstiftarna* 65), so her position on the rights of immigrants is unclear. Elin's silence here is part of a recurrent tendency in the *Blood Rain* series that leaves negative portrayals of immigrants and immigration unchecked. The series is told in the third-person objective with a focus on Elin's actions and reactions. Since readers are not privy to Elin's thoughts, the series maintains a distance regarding Elin's beliefs and worldview, including her conception of the immigrants.

Significantly, when she is considering accepting a high-level political appointment, Elin is pressed by her aunt about her intended response toward the three hundred thousand Balkan and Middle Eastern immigrants who live in Sweden's closed area:

> People have settled down there despite the fact that it is forbidden. The settlers say that they would rather die of leukemia in Sweden than of thirst and starvation in their home countries. What kind of healthcare are the three hundred thousand entitled to? The settlers have made their own laws and have their own militia. Is the closed area even a part of Sweden anymore? What are you going to do about that question [. . .]? (*De älskande* 60–61)

Elin responds that she is unsure what action to take (*De älskande* 61). Elin counters neither her aunt's depiction of the immigrants nor her assertion that the immigrants have created a society of their own within Sweden. Consequently, she silently accepts a rhetoric that can be seen as part of the hegemonic domain's legitimizing of the continued containment of the immigrants within the closed area. Karin suggests that perhaps this is not even a part of Sweden anymore (*De älskande* 61), which further underlines the distinction between an "us" that has access to citizenship rights and a "them" that is denied these rights. As a consequence, she raises the question of whether or not the immigrants are the responsibility of Swedish politicians.

One example of the particular writing style of the *Blood Rain* series, where slurs and racist comments are followed by gaps or changes in topic, occurs when a character uses the racist slur "svartskallar" ("black skulls") in a summary of what has happened in a particular part of Stockholm in the last twenty years (*De levande* 321).[7] The summary is placed at the very end of a section, and the next section begins with a description of a flight route (321). Thus, neither Elin nor any other character criticizes the choice of words. Even though the particular writing style of the book, which never directly addresses Elin's thoughts, gives room to interpret her as critical even when she does not speak up or protest—as a gap in the text that readers are supposed to fill in with a quiet critique—these instances strongly support an interpretation of Elin as a white politician who does not feel obliged to counteract racist statements and words, thereby indirectly accepting a racist worldview. Even if her silence is interpreted as a silent critique of the view of the immigrants, her white privilege is still underscored by the luxury of her being able to stay silent.

One further example of how Elin uses her political platform neither to stand up against racial oppression nor to challenge the hegemonic domain's conception of immigrants as different from Swedes is a visit to a racially segregated part of Stockholm. The leader promotes an ultranationalistic ideology: only people who match his definition of Swedishness are allowed to exist in Sweden (*De levande* 342–43). During this visit, Elin does not criticize this ideology or the violent and antidemocratic ways in which the area is governed. Since she is not a target for the leader's racist ideology and punishments, she has the luxury of remaining silent. When her political opponents from a nationalist right-wing party question Elin's decision to even visit this place, "Elin has troubles dealing with the questions" (*De levande* 418). Her attempts to answer the questions are not described, creating yet another gap in the depiction of Elin's standpoint. The visit clarifies that Elin's silence extends even to overt racism. The *Blood Rain* series thus suggests that staying silent about oppression is acceptable even for someone who has a lot of political power to work for a change in both the immigrants' situation and the racist discourse that legitimizes it.

Thus far, I have focused on the hegemonic domain's construction of the other and how the structural and disciplinary domains support this worldview. The interpersonal domain is highlighted when a flood forces hundreds of immigrants to leave the area where they have settled and go to a nearby village on the other side of the mountains. Elin visits the village to assist in aid distribution (*De levande* 443–45). When Elin hears one villager calculating how much profit the village could make if it created small houses for up to sixty people, she still remains silent (*De levande* 445). The narrative only clarifies that she catches the man's eye—something that could be interpreted either as agreement or a critique. In the latter interpretation it represents yet another instance of Elin's silence. This is Elin's only direct interaction with the immigrants. However, the incident does not affect how she deals with immigration in her role as a politician. She takes no stand against those who plan to profit from the immigrants' liminal status, puts forth no new policies that could affect the organization of the structural domain, and voices no challenge to the hegemonic domain's discourse about immigration or immigrants' rights, protections, and status as Swedish citizens.

While being interviewed when she has been the prime minister for several years, Elin confesses that the politicians have failed to help the immigrants, thereby commenting on her approach in previous books:

> The never-ending flows of immigrants cause us a lot of pain since they have forced us to look ourselves in the eyes and confess that our own loved ones are worth more to us than people we don't know. The proclamations of humans' equal rights turned out to be just that, proclamations and fancy talk. Now reality has caught up with us and we humans turn out to be just as egoistic and self-preserving as many of us didn't want to think that we were. (*De älskande* 267)

This is the closest to a recognition and a critique of the hegemonic domain's legitimizing principles for not doing anything to help the immigrants. Instead of arguing that institutional access (the structural domain) and hierarchies (the disciplinary domain) need to change, Elin reifies the hegemonic domain's ideologies by reinscribing and stabilizing the boundaries between "us" (the Swedes) and "them" (the immigrants). This ideological distinction is upheld through the structural domain by how the country's physical border efficiently prevents immigrants from entering Sweden: there is an electric fence, and anyone found within ten meters of it is imprisoned (*De älskande* 37).

The quote above suggests that it is impossible to extend human rights to all humans, which leads to the problematic conclusion that there is no value in trying to destabilize boundaries between "us" and "them" or to challenge the hegemonic domain's legitimization of immigrant oppression. The hegemonic culture's definition of the immigrants as "the other" is not only accepted but also reinforced. Contrary to her adolescent self, who believed in the possibility to solve the environmental issues (*Lagstiftarna* 16), the adult Elin has embraced the position that it is impossible to make a profound change to society, particularly regarding social justice, thus reaching the same conclusion as the adolescents in Trites's realist material: you have to accept the status quo in order to become an adult (Trites xii). "Instead of challenging the status quo, Elin protects it" (Alkestrand, "Adolescent" 219), and she thus silently accepts and reinforces a worldview wherein immigrants are different from "us" and therefore are not entitled to the same privileges as Swedish citizens. Her silence becomes part of the hegemonic domain's efforts to keep the distinction between "us" and "them" intact, thereby reinforcing white privilege.

Destabilizing Race Hierarchies in the *Eleria* Trilogy

As in the *Blood Rain* series, the *Eleria* trilogy presents a society of "us" that coheres in opposition to a clearly defined "them." However, the *Eleria* trilogy problematizes and destabilizes this distinction: it gives an in-depth depiction of how the hegemonic domain affects the structural, disciplinary, and interpersonal domains and how counterhegemonic knowledge can be used to interrogate and rebel against racial segregation established by hegemony. Eleria, or Ria, transitions from identifying with the society where she grew up to feeling like she belongs with "the other," becoming a rebel who advocates for a new society where a hierarchical division of people is erased. The trilogy is told in the first person, emphasizing Ria's thoughts, including changes in her worldview and how she herself is affected by a clearly defined racist discourse that positions one culture as superior and one as inferior. Consequently, it portrays racism and racial oppression in a more personal manner than the *Blood Rain* series, putting much more emphasis on how differences are established and legitimized based on stereotypes about oppressed groups. It also expresses hope in the possibility of creating an equal society.

Eighteen-year-old Ria lives in one of several glass spheres that were built to save humanity from the effects of a major volcanic eruption (*Sveket* 8). She is ranked seventh on a list of the young academics, the future leaders of the spheres (*Sveket* 14). The ranking system divides society into different classes, with academics and political leaders at the top and physical laborers at the bottom (*Sveket* 14, 15, 229). Ria is both a highly regarded academic and thought to be a "vitro," a child genetically engineered without parents or a family and raised by a sphere representative (*Sveket* 32). Vitros occupy a privileged position compared to naturally conceived children, who are defined as limited by their ancestry and their parents' upbringing (*Sammansvärjningen* 71–72). Thus, Ria is privileged due to both her ranking and her ancestry, which create an intersection between class and heritage.

Ria's whole life changes when she escapes an assassination attempt by the sphere leaders (*Sveket* 111). She and some other students are taken as prisoners by one of the clans who live outside of the spheres (*Sveket* 188, 200). Members of the clans are known by the pejorative term "prims," which denotes the perceived primitivism of their culture (*Sammansvärjningen* 5). A race hierarchy is established in which the sphere people figure at the top, and the clans are dehumanized. The two cultures are described as superior and inferior; ethnicity is used as a basis for this racist discourse. Children who are born in the clans but raised in sphere society are positioned as a part of the superior culture (*Sveket* 33), so acculturation appears more important than birth origin. Nonetheless, the sphere society utilizes a racist discourse about "the other" to legitimize its actions against the clans.

The clans also have preconceived opinions about the "darlings" from the spheres. Their guards are seen as brutal and violent, and the rest are assumed to take all resources and lack survival skills since most of them have never experienced the world outside of the spheres (*Sveket* 189, 227). In the clan society, work is gendered (*Sveket* 378), and Ria's femininity and lack of physical strength position her with more vulnerability. A character's intersectional subject position can change drastically in different cultural contexts, and each character must therefore be analyzed in relation to the specific fictional context(s) in which they are positioned (Alkestrand, and Owen 67). Two major differences in Ria's intersectional subject position within the clan society are that she no longer enjoys benefits connected to a high rank and that she finds out that she was born in the clans and stolen by the sphere people as an infant (*Sammansvärjningen* 416–17). Hence, her class privileges from the sphere both as a vitro and highly ranked are lost. Instead, she has to survive in the cold environment and live without the comforts of for example technology and heating.

While the clans and the sphere people are not distinguished by skin color—in fact, skin color is never explicitly described for any character apart from a vague description of Ria as "pale" with chestnut hair (*Sveket* 20)—a racist discourse positions the sphere people as superior to the "prims" due to the respective group's cultural background. Thus, ethnicity is used as the basis for racism. However, the trilogy destabilizes the boundary between "us" and "them" by challenging and transgressing hegemonic discourses about "the other." This is true for Ria and her fellow students, who realize both that the description of the clans is inaccurate and that their own society is not that benign or democratic. It is also true for the clan people, who get to know the students as individuals. In what follows, I analyze how hegemonic knowledge about the two cultures is constructed, challenged and transgressed through the portrayal of Ria's changing worldview and self-definition.

The *Eleria* trilogy utilizes the physical separation of the spheres and the clans to illustrate how the structural domain establishes privileges for some while denying them to others (cf. Collins 277). Warmth, safety (*Sveket* 26), and education (*Sammansvärjningen* 14) are just a few examples of Ria's privileges.

Her high rank gives her access to even more comforts, such as more advanced healthcare (*Sammansvärjningen* 136). The clans have to survive in the cold, hunt and collect their own food, and try to survive attacks both from other clans and from sphere guards, who kill clan members and steal clan children (*Sveket* 194, 250–51; *Slutet* 203). Their limited material resources position them not just as an inferior culture but as lower in the class hierarchy, highlighting an intersection between ethnicity and class. While the sphere people have citizenship rights, the clans do not. The clans are excluded entirely from the privileges of sphere society: no clan people are allowed within the spheres, and sphere guards are instructed to use deadly force against them (*Sveket* 194).

The oppression of is managed via the disciplinary domain. While the rules of the sphere society protect sphere people who adhere to the rules, surveillance is used extensively as a means to control the sphere people (*Sveket* 202). Surveillance and rules are also used to justify the abuse and oppression of the clans. The sphere guards kill all clan members and colonize their land (*Sveket* 267; *Sammansvärjningen* 280). The exclusion of the clan people from sphere society is legitimized through the hegemonic domain's construction of the clans as unintelligent (*Sveket* 230), animallike (*Sveket* 214, 236), filthy savages (*Sveket* 233, 249), violent murderers, and cannibals (*Sveket* 194), who rob the spheres' supply transports (*Sveket* 19), leave their own children in the snow for the sphere people to rescue (*Sveket* 364), and kill students (*Sveket* 6). The discursive construction of the clans as a "them," as the opposite of the cultivated "us," is similar to Said's description of the Orient as the West's other (13). This hegemonic knowledge is used to justify the spheres' dominance by constructing the clans as the opposite of the cultivated and moral sphere people. The goal is to colonize clan land as soon as it has once again become inhabitable.

When Ria first meets the people from the clans, her hegemonic knowledge profoundly affects her views of them, but she soon realizes that perception is inaccurate. According to Collins, "the interpersonal domain functions through routinized, day-to-day practices of how people treat one another" (287). In Ria's case, the interpersonal interaction with the clan people eventually leads to her challenging hegemonic knowledge about them. Thus, the interpersonal interactions counter the hegemonic domain's legitimizing practices, enabling Ria to change her worldview while creating antihegemonic knowledge.

Ria's transition from identifying with "us" (sphere) to "them" (clan) is closely tied to two processes. First, Ria gains accurate knowledge about both the spheres and the clans and uses that knowledge to challenge the depiction of the clans that is promoted by the hegemonic domain in the spheres. Second, Ria experiences increased emotional attachment to the clan society when she falls in love with a clan member and finds out about her true heritage (*Slutet*

202–3). When a surveillance tool from the spheres appears, she realizes that "[i]n this case, we [the students] are on the same side as the *prims* [italics mine]" (*Sveket* 208) since she knows that the spheres want to find the students and kill them. Thus, Ria starts questioning the conception of the "prims."

One of the clan members, Sandor, openly challenges the hegemonic knowledge that Ria has been taught in the spheres: "Do we live up to the image of primitive animals in furs?," but Ria avoids answering this question by redirecting the conversation to a discussion about the term "darlings" (*Sveket* 227). The silence, when faced with the racist worldview in this explicit way, is similar to how Elin does not speak up against racism in the *Blood Rain* series. The main difference is that while Elin's silence is constant until the very end of the final book when she expresses her lack of hope in creating a less divided society, Ria's worldview is gradually changed. Ria realizes that the clan people are intelligent, hard-working, creative, and caring people, who have been severely abused and oppressed by the spheres. She learns, for instance, that the spheres infect "help packages" with a disease that kills half a clan (*Sveket* 251) and that they have used clan people as slaves in mines (*Sveket* 300–1, 377). Thus, Ria's hegemonic knowledge is challenged throughout the trilogy, while Elin remains passive in the face of racism despite her political power to effect, or at least initiate, a change.

The clan people themselves distinguish their own clan and some other peaceful clans from many others that they perceive as brutal and violent killers (*Sveket* 220, 250–51), while the spheres have grouped all the clans together in order to legitimize their treatment of them and define them as "the other." Hence, the trilogy highlights how false and homogenizing constructions of otherness have direct and devastating consequences for how people relate to each other, which is a conclusion that Said highlights in relation to Orientalism (13).

The early stages of Ria's transition from "us" to "them" is supported by the insight that it is possible to change identities and join the clan. At this point she does not know that she was born in a clan. Ria describes herself as two different people: the one from the spheres who denies this possibility, and the other who is no longer surprised by the violent actions of the spheres (*Sveket* 267). Ria's mental transition is highlighted by how she sometimes stops herself from uttering the word "prims" (*Sveket* 269, 303). This process is further underscored by her growing attraction to Sandor (*Sveket* 276). Due to her positionality at the intersection of ethnicity and class, Ria initially considers herself superior to Sandor: she belongs with the elite of the Borwin academy, and he is "just a prim" (*Sveket* 229). However, she soon begins to consider whether she could also switch sides (*Sveket* 326), challenging the hegemonic domain's positioning of the clans as inferior due to an intersection between ethnicity and class.

By the end of the first book, Ria's notion of self has shifted from sphere to clan. When another student argues that it is time for "them"—that is, the sphere society—to experience the conspiracy they have unfairly accused the students of committing, Ria agrees (*Sveket* 431). Her transition becomes even more manifest in the second book, *Sammansvärjningen* (2015). She still differentiates between the clans and the spheres (*Sammansvärjningen* 17), but throughout the book she gradually but continually rejects sphere society as more information comes to light that challenges her hegemonic knowledge. Sandor clarifies that Ria "does not belong to the sphere people anymore" after she warns the clan that the sphere food that they have stolen is likely to be poisoned and thereby saves the clan from extinction (*Sammansvärjningen* 112). When she uses the word "darlings" about the sphere people for the first time, she wonders if this is a definitive end to her identifying as one of them (*Sammansvärjningen* 139)—a clear indication of her mental transition.

A trip to a sphere society to investigate the assassination attempt leads to an even more profound questioning of sphere organization, institutions, and rules, that is, the structural and the disciplinary domains' power distribution. Ria enters the sphere undercover as a working-class girl and soon realizes that the living conditions of this class are really poor (*Sammansvärjningen* 268–69, 320). She also gets insight into the disparity of career opportunities for naturally conceived children and vitros (*Sammansvärjningen* 302). These aspects of the sphere society further underscore how heritage is used to oppress portions of the population. The class differences become another reason for Ria to challenge the hegemonic domain's oppression via a rebellion.

Ria's antihegemonic knowledge about how the spheres mistreat and abuse not only the clans but also parts of the sphere population becomes her number one weapon in a righteous rebellion against the spheres. She rebels in order to defend "democratic values and challenge adults and institutions which are portrayed as corrupt and blinded by power" (Alkestrand, "Righteous" 109), most specifically by challenging the racial oppression of the clans through a revelation of antihegemonic knowledge about the spheres' abuse of the clans (*Sammansvärjningen* 374). When her fellow student says that their lives could be the same again if they can convince the spheres that they have not committed any crimes, Ria strongly underscores that she could never go back to pretending that she does not have access to the antihegemonic knowledge about the clans: "And everything that we have found out, will you stay quiet about it? Forget it? The mass murders of the clans that Lennis [a former sphere guard] have told us about?" (*Sammansvärjningen* 94). For Ria, knowledge of the spheres' crimes makes it impossible to identify with that group. She is initially hesitant about the possibilities of a rebellion

(*Sammansvärjningen* 144). This changes when she visits the sphere society Vienna 2 and sees that the clans and the sphere people are interacting with each other just outside of the sphere; "It feels like a beginning" for a new society, where the boundaries between the spheres and the clans are destabilized (*Sammansvärjningen* 326).

Ria's righteous rebellion is also directed against the clan "preserver" Quirin, who has infected clan children with a virus that does not break out until late adolescence (*Sammansvärjningen* 416–17). A former sphere president told a group of scientists, including Quirin's grandfather, to develop the virus, but the researchers found out that it was meant to be used to kill clan members and escaped to a clan, bringing their research and the virus with them (*Sammansvärjningen* 414–15). Quirin's plan is to use the children who have been stolen by the spheres as biological weapons that spread the virus in the spheres as a way to avenge the robberies of children that the sphere guards have committed (*Sammansvärjningen* 417). The children that are not stolen by the spheres are given an antidote (417). Ria and the rest of the students have been infected with the virus as infants (*Sammansvärjningen* 417). Sandor has already given Ria the antidote (*Sammansvärjningen* 230), but her unknowing and contagious fellow students are positioned in a sphere, posing a deadly threat both to the sphere people and themselves (*Sammansvärjningen* 423). Ria demands access to the antidote and threatens to reveal Quirin's actions to the clan people but is unsuccessful (*Sammansvärjningen* 423). Since no side is inherently good or evil (*Sammansvärjningen* 425), Ria works to challenge both groups and to establish an all-encompassing "us," within which the spheres and the clans begin to communicate and cooperate, moving beyond their perceptions of "the other."

In her righteous rebellion in the final book, *Slutet* (2016), Ria chooses words and the truth as her weapons instead of more violence and death. Her fellow student Aureljo is prepared to spread the virus to avenge the sphere society (*Slutet* 397, 400). Ria herself briefly considers this option since she knows that it is just a matter of time before the sphere guards start to "colonialize" the clans' land and to kill clan members (*Slutet* 233–34). However, she is not prepared to sacrifice innocent sphere people who do not know anything about the sphere guards' treatment of the clans: "I won't waste any lives that I can save" (*Slutet* 234). Instead, she seeks a different, peaceful way of defeating the spheres and preventing them from using the advanced weapons that they have transported to the area of the clan that Ria has been staying with for some time (*Slutet* 241). In the end, Ria's strategy is successful, while Aureljo has gone insane because of the virus (*Slutet* 440). He is killed by Ria's biological sister when Ria cannot convince herself to do it (*Slutet* 442–43).

Ria achieves her righteous rebellion with help from the other students and some of the clan people by showing a secret video that contains antihegemonic knowledge: the founder of the spheres set off bombs to kill off most of the world's population because of the lack of resources and the environmental destruction (*Slutet* 391, 468). He gathered the people who believed in his prediction of a major volcano eruption in spheres and killed the rest (*Slutet* 391–94). The founder never intended for those outside of the spheres to thrive; on the contrary, he urged guards to give all available resources to the people living in the spheres and to kill the "savages" living outside when the environment had begun to heal (*Slutet* 394).[8] Ria utilizes her power of convincing people to stall an attack on the clans (*Slutet* 424), and antihegemonic knowledge about the founder and the guards' crimes is Ria's special weapon—a weapon that "can cut sharper and stab deeper than all knives" (*Slutet* 461). After her rebellion, there are uprisings against the current regime in several spheres (*Slutet* 486), and some spheres are opened up for everyone, those from both spheres and clans (*Slutet* 488). The trilogy highlights that the racism against the clans does not disappear immediately (*Slutet* 491) and that the distinction between "us" and "them" needs to be continuously challenged, but Ria is hopeful: "[T]here is a chance" that things may change (*Slutet* 508).

The *Eleria* trilogy portrays an intricate matrix of domination that the protagonist has a pressing personal interest in challenging. Ria moves from buying into the hegemonic domain's construction of the clan people as a violent "other" toward new, antihegemonic knowledge about the sphere's abuse and interaction directly with clan people. This interaction, in particular, proves her prejudices and the stereotypical view of the clans to be wrong. Changes in her worldview are portrayed as directly connected to a righteous rebellion that challenges the status quo and effects change regarding the structural and disciplinary domains' oppression of the clans.

Conclusion

The *Blood Rain* series and the *Eleria* trilogy represent two very different approaches to racism and racial oppression within YA dystopias available in Swedish. While the *Eleria* trilogy problematizes the hegemonic domain's discourses that legitimize racial oppression, the *Blood Rain* series does not. Instead, the protagonist of the *Blood Rain* series stays silent when faced with racism, thereby clarifying her white privilege of not being affected by racism on a personal level. Compared to the *Blood Rain* series, in which Elin has political power to do something about the immigrants' situation but meets that oppression with silence, the *Eleria* trilogy thoroughly interrogates and problematizes the construction of hegemonic assumptions about the clans that rely on a racist worldview. While the boundaries between "us" and "them" are stabilized throughout the *Blood Rain* series and, in particular, in Elin's speech about how politicians have failed to uphold human rights because humans care more about the people they know ("us") than about strangers ("them") in the final book in the series, the *Eleria* trilogy portrays an ending in which there is a potential for the hegemonic domain's oppression of the clans to be destabilized and perhaps even erased. Whereas the *Blood Rain* series does not argue against racism, the *Eleria* trilogy strongly advocates challenging racist views and rebelling against racial oppression.

Further research regarding how YA dystopias stemming from various cultural contexts and written in different languages depict racial oppression, racism, and white privilege could examine the historical consciousness of different countries and how authors create future worlds in relation to their contemporary cultural context. As Klas-Göran Karlsson argues, "[H]istorical consciousness is a mental procedure in which the contemporary human being orientates him-herself [sic] and his/her [sic] life situation temporally, in the light of experiences and knowledge of the past, and of expectations for the future" (43).[9] My analysis of the *Blood Rain* series and the *Eleria* trilogy indicates that this type of research, in which the events from the past are fictionalized and unpacked in the present as a way to look toward the future, is especially relevant regarding YA dystopias, with their focus on future societies that in many ways relate to specific historical and contemporary cultural contexts.

Notes

1. I define YA dystopias as books marketed for young readers "in which the ideals for improvement have gone tragically amok," portraying futures in which institutions are oppressive, and free will is often a concept of the past (Hintz and Ostry 3).

2. None of these texts is available in English translation.

3. While neither Elin's nor any other characters' skin color is explicitly stated, she is neither described nor coded as a person of color. Other characters' cultural background is indicated by their names, and since both Elin's first and last name are distinctly Swedish, Elin and Holme, I interpret her as ethnically Swedish, which equals being white in a Swedish context: "[B]eing white constitutes the central core and the master signifier of Swedishness, and thus of being Swedish" (Hübinette and Lundström 426).

4. For an analysis of these intersections with a focus on aetonormative power structures, see (Alkestrand, "Adolescent").

5. Compare Richard Dyer's analysis of how whiteness is equaled with "ordinariness, not a particular race, just the human race" in Western media (Dyer blurb).

6. All translations from Swedish are my own.

7. "Svartskalle" is a pejorative term for someone who has dark skin or dark hair, especially used about "foreigners" ("Svartskalle" in SAOB). While the use of the word is slightly less controversial than the use of the n-word within an American context, it is one of the main racist slurs in the Swedish language. For a discussion of racial slurs in a Swedish context, see Hübinette.

8. For a Swedish language analysis of the connection between a lack of social sustainability, the racist discourse about the clan people, and the aetonormative power abuse of children and adolescents in the *Eleria* trilogy, see (Alkestrand, "Bristen").

9. See Zander and Frohnert, respectively, for texts that aim to explain how the memory of the Holocaust has affected different countries.

Works Cited

Alkestrand, Malin. "Adolescent Killer, Politician and Mother: Age-Related Ideologies in the Dystopian Future Sweden of Mats Wahls' *Blood Rain* Series." Manuscript submitted for publication, 2019.

Alkestrand, Malin. "Bristen på social hållbarhet i framtiden: Ugdomsdystopin Eleriatrilogins didaktiska potential [The lack of social sustainability in the future: The didactic potential of the YA dystopia The Eleria trilogy.]" *Didaktiska perspektiv på hållbarhetsteman i barn- och ungdomslitteratur* [Didactical perspectives on sustainability themes in childrens' and YA literature], edited by Corina Löwe and Åsa Nilsson Skåve, Natur & Kultur, 2020, pp. 164–85.

Alkestrand, Malin. "Righteous Rebellion in Fantasy and Science Fiction for the Young." *Hype: Bestsellers and Literary Culture*, edited by Jon Helgason, Sara Kärrholm, and Ann Steiner, Nordic Academic Press, 2014, pp. 109–26.

Alkestrand, Malin, and Christopher Owen. "A Cognitive Analysis of Characters in Swedish and Anglophone Children's Fantasy Literature." *International Research in Children's Literature*, vol. 11, no. 1, 2018, pp. 65–79.

Collins, Patricia Hill. *Black Feminist Thought: Knowledge, Consciousness, and the Politics of Empowerment*. Revised Tenth Anniversary Edition. Routledge, 2000.

Couzelis, Mary J. "The Future Is Pale: Race in Contemporary Young Adult Dystopian Novels." *Utopian and Dystopian Writing for Children and Young Adults*, edited by Balaka Basu, Katherine R. Broad, and Carrie Hintz, Routledge, 2003, pp. 131–44.

Crenshaw, Kimberle. "Demarginalizing the Intersection of Race and Sex: A Black Feminist Critique of Antidiscrimination Doctrine, Feminist Theory and Antiracist Politics." *U. Chi. Legal F*, 1989, pp. 139–67.

Day, Sara K., Miranda A. Green-Barteet, and Amy L. Montz. "Introduction." *Female Rebellion in Young Adult Dystopian Fiction*, edited by Sara K. Day, Miranda A. Green-Barteet, and Amy L. Montz, Ashgate, 2014, pp. 1–16.

Dyer, Richard. *White*. Routledge, 1997.

Feagin, Joe, and Sean Elias. "Rethinking Racial Formation Theory: A Systemic Racism Critique." *Ethnic and Racial Studies*, vol. 36, no. 6, 2013, pp. 931–60. *Taylor & Francis Online*, DOI: 10.1080/01419870.2012.669839.

Frohnert, Pär. "The Presence of the Holocaust: *Vergangenheitsbewältung* in West Germany, East Germany and Austria." *Echoes of the Holocaust: Historical Cultures in Contemporary Europe*, edited by Klas-Göran Karlsson and Ulf Zander, Nordic Academic Press, 2003, pp. 81–114.

Hintz, Carrie, and Elaine Ostry. "Introduction." *Utopian and Dystopian Writing for Children and Young Adults*, edited by Carrie Hintz and Elaine Ostry, Routledge, 2003, pp. 1–20.

Hübinette, Tobias. "Swedish antiracism and white melancholia: Racial words in a post-racial society." *Ethnicity and Race in a Changing World*, vol. 4, no. 1, 2013, pp. 24–33. *Open Library Manchester*, DOI: 10.7227/ERCW.4.1.2.

Hübinette, Tobias, and Catrin Lundström. "Three phases of hegemonic whiteness: understanding racial temporalities in Sweden." *Social Identities*, vol. 20, no. 6, 2014, pp. 423–37. *Taylor & Francis Online*, DOI: 10.1080/08038740.2010.547835.

Karlsson, Klas-Göran. "The Holocaust as a Problem of Historical Culture: Theoretical and Analytical Challenges." *Echoes of the Holocaust: Historical Culture in Contemporary Europe*, edited by Klas-Göran Karlsson and Ulf Zander, Nordic Academic Press, 2003, pp. 9–57.

Omi, Michael, and Howard Winant. "Resistance Is Futile?: A Response to Feagin and Elias." *Ethnic and Racial Studies*, vol. 36, no. 6, 2013, pp. 961–73. *Taylor & Francis Online*, DOI: 10.1080/01419870.2012.715177.

Owen, Christopher. *Systemic Oppression in Contemporary Children's Fantastika Literature.* Doctoral dissertation, Anglia Ruskin University, Submitted in September 2019.

Poznanski, Ursula. *Sammansvärjningen* [The conspiracy]. Translated by Sofia Lindelöf, Opal, 2015.

Poznanski, Ursula. *Slutet* [The end]. Translated by Sofia Lindelöf, Opal, 2016.

Poznanski, Ursula. *Sveket* [The betrayal]. Translated by Sofia Lindelöf, Opal, 2014.

Said, Edward W. *Orientalism*. 1978. Routledge & Kegan Paul, 1980.

"Svartskalle." *Svenska Akademins ordbok* [The Swedish academy's wordbook], 1 Oct. 2018, www.saob.se/artikel/?seek=svartskalle&pz=1#U_S14717_239458.

Trites, Roberta Seelinger. *Disturbing the Universe: Power and Repression in Adolescent Literature.* University of Iowa Press, 2000.

Wahl, Mats. *De älskande* [The loving]. Natur and Kultur, 2017.

Wahl, Mats. *Krigarna* [The warriors]. Natur and Kultur, 2014.

Wahl, Mats. *Lagstiftarna* [The lawmakers]. Natur and Kultur, 2015.

Wahl, Mats. *De levande* [The living]. Natur and Kultur, 2016.

Wahl, Mats. *Ryttarna* [The riders]. Natur and Kultur, 2014.

Yuval-Davis, Nira. "Intersectionality and Feminist Politics." *European Journal of Women's Studies*, vol. 13, no. 3, 2006, pp. 193–209. *Sage Journals*, DOI: 10.1177/1350506806065752.

Zander, Ulf. "To Rescue or Be Rescued: The Liberation of Bergen-Belsen and the White Buses in British and Swedish Historical Culture." *The Holocaust-Post-War Battlefields: Genocide as Historical Culture*, edited by Klas-Göran Karlsson and Ulf Zander, Sekel, 2006, pp. 343–83.

Postracial Futures and Colorblind Ideology
The Cyborg as Racialized Metaphor in Marissa Meyer's Lunar Chronicles Series

Sierra Hale

As a genre that, at its inception, was mostly written and read by white men, science fiction (SF) has been plagued by racism and sexism. As Sharon DeGraw's *The Subject of Race in American Science Fiction* explains, when SF writing first gained prominence in the United States via magazine serials in the 1920s, it was predominantly written by white male writers for white male readers. This led to SF featuring white Western male perspectives emphasizing masculine heroism, frontier glorification, and, most significantly, a penchant for xenophobia and fear/mistrust of people of color.[1]

However, as the genre has developed, it has also diversified. Today's SF features more women writers and writers of color than ever before. Subsequently, SF literature today features more well-rounded female protagonists with agency and more series that feature complex nonwhite protagonists.

Despite this diversity, some critics still see inherent problems with the genre's treatment of race. In particular, they've pointed to SF's common assumption of postracial futures as espousing a problematic "color blind" treatment of race. In "Aliens, Cyborgs, and Other Invisible Men," Ximena Gallardo C. addresses this issue in Hollywood's treatment of Black actors in SF and demands acknowledgment of societal racialization rather than imagining postracial futures: "This awareness of the ongoing and permanent significance of race is especially needed at the present time to counteract the neo-conservative rearticulation of the American Civil Rights movement's demands for racial equality and justice into proclamations of the US as a color-blind, post-racial, multicultural society, a hegemonic racial ideology that perpetuates white dominance" (220). She associates postracial spaces in SF with imposing a "whitening gloss" on the future of race relations in order to ease white anxieties about contemporary race relations (244). Many of her examples illustrate how attempts to depict a future where race no longer matters are problematized by connections contemporary readers will necessarily make to their own society—connections overlooked by white filmmakers' willful ignorance of contemporary and historic racial dynamics.

Susan Louise Stewart notes similar problems in Lois Lowry's *The Giver*, a YASF novel that champions societal difference. Stewart demonstrates how the novel reinforces Western cultural ideology without inviting readers to critique that ideology, arguing *The Giver* "does little to challenge some concepts that under close inspection are problematic" (32). For example, it assumes a future in which all individuals have physically assimilated to a white standard. While the novel recognizes that the lack of diversity is problematic, Stewart argues that the way Jonas conceptualizes his society's homogeneity entirely in terms of lack of choice rather than physical difference shuts down any potential discussion of racial implications. She also notes that the novel's two socially rebellious heroes are differentiated by their shared characteristic of light eyes, further problematizing the novel's stance on racial issues. Stewart concludes that while Lowry's implicit message about race seemingly promotes racial diversity and multiculturalism, her explicit depictions of race contradict this message.

Stewart's work on *The Giver* analyzes the novel's "ethnoscape," a term coined by Isiah Lavender in *Race in American Science Fiction*. According to Lavender, "The writer constructs a socio-spatial environment in which to tell a story, but the reader can reconfigure those arrangements, draw out the assumptions and implications of the text to perceive its ethnoscape" (158). In other words, an SF novel's ethnoscape establishes the racial politics the reader infers from world-building details the author provides. Lavender posits the ethnoscape as a way to understand how race operates implicitly within SF texts and argues that analyzing a work's ethnoscape allows critics to see how the world of a text can contradict its stated message.

Postracial settings in SF necessarily create problematic ethnoscapes. They depict a raceless generic idea of difference that writers assume readers will equate specifically to racial difference, but the obfuscation of race often prevents this from happening. These spaces also tend toward problematic ethnoscapes that contradict antiracist messages the author attempts to convey.

Focusing on this intersection of postracial spaces and problematic ethnoscapes, this essay critiques Marissa Meyer's bestselling YASF Lunar Chronicles series.[2] The series, much like *The Giver*, features an implicit message supporting diversity and antiracism that becomes problematized due to its racialized ethnoscape and colorblind ideology. The series attempts to deal with racial issues by using cyborgs as metaphors for people of color and imbuing the series with antiracist messages about society's unfair treatment of minorities. Despite the partial success of Meyer's metaphors, however, the contradiction between the texts' antiracist messages and its problematic ethnoscape creates at best incongruity, at worst inherent racism. Analyzing the treatment of race in the Lunar Chronicles demonstrates how the use of postracial spaces that espouse a colorblind ideology problematizes SF that deals with difference.

Within SF criticism, important metaphoric connections have been established over time between the figure of the cyborg and the person of color in Western society. To start, cyborgs have been associated with larger societal forces acting upon the individual in oppressive ways. In her foundational work, "A Cyborg Manifesto," Donna Haraway reads the cyborg as a hybrid being upon whom cultural and state power is exerted. Victoria Flanagan's chapter on cyborgs in *Technology and Identity in Young Adult Fiction* deepens our understanding of the cyborg's connection to the body and oppression. She argues that the cyborg represents the concept of "embodiment" and forces privileged readers to reconcile with the way the state acts upon the bodies of the disenfranchised. She quotes Vint, who states, "The ability to construct the body as passé is a position available only to those privileged to think of their (white, male, straight, non-working-class) bodies as the norm. This option does not exist ... for those whose lives continue to be structured by racist, sexist, homophobic, and other body-based discourses of discrimination" (106). The embodiment of the cyborg challenges racial ignorance by reminding readers that while privileged people can avoid caring about their bodies, those without privilege are very much at the mercy of their bodies and how those bodies are treated by society.[3]

But within the cyborg metaphor is also the potential for change. Haraway sees the cyborg as a symbol of social upheaval and potential change due to its unique combination of outside control of the body and individual free will. Feminist critic June Deery views the cyborg as inherently interrogative, arguing that of the various forms of posthumans from robots to AI, "the embodied cyborg provokes more questions about body, gender, reproduction, kinship, and cultural identity" (92). In *Self-Wired*, Lisa Yaszek also reads the cyborg as representing the potential for increased social possibility. Yaszek paraphrases "medical experts" Manfred Clynes and Nathan Kline, who believed "this hypothetical hybrid being—'the cyborg'—marked the beginning of an era in which technological extension would free individuals from the biological constraints that had previously defined (and circumscribed) 'humanity' itself" (155).

Other SF critics have taken this idea further and applied it specifically to people of color. Lavender argues that "[t]he deliberate intersection of man and machine raises issues of identity that are somewhat similar to questions of race and ethnicity ... Informed imaginings about these technology-driven ethnicities can offer insight on otherhood" (186.) Lavender's interpretation of the human-machine hybrid allows readers to interpret the fusion of machine and human as a metaphor for how systematic racialized structures restrict or oppress the othered individual. More specifically, in her article "The Mulatto Cyborg: Imagining a Racial Future," Leilani Nishime reads the cyborg in SF as a symbolic representation of the mixed-race individual, describing three different "models" of cyborgs in cinema as being representative of a progression of self-acceptance on the part of mixed race individuals. In total, the cyborg functions as a symbolic figure for the socially racialized individual and as a physical body upon which institutional power and privilege are enacted, questioned, and potentially overthrown. These symbolic ties are highlighted by Meyer's construction of the cyborg.

Set several centuries in Earth's future, Meyer's Lunar Chronicles series imagines that cyborgs have become part of Earth's population and that former Earth colonists on the moon have evolved into a separate alien species called "Lunars." The aliens are ruled by a ruthless, power-hungry queen who aims to conquer Earth via enforced political alliance or violent takeover. Amidst these interstellar political tensions, the novels feature a female cyborg protagonist named Cinder who lives in New Beijing. At the end of the series' first novel, Cinder discovers that she is the missing Lunar princess and rightful heir. With a band of outlaws including Earthen/Lunar hybrid Scarlett, genetically engineered Lunar soldier Wolf, and tech savvy captive Cress, Cinder travels the world making plans to overthrow Queen Levana and retake her planet. In the process, she rediscovers forgotten parts of her life and reconciles her past and present identities.

Throughout this journey, Cinder confronts society's fear of her and faces discrimination for being a cyborg. Cyborgs are considered second-class citizens and denied basic rights. The way Meyer characterizes the systematic oppression and class struggle cyborgs face provides a direct connection to the way segregation and discrimination function in the United States.[4] One way this oppression is conveyed is through the laws governing the ownership and conduct of cyborgs. The state's view of cyborg rights is demonstrated by the "cyborg draft" in which they become test subjects for vaccines. Cinder states plainly that "nobody survives the testing" (*Cinder* 66). The official rationale is that cyborgs are of a lesser value and don't have the same rights as non-cyborgs: "[I]t was really just a reminder that cyborgs were not like everyone else...It's only right that they should be the first to give up their lives in search for the cure" (*Cinder* 29). One of the scientists justifies the draft, explaining, "It's better than testing on people" (*Cinder* 70). The draft establishes cyborgs as subject to state-enforced oppression and shows how this kind of oppression becomes accepted. Cinder questions her use as fodder within the system and thereby encourages readers to do the same. When told she is performing "a great service" for her "fellow citizens," Cinder responds, "Yeah? And what'd they ever do for me?" (*Cinder* 79). Cinder resents being forced to sacrifice for a society that oppresses and discriminates against her. Both the use of "citizens" and the militaristic language in this scene are significant as they directly tie Cinder's anger to both her individual situation and her position within the political institution.

Cinder's recognition of how discrimination is built into the social and legal system shows readers how contemporary racism functions on an institutional level. As critic Steve Martinot emphasizes, institutional structures are inherent in the process of racialization, taking "the form of the white para-political state ... These all function to sustain and valorize the coherence and cohesion of the white cultural environment" (173–74). Meyer's series goes beyond describing the experience of individual discrimination and creates a system that allows the reader to see how racism functions on a larger political scale.

New Beijing's legal system also denies cyborgs freedom within society, effectively enslaving them. Functionally, Cinder's cyborg status renders her legally subordinate to her stepmother, and she is both enslaved to her family and by the state, which sees her as a piece of property that can be bought and sold. This legal discrimination is reflected in reality. In "Darkness Made Visible: Law, Metaphor, and the Racial Self," D. Marvin Jones analyzes how US legal decisions are affected by race, explaining, "The idea of race as a natural, objective demarcation of difference between groups is the lens through which courts continue to view claims by blacks" (66). In his work, Jones demonstrates a legal disparity between Blacks and whites in the US and shows how the racial biases of the legal system unfairly punish Black citizens.

While this system of ownership explains why Meyer's Cinderella figure works as a slave for her family, the fact that Meyer's system spans society indicates a deeper message about social injustice. As the series' perspective is namely that of the othered individual, the oppressive structures of Meyer's world are designed to invite the reader to recognize and feel outrage at social injustice. Though the reader only gets Cinder's perspective, the novel establishes the pandemic nature of cyborg oppression. The novel makes it clear that the oppression of cyborgs is systemic and that as a cyborg, wherever she flees, Cinder will retain the same legal status of property she has in New Beijing.

Due to this legal system (or helping to create it), the novel describes rampant discrimination against cyborgs throughout society. Early in the first novel, Cinder is marked as a social outcast when a woman pulls her son away from Cinder's booth: "Sacha met Cinder's gaze, knotted her lips, then grabbed her son by the arm and spun away … 'It's not like wires are contagious,' Cinder muttered" (*Cinder* 5). This short scene indicates the thematic importance Meyer places on the social discrimination Cinder faces as a cyborg. While Cinder is, of course, resentful of her treatment, her response is one of resignation, indicating that she is accustomed to this type of discrimination. Meyer's readers experience the same fear and tension that Cinder does as she worries that Prince Kai, Cinder's love interest, will discover she is a cyborg. When he helps her at the hospital, Cinder braces herself to be rejected by him upon discovery: "She could already imagine how quickly Kai would pull away from her when the doctor told him he was supporting a cyborg" (*Cinder* 123). Her apprehension is validated when he reacts negatively toward her x-rays: "Cinder squeezed her fists together, nerves twisting in the base of her stomach as Kai recoiled from the image" (*Cinder* 126). Both of these instances, along with the many others focused on Cinder's fear that others will discover she is a cyborg, demonstrate the extent of the social divide between those who are fully human and those who are cyborg, as well as the extent to which Cinder herself has internalized this divide. Cinder's internal struggle recalls W. E. B. DuBois's concept of "double consciousness," a state of mind experienced by African Americans that he describes as "this sense of always looking at one's self through the eyes of others, of measuring one's soul by the tape of a world that looks on in amused contempt and pity" (9). It's a reaction to the racialization created by white society that not only ascribes the negative aspects of race to those who are perceived as other, but also changes the way racialized individuals view themselves. Much like people of color who experience systems of institutional racism, Cinder consciously recognizes the injustice of her position legally and politically, but she also sees herself as lesser through society's prejudicial lens. The series' message for readers about discrimination manifests particularly via the tension the text creates over Cinder's fears of discovery. This dramatic pressure invites readers to sympathize with Cinder and lament the discrimination she faces due to a perceived biological difference.

Integral to Cinder's attempts to hinder discrimination are the ways that cyborgs in the series can or cannot "pass" as humans. This attention to passing furthers the connection between cyborgs and individuals of mixed race.

Cinder spends most of the first novel attempting to pass as human. She uses clothing, particularly wearing gloves, to conceal the fact that she is a cyborg, often pulling at her gloves when she is nervous of discovery. When Cinder's gloves and boots are forcibly removed, she puts both back on as soon as she is able: "With her synthetic limbs covered and a weapon in hand, she felt better" (*Cinder* 94). Passing is a practice most often associated with multicultural communities in the United States and is typically a reaction to racial discrimination. Nadine Ehlers defines passing in *Racial Imperatives* as "the subject who executes a 'crossing-over' of any line or border that separates social groups" (56) and states, "The terminology 'passing' is most often utilized to denote the action of an individual who, based on genotype is defined as black, but crosses the racial line into whiteness through winning acceptance as white" (56). While Cinder's behavior fits into Ehler's more general definition, it also closely mirrors the Black-white specific passing Ehler identifies.

Due to her high percentage of mechanical parts and wiring, Cinder has a more difficult time passing than most. In one telling scene, Cinder's body is x-rayed, and a holographic screen proclaims her cyborg percentage: "RATIO: 36.28%. She was 36.28 percent not human" (*Cinder* 82). This scene alludes to the notorious one-drop rule that governed the status of African Americans. Historian Nikki Khanna explains the context for the one-drop rule: "To deal with the growing number of multiracial children, an informal one-drop rule was born in the South—anyone with any known trace of black blood was considered black" (98), thereby allowing white Southerners to disenfranchise individuals who either looked Black or had any African ancestry. Cinder's high percentage of synthetic body parts proves that she can be categorized firmly as a cyborg, just as one's "blood" or ancestry allowed the US government to determine citizens' ethnicity. Khanna points out that the one-drop rule still influences American perceptions of race today. She quotes Mary Water's research, which demonstrates that "Black Americans ... are highly constrained to identify as black, without other options available to them, even when they believe or know that their forbearers included many non-blacks" (100). Cinder's determination to keep her cyborg body parts covered underscores that Cinder sees herself as mostly robotic even though she's actually mostly human. Ultimately, the discrimination Cinder faces demonstrates that she fails to pass. Society views Cinder as a cyborg first and foremost, even though she often does not look like one.

While the first novel deals with Cinder's attempts to pass, subsequent novels focus on Cinder's self-acceptance and reconciliation of being Lunar and a cyborg, and, ultimately, her rejection of "passing." At one crucial moment in *Scarlet*, Cinder uses her Lunar glamour to create an illusion of a human hand to hide her cyborg one. For Cinder, this is the ultimate means of passing; she can bewitch everyone she meets to believe that she is fully "human." Initially, Cinder is overjoyed: "She did not need gloves anymore. ... No one would ever know she was cyborg again" (196). Almost immediately, Cinder's bionic wiring detects the lie. She connects Levana's use of glamour in order to trick people and gain power with her own newly discovered ability to successfully pass and decides that she would rather live authentically: "If this was her chance to decide who she was, who she wanted to be, then the first decision was an easy one. She would never be like Queen Levana" (197). Meyer equates Lunar glamour with the ability to pass—to be able to overcome the social perception of difference and be accepted and revered by a society that sees difference as a legal cause for oppression. Most scholarly sources treat passing as a neutral behavior, pointing out that passing can be both voluntary and involuntary. Ehler provides several valid reasons one might voluntarily pass as white, including "the desire to escape social disadvantage ... to gain economic advantage that was denied to black subjects as a result of discriminatory practices, or to temporarily access certain rights that would be denied to a visibly black subject" (57). Throughout the first book, Cinder attempts to pass as human for these very same reasons; however, interestingly, when Cinder rejects the idea of passing and refuses to hide her cybernetic parts, Meyer takes a stance on racial passing that connects it with lying and rejects it as representing a lack of authenticity.

Since the cyborg is a metaphor for the raced or mixed-race person, the novel's focus on the romantic relationship between Cinder and Kai appears to promote, or at least accept, miscegenation. Throughout the series, especially in the first novel, Cinder worries that if Kai discovers she is a cyborg, he will reject her as unworthy of romantic attention. At the end of the first novel, when Cinder is revealed as both cyborg and Lunar, Kai's reaction is negative. He immediately compares her to Queen Levana, saying: "You're even more painful to look at than she is" (*Cinder* 368). It's unclear whether Kai's dismayed reaction is due to the revelation of Cinder's cyborg status, her Lunar status, or a combination of both, but Cinder attributes Kai's negative response to her bionic parts, noting his distraction as she's carried off by the guards: "[H]e didn't look at her as she was dragged past him. His eyes were locked on the dirty steel foot clasped in both hands" (369). However, despite the initial tension over miscegenation the series presents, it ultimately promotes Cinder and Kai's relationship with a romantic reunion at the third book's conclusion. Their relationship is made explicitly reproductive by a curious scene that focuses on the functionality of Cinder's reproductive organs: "You know, lots of female cyborgs are left infertile because of the invasive procedures, but from the looks of it, I don't suspect you will have any problems" (*Cinder* 116). It's interesting that the novel takes time to explicitly point out Cinder's ability to have children with Kai, especially since the series limits sexual contact. This focus on reproductive viability could point to the novel's stance on miscegenation. The series not only encourages romance between cyborg and human—read white and nonwhite—but also validates their sexual potential.

As demonstrated, Meyer's cyborg functions as a metaphor for race. The series establishes the cyborg as a stand-in for the person of color and then creates empathy for its protagonist via a thematic discussion of the systematic oppression and injustice she faces due to her perceived biological difference. The message is also one of social progress. In the third book, the laws governing the control of cyborgs are recognized as violating human rights and are partially repealed. Perhaps recognizing the impossibility of "solving race" in one move, Meyer renders the results of Cinder's attempts to ban legal cyborg discrimination as ambiguous by positioning other world leaders as reluctant to end discrimination in their countries.

While Meyer's message about the institutional and social ramifications of prejudice is inherently antiracist, it's is complicated by the series' lack of historical context and problematic ethnoscape. According to Lavender, the fundamental reason we can read race into cyborg interactions is that "[t]hese beings pose problems for posthuman civilization where racial difference as we might recognize it is outmoded because our relations with them are potential repetitions of the discrimination and domination we have already lived through" (190). In other words, in SF, the systematic racial discrimination, prejudice, and oppression that exist in contemporary American society are displaced onto technological beings. The reader is meant to recognize this process as a repetition of an existing cycle in humanity's future rather than as an implicit metaphor. However, as Gallardo points out, contemporary SF often fails to provide a historical context linking metaphorical oppression with lived oppression. In particular, she notes the lack of association between systems of slavery depicted in SF with African slavery, calling the association "a scenario that Hollywood SF cinema—apparently partaking in America's historical amnesia when it comes to slavery—has been notoriously deficient at portraying in films" (24). The problem, then, is that while SF creators often use futuristic racial metaphors within postracial spaces to create antiracist messages for contemporary audiences, the futuristic oppression depicted is detached from actual racial oppression and the message is lost.

The reader's recognition of the cyborg as a metaphor for contemporary race relations is hampered in Meyer's series by the fact that humanity's history of oppression is never acknowledged. This is an obvious gap because Meyer's series takes place on Earth, not an imagined planet. The geographic locations that characters inhabit (the three books are set, respectively, in China, France, and Africa—a specific African country is never identified) have experienced the violence of imperialism and the pain of discrimination and segregation. In the series, the same racial problems are repeated in different forms in the same locales with no recognition of that history. The series aims to create an antiracist message for its reader, but it doesn't link the oppression of the future with that of the past and present. This link would strongly reinforce its message and create a greater possibility for social change. Its absence is a serious misstep.

Joseph Francavilla's essay "The Android as *Doppelganger*," in which he examines the replicants from Ridley Scott's *Blade Runner*, helps us understand the potential rationale behind the use of postracial spaces. He states, "Contemporary Science Fiction's view of the android or replicant as a persecuted being deprived of human rights may reflect our culture's projected guilt over the exploitation, conquest, enslavement, and extermination of other races and nationalities in history" (9). Here, Francavilla implies that for white SF writers and readers, it's easier to deal with white culture's history of racial oppression by separating that oppression from race itself. If we accept this premise, it may be subconscious guilt that prevents white SF writers from including references to humanity's history of racial oppression in works that clearly deal with it thematically. Failing to do so also absolves white SF readers of the guilt they may feel reading SF that deals explicitly with the history of racial oppression and contemporary racial discrimination. Metaphors of race allow white readers to feel catharsis of difference triumphing over oppression without the internal crisis of connecting that struggle with their own society. For this reason, dealing with racial issues solely in metaphor obscures and potentially undoes any positive message about race contained in the text by preventing fruitful connections from being made between the oppression in the text and oppression in society.

Aside from Meyer's emphasis on a postracial future, several contradictions within her series' ethnoscape complicate and problematize her messages about race. Along with absence of race, all socio/cultural aspects of global culture appear to have assimilated to a Western standard. While each novel takes place in different global settings, the cultures described are very similar. For example, characters in different geographical settings can communicate with each other because almost everyone speaks English. Cinder is from the Eastern Commonwealth, Scarlet is from France, Thorne is from the United States, and Cress and Wolf are from Luna. But they can communicate with each other without using translating technology or having learned other languages. That the default language is English is easy for the reader to assume as the book is written in English, but there are also subtle clues. Cress—attuned to Earth's history—listens to operas in other languages that she doesn't know (likely Italian and French), and she and Thorne cannot understand the tribespeople living in Africa. Presumably in a future in which difference is eradicated and race no longer matters, everyone (even an alien colony) would speak the same language—that the language is English privileges white, Western culture and contradicts the series' message about diversity.

The ethnoscape of the series also includes racially problematic depictions of global politics. In the future that Meyer envisions, all Asian countries are fused into one empire. While the United States, England, and Canada are depicted as separate nations, all forty-eight countries in Asia are collapsed into one country that shares a similar culture and values. Meyer's ethnoscape clearly demonstrates a Western cultural bias that individualizes Western cultures while generalizing non-Western cultures.

But Meyer's depiction of a unified Asia pales in comparison to her depiction of Africa—also apparently unified, though in this case it seems less like a purposeful stroke on the author's part and more a Western ethnocentrism that sees all the countries of Africa as the same. In a future where technology is readily available and race no longer matters, Africa is the only continent that speaks a language other than English that the series' main characters cannot understand. The series also depicts Africa as primitive. The characters visit places lacking modern technology and architecture, and the people are described as largely nomadic. While the other nations are depicted as futuristic and modern with a unified language, Africa is depicted as technologically primitive and isolated. Meyer's image of Africa corresponds to the stereotypical racist image of Africa that pervades much of contemporary Western thought and does the most to contradict her antiracist message. Unfortunately, the explicit descriptions and details of Meyer's racist ethnoscape are more apparent to readers than the metaphoric message Meyer uses the cyborg to create. By their nature, explicit details and messages are easier to pick up on than implicit ones, so authors of SF and especially YASF must recognize and correct problems in their explicit ethnoscapes.

The series' lack of connection between futuristic oppression and lived oppression and the contradictions apparent in Meyer's ethnoscape are two factors that seriously compromise its seemingly productive messages about race. A third factor—one that underlies the previous two—is how the SF world created in the Lunar Chronicles relies on colorblind ideology.

"Color-blindness" is a predominant white mode of thought, according to Donna L. Gilton in her book *Multicultural and Ethnic Children's Literature in the United States*. Gilton explains colorblindness as assuming or promoting the mindset that "we will have racial reconciliation once we ignore race and forget past discrimination" (17). On its surface, colorblindness appears helpful, even progressive. Gilton notes that colorblind ideology is largely responsible for the creation of antidiscrimination legislation during the civil rights movement and for repealing laws that prohibited interracial marriage. However, colorblind ideology is inherently flawed. First and foremost, it creates false ideas about contemporary race relations. As Gilton argues, colorblindness ignores past and present racism—assuming that the civil rights movement solved racial issues—and denies the existence of ethnocentrism. She also states that one of the worst ramifications of colorblindness is that it "can render people of color and their concerns invisible" (17).

In literature, colorblindness is used to create spaces in which race is dealt with purely thematically or metaphorically via characters who are othered in some way. Lavender calls this phenomenon "science fiction's frequent assumption of a colorblind future" (157) and describes how this colorblindness has historically manifested in SF: "sf has been largely 'colorblind,' depicting racial discrimination as a relic of the past and race as a biological fiction" (18). Meyer creates a postracial world in which race is explored via the metaphor of the cyborg, while race in terms of skin color and/or cultural difference is largely ignored. Meyer's ethnoscape implies that in future society, racial differences will no longer matter. As Lavender's description of the field makes clear, Meyer's world is similar to many SF worlds. DeGraw notes that both George Schuyler's and Samuel Delany's science fiction has been categorized as postracial in that their works exist in futures where race ceases to be a concern. She explains that this idea comes partially from science itself. If, as science tells us, race is not biologically determined but socially constructed, then there could come a time when social meanings about racialized peoples are no longer relevant. These worlds erase racial difference in terms of social stereotypes and racial discrimination as determined by skin color both from the futuristic world and its historic past.

These postracial worlds lead to glaring problems with racial representation. DeGraw provides an excellent, concise summary of some of the issues involved with SF authors espousing colorblind ideologies and transforming real world racial issues into metaphors: "[S]uch fictional transformation also suppresses the importance of race to human society. The real prejudice and oppression experienced by many groups is eclipsed and any explicit discussion of race is effectively forestalled. Simultaneously, the guilt of oppressors is obscured and any redress of grievances becomes more difficult" (16). Her concerns about the erasure of historical and contemporary racism and the obfuscation of the concerns of people of color echo Gilton's. Talking about race only through fictional cyborg hybrids removes the problem from its social and political context and distances it from the lived experiences of those who face discrimination and oppression. This removal makes it more difficult to have conversations about racial politics and potentially inspire social change.

The racial composition of Meyer's world demonstrates the series' color-blind ideology. One of the major critiques in children's literature is that it often whitewashes its fictional worlds. In "Children's Books: Still an All-White World?" Kathleen Horning states that "children's literature still represents a mostly white world in a real one that's becoming increasingly diverse." This is also true of SF. DeGraw, Lavender, and Delany base their studies of race in SF on the fact that nonwhite characters in the genre are few and far between. SF is necessarily political in nature, but Lavender points out that these political dialogues often occur from "a somewhat generic white space" (7).

The Lunar Chronicles generally follows this trend. A reader could easily surmise that Meyer entirely separates skin color from her concept of race, as the different races (Lunar and Earthen) both feature characters of multiple skin tones. Meyer typically either describes characters briefly once and then never again or fails to describe characters' appearances at all. Dr. Erland, for example, is a major character who plays a significant role in all three books and is only described once, when Meyer notes that he has grey hair. It is difficult to infer the race of characters who are not described. Even typical markers of race as connected to ethnicity are missing. Cinder believes she was born in New Beijing to Asian parents, but she learns that she is actually a Lunar. However, she looks just like everyone else in New Beijing (aside from being a cyborg), and there are no physical markers that she's either alien or not Asian because those types of physical markers don't exist in Meyer's ethnoscape.

Readers can only find explicit references to characters who are raced on Meyer's personal blog, where she offers physical descriptions of most characters.[5] According to the blog, Thorne, Scarlet, Cress, and Jacin are all Caucasian, Kai is Asian, Winter is Black, Wolf is "olive-toned skin—think Middle Eastern," and Cinder is "mixed ethnicity—Asian/Caucasian?" As the last two entries indicate, even with Meyer's own racial labeling, it's difficult to determine the race of her characters. The fact that she includes prominent nonwhite characters potentially demonstrates an effort to create a multicultural and inclusive series. However, her inattention to her characters' races—particularly the question mark after Cinder's description—indicates that her characters' races are unimportant.[6]

There are several reasons that giving brief, vague descriptions of characters' races is problematic. For one, readers are unlikely to recognize any implicit diversity an author attempts to include within a novel. One could easily read the word "dark" indicating a character's skin color once, but if it's never alluded to in any way again, it's quickly forgotten. Readers often imagine themselves or people like themselves into novels whenever they are able, and minuscule descriptions allow them to do so. This becomes especially problematic for white readers, as Stewart suggests in her analysis of *The Giver*: "My reading is very clearly guided by my cultural assumptions as a white reader. I have done precisely what a reader does. I have projected my own knowledge and my own light-skinned, blue-eyed image upon that which remains open and lacks description. I filled in the gaps, and I did it with my own cultural history" (28). For the white reader, for whom race is so socially normalized as to feel nonexistent and whose imagined space often defaults to all-white, there's a risk that any diversity could be erased. It then becomes more difficult for readers to connect Meyer's implicit, thematic messages of antiracism with a real-world counterpoint. In this way, when writers whose books include thematic messages about racial inequality provide their readers with brief or nonexistent character descriptions, it can lead to negating of those messages.

Flanagan's model of successful cyborg figures in YA is helpful to examine here. Flanagan's successful cyborg depictions remove women's organic bodies and replace them with cybernetic ones, forcing the protagonists to relearn what it means to be embodied women. This allows for a transgressive view of what female subject development and female embodiment look like. Meyer's depiction of the cyborg, though she connects it to race rather than gender, does not follow this model and is less successful for two reasons. One is that Cinder doesn't remember anything before she became a cyborg and thus cannot interrogate her own position to the level of critique. The other is that Cinder herself is not explicitly "raced"; therefore, she does not transgress the reader's understanding of the "raced" body.

The problems of Meyer's racial message come from the fact that, following a colorblind ideology, she removes race from its historical roots as well as falling into Western racial stereotypes. The effect at best convolutes and at worst potentially erases the series' tolerant messages about race. Yet while this essay focuses on the Lunar Chronicles, as I have attempted to convey by providing an SF-based theoretical context Meyer is merely working within the conventions of a genre that often either relegates race as a nonfactor or creates metaphors for race within a race-less, whitewashed background. And as Charles Gallagher argues in "Racial Formation," colorblindness is the dominant mode of white understanding of race relations today. He states, "Whites perceive themselves, according to one account, as being part of a distinctly different, colorblind, sympathetic generation that has learned to look beyond 'the color of the skin' to 'the beauty within'" (6). The problem of this mode of thought for the SF genre is clear. SF often deals explicitly with "difference" and depicts how societies create systems of injustice and oppression based on this difference.

Nevertheless, by situating these discussions almost exclusively within postracial spaces, "difference" becomes separated from "difference created by race." Postracial spaces may seem progressive, but the underlying colorblind ideology that allows for their creation is insidious. Displacing racial tensions into postracial spaces and figures creates a colorblindness that undercuts the otherwise noble intentions of the texts.

Understanding the problems of colorblind ideology in postracial SF universes is an important first step in eliminating this mode of thought from the genre and allowing important, socially positive messages to come through. Martinot cautions that choosing to ignore the implications of race, as using postracial spaces allows SF writers to do, makes one complicit in the institutional racism that pervades society: "For the white antiracist, there is an ethics involved in not seeing below the surface ... in ignoring the underlying social machinery or taking it for granted. If the history of that machinery is part of the history of white people themselves, then their ethics of not seeing it becomes part of the ethics of the machine" (3). Not considering the myriad ways race affects society can contribute to the continuation of racial oppression. Doing so confuses and potentially counteracts positive messages about race that SF writers attempt to convey to readers through metaphors of difference.

It's important to remember that the ability to ignore race is only available to white people; it's often not possible for people of color to close their eyes the effects of racialization on their daily lives. To envision a world where race no longer matters is to discount the experiences of contemporary readers of color and detach well-meaning intentions for furthering social justice from the realities of society. SF is a genre rife with meaningful possibility for our future, though white writers in the SF genre can't forget to make room for racial difference within that future, as nonwhite SF authors have been doing for decades.

Notes

1. See also Samuel Delany's "Racism in Science Fiction" and Isiah Lavender III's *Race in American Science Fiction*.

2. At the time of this essay's original composition, only three books in the Lunar Chronicles had been published: *Cinder*, *Scarlett*, and *Cress*. Later, some material was added to acknowledge the then-recent publication of *Winter*. Thus, the scope of this essay is primarily the first three novels; subsequent prequels, sequels, and graphic novels were not formally analyzed or included.

3. It's important here to distinguish between "care for the body" in terms of self-perception and self-esteem versus "care for the body" in terms of degree of autonomy, safety, and social currency. Certainly, white people care for their bodies in terms of health and appearance, and they face pressure to conform to societal ideals. However, this is very different from the ways

people of color are often made to fear for their personal safety and freedoms when institutionalized racism and discrimination reinforce their minority status.

4. Cinder's societal and personal position as a cyborg can potentially be viewed through multiple identity lenses. Throughout the first book, the disadvantages she faces as a cyborg are repeatedly linked to economic disadvantage, connecting Cinder's plight to contemporary class struggle. Jennifer Mitchell reads Cinder's fractured cyborg identity and interspecies romance with Kai as a metaphor for queerness. However, it's important to remember that Cinder's compromised legal and political status is based not on economic wealth but solely on perceived biological difference, aligning her status as a cyborg most clearly with race.

5. Meyer's blog has since been updated, and these character descriptions have been removed.

6. The one exception some readers of the series may point to here is Winter, who becomes a prominent character in the fourth and final book of the series. Unlike the other characters, Winter's brown skin is made visible to the reader through multiple textual references and the image of her hand on the front cover. Meyer's move to clearly identify Winter as Black and emphasize her physical beauty as her defining characteristic clearly serves to counter Western stereotypes of beauty as something that is exclusively white. It's a positive social message that challenges racialized Western beauty standards. However, there's no connection between Cinder's social and legal plight and Winter's portrayal as a Black character. While *Winter* offers readers a positive racial message and an attempt to include diversity, Winter's portrayal still demonstrates a colorblind ideology as her ability to seamlessly and positively blend in with the rest of her society further obscures the connection between race and societal discrimination in the series' focus on cyborg rights.

Works Cited

Deery, June. "The Biopolitics of Cyberspace: Percy Hacks Gibson." *Future Females, the Next Generation: New Voices and Velocities in Feminist Science Fiction Criticism*, edited by Marleen S. Barr, Rowman & Littlefield, 2000, pp. 87–108.

DeGraw, Sharon. *The Subject of Race in American Science Fiction*. Routledge, 2007.

Delany, Samuel. "Racism in Science Fiction." *The New York Review of Science Fiction*, vol. 10, no. 2, 1998, pp. 1, 16–20.

Du Bois, W. E. B. *The Souls of Black Folk*. 1903. Edited by Brent Hayes Edwards, Oxford University Press, 2007.

Ehlers, Nadine. "Passing through Racial Performatives." *Racial Imperatives: Discipline, Performativity, and Struggles Against Subjection*, Indiana University Press, 2012, pp. 51–72.

Flanagan, Victoria. *Technology and Identity in Young Adult Fiction*. Macmillan, 2014.

Francavilla, Joseph. "The Android as Doppelganger." *Retrofitting Blade Runner: Issues in Ridley Scott's* Blade Runner *and Phillip K. Dick's* Do Androids Dream of Electric Sheep?, edited by Judith Kerman, The University of Wisconsin Press, 1997, pp. 4–14.

Gallagher, Charles A. "White Racial Formation: Into the Twenty-First Century." *Critical White Studies: Looking behind the Mirror*, edited by Richard Delgado and Jean Stefancic, Temple University Press, 1997, pp. 6–11.

Gallardo C., Ximena. "Aliens, Cyborgs, and Other Invisible Men: Hollywood's Solutions to the Black 'Problem' in SF Cinema." *Science Fiction Film and Television*, vol. 62, no. 2, 2013, pp. 219–51.

Gilton, Donna L. *Multicultural and Ethnic Children's Literature in the United States*. Scarecrow Press, 2007.
Haraway, Donna J. "A Cyborg Manifesto: Science, Technology, and Socialist-Feminism in the Late Twentieth Century." *Cultural Theory: An Anthology*, edited by Imre Szeman and Timothy Kaposy, Wiley-Blackwell, 2011, pp. 454–71.
Horning, Kathleen T. "Children's Books: Still an All-White World?" *School Library Journal*, 1 May 2014, http://www.slj.com/2014/05/diversity/childrens-books-still-an-all-white-world/#_. Accessed 15 November 2017.
Jones, D. Marvin. "Darkness Made Visible: Law, Metaphor, and the Racial Self." *Critical White Studies: Looking behind the Mirror*, edited by Richard Delgado and Jean Stefancic, Temple University Press, 1997, pp. 66–78.
Khanna, Nikki. "'IF YOU'RE HALF BLACK, YOU'RE JUST BLACK': Reflected Appraisals and the Persistence of the One-Drop Rule." *The Sociological Quarterly*, vol. 51, no. 1, 2010, pp. 96–121.
Larrick, Nancy. "The All-White World of Children's Books." *Saturday Review*, 11 Sept. 1965, pp. 63–65.
Lavender, Isiah III. *Race in American Science Fiction*. Indiana University Press, 2011.
Martinot, Steve. *The Machinery of Whiteness: Studies in the Structure of Racialization*. Temple University Press, 2010.
Meyer, Marissa. *Cinder*. Feiwel and Friends, 2012.
Meyer, Marissa. *Cress*. Feiwel and Friends, 2014.
Meyer, Marissa. *Scarlet*. Feiwel and Friends, 2013.
Meyer, Marissa. *Winter*. Feiwel and Friends, 2015.
Mitchell, Jennifer. "'A girl. A machine. A freak.': A Consideration of Contemporary Queer Composites." *Bookbird: A Journal of International Children's Literature*, vol. 52, no. 1, 2014, pp. 51–62.
Nishime, Leilani. "The Mulatto Cyborg: Imagining a Multiracial Future." *Cinema Journal*, vol. 44, no. 2, 2005, pp. 34–49.
Stewart, Susan Louise. "A Return to Normal: Lois Lowry's *The Giver*." *The Lion and the Unicorn*, vol. 31, no. 1, 2007, pp. 21–35.

III
LINEAGES OF WHITENESS

"I've Connected with Them"
Racial Stereotyping and White Appropriation in the Chaos Walking Trilogy
Meghan Gilbert-Hickey

Recent YA dystopian fiction and film presents alternative futures in which communities, nations, and even entire planets are saved by strong-willed teenagers who persevere despite adversity. These teen rebel/leaders learn—and, subsequently, teach—lessons of equality, pushing back against heteronormative roles of gender and sexuality. However, the vast majority of those novels and series that are granted major media attention and franchise opportunities privilege the white female and/or queer experience over more intersectional identities, particularly those defined by race. One notable example is Patrick Ness's Chaos Walking trilogy, a successful trilogy that has been optioned for a major motion picture starring big-name white leads.

In Chaos Walking, Ness problematizes the normalized heteropatriarchal family configuration while simultaneously calling out the settler colonial mindset that undergirds this configuration. In this chapter, I argue, however, that as sympathetic as Ness's portrayals of his Indigenous characters and characters of color are, the trilogy ultimately replicates structures of both settler colonialism and Western racism. His portrayals of two major characters of color, Bradley and the Return, whitewash racialized histories of power imbalance, romanticize and stereotype Indigenous populations and people of color, and reify the normalized centrality of the white perspective, particular that of the liberal, white middle-class. Thus, Chaos Walking is, at best, an incomplete critique of Western power imbalances and, at worst, an insidious investigation of normativity that privileges discussion of gender and sexuality at the expense of racial discourse.

Throughout the trilogy—particularly the second and third novels, *The Ask and the Answer* and *Monsters of Men*—Ness investigates and condemns settler colonialism as a justification for violence. *Monsters of Men* takes this project up in earnest, with the inclusion of several subsections written from the perspective of the Return, a member of the Indigenous group the Land (called the Spackle by the settlers), who has served as a slave to a settler master and returns to the community of the Land, the sole survivor of a bloody massacre.

The trilogy's opening novel, *Chaos Walking*, tells the story of Todd Hewitt, the last young boy in Prentisstown. Todd is told that his mother was the last of the Prentisstown women to die of a "woman-killing germ" released on the town in a biological attack spearheaded by the natives of New World, the planet upon which Todd's family has settled. Todd is taken in by his neighbors, Ben and Cillian, two romantically partnered men. It is significant that Ben and Cillian partnered not in response to the impossibility of a heterosexual match, due to the absence of women, but long before they, along with Todd's biological parents, settled on New World. "Story is," Todd narrates,

> my ma was friends with Ben before they left for New World, [and] they were both members of the Church when the offer of leaving and starting up a settlement was made. Ma convinced Pa and Ben convinced Cillian and when the ships landed and the settlement started, it was my ma and pa who raised sheep on the next farm over from Ben and Cillian growing wheat and it was all friendly and nice. (Ness, *Knife* 33–34)

In actuality, the men of Prentisstown were infected with a New World disease, which caused their thoughts to be projected onto all other sentient beings. For a reason unknown to New World settlers, women are immune from the disease. Whereas other communities of New World settlers were able to cope, emotionally, with the disease and its symptoms, the men of Prentisstown became paranoid about the women knowing all of their inner "Noise." After a period of increasing unrest and rise of religious zealotry, Todd is told, some of the men killed all of the women, thereby providing a fictional enactment of Margaret Atwood's claim that, whereas men are afraid that women will laugh at them, women are afraid that men will kill them (413).

Ness's desire to highlight and deconstruct misogyny is significant, given the way he fails to interrogate fully the intersectional identities he creates throughout the trilogy. Even as they fall victim to the heatedly misogynist preaching of their pastor, however, and even though none of the other men choose a queer coupling over single life, the men of Prentisstown voice no objection to either the romantic relationship of Ben and Cillian or their adoptive co-parenting of Todd. The queer(ed) nuclear family is accepted, so long as its three members remain participants in the town's goings-on. Ness normalizes the family without any examination of what it might be like to be nonnormative in a community ruled by religious zealots. Further, Ben, Cillian, and Todd remain a smaller part of a violent settler society, once privileged and willing to go to violent extremes to maintain a semblance of that privilege. Following a war between the Land and the settlers of New World, a peace treaty requires all prisoners of war, as well as their subsequent offspring, to become slaves of Haven, New World's major city.

With his inclusion of Haven, Ness condemns violent settler colonialism, particularly as it involves slavery. As Curtis Marez recounts, the United States has a longstanding history of settler colonialism and Indigenous slavery, including "direct labor exploitation but also the forced reservationing of Comanches, Kiowas, Navajos, Apaches and others in the 1860s and 1870s; the transportation of so-called Indian war criminals, who were forced to work on prison plantations in Alabama and Florida during the 1870s and 1880s" (338). Ness draws upon this history to create the trilogy's slave narrative, but he removes race from his analysis of settler colonialism by making the Land a white-skinned Indigenous alien species. He both whitewashes the history and replicates it by dehumanizing those who have been exploited in both contemporary and historical contexts and the trilogy he creates. This whitewashing is especially insidious in a trilogy, like Chaos Walking, that is purported to be progressive in its undermining of normalizing social structures. At its base, Ness undermines his challenge of the heteronormative nuclear family with his racial complicity.

Using several characters, most notably new settler Viola and her mentor, Bradley, Ness appears to argue against settler colonialism and the violence that supports it. Regarding the Land, Viola says,

> "The only one I met was gentle and much more frightened of humans that the humans here seem to be of them."
> "You didn't fight them in a war," Mistress Coyle says.
> "I also didn't enslave them." (Ness, *Monsters* 36)

Teenaged Viola, representing a new generation of settlers coming to New World, judges those who came before her and argues for a new kind of colonialism—one that, apparently, steals Indigenous land, but does so in a gentler, more collaborative manner. Shannon Sullivan, in *Good White People: The Problem with Middle-Class White Anti-Racism*, intervenes into the heightened racial tensions within Chaos Walking, especially the fact that wealthy, educated newcomer Viola is chosen as the community's Peacekeeper, even though she is still a child. Sullivan's work provides us with a way to understand this moment in the text with her argument that, in American culture,

> One of the main ways that white class hierarchies operate is through the production and display of white middle-class moral goodness. This is achieved by establishing the moral badness of poor and lower-class white people. Lower-class white people supposedly are the retrograde white people who still believe and act in racist ways; they are the real problem when it comes to lingering racism in our enlightened times. Knowing this, white middle-class liberals know and/or take steps to ensure that they are different in kind than the white lower class, and this process of othering secures white liberals' status as good. Those white people (the lower class) are racist; we middle-class whites are not like them; therefore we are not racist. At the heart of this anti-racism, however, is not necessarily an attempt to eliminate racial injustice—which, to be successful, might involve strategies or tactics that don't make white people look or feel morally good—but a desire to be recognized as Not Racist, perhaps especially by people of color. (5)

It is unsurprising, then, that Ness makes use of the more sophisticated, cosmopolitan Viola, educated, well-mannered, and elite, a newcomer who immediately takes umbrage with the anti-Indigenous individuals she discovers in Todd's poor, rural community and other earlier New World settlements. In setting up a dichotomy between uneducated, rural, racially violent settlers and educated, urban, seemingly open-minded newcomers, Ness not only participates in but also reifies the kind of scapegoating and blame that Sullivan highlights and critiques. Ness forwards a classist agenda through which poor, uneducated whites are marked with the stigma of racism in order for more normative, middle-class individuals and communities to escape the stain of being racist.

Like Viola, Bradley, a new arrival on New World who leads the team to ready a new settlement, opposes the violence associated with colonizing New World while wholly supporting the colonization itself. When asked if he will join the present war between the groups, he replies, "And have our first action here be killing hundreds of the local species, the local intelligent species that, in case you're forgetting, we're going to have to live with for the rest of our lives?" (Ness, *Monsters* 51–52). "[W]e start our new life here as conquerors and you'll be setting up brand new wars for generations to come" (Ness, *Monsters* 55). It is Bradley and Viola who broker the ultimate peace treaty between the Land and the settlers, new and old, thereby ending the trilogy with a New

World in peace. But both characters operate in terms of their willingness to appropriate New World. The Land, one must assume, would just as well keep their properties intact and only agree to a treaty in order to avoid war; thus, Viola and Bradley's mission of settling the Land's planet via a peace treaty is, in itself, a significant violence.

Bradley is one of the texts' few brown-skinned characters.[1] Ness might be gesturing toward the notion that Bradley, as a person of color, may be uniquely insightful in dismantling long-held colonial subjugation. Indeed, the more hawkish members of his new community dub Bradley "The Humanitarian," a title that is meant to be derogatory. However, readers may see Bradley's characterization as Ness's attempt to overturn stereotypes of Black men as violent and dangerous.[2] Bradley is more than once described as gentle and kind, and he does not challenge these characteristics during the trilogy.

It is not until the trilogy's final installment that the reader discovers Bradley's Blackness, through the eyes of Viola: "I pull a little away from Bradley and the light catches his face and I see him, really *see* him, see his kind brown eyes, his skin the same dark shade that Corinne's was, his short curly hair, greying at the temples, Bradley who was always my favourite on the convoy, who used to teach me arts and maths" (*Monsters* 30). The reader is only familiar with Bradley through Viola's memories, but they know of his wisdom, his warmth, and his ability to help Viola process the struggles of adolescence. However, it is not until he is reunited with her that Viola "*sees*" Bradley's racialized appearance. Here, Ness operates under the assumptions of colorblindness in his characterization of Bradley; Viola—and, thus the reader—doesn't "see" Bradley's race because, despite it, he is just like her. Critical race theorists have long argued against colorblindness, as it only serves to further empower the normalized culture by shutting down discourses of racialized difference.[3] *New York Times* writer Jennifer Harvey underscores the assumptions that colorblindness allows for:

> Not realizing the pollution is there doesn't mean it doesn't affect you. White children are exposed to racism daily. If we parents don't point it out, show how it works and teach why it is false, over time our children are more likely to accept racist messages at face value. When they see racial inequality—when the only doctors or teachers they see are white, or fewer kids in accelerated classes are black, for example—they won't blame racism. Instead, they'll blame people of color for somehow falling short.

Just as white parents' avoidance of conversations about racism inadvertently perpetuates discrimination, so, too, does Ness's position that Viola doesn't "see" Bradley's raced image. Further, as Chaos Walking is geared toward a YA audience, Ness's use of colorblindness reinforces the notion that discussions of racialized experience—like queerness or other intersectional identities—aren't important, that they should be silenced.

Ness's colorblindness is particularly troubling as he simultaneously uses racialized discourse and a history of Western discomfort with Black excess and Black sexuality in his characterization of Bradley. After a brief tenure in New World, Bradley develops Noise, so his thoughts become audible to everyone around him. As Men become accustomed to Noise, they develop strategies to quiet their own as a way to maintain some small level of privacy. Bradley and those around him became increasingly uncomfortable because of the loud clumsiness of his new Noise. Bradley rues his own loudness, and this excess is echoed by those around him (*Monsters* 127). Viola tells him, "You *will* get used to it," and, when he meets the leadership of the Land, they call him "loud and chaotic" (*Monsters* 127, 345). Although Bradley's Noise is especially loud and disorganized only because it is new, the others characterize it as excessive. Thus, I want to emphasize how his uncontained Noise is typical of Western cultural depictions of people of color. Juana María Rodríguez calls attention to the racialized reading of othered bodies, "often represented, if not identified, by our seemingly over-the-top gestures, ... bodies betraying—or gleefully luxuriating in—... intentions to exceed the norms of proper corporeal containment. ... Our racialized excess is already read as queer, outside norms of what is useful or productive" (2). Viola may rarely see Bradley's Blackness when she looks at him; however, no one can ignore his over-the-top Noise, a symptom not only of the New World disease but also of a white Western ideology that reads people of color as excessive and improper.

Bradley and those around him are especially uncomfortable with a particular strain of his thinking: Bradley is sexually attracted to Simone, the leader of the other ship on the settler mission. While the explicit nature of his thoughts, in general, is what makes Bradley's noise so difficult to tolerate, I contend there is more to their discomfort. Simone, the object of Bradley's desire, is described as "beautiful and smart," with "freckled skin" and "red hair tied back in a ponytail" (*Monsters* 30). Although—or, perhaps, because—her skin is unmarked by a racial description, readers assume that Simone is white.[4] Therefore, Bradley is a Black man having audible, sexual fantasies about a white woman, and this transgressive act—a Black man actively fantasizing about a white woman—makes him and those him around him uncomfortable. As historian Leon F. Litwack reminds us, the United States has a long and troubled history of Black men accused of and punished for raping white women, to such a degree that "[f]or a black man, a sexual advance to a white woman was a certain invitation to a tortured death" (344).

In *White Women, Rape, and the Power of Race in Virginia, 1900–1960*, Lisa Lindquist Dorr concludes that the trials of Black men accused of raping white women had one sole purpose: to "diffuse the furor usually awakened by the alleged assault" (5). More contemporary events demonstrate that little has changed in the public's misplaced fear of violent Black male sexuality. C. Riley Snorton's *Nobody Is Supposed to Know: Black Sexuality on the Down Low*, for instance, examines the white panic triggered by the case of Nushawn Williams, an HIV-positive Black man who confessed to having unprotected sex with up to three hundred girls and women, many of whom were white, in New York State in the 1990s (27). Bradley's now-legible fantasies about a white woman, and the ways those fantasies are the source of shame on both sides of the relationship, are easily read as part of this history of policing Black masculine desire.

Because he is a pacifist on a planet at war, Bradley's ideas are often dismissed, sometimes violently. Ness shows Bradley's white peers talking over him, until he snaps in frustration (*Monsters* 49, 51). His "Humanitarian" title is given to him by an angry white civilian, and it catches on as the people he attempts to lead become more and more frustrated with the status quo:

> "Is there trouble outside?" [Viola] asked.
> Bradley just frowned, his Noise full of images of people getting into his face, calling him the Humanitarian.
> Some of them spitting on him. (*Monsters* 245–46)

Again, Ness's portrayal of Bradley here is sympathetic. Bradley's colleagues and the violent, hawkish crowds they attempt to contain are in the wrong repeatedly throughout the trilogy, and Bradley is rewarded for his correct views by joining Viola in the small convoy that makes peace for the planet. However, in purporting to take up a colorblind ideology while simultaneously reinscribing a long history of racialized violence in which white Western citizens spit on their Black counterparts, Ness both reflects and normalizes these kinds of racist actions and discourse.[5] Thus, Bradley is alternately portrayed as the gentle humanitarian and the uncontrollable sexual aggressor. In both roles, he is frequently dismissed and disrespected, sometimes violently. In many cases throughout the trilogy, Ness works to discredit racist assumptions about Black men. However, by positioning himself as a colorblind author who trades on a history of Western racism and, moreover, makes use of Western anxiety over the sexual appetites of Black men, he undermines this important work, rendering it complicated and incomplete, at best, and insidious, at worst.

Bradley is not the only character of color who is effectively silenced. Ness similarly obfuscates the Return, a character whose voice is much more central to the trilogy. The organization of *Monsters of Men* builds on that of the trilogy's first two books—a progression that is telling and deserves some explanation. In *The Knife of Never Letting Go*, Ness writes solely from Todd's perspective; then, in *The Ask and the Answer*, the trilogy's second text, he alternates sections between Todd and Viola. In *Monsters of Men*, however, the Return—who, until this text has been identified not by his name but by the number of the identification band forcefully attached to his arm, 1017—closes each chapter from his perspective. Todd and Viola alternate brief sections in every chapter, which average fifty pages in length, and then the Return voices a separate, ten-to fifteen-page subchapter. Most sections of the book have two main chapters: one beginning with Todd's perspective and one with Viola's. The result of these narrative decisions is that, while its inclusion is a notable departure for the trilogy, the Return's perspective is not only brief but also buried—a narrative afterthought. Thus, Ness's writing of the Return exhibits what Isiah Lavender III argues is talk about race and oppression "from a privileged if somewhat generic white space" (8). Helen Young's work on fantasy examines similar "habits of whiteness." Young argues the following: "Those habits take multiple forms: some are to do with the bodies which have traditionally dominated its spaces—in both the real and imagined worlds; some with the voices that are most audible; and some with the kinds of sources which inspire imagined worlds, and the ways that they are used" (10). The organization and accessibility of *Monsters of Men* exemplify, visually and logically, the ways in which both the body and the voice of the Return are less present, less audible, despite Ness's decision to include his perspective in the text.

Moreover, just as Ness's characterization of Bradley is both colorblind and built upon Western structural racism, his interpretation of indigeneity via the Return enacts a similar violence. First, it is notable that, like all of the Land, the Return is distinguished by his bright white skin and the lichen-based protective layer—described as similar to clothing—that grows on it (Ness, *Monsters* 197). In giving the Return white skin, Ness fails to engage with the racial aspects of slavery typical to the West. In "Black and Brown Boys in Young Adult Dystopias: Racialized Docility in the *Hunger Games* Trilogy and The Lunar Chronicles," Miranda A. Green-Barteet and I trace the literary whitewashing of American slavery in Marissa Meyer's Lunar Chronicles series and argue,

> In her erasure of the African American history and positioning of Cinder as the white subject of culturally racialized discipline, Meyer perpetuates [Richard] Dyer's notion that the insidious power of whiteness lies in its desire to represent

all of human experience. In The Lunar Chronicles, slavery and civil rights are not part of the African American experience. Rather they have been co-opted by cyborgs and their white representative, Cinder. (14–15)

Likewise, Ness's whitewashing of Indigenous positionality transforms indigeneity into a kind of voiceless subaltern experience and posits the author himself as speaking on behalf of an oppressed group of which he has limited first-hand knowledge. Marez argues, "Echoing the history of official US discourses and practices that projected Indian disappearance, science fiction imaginatively removes Indian people from speculation about the future. Along with other imperialist discourses, it suggests that there is no future in being Indian" (336). That this erasure occurs while Ness simultaneously makes use of United States settler colonial history is especially disquieting.

Additionally, I want to underscore the racialized nature of the Land's non-physical descriptors, the ways in which, rhetorically, the members of the Land—both enslaved and free—are dehumanized and transformed, in settler culture, from subject to object. Significantly, the Land is referred to, by settlers, as "Spackle," New World's "indigenous species," "vicious in battle" (Ness, *Monsters* 36).[6] The redefinition of this Indigenous group, of course, asks the reader to recall American settlers' renaming of various Indigenous tribes as one mislabeled group—Indian—and the terms "species" and "vicious" evoke the kind of beastly, objectifying rhetoric used to describe these groups during the era of colony, as well as long after.

Interestingly, Ness partners the Return with a male significant other. Like Ben and Cillian's relationship, this partnership is unremarkable within the narrative. That the Return's "one in particular" is another man is mentioned only once, after his death: "*You miss him*, the Sky shows. *You loved him*" (Ness, *Monsters* 271). Just as he does with his descriptions of Bradley's brown skin, Ness makes the Return's sexual identity seem unremarkable. After a cursory reading of this relationship, one might argue that gay partnerships within the trilogy are treated equally and that the existence of two such relationships within the narrative serves to destabilize the heteronormative mindset upon which much colonial power was built. However, the heteronormativity of settler communities depends, in large part, on the queered othering of their Indigenous counterparts. Mark Rifkin's work in *Settler Common Sense: Queerness and Everyday Colonialism in the American Renaissance* underscores how settlers labeled and policed native sexuality, thereby producing Indigenous subjects who were both always already queered and forced, through state sanctioned violence, to participate in straight identities and communities. Thus, the relationship between the Return and his "one" in particular, not unlike settler notions about a "vicious" "species" of natives, trades on assumptions of indigeneity that serve as the framework for settler violence.

In this instance—and, by and large, all other instances—Ness uses the voice of the Return to present a white Western view of this Indigenous community that is steeped in romanticized stereotypes. The Land call themselves such because of their connection to the planet. After Ben is temporarily taken captive and healed by the Land, he returns to Todd and explains the group's true nature: "Spackle speak the voice of this planet. They live within it. And now, because of how long I was immersed in that voice, I do, too. I've connected with them" (Ness, *Monsters* 452). Ness romanticizes that the Land, as the Indigenous population, are more connected to the natural world, as evidenced by their embrace of the Noise "germ" and their use of Noise to create a voiceless language that speaks both to and for all other members of the group. The voices of the Land connect "to each other to form the one voice" (Ness, *Monsters* 268): "one big voice, evolved to fit this world perfectly, connecting them all. [. . .] All those individuals, speaking as one. Like the voice of this whole world, right inside your head" (Ness, *Monsters* 175–76). Critics such as Christine Morris, Mary Weinkauf, and Lorenzo Veracini show how Indigenous identity is all too often romanticized as spiritually connected both to each other and to nature in social culture and the popular literature that stems from it. In particular, the Native American/Indian experience is characterized, in these venues, as the Noble Savage, wild and unfettered, one with the land and with the community.[7] Work like that by Veracini, Scott Morgensen, and Mark Rifkin undermines this normative impulse by recentering Indigenous identities and epistemologies and making them present, not romantically historicized.

It is also significant that Ben, a white settler, feels "connected with them" after only a brief time in the Land's captivity. Marez argues, "From the long view of continual conquest, representations of alien abduction revisit histories of Indian slavery in response to contemporary contexts that call into question the property rights and entitlements of white North Americans. ... This suggests that the larger cultural obsession with alien contact and abduction ... speaks to the continuing influence of Indian slave histories in the form of an appropriative identification with Indians" (345). Marez notes that this is "identification with the slave in order to reinforce ideologies of mastery" (345), and, I argue, it is the sort of identification that we see both in Ben's assumption that he has connected with the Land—a notion that the text does little to dispel—and Ness's own employment of a romanticized, essentialized portrayal of the Land as an Indigenous group. For it is not only Ben that claims a connection with the Land; the group's leadership accepts the connection as well:

> And just because he speaks with our voice, I showed, does not mean he is one of us.
> Does it not? The Sky asked. What is the Land if not its voice?
> I looked back at him. Sure you are not suggesting—? (Ness, *Monsters* 422–23)

The Sky is the appointed leader of the Land, and, by this point in the novel, the Return is being groomed as his replacement. This conversation between them, told from the Return's perspective, pushes back somewhat against the notion that Ben has become one with the Land simply by learning its language. Later, the Return confronts Ben directly, telling him, "You have spoken in our voice for a fraction of your life. You are not us. You will never be us," but Ben counters, "As long as there is an us and a them, [...] the Land will never be safe" (Ness, *Monsters* 509–10). We see here that the Return's resistance to a connection with Ben and his white settler community isn't the means by which Ness voices a complication of that dictate. Ben's message of unity—unity voiced by white settler leadership with little regard for Indigenous sovereignty—is the message that prevails.

By the trilogy's close, the reader finds that the Return has learned a lesson of forgiveness and peace. The Return has the opportunity to kill Todd, the figure upon whom the Return focuses his righteous anger. Clearly, Todd is complicit in settler violence. Manipulated by the evil president of New World, Todd is the man who attaches a painful identification band to the Return's arm before his escape (Ness, *Ask* 183). Todd violently beats the Return (Ness, *Ask* 267). But he also saves him from an explosion and is instrumental in his escape from slavery and return to the Land (Ness, *Ask* 211, 310). In fact, Todd's guilt over his complicity is both what spurs him to act on behalf of the Return and the reason he is the target of the Return's anger:

> He is worse than the others, I show. He is worst of all of them.
> *Because*—
> Because he knew he was doing wrong. He felt the pain of his actions—
> But he did not amend them, shows the Sky.
> The rest are worth as much as their pack animals, I show, but worst is the one who knows better and does nothing. (84)

However, the Return finds that he cannot kill Todd when the opportunity arises because of this very guilt:

> I saw the Knife again for the flawed Clearing that he was, and as the Source forgave the Knife, as the Source provided absolution for everything the Knife had done—
>
> For everything *Todd* had done—
>
> I felt my voice provide it, too, I felt my voice join with the Source's and offer my own forgiveness, offer to let go and forget every wrong he had done to me, every wrong he had done to our people—
>
> Because I could see through the Source's voice how the Knife punishes himself for his crimes more than I ever could—. (Ness, *Monsters* 475)

Notably, the Return corrects himself in this passage, referring to Todd by his given name, rather than the Knife, the name the Return has given him. Neither Todd nor any member of his community returns that gesture of respect—they never refer to the Return by his given name. They continue to call him 1017—the number inscribed on the slave armband that he wears—and the Land is still Spackle in all settler voices and thoughts throughout the trilogy.

Todd is dubbed "the Knife" because he fatally stabs a member of the Land early in *The Knife of Never Letting Go* in what might be self-defense. Todd spends the remainder of the trilogy struggling with the guilt of this murder, although he is reassured that killing a "Spackle" isn't the same thing as killing a man. Once again, we see the racialized violence Ness perpetuates by dehumanizing the Land while simultaneously using their experience to explore both white guilt and white appropriation of Indigenous suffering.

Moreover, once unified with Ben (whom the Return calls the Source), the Return takes up Ben's forgiveness of Todd as his own, allowing that Todd's feelings of guilt are enough to atone for generations of settler violence. In this passage, Ben's perspective takes over. The Return, it seems, has nearly no choice regarding whether to dispense forgiveness. He feels himself forgiving, rather than actively choosing to forgive. As Ben absolves Todd, so must the Return. It is in this seemingly benign moment that we have the clearest sense of the centrality of the white perspective in the text. Ness's sympathies lie not with the Return or the Land, individually or collectively. Rather, Ness sides with those settlers who feel guilt for their actions, those who would offer up peace as a way to keep both their land and their lives. As Sullivan argues, "good white liberals often use their guilt and shame ... to efface their own complicity in white racism and white domination" (6). Ultimately, Ness determines that Todd's shame is enough to absolve him of his complicity and, thus, helps him evade punishment for his actions.

The Return's eventual forgiveness of Todd—like Ben's connection to the Land, as well as the racialized and sexualized characterizations of the Return and Bradley—points toward the prioritizing of the white perspective in Ness's Chaos Walking trilogy. This white perspective perpetuates violence toward Indigenous populations and people of color in several ways. First, it trades on racialized stereotypes of both groups and fails to depict intersectionality, sometimes using romanticized characterizations of identity and sometimes displaying anxious judgments on racialized characters without unpacking them as such. Second, it foregrounds white guilt about racialized violence rather than experiences of that violence by Indigenous people and people of color. Finally, it implicitly argues that white guilt should suffice—that guilt for complicity in white violence renders Todd, Ben, and other "good" white characters innocent of those very crimes.

Indigenous queer critiques, like those by Qwo-Li Driskill, Chris Finley, Brian Joseph Gilley, and Scott Lauria Morgensen in *Queer Indigenous Studies: Critical Interventions in Theory, Politics, and Literature,* argue that colonialism cannot be dismantled without a simultaneous deconstruction of heteropatriarchy, the foundation upon which Western power structures are built. Driskill's essay in that collection demonstrates the ways that Cherokee Two-Spirit identity "refers specifically to a different way of thinking, feeling, and being that is outside of men's and women's traditional roles" (98). He points to contemporary Native American antiqueer sentiments, which have led some to deny the history of Two-Spirit culture, and underscores the settler colonial lineage of that type of heteronorming thought. In their introduction, all four editors call for the joint deconstruction of settler heteropatriarchy:

> What we should share in common, however, is a commitment to our communities and to larger decolonial struggles, understanding that colonial heteropatriarchy injures all of us. Decolonial movements of Indigenous GLBTQ2 people that replicate sexism, transphobia, and biphobia in our communities are—in fact—not decolonial at all. We must realize that in order for our projects to be successful in intervening and interrupting oppression, we must become allies to one another in our struggles. (Driskill, Finley, Gilley, and Morgensen 18–19)

Here, we can see the strong link between the colonizing of Indigenous groups and power structures based on varied access to white, masculine, heteronormative identity. To Driskill, Finley, Gilley, and Morgensen, movements that attempt to explode one of these power imbalances while upholding—even reifying—the others are inherently colonial, as they maintain imbalance based on identity.

In Chaos Walking, however, Ness makes the opposite error. Although he works to destabilize heteronormative families and communities, he implicitly upholds systems of racism and colonial control that utilize heteronormativity to maintain authority. Thus, the trilogy is, at best, an incomplete critique of power imbalances. At worst, Chaos Walking tells its readers that gender and sexual sovereignty trump race discrimination and that the absence of physical violence is the same thing as equality.

Notes

1. Another notable exception is Corinne, a healer's assistant who, until her untimely death, vehemently protects and cares for patients and loved ones.

2. For more on the racialized depictions of Black and brown men in YA dystopias, see Green-Barteet and Gilbert-Hickey's "Black and Brown Boys: Racialized Docility in *The Hunger Games* and *The Lunar Chronicles*" and Mary J. Couzelis's "The Future Is Pale: Race in Contemporary Young Adult Dystopian Novels."

3. See Michelle Alexander's *The New Jim Crow: Mass Incarceration in the Age of Colorblindness*; Ruth Frankenberg's *White Women, Race Matters: The Social Construction of Whiteness*; and Shannon Sullivan's *Good White People: The Problem with Middle-Class White Anti-Racism* for more on the perils of colorblindness.

4. For more on bodies marked and unmarked by race, gender, and other norming categories, see Wayne Brekhus's "A Sociology of the Unmarked" and Linda R. Waugh's "Marked and unmarked: A Choice between Unequals in Semiotic Structure."

5. White individuals or crowds have, throughout American history, spit on people of color to show disrespect. As recently as October 2015, a member of a white crowd at a Donald Trump rally spit in the face of a man of color who attended the rally to protest (Mathis-Lilley).

6. The name "Spackle" comes from colonists' appropriation of the Indigenous language: *es'Paqili* means "the People." New World settlers change the spelling but keep the pronunciation more or less the same. However, this is not the word the Land uses to describe themselves but is, instead, "the only written words anyone's ever seen in the spack language" (Ness, *Knife* 15). Thus, the label is not only misrepresentative but also reductive, as it assumes that the only visible word might stand in for all words. Further, as spackle, in American English, refers to a tacky substance used to fill holes or cracks, readers might discern, in the name "Spackle," the ways in which New World settlers scapegoat the Land to provide critical distance between themselves and their violent actions. As spackle fills cracks in a wall, then, Spackle are used to fill the cracks in New World settlers' collective psyche ("Spackle").

7. For more on the figure of the Noble Savage in colonial discourse, see Gaile McGregor's *The Noble Savage in the New World Garden: Notes Toward a Syntactics of Place*. For more on the stereotypes of Indigenous populations in YA fiction, see Paulette F. Molin's *American Indian Themes in Young Adult Literature*.

Works Cited

Alexander, Michelle. *The New Jim Crow: Mass Incarceration in the Age of Colorblindness*. New Press, 2012.

Brekhus, Wayne. "A Sociology of the Unmarked." *Sociological Theory*, vol. 16, no. 1, 1998, pp. 34–51.

Couzelis, Mary J. "The Future Is Pale: Race in Contemporary Young Adult Dystopian Novels." *Contemporary Dystopian Fiction for Young Adults: Brave New Teenagers*, edited by Balaka Basu, Katherine R. Broad, and Carrie Hintz, Routledge, 2013, pp. 131–44.

Dorr, Lisa Lindquist. *White Women, Rape, and the Power of Race in Virginia, 1900–1960*. University of North Carolina Press, 2004.

Driskill, Qwo-Li. "Situating Two-Spirit and Queer Indigenous Movements—Asegi Ayetl: Cherokee Two-Spirit People Reimagining Nation." *Queer Indigenous Studies: Critical Interventions in Theory, Politics, and Literature*, edited by Qwo-Li Driskill, Chris Finley, Brian Joseph Gilley, and Scott Lauria Morgensen. University of Arizona Press, 2011, pp. 97–112.

Driskill, Qwo-Li, Chris Finley, Brian Joseph Gilley, and Scott Lauria Morgensen. "Introduction." *Queer Indigenous Studies: Critical Interventions in Theory, Politics, and Literature*, edited by Qwo-Li Driskill, Chris Finley, Brian Joseph Gilley, and Scott Lauria Morgensen. University of Arizona Press, 2011, pp. 1–30.

Driskill, Qwo-Li, Chris Finley, Brian Joseph Gilley, and Scott Lauria Morgensen, eds. *Queer Indigenous Studies: Critical Interventions in Theory, Politics, and Literature*. University of Arizona Press, 2011.

Dyer, Richard. *White: Essays on Race and Culture*. Routledge, 1997.

Frankenberg, Ruth. *White Women, Race Matters: The Social Construction of Whiteness*. University of Minnesota Press, 1993.

Green-Barteet, Miranda A., and Meghan Gilbert-Hickey. "Black and Brown Boys in Young Adult Dystopias: Racialized Docility in The Hunger Games Trilogy and The Lunar Chronicles." *Red Feather*, vol. 8, no. 2 (2017).

Harvey, Jennifer. "Are We Raising Racists?" *New York Times* 14 Mar. 2017. https://www.nytimes.com/2017/03/14/opinion/are-we-raising-racists.html. Accessed 22 Mar. 2017.

Lavender, Isiah. *Race in American Science Fiction*. Indiana University Press, 2011.

Litwack, Leon F. *Trouble in Mind: Black Southerners in the Age of Jim Crow*. Vintage, 1999.

Marez, Curtis. "Aliens and Indians: Science Fiction, Prophetic Photography and Near-Future Visions." *Journal of Visual Culture*, vol. 3, no. 3, 2004, pp. 336–52.

Mathis-Lilley, Ben. "A Continually Growing List of Violent Incidents at Trump Events." *Slate* 25 Apr. 2016. http://www.slate.com/blogs/the_slatest/2016/03/02/a_list_of_violent_incidents_at_donald_trump_rallies_and_events.html. Accessed 29 Jul. 2017.

McGregor, Gaile. *The Noble Savage in the New World Garden: Notes toward a Syntactics of Place*. University of Toronto Press, 1988.

Molin, Paulette F. *American Indian Themes in Young Adult Literature*. Scarecrow, 2005.

Morris, Christine. "Indians and Other Aliens: A Native American View of Science Fiction." *Extrapolation*, vol. 20, no. 4, 1979, pp. 301–7.

Ness, Patrick. *The Ask and the Answer*. Candlewick, 2010. Kindle Edition.

Ness, Patrick. *The Knife of Never Letting Go*. Candlewick, 2010. Kindle Edition.

Ness, Patrick. *Monsters of Men*. Candlewick, 2010. Kindle Edition.

Rifkin, Mark. *Settler Common Sense: Queerness and Everyday Colonialism in the American Renaissance*. University of Minnesota Press, 2014.

Rodríguez, Juana María. *Sexual Futures, Queer Gestures, and Other Latina Longings*. New York University Press, 2014.

Snorton, C. Riley. *Nobody Is Supposed to Know: Black Sexuality on the Down Low*. University of Minnesota Press, 2014.

"Spackle." *Merriam-Webster*. https://www.merriam-webster.com/dictionary/spackle. Accessed 5 Oct. 2017.

Sullivan, Shannon. *Good White People: The Problem with Middle-Class White Anti-Racism*. State University of New York Press, 2014.

Veracini, Lorenzo. "District 9 and Avatar: Science Fiction and Settler Colonialism." *Journal of Intercultural Studies*, vol. 32, no. 4, 2011, pp. 355–67.

Veracini, Lorenzo. *The Settler Colonial Present*. Palgrave Macmillan, 2015.

Waugh, Linda R. "Marked and Unmarked: A Choice between Unequals in Semiotic Structure." *Semiotica* vol. 38, 1982, pp. 299–318.

Weinkauf, Mary. "The Indian in Science Fiction." *Extrapolation*, vol. 20, no. 4, 1979, pp. 308–20.

Young, Helen. *Race and Popular Fantasy Literature: Habits of Whiteness*. Routledge, 2015.

Asian Masculinity, Eurasian Identity, and Whiteness in Cassandra Clare's Infernal Devices Trilogy[1]

Elizabeth Ho

The Infernal Devices trilogy—*Clockwork Angel* (2010), *Clockwork Prince* (2011), and *Clockwork Princess* (2013)—is a prequel to Clare's wildly popular Mortal Instruments (2007–2014) series. In 1878, seventeen-year old orphan Tessa Gray leaves her home in New York after the death of her aunt to join her brother, Nate, in London. Upon arrival, the repulsive Dark sisters intercept Tessa and imprison her in their Limehouse home where she is forced to endure torturous training to manifest her talent as a shape-shifter. A mysterious man known only as "the Magister" sponsors her training and, she soon learns, also wants her as his bride (Clare, *Angel* 31). On the day of her supposed wedding, Tessa is rescued by Shadowhunters, Nephilim warriors, drawn to Limehouse by a surge in the number of strange deaths and supernatural energy. Tessa becomes immediately attracted to the handsome and dashing Will Herondale, who helps her fight her way out of the Dark house guarded by its automaton servants, the prototypes of the clockwork army of "Infernal Devices" (Clare, *Princess* 50) that the Magister will command to destroy the global Shadowhunter hegemony known as the Clave. As Tessa forms the only link to identifying and capturing the Magister, she takes refuge at the Institute, the headquarters of the London branch of the Clave. There, Tessa meets Jem Carstairs, Will's partner or "*parabatai*" (Clare, *Angel*, 212), a Eurasian boy from Shanghai with a devastating illness that requires the constant but deadly ingestion of the demon drug "*yin fen*" (Clare, *Prince* 194). Banded together, the trio embarks on a quest to hunt down the Magister, prevent his Infernal Devices from destroying the Nephilim, and discover the origins of Tessa's extraordinary powers as a shape-shifting immortal. Together, the inhabitants of the Victorian Institute—the Fairchilds, Herondales, Carstairs, and Grays—are the Victorian ancestors of the twenty-first-century protagonists of the *Mortal Instruments*.

Clare's novels, in general, advocate a postracial (and prosame-sex) agenda: they suggest that her characters and her readers have moved beyond race thanks to the advances of the civil rights movement, the decline in racism, an increase in interracial relationships, and people who identify as mixed race. Read together, the Infernal Devices trilogy, with its epilogue set in 2008, and the Mortal Instruments series posit that, if a postracial era is a fantasy we have not yet inhabited in the present, then *this* nineteenth century, however fantastical, can be the imaginary past for *that* imagined future. Parsing Brian McHale's analysis of steampunk's temporality, the novels help to "historicize our present by reimagining it as *an alternative future for a past that never happened*; it makes us aware of our historical situation by imagining the past otherwise" (McHale 223). As Infernal Devices shapes its version of the nineteenth century in order to bring about its vision of a multicultural future, can its characters (and primarily YA readers) bridge racial boundaries and take into account the significance of the Victorian colonial past that underlies racial categories and hierarchies in the present? What race work does the return to the Victorian provide or hinder in mainstream, massively popular YA fiction such as the *Infernal Devices*? In this paper, I explore the relationship between whiteness, Eurasian identity, and masculinity by showing how, without a more thoughtful ethics of appropriation, the deployment of the Victorian can reinforce, rather than critique, discourses of whiteness and racism that bleed from the past into present and, it seems, beyond the books themselves.

If the conventional and most simplistic definition of neo-Victorianism is a subgenre "*self-consciously engaged with the act of (re)interpretation, (re)discovery, (re)vision concerning the Victorians*" (Heilman and Llewellyn 4), then the Infernal Devices provides neo-Victorian studies with an interesting example as the series works, like the steampunk genre it also inhabits, as a wildly unrestrained appropriation of the most token collection of details about the Victorian era, including some of the perennial concerns of neo-Victorian studies. Like many neo-Victorian characters, Victorian Shadowhunters struggle with decorum and corsets. They are concerned about threats to the British Empire, such as the opium trade and the evil Magister, who the Shadowhunters discover is really the "tai pan," Axel Mortmain, with ties to "Hong Kong, Shanghai, Tianjin" (Clare, *Angel* 149). Postcolonial themes are introduced with Downworlders (warlocks, faeries, demons, and werewolves) who have signed tenuous Accords of governance with the Shadowhunters, the self-appointed guardians of the Shadow World, which is hidden by glamours from intruding into its "mundane" counterpart. In a nod to Michel Foucault, the trilogy celebrates homosexuality in the nineteenth century by situating Clare's most beloved queer character, Magnus Bane, within the Aestheticism movement.[2] Aside from the many references to Victorian literature and epigraphs taken from Victorian poetry, the series also rewrites Charles Dickens's *A Tale of Two Cities* (1859), eschewing its political and historical themes for a more simplistic emphasis on love and sacrifice. Despite the fact that Clare claims she lived "in a bubble of the Victorian era" in order to write the series (*Phantastik-Couch*), the trilogy does come across as "neo-Victorian-lite," merely hitting on various Victorian touchpoints without much critical commentary. However, the Infernal Devices can be considered neo-Victorianism for a specific YA audience: young; often female; media and tech savvy; a powerful demographic comfortable with mass consumption; adept in bowdlerized MTV adaptations of literary works, who might have come to Victorian fiction via *Twilight* (2005) and the Victorian era through Philip Pullman's *Sally Lockhart Quartet* (1985–1988); untroubled by anachronism and inauthenticity; equal parts critical reader and fan. In fact, as I have argued elsewhere, if neo-Victorianism is constructed out of a global memory of what "the Victorian" means or stands for, then the series can be considered a "deliberate misreading, reconstruction or staged return of the nineteenth century in and for the [YA] present across genres and media" (Ho 5). As the Infernal Devices suggests, in its own lexicon, a "mundane," perhaps "adult" version of the Victorian, exists—under the purview of neo-Victorian studies and high neo-Victorian literature—alongside the Shadowhunter or YA version that plays fast and loose with historical detail and authenticity. As Charlotte, the young leader of the London Institute, studies a globe marking the boundaries of the "mundane" British Empire, she muses, "their world was not the same shape as the one she knew" (Clare, *Angel* 131). While such "lite-ness" can be considered a weakness of the series, I argue that it serves an important neo-Victorian function: to strategically mis-remember the Victorian past in order to conjure into being the novels' vision of a postracial future.

Clare's series can be contextualized within a range of YA historical novels set in the global nineteenth century. The focus in many YA series, such as the *Gemma Doyle* novels (2003–2007) or Gail Garriger's *Parasol Protectorate* (2009–2012) and *Finishing School* books (2013–2015), has been the agency of the heroine and the relevance of Victorian girlhood to twenty-first century female readers of all ages. The Infernal Devices can be read in tandem with these concerns; viewing the novel through Tessa's perspective, we can regard her shape-shifting and choice of partner as a quest for self-knowledge, and share her success in overcoming the patriarchal constraints of both the Victorian era and the Shadowhunter organization. Read in this light, Tessa fulfills the mandate of protagonists of YA historical fiction who "in confronting their respective circumstances and challenging the dominant structures of their society, each assumes more control of his or her life, gaining unanticipated strength" (Brown and St Clair 4). However, the *Infernal Devices*' investment in an interracial romance draws our attention away from Tessa's development as a heroine and towards the romance of race.

What might be gained by entering the Infernal Devices on the side of James Carstairs? Born to a Chinese mother and a British father who "met in London" before moving to Shanghai (Clare, *Angel* 109), Jem, or "Jian" in Chinese (Clare, *Angel* 345), is visually arresting. In her first encounter with him, Tessa notices that his hair is "an odd bright silver color, like an untarnished shilling. His eyes were the same silver, and his fine-boned face was angular, the slight curve of his eyes the only clue to his heritage" (Clare, *Angel* 9). That the slant of his eyes forms the only marker of Jem's heritage might be disturbing to a twenty-first-century reader. Yet Clare does not explicitly reveal Jem's ethnicity until Tessa is "startled" by it a hundred pages later: "If Jem's mother had been Chinese, then so was he, wasn't he? She knew there were Chinese immigrants in New York—they mostly worked in laundries or sold hand-rolled cigars from stands on the street. She had never seen one of them who looked anything like Jem, with his odd silvery hair and eyes" (Clare, *Angel* 109). It would have been rare for Tessa to see a Chinese woman in New York given that they were effectively barred from entering the United States by a selection of "immigrant acts" (Lowe 9), including the Page Law in 1875, a "startling" fact that Clare elides by referring to them collectively as "Chinese immigrants." Further "startling" may be Tessa's misreading of Jem's ethnicity: he is not Chinese, as Tessa thinks, but Eurasian. She discovers that Jem came to England after the brutal murder of both of his parents because "my father was British. I spoke English. It seemed reasonable" (Clare, *Angel* 325). Instead of identifying with his Chinese mother, Jem finds a more "reasonable" rapport with the country and language of his English father despite moving easily between English and Mandarin.

Tortured for days by the demon that slaughtered his family, Jem was forced to ingest large quantities of the demon drug *yin fen*. Unable to be weaned off the poison even with powerful spells, Jem is doomed to addiction and a "slow death" (Clare, *Angel* 346). Jem's dependency on *yin fen* weakens his body and "drains the color from [his] eyes and hair, even [his] skin" so that he appears "so ghostly" (Clare, *Angel* 347). To enter successfully into Victorian English society, the novels suggest, requires such a "ghosting" or alignment with the dominant culture and language coupled with transformation into an even whiter version of oneself that mirrors the values of the imperial center (Young 180). To retain his membership in Shadowhunter society means that Jem must fight skillfully, his short bursts of strength buoyed by the very drug that also whitens his skin. While Jem outwardly adopts the label of an "honorary European" (Young 178), he must also master the skills and codes of the Shadowhunter world in order to assure his rights and privileges by battling the demon others to which he feels no affinity. It can be argued, then, using Adrian Valdez Young's analysis of the colonial logic of whiteness, that Jem, as a Shadowhunter, protects his "tentative status through acts of vigilance and exclusion of one's external and internal native, *other*" (180). As authenticity is not Clare's goal, the series does not attempt a detailed recuperation of the history of mixed-race identities that emerged when people traveled and forged bonds between empires of the nineteenth century. Instead, representing Jem's hybridity as a supernatural shifting between otherness and whiteness ensures a forgetting of racial history that, I will argue, authorizes the predilection to whitewash his character in Infernal Devices fandom.

Clare's allegiance to the supernatural romance plot tends to supersede an explicitly neo-Victorian project: retrieving a version of the nineteenth century that could present and explain a wealth of nineteenth-century antimiscegenation laws and other racial prohibitions to a contemporary YA audience. For example, Emma Jinhua Teng begins her narrative of racial hybridity in the nineteenth century during the First Opium War (1838–42) when Chinese ports and trade routes were forcibly opened up by Western powers and so-called "unequal treaties" were signed between China and the West. As a result of this competition between empires, the nineteenth century viewed from Asian eyes forms the largest migration of Chinese around the globe. In China, Teng continues, Eurasian children were often born out of unequal situations of power, left unrecognized and illegitimate as the result of "temporary alliances" (28). Eurasian offspring were often the issue of European diplomats, merchants, sailors, consuls, and missionaries who married or, more than likely, fathered children with their temporary Chinese "wives." At the same time that Europeans and Americans objected to mixed-race children on the grounds of miscegenation, in China, "ostracism of mixed race couples and their Eurasian children served as a form of social sanctioning that punished those who violated the taboo against crossing racial boundaries" (Teng 164). The Chinese, who feared "dilution" and illegitimacy, often made distinctions between the racial and cultural superiority of Eurasian offspring fathered by Chinese rather than European men (Teng 152). In her comparative study of interracial families during the nineteenth century, or "an earlier age of globalization" (Teng 24), Teng argues that there were two strands of dominant thinking about "amalgamation": one led to "hybrid degeneracy and abnormality," and the other fostered "the belief that racial crossing was eugenic [and] gave rise to ideas of hybrid vigor and racial improvement" (24). Attitudes towards mixed-race people swung between these two poles of problem and promise. While Jem's portrayal as a Eurasian is similarly characterized by race and shame, readers have little to no access to this history of mixed race in the *Infernal Devices*. Voided of historical depth, the novels' "lite" version of the Victorian does not necessarily archive a significant cultural memory for a mixed-race or Asian YA reader seeking identification with Jem.

The inspiration for Jem's character, according to Clare, came from her research into the Opium Wars and the idea "that for a large part of the Victorian era the British Empire was the biggest drug dealer on the planet" (*twilightseriestheories*). In the novels, opium becomes not a "mundane" historical fact but one of the few opportunities for readers to, metaphorically, encounter China. Drawing on the ill repute of opium fictionalized by nineteenth-century novels, the demon drug, *yin fen*, can only be obtained "from a warlock dealer in Limehouse" (Clare, *Angel* 347). Later we learn that Mortmain has monopolized the supply of *yin fen* in the country, using it to enslave werewolves and as a ploy to draw the London Shadowhunters out of their fortress in their concern for Jem's life. The *yin fen* den becomes a place where Jem and Tessa must confront their anxieties about race and gender via the orientalist imagery of exoticism and sexuality and the rhetoric of contamination. Chasing Will, who has gone in search of drug-induced escape, Tessa and Jem end up at a storefront in the East End and are guided through its smoky, red interior by a woman with "black hair piled on her head, kept in place by a pair of gold chopsticks. Her skin was very pale, her eyes rimmed with kohl—but on closer examination Tessa realized she was white, not foreign" (Clare, *Prince* 192). A few beats later, the woman's clothing parts to reveal a "slender forked tail" (Clare *Prince* 193), and Tessa realizes that she is a warlock. Tessa automatically Sinicizes this warlock woman who, despite being "not foreign," can nonetheless be literalized into the Oriental stereotype of the dragon lady. The novel's supernatural qualities allow readers to gloss over a neo-Victorian argument that might show how the representation of the warlock woman belongs to "a tradition of imperialist images that commodify, objectify and fetishize the bodies of Asian women" (Shimizu 3). However, the neo-Victorian project is curtailed, its didactic function "lite-ned," because, as Jem tells Tessa, this is *not* an opium den (Clare, *Prince* 193). The novels must rehabilitate the opium/*yin fen* den and its disorderly, sexualized parody of domesticity and care in favor of heterosexual, interracial normativity using methods other than neo-Victorian mnemic strategies.

The Infernal Devices finds it difficult to correct by being historical when illegitimacy, deleted records or unrecorded lives, and other forms of erasure and fantasy constitute both a mixed-race archive and cultural memory. As a substitute for history, the series opts to explore its theme of race mixing and multiculturalism by depicting a variety of supernatural hybrid characters such as the warlock woman at the *yin fen* den. Clare relies on what Alexandra Hidalgo has called "metaphorical race" in her study of Stephenie Meyer's *Twilight* novels (79). A common strategy in YA supernatural fiction, "metaphorical race" depends on the use of supernatural characters—vampires, werewolves, and the like—to serve, with greater or lesser success, as imaginary solutions to real racial problems. Explaining the existence of Shadowhunters to Tessa in *Clockwork Angel*, Charlotte refers to Nephilim as "a race, if you will, of people, people with special abilities. We are stronger and swifter than most humans" (Clare, *Angel* 65). To marry outside of the Nephilim, as Will's father did, is possible, but the Shadowhunter/mundane or "interracial" couple risks ostracization, or, at worst, excommunication from the Clave. Even then, as Jem explains to a shocked Tessa, Shadowhunters can still "lay claim" to hybrid, "mixed-race" children because "Nephilim blood is dominant" (Clare, *Angel* 323). Jem nonetheless finds solace in his Nephilim blood as it helps him transcend race; "when other Nephilim look at me" he reveals, "they see only a Shadowhunter. Not like mundanes, who look at me and see a boy who is not entirely foreign but not quite like them either" (Clare, *Angel* 326). In signing the Accords, the "laws that govern peace among Downworlders" (Clare, *Angel* 66), Nephilim have taken on a postimperial role to "safeguard the Covenant Law" and police the Shadow World (Clare, *Angel* 66). Yet resistance towards them is strong, and the Nephilim must adapt and reform lest their "proud isolation" and "insular" ways prevent them from transforming into an inclusive society (Clare, *Angel* 247, 313), moving away from thinking "whether something is good for the Nephilim or bad for the Nephilim" and closer to asking "whether or not it is good or bad for the world" (Clare, *Angel* 313). Closer, in other words, to what Alfred J. Lopez has called a "postcolonial whiteness" or a "number of post-empire, post-mastery whitenesses attempting to examine themselves in relation to histories of oppression and hegemony of their others" (6). The novels challenge their characters and readers to see like Nephilim: only then will the "white but not quite" rhetoric of Jem's Eurasianness be erased in favor of the ease of belonging. But readers must also be critical because to see like some Nephilim also means misogyny and the valuing of blood rather than race. The Nephilim's emphasis on parentage and bloodlines, specifically Tessa's warlock/Nephilim hybrid origins, eugenically engineered in a prior generation by none other than Mortmain, and the possibility of her subsequent sterility, "in the manner of mules and other crossbreeds" (Clare, *Angel* 472), is couched in terms of "blood quantum" or, more familiarly, the "one-drop rule." The danger and excessiveness of categorizing the world through blood can be seen in Starkweather's archive of "spoils" at the York Institute replete with pelts, fangs, skin and other trophies of the Nephilim's "race" war with Downworlders (Clare, *Prince* 112). Focusing on metaphorical race allows Clare to inject a range of nineteenth century racial discourses into her novels regardless of historical, geographical, or contextual shifts in the criteria of racial belonging while championing marital free choice and the supposedly transgressive politics of love.

Turning to romance allows Clare to transform "political questions of difference" into what Susan Koshy calls the "simulacrum of a 'universal' language of the human heart" (21). Koshy describes how the romance plot in late-nineteenth century America served the national project by providing affective and cultural work at a time of crisis that could knit immigrants into a national story that as yet lacked tradition, historical foundations, and narratives of legitimacy. Her argument can serve to highlight how important "narratives of interracial desire" can *still* be in forging commonalities for a postracial future that, many would argue, similarly lacks an actual genealogy (Koshy 20). Like Meyer's Bella or Suzanne Collins's Katniss, Tessa must also choose between two men whose characteristics, often racial, symbolically define what the novels value.[2] Choosing Will gives Tessa sexual passion, health, vitality, and adventure along with the solidification of her white privilege. As a mate, Jem offers Tessa intense kindness (Clare, *Prince* 344, 429), gentleness, and selflessness (Clare, *Prince* 429). Indeed, Jem feels an affinity with Kwan Yin, the Chinese goddess of love and compassion. Without further probing, the novels reinforce the stereotype that white males dare, while Asians care. But further analysis reveals a more complex dynamic of interracial intimacy. Entering into a relationship forces Jem and Tessa to negotiate a deeply ingrained racial hierarchy. In their romantic encounters, they are called upon to resist the scenario in which Tessa is the dominant white partner and Jem the racialized other. In moments of intimacy, Tessa takes on an active role, so much so that she frets that her forwardness has offended him. Rendered unthreatening by his passivity and "uncertainty" (Clare, *Prince* 206), Jem elicits an overwhelming "tenderness" in Tessa (Clare *Prince*, 206). She feels the "same responsibility of enormous care now…here was something that was as breakable as it was lovely" (Clare, *Prince* 208). Yet, Jem's *yin fen* often disrupts their attempts at physical intimacy; in one scene, he "jerked back, a look of horror on his face…The lacquer box that held his drugs had fallen and broken open. A thick layer of shining powder lay across the floor" (Clare, *Prince* 209). How can this couple overcome that "look of horror" at the sudden appearance of history and Jem's Chineseness?

The series attempts to forestall that "look of horror" by denaturalizing whiteness as a category. A neo-Victorian novel with a postcolonial agenda could, in addition to looking deeply at race, interrogate whiteness as a "colonial structure or privilege" since evoking the Victorian offers an opportunity to "restage and dramatize white European complicity in the nineteenth century in and for the present" (Ho 12). For the Infernal Devices trilogy to bring about the postracial future of the later Mortal Instruments novels, whiteness cannot remain an unmarked norm. Since Jem edges slowly along the continuum into a whiteness that results in his possible death, Tessa's white womanhood cannot remain intact either. Thus, while Jem's raced body bears the marks of his hybridity, Tessa's unmarked body is remarked upon throughout the novel. As the Shadowhunter bloodline had been concealed from both mother and child, Tessa was not initiated with the marking of runes on her body. Without the telltale Shadowhunter markings and without any external warlock attributes, "wings, or hooves, or webbed toes" (Clare, *Angel* 66), Tessa's ethnicity, like Will's Welshness, remains invisible. This allows Tessa to pass as white in part via the privilege of her shape-shifting as well as her ambivalent relationship to Victorian femininity. Tessa finds herself contemplating "would it be possible to Change just one small part of herself, give herself shimmering hair, or perhaps a slimmer waist or fuller lips?" (Clare, *Prince* 341). Problematically, Tessa rarely shape shifts beyond her gender in a significant way and never experiments beyond her race, except for a short time as the vampire Camille. Taken at face value, Tessa can be considered an unmarked, feminine cultural norm against which Jem and others are constructed. However, Tessa's part-demon, part-Shadowhunter blood makes her a "new kind of Shadowhunter" more attuned to otherness, and, as Charlotte's husband tells her, "new is not always a bad thing" especially if it brings about transformation (Clare, *Princess* 465). Like Jem, Tessa is regarded as both problem and promise.

While Tessa remains under scrutiny throughout the novels, it is Jessamine Lovelace's body that bears the brunt of the novels' punishment of those unwilling or unable to embrace the Nephilim's multiracial potential. Another orphan of the Institute and reluctant Shadowhunter, Jessamine, described as a beautiful "English rose" (Clare, *Angel* 73), simply wants an "ordinary life" as a Victorian wife who "preside[s] over lovely homes" and provides her husband with "uplift and comfort" by surrounding him with her "gentle and angelic presence" (Clare, *Angel* 142). The novels find Jessamine's desire to enter the white, middle-class "cult of domesticity" suspicious and counterproductive to the discourse of hybridity that runs through the texts. Jessamine's hatred for her Nephilim blood causes her to betray the Clave, aiding Mortmain by passing him information from the Institute and leaving it and Tessa vulnerable to attack. Tortured by the Silent Brothers for her crimes and imprisoned in the Silent City, Jessamine dies a violent death because she "did not wish to be a Shadowhunter" and eventually becomes a ghost guarding the Institute (Clare, *Princess* 530). In the massive battle over the future of Idris, the Nephilim homeland, fought in the present-day of the *Mortal Instrument* series, Jessamine, we learn, continues her vigil. As a spectral presence or "unfinished business" (Clare, *Princess* 529), Jessamine becomes a version of the Victorian past that persists in the present, an unwanted but acknowledged whiteness that pays penance by protecting the sanctuary of the Institute.

Jem's "ghostly" whiteness mirrors Jessamine's reappearance in the present as a "spectral trace" of the whiteness of the Victorian past (Arias and Pulham xvi). Rather than ghostly revenant, I claim Jem as a neo-Victorian *body* capable of holding in tension the anachronistic racial forces that the series places upon him. Orientalized, feminized, and consistently on the verge of disappearance, Jem's nineteenth-century Eurasian body is constructed almost exclusively by contemporary stereotypes of Asian (-American) masculinity. In the same scene at the *yin fen* den, for example, Jem is so distracted by the squalor of addiction that Tessa threatens to Change into him so that she can single-handedly carry an unconscious Will out of the establishment, "and then everyone here will see what you look like in a dress" (Clare, *Prince* 196). Significantly, while Jem is incapacitated by what he fears the most, being "weakened" by addiction (Clare, *Prince* 345), Tessa threatens him with feminization, a stereotype of Asian-American men in the present. At the same time, the text intimates that Jem is threatened by another demon: Yellow Peril, a nineteenth century stereotype, which posits Asian men as "fiendish, effeminate, cunning opium smokers who secretly fantasize about raping white women" (Pon 96). In many ways, Jem represents what Jeffrey Santa Ana has called "feeling ancestral," his term for the "dialectic between the celebratory color blindness of racial mixture in global commerce, on the one hand, and cultural memory in the empathic and often painful identification with heritage and genealogy, on the other" (459). As an "ancestor" to the characters in *The Mortal Instruments*, Jem retains a slim access point to a unique Eurasian history, rooted in the nineteenth century, and a future-driven understanding of racial mixture. It is this duality that makes him a neo-Victorian.

The novels achieve their race-work goals by persuading YA readers to find in Jem a desirable and attractive alternative to Will's heteronormative masculinity. The novels must do this by using and then overcoming sexualized gender and racial stereotypes about Asian manhood, such as Orientalism and miscegenation, which originated in the nineteenth century. For example, the first time Tessa meets Jem, he is described diminutively as a "boy…too slight to be a grown man" (Clare, *Angel* 106). Throughout the series, the word most associated with Jem is "slender" (Clare *Angel*, 107). Characters often compare him to other women; for example, Tessa sees similarities between Jem and another Chinese Clave member: "her face was like Jem's—the same delicately beautiful features, the same curves to her eyes and cheek-bones, though where his hair and eyes were silver, hers were dark" (Clare, *Prince* 22). Dying from withdrawal, Jem reminds Sophie of a consumptive woman (Clare, *Princess* 285). In contrast to Jem's slender and sickly appearance, Tessa finds Will's physicality to be "hard and smooth" (Clare, *Angel* 297), all "fierce colors and repressed fire" (Clare *Prince*, 139). With Jem's weakened physical state, Tessa has to be incredibly gentle with him. In one scene, Jem appears "light, hollow-boned like a bird" (Clare, *Prince* 206). In another, he is "sharp, too sharp, the bones of his face, the pulse of his blood too close to the surface of the sin, collarbones as hard as a metal necklace" (Clare, *Princess* 191). Emasculated by his lack of access to Victorian patriarchy and made racially abject by an albeit occluded history of inequality and racism, Jem's masculinity becomes visible and affirmed only when he competes against Will and seems to win Tessa.

Jem is also queered by frequent comparisons to Will's white, hegemonic masculinity; their *parabatai* pairing serves only to reinforce stereotypes of Asian effeminacy. "Even in a blatantly heterosexual love story," Nguyen Tan Hoang argues, "Asian male sexual potency continues to be informed by bottomhood" (112), a term he uses to describe the queering of Asian males even as they lay claim to normative masculinity or sexual prowess. A version of David Eng's influential concept of "racial castration" in which "Asian American male subjectivity is psychically and materially constrained by a crossing of racial difference with homosexuality" (Eng 14), bottomhood has the potential to attach itself at will to even Asian, heterosexual masculinity. In the Infernal Devices/Mortal Instruments universe, *parabatai* are militaristic soulmates, which, when it occurs between men, is a relationship valued because they are "more than brothers" (Clare, *Princess* 244), consisting of "loyalty and love, unclouded by doubt" (Clare, *Princess* 410). While romantic love between *parabatai* is forbidden by Shadowhunter law, homosexuality is nonetheless implied by comparing the *parabatai* bond to the "covenant" between Jonathan and David (Clare, *Prince* 97). Even Tessa "placidly" notes that the *parabatai* bond between Jem and Will "is like being married, isn't it?" (Clare, *Prince* 98). It is important to remember that Clare's YA audience is, thanks to the global marketing of "YA" products, fluent in transnational romance genres. Jem's feminized appearance and the queer elements of the *parabatai* bond tap into an alternative Asian masculinity much prized by female readers of all nationalities: the so-called "beautiful boy" (*bishonen*) of Japanese "boys love" (BL) manga. Despite its "romantic or homoerotic" content, Kam Louie argues, BL narratives were "created and consumed by women" eager to embrace a "fantasy world in which men are feminized and related to each other in loving rather than competitive ways" (934). As BL is a genre written primarily by women for women, Louie lauds the power that female readers and consumers have in defining desirable masculine ideals (937). Reading Jem positively through this transnational lens illustrates how responding to YA fiction requires casting a wider interpretive net than the canon of Asian American studies.

Readers join #teamjem for precisely these qualities of the "perfect bookboyfriend" ("Best Book Boyfriends"); they are drawn specifically to Jem's patience, loyalty, respect for men and women, sensitivity, and shyness. And comments like this are common: "It only goes to show he cares about people other than himself. He cares about what's going on in their lives and wants to be there when he's needed. Especially when it comes to Tessa and Will—he wants to be the shoulder you cry on!" ("Team Jem v. Team Will"). Although these are feminized descriptors, Celine Parrenas Shimizu, like Louie, argues for a more liberatory way to think through how Asian men are constrained by "straitjacket masculinities" such as effeminacy, queerness, and lack. Instead, they can "assert[ing] the presence of both vulnerability and strength…forge manhoods that care for others. They invest in the most rewarding of relations beyond propping up the self" (4). If Will takes center stage as the "brighter burning star, the one to catch attention," Jem emerges as the "steady flame, unwavering and honest" (Clare, *Prince* 358). Certainly Jem's "steady" nature, his gentleness and fierce protection of both Will and Tessa, his eventual absorption into the Silent Brothers, and their mission of pastoral and medical care fulfill Shimizu's concept of an "ethical manhood" (Shimizu 9). If this contemporary racework can be achieved in the supposedly more repressive, racist Victorian past, what more can be achieved in the present?

The Infernal Devices trilogy constructs the Victorian as a locus of both racial inequality in the past and the "rupture" that leads to new postmodern identities and, in this case, a multicultural future (Kucich and Sadoff xv). However, as I have demonstrated, maintaining the centrality of whiteness can be a side effect of deploying the Victorian, made further pronounced by the novels' neo-Victorian-liteness. The racial issues of the Infernal Devices remain unresolved until the epilogue, set in 2008, when an immortal Tessa rekindles her relationship with Jem, now re-Sinicized, after centuries of service as a Silent Brother. After joining the Silent Brothers in an effort to save his own life, Jem's illness was gradually reversed, "his hair was no longer pure silver—streaks of it had darkened to black-brown, no doubt the color he had been born with" (Clare, *Princess* 488), and, although he gains the Brothers' immortality, his vows forbid him from participating in the mortal world. Yet, even in this state and renamed Brother Zachariah, Jem in the nineteenth century can still never be "quite as they are" (Clare, *Princess* 493). In the epilogue, however, Tessa and Jem become true neo-Victorians. Both are anachronisms, remnants of the Victorian in the twenty-first century present. Released from the Brotherhood by events detailed in *City of Heavenly Fire* (2014), the last volume of the Mortal Instruments series, Jem becomes mortal and, finally, Eurasian. In the twenty-first century, Jem finally has "raven-black hair...dark brown eyes with glints of gold in the irises. Once his skin had been pale; now it had a flush of color to it" (Clare, *Princess* 555). Now a fully embodied person of color, the novel suggests, Jem can renew his vows of love to Tessa and they can embark on their new life together as an interracial couple.

Clearly, the multicultural future in the epilogue of the Infernal Devices also forms the idealistic postracial present of the Mortal Instruments series. In *City of Heavenly Fire*, however, where we eventually learn the source of Jem's cure (he is rescued by a descendent of Will and Tessa, Jace Wayland, and cauterized by Jace's sacred fire), no mention is made of Jem's Eurasianess. For practical reasons, Clare needed to obscure Jem's ethnicity to maintain the ambiguity of the Zachariah/Jem pairing in *City of Heavenly Fire*. Physical descriptions of Jem are thus kept to a minimum; he is, as Isabelle says, of course, "hot" (Clare, *Fire* 318), but his features are reduced to "dark hair" and a "high-cheekboned face" (Clare, *Fire* 240, 703). If readers had not read *Infernal Devices*, the nineteenth-century past—the key to Jem's racial identity—would remain hidden. As Clare herself comments regarding a reader's questions about spoilers, in *City of Heavenly Fire*, "[Zacariah] could be Will or Jem—if you've never read *ID*, he could literally be anyone. In fact, as he has dark hair and Jem is introduced as blond, it seems to point to Will" ("The Infernal Devices"). Outside of practical plot concerns, the erasure of all markers of race in *City of Heavenly Fire* raises questions about Jem and Tessa's function as emissaries of the Victorian in the present. While they serve as a form of elision between the two worlds and temporalities of the series, Tessa and Jem also function as ellipses, omitting the historical conditions of racism and inequality faced by Eurasians past and present that I have briefly traced in this essay. Significantly, when the couple meets the next Carstairs generation, they intentionally remain silent about their identities and history. The Jem that appears in *City of Heavenly Fire*, it can be argued, has been utterly decontextualized from even his neo-Victorian-lite historicity.

The postracial present of the Mortal Instruments unmoored from a neo-Victorian past authorizes fans to, consciously or not, whitewash the Eurasian characters of the series such as Jem and, to a lesser extent, Magnus Bane. The controversy over whitewashing arose in public forums where readers voiced their preferences for "fan-casting" characters in the novel. When the Mortal Instruments movie, *City of Bones* (2013), was under discussion, Clare was adamant that no race bending would occur and that an Asian or Eurasian actor must play Magnus Bane. An explicitly gay character, Magnus is a high warlock born out of an earlier moment of colonialism in Dutch Batavia to a mixed-race mother and a demon of hell. While Clare was "somewhat disturbed by the eagerness" of her fans "to try to paint Magnus as white, or whiter, when he clearly is not" ("Magnus"), an ethnically Asian, Taiwanese-Canadian actor, Godfrey Gao was eventually cast in the part to the delight of many fans and Clare herself. When the Infernal Devices trilogy was published, Clare insisted that an Asian model be used for the cover of *Clockwork Prince*, rejecting outright any attempt to disguise the character's ethnicity for marketability. The response to accurately portraying Jem's Chinese heritage has been overwhelmingly positive, with many readers thankful for the diversity and the representation and recognition that Jem affords them.[4] Yet, the whitewashing controversy in Mortal Instruments extended into fan-casting debates over which actor would portray Jem Carstairs, *if* there were to be a movie adaptation. Readers have informed Clare of their surprise and even displeasure at "discovering" that Jem is "Chinese":

> He speaks Chinese, he is from China, he is portrayed on the cover of *Clockwork Prince* by an Asian model. And yet people still come up to me and say—or Tweet me and say—that they were shocked to hear he was Asian, or even that they are *displeased* that he is Asian. I have had people come up at signings and say "My Jem isn't Chinese." Well, then, he isn't Jem. Or they will ask me if he "looks Asian" and say they think Mitch Hewer would be great to play him if there was a film. ("The Mortal Interview")

Careless (or willful) reading and the preference for Mitch Hewer, a "white british guy" ("Prouvairy"), infuriated other readers who took to their blogs and fan sites to voice complaints and plead with fellow fans to "please just acknowledge that [Jem] is Asian and stop using Mitch Hewer for him?|" ("alohomorashlie"). Yet even more fans took offense at Clare's and others' use of "Asian" and "Chinese" exclusively to describe a character that is clearly Eurasian. In response to "Sparky's" impassioned blog post about the negative Asian stereotypes that constrain and diminish the development of Jem and Magnus as characters "of color" ("Asian Characters"), "Andre" argued that this designation "reinforce[s] the notion that white means you must be 'pure' if there is someone non-white in your ancestry you cannot be white" (Comments on "Asian

Characters"). Ignoring his hybridity, "Andre" implies, curtails Jem's ability to choose or opt out of his affiliations. Ignoring Jem's inability to pass for white, however, also denies the scopic regime that governs the identification with "mixed race" as a category. Moving beyond the debate of white/not white, I suggest that these comments document how fans react to the realization that the postracial vision of the novels require an "ambiguous" Jem whose race we do not and should not see precisely because we have supposedly come so far from the Victorian past. That reactions range from whitewashing to a critique of how much Jem can be considered a political representative for ethnic affirmation underscores how "Victorian" we still may be about race and whiteness and how mixed-race narratives have been scripted to privilege an ambiguity that can be more easily assimilated into multiculturalism.[5]

The Victorian setting of the Infernal Devices is problematically yet inextricably aligned with the series' vision of a postracial present/future. On the one hand, the Victorian past has the potential to reveal the colonial formations that inform mixed-raced narratives in the present. On the other hand, while Clare claims that she has gone to great lengths to research the Victorian era, the "liteness" of her Victorianism and reliance on the supernatural form a strategic forgetting that obscures colonial formations in order to bring about the 2008 epilogue and, eventually, the *Mortal Instruments*. As a result, the Infernal Devices loses its potential to help a new generation of readers negotiate being mixed race. As Adrian Carton notes, "what it means to be mixed-race could have refreshed relevance in cosmopolitan communities where new generations now face older categorical questions and revived dilemmas about the meanings of hybridity and cultural difference that might benefit from the perspective of historical hindsight" (vi). At the end of the *Infernal Devices*, Jem's "perfect book boyfriend" qualities, his "ethical manhood" coupled with Tessa's attributes as a YA heroine herald an optimistic future where racial equality exists. For a neo-Victorianist, however, this future comes at the expense of a more nuanced representation of the nineteenth-century past or the "perspective of historical hindsight."

Notes

1. Republished with permission of Taylor and Francis Group LLC Books, from *The Victorian Era in Twenty-First Century Children's and Adolescent Literature and Culture*, edited by Sara K. Day and Sonya Sawyer Fritz, 2018; permission conveyed through Copyright Clearance Center, Inc.

2. In an interview with *VH1*, Clare discusses her research on the Victorians; they were, she says, "much less hung up and repressed than we think of them as" (Weiss n.p.). Whether Clare read Foucault's "repressive hypothesis" cannot be confirmed, but his highly influential rereading

of the Victorians, including isolating 1870 as the magic date when the homosexual emerged as a "species," has certainly entered into popular culture and mainstream neo-Victorianism.

3. See Natalie Wilson's chapter, "Civilized Vampires Versus Savage Werewolves: Race and Ethnicity in the Twilight Series," in *Bitten by Twilight: Youth Culture, Media and the Vampire Franchise*, in which she argues that the Cullen family represents white privilege and values to which Bella ultimately assents. See also Rachel E. Dubrofsky and Emily D. Ryalls's essay "*The Hunger Games*: Performing Not-performing to Authenticate Femininity and Whiteness," in which they argue that the movie version of Katniss Everdeen presents a healthy, natural, and authentic feminine that, in its heroicism, is valued as whiteness.

4. Clare has been vocal about race bending and whitewashing on multiple online venues, including her own blog and often chronicles her fight to maintain control over the casting of her characters in *City of Bones* and the models used for her book covers. Readers have been appreciative of her efforts; in an interview for Racebending.com, Clare tells how "I've had parents come up to me and say 'My son is biracial and this is the only book cover I have that represents someone who looks like him'" ('The Mortal Interview').

5. Michele Elam's book, *The Souls of Mixed Folk*, focuses on contemporary Black/white mixed-raced narratives; however, her argument serves to highlight similar issues for those identified as Eurasian. Discussing the politics of mixed-race representation, she writes, "when mixed race advocacy groups argue for visible representation, they frequently enlist people to represent them who meet the tacit criteria of ambiguity. The result of this silent norming is that people who wish to self-identify as mixed but do not appear ambiguous—or ambiguous enough…are less suited to serve as political representatives" (24).

Works Cited

"alohomorashlie." "Listen Infernal Devices Fandom. I usually like you. Really. I usually do." *In a City of Love Light*, https://biblioceraptor.tumblr.com/post/23224466541/in-a-city-love-light-listen-infernal-devices, Accessed 14 Feb. 2015.

"Andre." Comment on "Asian Characters in Cassandra Clare's Shadow Hunters World." *Fangs for the Fantasy*, 29 March 2013. http://www.fangsforthefantasy.com/2013/03/asian-characters-in-cassandra-clares.html, Accessed 5 March 2015.

Arias, Rosario and Patricia Pulham. "Introduction." *Haunting and Spectrality in Neo-Victorian Fiction: Possessing the Past*, edited by Rosario Arias and Patricia Pulham, Palgrave Macmillan, 2010, pp. xi–xxvi.

Brown, Joanne, and Nancy St. Clair. *The Distant Mirror: Reflections on Young Adult Historical Fiction*. Scarecrow Press, 2006.

Carton, Adrian. *Mixed-Race and Modernity in Colonial India: Changing Concepts of Hybridity Across Empires*. Routledge, 2012.

Clare, Cassandra. "Cassandra Clare Interview." *Twilightseriestheories*. 8 Sept. 2010, https://twilightseriestheories.com/2010/09/08/cassandra-clare-interview/, Accessed 20 Feb. 2015.

Clare, Cassandra. *City of Heavenly Fire*. Walker Books, 2014.

Clare, Cassandra. *Clockwork Angel*. Walker Books, 2010.

Clare, Cassandra. *Clockwork Prince*. Walker Books, 2011.

Clare, Cassandra. *Clockwork Princess*. Walker Books, 2013.

Clare, Cassandra. "The Infernal Devices in The Mortal Instruments." *Shadowhunters*. https://cassandraclare.tumblr.com/post/88705596004/the-infernal-devices-in-the-mortal-instruments, Accessed 24 March 2015.

Clare, Cassandra. "Interview with Cassandra Clare." Interview by Eva Berg Schneider and Verena Wolf. *Phantastik-Couch*. April 2012, https://www.phantastik-couch.de/magazin /interview/archiv-2013–2010/04-2012-cassandra-clare-engl-ov/, Accessed 20 Feb. 2015.

Clare, Cassandra. "Magnus." *Shadowhunters*. https://cassandraclare.tumblr.com/post /23181390945/magnus, Accessed 17 March 2015.

Clare, Cassandra. "The Mortal Interview: Cassandra Clare on Diversity." Interview by Gabriel Canada. *Racebending.com*. 18 October 2012, http://www.racebending.com/v4/featured /mortal-instruments-casting-diversi/. Accessed 2 Feb. 2015.

Dubrofsky, Rachel E., and Emily D. Ryalls. "The Hunger Games: Performing Not-Performing to Authenticate Femininity and Whiteness." *Critical Studies in Media Communication*, vol. 31, no. 5, 2014, pp. 395–409.

Elam, Michele. *The Souls of Mixed Folk: Race, Politics, and Aesthetics in the New Millennium*. Stanford University Press, 2011.

Eng, David L. *Racial Castration: Managing Masculinity in Asian America*. Duke University Press, 2001.

"Erin." "Team Jem v. Team Will—The Infernal Devices by Cassandra Clare." *Eleusinian Mysteries*. 8 Feb. 2012, http://eleusinianmysteriesofreading.blogspot.com/2012/02/team -jem-vs-team-will-infernal-devices.html, Accessed 12 March 2015.

Fritz, Sonya Sawyer. "Double Lives: Neo-Victorian Girlhood in the Fiction of Libba Bray and Nancy Springer." *Neo-Victorian Studies*, vol. 5, no. 1, 2012, pp. 38–59.

Heilmann, Ann, and Mark Llewellyn. "Introduction." *Neo-Victorianism: The Victorians in the Twenty-First Century, 1999–2009*, edited by Heilmann and Llewellyn, Palgrave Macmillan, 2010, pp. 1–32.

Hidalgo, Alexandra. "Bridges, Nodes and Bare Life: Race in the "Twilight" Saga." *Genre, Reception, and Adaptation in the Twilight Series*, edited by Anne Morey, Ashgate, 2012, pp. 79–94.

Ho, Elizabeth. *Neo-Victorianism and the Memory of Empire*. Continuum, 2012.

Koshy, Susan. *Sexual Naturalization: Asian Americans and Miscegenation*. Stanford University Press, 2004.

Kucich, John, and Dianne F. Sadoff. "Introduction." *Victorian Afterlife: Postmodern Culture Rewrites the Nineteenth Century*, edited by Kucich and Sadoff, University of Minnesota Press, 2000, pp. ix–xxx.

López, Alfred J. "Introduction: Whiteness after Empire." *Postcolonial Whiteness: A Critical Reader on Race and Empire*, edited by Alfred J. López, State University of New York Press, 2005, pp. 1–30.

Louie, Kam. "Popular Culture and Masculinity Ideals in East Asia, with Special Reference to China." *Journal of Asian Studies*, vol. 71, no. 4, 2012, pp. 929–43.

Lowe, Lisa. *Immigrant Acts: On Asian American Cultural Politics*. Duke University Press, 1996.

McHale, Brian. "Difference Engines." *ANQ: A Quarterly Journal of Short Articles, Notes, and Reviews*, vol. 5, no. 4, 1992, pp. 220–23.

Nguyen, Tan Hoang. *A View from the Bottom: Asian American Masculinity and Sexual Representation*. Duke University Press, 2014.

Pon, Gordon. "Queering Asian Masculinities and Transnationalism: Implications for Anti-Oppression and Consciousness-Raising." *Troubled Masculinities: Reimagining Urban Men*, edited by Ken Moffat, University of Toronto Press, 2012, pp. 93–108.

"Prouvairy." *Damn, Lay Off the Bleach*. 14 March 2013, http://damnlayoffthebleach.tumblr.com /post/45366427533/the-infernal-devices-mortal-instruments-fandoms#notes, Accessed 23 Feb. 2015.

Santa Ana, Jeffrey. "Feeling Ancestral: The Emotions of Mixed Race and Memory in Asian American Cultural Productions." *Positions*, vol. 16, no. 2, 2008, pp. 457–82.

Shimizu, Celine Parreñas. *The Hypersexuality of Race: Performing AsianAmerican Women on Screen and Scene*. Duke University Press, 2007.

Shimizu, Celine Parreñas. *Straitjacket Sexualities: Unbinding Asian American Manhoods in the Movies*. Stanford University Press, 2012.

"Sparky." "Asian Characters in Cassandra Clare's Shadow Hunters World." *Fangs for the Fantasy*. 29 March 2013, http://www.fangsforthefantasy.com/2013/03/asian-characters-in-cassandra-clares.html, Accessed 5 March 2015.

Stetz, Margaret D. "The 'My Story' Series: A Neo-Victorian Education in Feminism." *Neo-Victorianism and Feminism: New Approaches*, vol. 6, no. 2, 2013, pp. 137–51.

"Tamie." "Best book boyfriends of 2012. *Bookish Temptations*. 17 December 2012, http://bookishtemptations.com/2012/12/17/best-book-boyfriends-of-2012/, Accessed 16 March 2015.

Teng, Emma Jinhua. *Eurasian: Mixed Identities in the United States, China, and Hong Kong, 1842–1943*. University of California Press, 2013.

Weiss, Sabrina Rojas. "Mortal Instruments Author Says Clockwork Prince Sexiness is 'Properly Victorian!'" *VH1 Celebrity*. 13 Dec. 2011, http://www.vh1.com/celebrity/2011-12-13/mortal-instruments-infernal-devices-clockwork-prince-sexiness-cassandra-clare/, Accessed 29 Feb. 2015.

Wilson, Natalie. "Civilized Vampires versus Savage Werewolves: Race and Ethnicity in the Twilight Series." *Bitten by Twilight: Youth Culture, Media, and the Vampire* Franchise, edited by Melissa A. Click, Jennifer Stevens Aubrey, and Elizabeth Behm-Morawitz, Peter Lang, 2010, pp. 55–70.

Young, Adriana Valdez. "Honorary Whiteness." *Asian Ethnicity*, vol. 10, no. 2, 2009, pp. 177–85.

Eugenics and the "Purity" of Memory Erasure
The Racial Coding of Dis/ability in the *Divergent* Series
Alex Polish

Following the whitewashing trend of many YA dystopian narratives to elide race and create a "postracial" world by displacing racial formations onto other factors such as alienness or different species, Veronica Roth's *Divergent* trilogy displaces race and racism onto eugenics and dis/ability.[1] While purporting to be "colorblind"—including several characters of color while erasing the structural racism that undoubtedly forms the racialized backdrop of the eugenics campaign that comes to be the focus of the trilogy's final installment, *Allegiant* (2013)—the series perpetuates racist and ableist assumptions by uncritically conflating race and dis/ability. Tris's white, able-bodied status as the "purest of the genetically pure" embodies the ways that refusing to explicitly discuss racism reinscribes images of able-bodied whiteness as the ultimate manifestation of genetic privilege.

In contrast to Tris, Nita, a genetically "damaged" leader of the rebellion against the US government's[2] Bureau of Genetic Welfare (which violently oppresses those considered to be "genetically damaged," GDs), is exotified, sexualized, and othered throughout the narrative. Through Nita's othering and *Allegiant*'s narrative structure, Roth creates a highly racialized world that purports to be colorblind. "Colorblindness," itself an ableist term when used out of context, is a privileged forgetting of race through refusing to acknowledge racism's pervasiveness. This forgetting is a constant theme of Roth's narrative, which ultimately advocates the privileged resolution of erasing memories of state legacies of racist, ableist violence. Tris's privilege manifests in the prioritization of her forced re-membering vis-à-vis PTSD-esque responses to discrete instances of trauma. While Tris's trauma should be validated, prioritizing her trauma elides the continuous, rather than discrete, structural trauma of those who are dually racialized and dis/abled in the narrative, resulting in the erasure of systematically imposed, oppression-based trauma through *Allegiant*'s forget-and-forgive narrative.

Focusing on the interaction between the Bureau of Genetic Welfare's oppression of those they label GD and the narrative's ultimate glorification of Divergence (the state of being genetically "pure"), this essay considers how race is dis/abled and how dis/ability is raced. I further consider whether contemporary readers disidentify with the characters in this text, where racial and dis/ability identities are clearly dependent, not upon inherent bodily traits but upon the given power structures of a society.

The trilogy's first two books, *Divergent* and *Insurgent*, treat Divergence as a special category, to be feared (for its power), hunted (because of the threat its power represents), and hailed (for the good it can do). Tris's Divergence is positioned as both key to and witness of the rebellion around her. When *Insurgent* ends with Divergence being revealed as something still unknown but special—the Divergent are the only people who can leave the city to "help" whoever has placed the factions there—the idea that Divergence is powerful and needed for everyone's survival is reinforced.

Allegiant, through a much more convoluted plot than the earlier novels, reveals this plea is false. Tris learns that her city, Chicago, was one of many experimental cities run by the US government's Bureau of Genetic Welfare. In these cities, people deemed "genetically damaged" were placed into a series of real-life, citywide simulations to "correct" their genes (Roth 223). After failing to correct all of humanity's perceived problems through genetic engineering, the Bureau isolated those who weren't "genetically pure" (GP) in experiment cities like Chicago and controlled their populations with several methods. Divergents, like Tris, are classified as GP. Everyone who isn't GP, the Bureau considers GD and consistently interprets the GDs' differences as a result of their genetic makeup.

Further, when GPs kill or assault GDs, they are rarely charged with anything beyond manslaughter: GDs are thereby killable, while GP life is valued above all else. Systemically discriminated against from multiple angles, GDs are actively punished for their nonnormative genetic structure. The Bureau, however, claims that everything it does is for the "greater good" of humanity (Roth 326).

Because of the intertwined dis/ability and racial politics of the Bureau's policies and particularly *Allegiant*'s narrative thrust, I first argue that by displacing ableism-inflected racism onto a purportedly colorblind eugenic ableism, Roth creates a racially inflected politic which unsettles essentialist[3] definitions of race and dis/ability. However, the narrative simultaneously reinscribes the violence of conflating racialization and dis/ablement. I then examine Nita, whom I identify as an exemplary figure of Roth's attempt to displace racism onto a colorblind, eugenics-based dis/ability politic. Nita's character arc reveals the narrative's dismissal of the lives of dis/abled women of color, framing Nita as less capable of combating her own oppression than white, genetically able-bodied Tris. The third section traces Tobias's subversive resistance to and embrace of his genetic damage. I conclude by suggesting that the trilogy, for all its flaws, leaves potential to disidentify with subtle pieces of the narrative to construct race and dis/ability as products of the oppressive structures that give bodies their hegemonic meaning.

Historicizing *Allegiant*: Eugenics in the United States

Given *Allegiant*'s narrative thrust, it is apt to draw connections between the Bureau's experiments on GDs and the widespread eugenics programs carried out by the US government throughout contemporary history. Threatened both by white "feeblemindedness" and POC of multiple abilities, white supremacist eugenics practices in the United States have aimed to eliminate the "tainted whiteness" of dis/abled white people along with the very personhood of all people of color (Stubblefield 163). According to Nirmala Erevelles and Andrea Minear, "Colonial ideologies conceiving of the colonized races as intrinsically degenerate sought to bring these 'bodies' under control via segregation and/or destruction. Such control was regarded as necessary for the public good" (133). Always emphasizing the public good, the United States has long sought to eliminate "degeneration" through protecting white able-bodiedness.

Eugenics-based policies that conflate race and dis/ability, while creating dis/abilities among POC communities, have held fast throughout US history since the term became popularized in the late nineteenth century. Since then,[4] the US government has used a combination of antimiscegenation laws, coerced sterilization, medical testing, restrictive immigration policies, environmental racism, and racialized welfare systems to contain the supposed contagion of POC in the United States (Ordover 16, 33; Washington 385; Stubblefield 164–67; Selden 236).

Eugenics and Allegiant's Colorblind Histories

Today, eugenics-based arguments are often couched in the rhetoric of genetics, and this word switch, without an actual change in fundamental ideology, is exemplified in *Allegiant*, which discusses genetics without explicitly mentioning the legacy of eugenics that gives the story its potential power. Indeed, the eugenic methods deployed throughout US history, including experimentation, selective breeding, violent medical intervention, segregation, and destruction vis-à-vis immediate killing, are all featured in *Allegiant*. Readers are told that people who are GDs and GPs aren't permitted to date each other and that LGBTQ people must keep their queer relationships under ominous wraps. Destruction, on unbelievable scales, is evident when the Bureau takes not only the lives but also the memories—the histories, the loves, the desires, the pains and the joys—of GD people subject to their experiments. However, the narrative never acknowledges the racial overtones of this eugenics legacy; as Suzanne Roszak asserts in her analysis of the trilogy, the narrative "do[es] not overtly name and give real weight to issues of race and ethnicity" (61).

This lack of acknowledgment persists despite the trilogy featuring characters whose skin is described in racialized terms. However, these characters' racial identities remain unacknowledged in Tris's world. Seemingly attempting to create a "postracial" society, Roth's erasure of explicit racism is problematic because she constructs an entire society based on eugenics, which is inextricable from racism. Insisting on a false sense of "colorblindness," *Allegiant*'s portrayal of racialization processes focuses exclusively on able-bodied GPs and dis/abled GDs and erases the legacy of violent racism that would have historically served as the foundation for the Bureau's experimentation programs. In essence, then, the narrative constitutes an advocacy for the deliberate racial forgetting involved in "colorblindness" and erasure of structural racism against people of color. Roth's books then draw lines of differences and oppressions based only on created differences and oppressions. This uncritical displacement whitewashes the legacy of racist violence that Tris and her fellow citizens inherited.

The violent, racist legacy is manifested through the Bureau's eugenic control over entire cities. Although the technologies and situations differ, the Bureau's experiments are undeniably similar to the US government's racially targeted eugenics programs. The Bureau even uses rhetoric similar to the contemporary US government's, emphasizing reproductive control in favor of the white, able-bodied public good. Indeed, the Bureau defines its "genetic healing" program as "a genetic engineering procedure resigned to correct the genes specified as 'damaged' on page three of this form" (Roth 223). David, the Bureau's leader, tells Tris that "the ability to make sacrifices for the greater good" is key for genetic purity. Like the contemporary US government, the Bureau understands the perpetuation of "pure" genes as more important than the killable, racialized and dis/abled people classified as GDs.

Further, like the contemporary US government, the Bureau recruited people to be genetically "healed" by taking advantage of a racially inflected class system in which many were starving. Tris's brother Caleb explains to her that "people joined the experiment so their families could escape extreme poverty—the families of the subjects were offered a monthly stipend for the subject's participation, for upward of ten years" (Roth 226). While this is not stated in the text, a program targeting impoverished people by economically coercing them into compliance with eugenics programs is likely to overwhelmingly target people of color, just as eugenics programs in contemporary United States have done (Ordover 127).

Indeed, economics has been the primary weapon used to force women of color to consent to sterilization in the contemporary United States (Ordover 159). Thus, economic coercion is used to further erase and justify the desire to keep the "purity" of whiteness from being contaminated. Along these lines, Stubblefield makes it clear that even in the first half of the twentieth century, when a majority of people sterilized for "feeblemindedness" were impoverished and white, the motivation was to eliminate the "tainted whiteness" that dis/ability represents. In other words, even when impoverished white people are targeted by eugenics policies in this country, protecting whiteness remains the priority (163).

This undertone of protecting whiteness even when targeting white people is important to understand in the purportedly "postracial" world of *Allegiant*. The lack of acknowledgment of this historical legacy manifests in the ways that memory operates in the novel: the Bureau's policies have made Tris and others forget the legacy of racism that their bodies bear, physically erasing any memories they had of themselves or their history and repopulating their memories with a doctored version of history that lacks any explicit references to racism that readers experienced. While they are told that "the peace and prosperity that had reigned in this country for nearly a century, it seemed advantageous to reduce the risk of [various] undesirable qualities showing up in our population by correcting them" (Roth 121). Since "undesirable qualities," when determined by a nation-state, are invariably determined by hegemonic norms, it is extremely likely that the "peace and prosperity" that the Bureau claims existed only for the privileged. Because this is not stated in the narrative, such a reading is by questioning the privileged status of GP government officials from whom this information comes.

Based on the narrative arc of *Allegiant*, however, readers are encouraged to willfully forget racialized oppression by not acknowledging racist and ableist violence. The novel, then, relies on a form of "colorblind" futurism, in which "the conditions that exist [in the imagined future] are presented as outcomes of current realities," yet those current realities are simultaneously erased or forgotten (Jackson 2). This willful forgetting is reinforced by the featuring characters of color who don't experience racial discrimination as a way to imagine that contemporary racism doesn't impact future or current US oppressions. While characters refer to brutal contemporary wars and even the Great Chicago Fire, no one ever mentions the racist, ableist eugenics experiments that preceded the Bureau's attempts to create "desirable" citizens (Roth 512). Through these erasures, the narrative concludes with Tris and other "good" GPs taking the lead in forcing "bad" GPs to "forget" how they oppressed and experimented on GDs. Since the happy ending is based on the premise that GPs will never remember that they used to be GPs, Roth seems to want readers to assume that people will stop talking publicly about past oppressions. Is the novel, then, implying that after a couple of generations of utopian "healing," the brutal legacy of GD oppression will be erased as the memories of contemporary racism were erased from Tris's society? Does the *Divergent* trilogy thus imply that it is "that easy" to "fix" racism, as long as there are noble white individuals, like Tris, who are willing to martyr themselves? Indeed, can only white, genetically "pure" individuals achieve martyrdom and successfully "heal" society?

According to the narrative, GD individuals seem to only be able to have a positive impact on the status quo when their actions are bolstered by GP actions (like Tris's). In the history that David tells, this is certainly the case: the only choices that GDs make in the version of history that he (and, by extension, the Bureau) presents as "choices" to subject themselves to genetic experimentation and memory erasure. With this knowledge, readers can perform a racially conscious interpretation of the Bureau's history to reveal the ways that the narrative implies that race did play a role in its conceptions, even though it erases the present-day impacts. Indeed, if the history that Bureau leader David provides is any indication, the eugenics program that the Bureau created involved "people [being] selected from the general population in large numbers, according to their background or behavior, and they were given the option to give a gift to our future generations, a genetic alteration that would make their descendants just a little bit better" (Roth 122).

As Emily Russell notes, there is a powerful "ideological weight attached to bodily difference as the over determining force of political participation for those marked as different" (4). In other words, the parameters of desirable behavior are likely to be governed by ideals that prohibit "anomalous bodies from full[y] access[ing] ... the national ideal" (4). In this formation, "undesirable behavior" is judged based largely on having an "undesirable background," so, undoubtedly, these ideals would be based on a dually racist and ableist conception of desire. David's telling Tris that the government selected people for eugenic experiments based on their "background" likely is a euphemism for the racially targeted origins of the Bureau's eugenic experiments. However, the narrative doesn't acknowledge this, so it perpetuates the same racism that eugenics was founded upon. As Mary J. Couzelis argues, "narratives where authors pretend racial tensions have been eliminated in the future risk trivializing contemporary encounters teens have with prejudice ... these novels perpetuate the hegemonic status quo of pretending race does not matter ... privilege[ing] the dominant race" (131–32).

This dominance is not abstract in the *Divergent* trilogy: it is embodied by the main character's selfhood. While the trilogy views the Bureau negatively, Roth's narrative ultimately legitimizes and valorizes the government's racist, ableist image of a desirable citizen: a white, genetically able-bodied blonde person. Tris's mother, who was blonde and pale, had, according to the Bureau, "nearly perfect" genes (Roth 153). Tris inherited her mother's genes, being able even to resist death serum. As Matthew tells her, this makes her even more Divergent as "most of the Divergent aren't as capable of resisting serums as you are" (157). By making several of Tris's friends people of color, Roth attempts to create a world in which contemporary racism has seemingly been eradicated. However, valorizing Tris and her mother suggests that whiteness, especially as it pertains to able-bodied "purity," is to achieve the martyrdom that Roth positions as necessary to creating change in society.

"To Them, a GD Is Expendable"

As is evident in the quote referenced in the subtitle above (Roth 235), the fallacies of the racism-erasing narrative structure can be exposed at the level of individual experiences, minds, passions, and bodies by analyzing the portrayal of Nita, a GD woman of color. Nita provides a possibility for disidentification with the text, taking on the role of revolutionary woman of color (albeit tokenized); additionally, attentiveness to her story arc allows readers to challenge the distorted version of history Tris (and the readers) receives from the Bureau.

However, her character arc also demonstrates how the Bureau renders women of color, who are considered dis/abled, disposable. This section juxtaposes Nita's group decisions with other GDs and her personal suffering with genetically "pure" individuals, specifically Matthew and Tris, and their related experiences. These comparative analyses reveal how the narrative reifies the erasure of women of color with dis/abilities, choosing instead to valorize the experiences of a white woman who is understood as genetically "pure." Individually, this performs the kind of racial forgetting that the Bureau mandates on a systematic scale.

Introduced from Tobias's perspective, Nita, a Bureau lab technician, drives *Allegiant*'s primary actions. Nita is "a girl with light brown skin" and eyes that are "dark, with the same sheen as a puddle of oil beneath a leaking engine" (Roth 168, 172). Firmly establishing Nita as a woman of color quickly narratively derails excitement about her intelligence, courage, and revolutionary passion for her people's freedom into scathing feelings about the perceived threat of this exoticized woman to Tobias's relationship with Tris.

Immediately upon being introduced, Nita is simultaneously delegitimized as a thinking person and established as Latina. Matthew, Nita's GP supervisor, tells Tris and Tobias, "This is Juanita, the lab technician" (Roth 168). She interrupts his next sentence, telling them, "Matthew's supervisor is the only person who calls me Juanita. Except Matthew, apparently" (168). While she clearly has a preferred name that she makes known, Matthew delegitimizes her, ignoring her preferences in the way he introduces her to both the characters and to readers and claiming an intimacy the she eschews. The readers never learn whether Matthew's supervisor also calls her "Juanita" without her consent or whether they have a closer relationship.

This lack of detail about Nita's personal life is consistent with the rest of the narrative. Nita is primarily represented as a passionate mouthpiece for the rebellion rather than a character about whom the readers are supposed to care. She rarely discusses anything other than genetic damage and government oppression. Thus, she is defined by her genetic dis/ability and becomes a representational figure for all other GDs fighting the government. These GDs also never seem to discuss anything else, unlike Tris, who frequently discusses her relationship, her brother, and her friendships. While other characters, including Matthew, are given full histories, Nita has no history; instead, she is dismissed by the narrative as a repetitive dispenser of the truth about the Bureau. She is the one who reveals to Tobias—and eventually, to Tris—the true impact of the Bureau's experiments and eugenics rhetoric, explaining that "the crimes they have committed against people like us are serious ... And hidden ... we're working against the Bureau, for good reasons, and we want you with us" (Roth 235). As she is always speaking for the collective, Nita is all cause.

While Roth's decision to render Nita as a two-dimensional character is arguably tokenizing, it is also possible to disidentify with her character arc to read the Bureau's history against the grain. Centralizing Nita as the exemplary figure of resistance instead of Tris, readers gain insight into the large-scale erasures that both the Bureau and the narrative create. Though the narrative defines Nita by her genetic dis/ability, Nita's presence and active resistance to the status quo enable identificatory practices that reframe the oppression of GDs as immediate and personal.

Disidentifying with Nita and centralizing her perspectives has implications for the larger narrative as well: through Nita's astute analysis of the Bureau, one can easily imagine a GD-perspective retort to the larger version of history that David gives Tris. He tells her that large-scale experiments with genetic alterations "manifested ... in ... the Purity War. A civil war, waged by those with damaged genes, against the government and everyone with pure genes. The Purity War caused a level of destruction formerly unheard of on American soil, eliminating almost half of the country's population" (Roth 123). Considering Nita's insights while reading this history yields a version of history that David may not be telling: Nita's perspective on the Bureau's current policies encourages a line of thinking that reframes the "civil war, waged by those with damaged genes" as a rebellion against a status quo that treated them as damaged in the first place. David does not say directly who caused the "level of destruction formerly unheard of," but given the current status quo, it is not hard to imagine a version of history that does not erase the oppression implied in the mere label of people having "damaged genes." Reframing the "Purity War" as a rebellion against an oppressive government that treats most of its people as damaged stock is particularly reasonable considering the rebellion that Nita and many of her fellow GDs are trying to initiate.

However, this against-the-grain perspective is not the one that the overarching narrative puts forth. True to the form in which Roth presents Nita, readers are supposed to take her at her word, which is challenged, rather than her experience. She was part of the Indianapolis experiment on GDs and tells Tris and Tobias that the idea of integrating with the greater population upon being released "felt too overwhelming ... [s]o I volunteered to come [to the Bureau]. I used to be a janitor. I'm moving through the ranks, I guess" (Roth 172). While readers here can detect hints of both Nita's potential for debilitating anxiety and sharp critique of the rigid class system that the Bureau has built around GD/GP identities, we receive no further insight into her life beyond a clinical report of the Indianapolis experiment.

Significantly, no one asks about her life either, perpetuating the erasure of histories of violence that dominates the narrative. This erasure strongly contrasts with characters' concern for Matthew's history, a GP and a man. Tobias asks Matthew later why he became involved in helping the GD cause, even though he does so through the lens of condemning any violence against GPs.

This establishes a dynamic in which Matthew, the privileged "ally," assumes that the only effective way to resist oppression is in a way privileged people approve of. Through Matthew's story, readers learn more about the ways that violence against GDs interacts with violence against women.

Readers also learn that Matthew's dismissiveness toward Nita is symptomatic of his dismissiveness of women generally. Matthew is presented as essentially "good" and even as heroic: he becomes close enough to Tris for her to think of him, among others, as she is fighting to stay alive amidst the death serum. However, he tells Tobias that "[t]here was this girl," a GD woman, who educated him about his GP privilege. After she was murdered by GPs, Matthew began helping GDs like Nita resist the system of GP supremacy. He does not describe falling in love with this unnamed woman because of her personality; rather, he says, "I was feeling rebellious, and there was something appealing about how forbidden it was, so she and I started dating" (427). The narrative neither questions nor challenged this masculinist, objectifying trope of exotifying racialized women. The sole horror of the story is supposed to, instead, rest in the Bureau's restriction on non-"optimal" sexual partnerships, as well as in the GPs who beat Matthew's GD girlfriend to death (427). The assailants only received community service, which the narrative justifiably portrays as horrifying for what it reveals about the value of GD lives, further reinforcing their disposability.

However, the sexual, gendered undertones of this attack are unstated: Matthew reports that his girlfriend was "beaten up," but, much like the Dauntless boys' attack on Tris in *Divergent* reveals, physical violence against women rarely occurs without overtones of sexual assault (Roth 427). The GD woman remains unnamed, rendering her story a disembodied example rather than a lived experience. Matthew's characterization of the relationship as "rebellious" further centralizes his own experience rather than those of the GD woman. This obscures, again, the larger issues at play by personalizing GD oppression only through the lens of GP individuals.

Furthermore, this incident hints at the antimiscegenation policies that emerge from the Bureau's eugenics-based logic. Matthew couldn't have a relationship with his unnamed GD lover because of the fear they might produce "impure" children. This rationale recalls contemporary history's antimiscegenation laws, which were based in fears of "tainting" whiteness; yet, this historical connection is never explicitly addressed, erasing it from the histories that Tris learns. This erasure is particularly troubling, given that contemporary state-funded campaigns for birth-control implants like Norplant have primarily targeted women of color, so much so that "given the disproportionate number of Black women undergoing the procedure, [state] sponsorship could translate into government sterilization of undesirables" (Ordover 183). The unique positioning of women (especially women of color) as dis/abled and, therefore, targeted for reproductive control—women like Matthew's former GD lover and Nita—is evident in the text but, in leaving Matthew's lover unnamed and refusing to give Nita a personal history, is erased.

Since Nita is framed as a dis/abled woman of color, it is necessary to ask what the narrative might be erasing from Nita's story, from Nita's motivations to risk her life to rebel against the government she works for. While resisting the idea that readers—and other characters—are entitled to intimate details about a dis/abled woman of color's intimate life, it is nonetheless important to highlight absence of such details from the text while characters like Tobias actively seek intimate details of genetically privileged Matthew's life. The contrast between these characters, who are introduced at the same time, epitomizes the ways Roth emphasizes characters with genetic privilege.

Furthermore, the narrative positions Matthew as inherently more heroic, honorable, and intelligent than Nita. When he reveals to Tris that Nita is planning to release death serum in the Bureau's compound—instead of the memory serum that she told Tobias she would release—he bemoans, "I thought I was helping her with something smarter" (Roth 282). Readers are encouraged to support his criticism of Nita's plan because Tris and Tobias's friend Uriah, to whom readers are likewise attached because of his role earlier in the series, is killed in Nita's attempt to release the serum.

Significantly, plans to resist the Bureau only work when Tris, a GP, is leading them. While Tris's friends, including Christina and Cara, are GDs who play important, albeit secondary, roles in resisting GP power toward the text's conclusion, their GD status is not emphasized. Christina angrily points out to Tris that, when no one will tell her Uriah's condition after he is injured in the explosion before the death serum attack, "they would tell *you*" (295). Christina, who is both GD and Black, calls out both Tris's "pure" status and, perhaps too, her racial privilege. Indeed, since the books are mainly from Tris's perspective and generally only highlight the skin shades of those who are othered racially, it is completely conceivable that racial oppression exists strongly in her time but that she is privileged enough to not report it in her narrative. It is quite conceivable that Christina's comment here, when considered with Nita's position in the narrative arc, offers readers some against-the-grain insight into perspectives that Tris is generally too privileged to notice.

However, primarily, the privileges that Christina calls out and that Nita devotes her energies to combating were not perceived as such throughout most of the books: the major, recognized acts of violence and oppression throughout most of the series occurred before either readers or characters were aware that to be Divergent is to be genetically "pure." While the experiment cities were atrocious manifestations of the Bureau's dehumanizing violence, these cities were positioned through the series first two books as being more dangerous for the hunted Divergent than for the more prevalent GDs. Nita's experience is, again, not only buried but delegitimized.

While many people of color in the Divergent fandom have actively advocated for the casting in the film version of *Allegiant* of Nita as a Latina woman, demonstrating the potential for marginalized peoples to disidentify powerfully with characters dismissed by narratives, the book itself does not encourage readers to empathize with Nita. Tobias, fearful that Tris will be threatened by her beauty, is always cautious around her. Tris, for her part, does not trust Nita once she finds out that Nita had spoken to Tobias alone. Tobias accuses Tris of being "suspicious of [Nita]'s motives just because she's pretty!" Indeed, Tris writes about how threatened she feels by the "pretty girl" (Roth 274, 258). Acknowledging that her genetic privilege can form a wedge between her and Tobias, she writes, "I don't want to spend time with Nita and Tobias together, knowing that her supposed genetic damage gives her something in common with him that I will never have" (260). Nita returns Tris's disdain, not trusting her because of her GP status: when she sees her with Tobias, intending to participate in their GD uprising, "her face tightens like she just tasted something bitter" (261).

The narrative doesn't provide the space to validate Nita's concern that Tris actually can't be trusted to—nor ethically should—lead a GD uprising, given her genetic privilege. Dismissing Nita's legitimate concerns, the narrative positions Nita as wrong (Uriah is killed by her plan) and Tris as right (she bravely gives her life to reset the memories of other GPs). In all distracting, exotifying sexual tension surrounding this young revolutionary, Nita herself nearly drowns in the glorification of (white) GP status (Tris). In doing so, honorable GPs are inadvertently framed as better and more capable than GDs in dismantling GP oppression of GDs. Inadvertently reinforcing the Bureau's insistence that GDs are genetically dis/abled, the narrative dismisses Nita and reinscribes violent assumptions onto her body.

By establishing GPs as better at combating the oppression of GDs than GDs themselves, the trilogy invalidates the insights that Nita—including her plan to release the death serum and her decision not to trust Tris and Tobias with the full details of her plan—potentially provides into the strategic and emotional importance of rage caused by systematic oppression. As Brittney Cooper of the Black Lives Matter movement explains,

> Violence is the effect, not the cause of the concentrated poverty that locks that many poor people up ... This kind of social mendacity about the way that

racism traumatizes black people individually and collectively is a festering sore, an undiagnosed cancer, a raging infection threatening to overtake every organ in our body politic ... We are tired of forgiving people because they most assuredly do know what they do.

While Tris, too, has been traumatized and hunted, both as an individual and part of a collective, once she arrives at the Bureau, she has only to recover, assuming that is possible, from the rage and danger she has experienced in the past. She would not, moving forward, be subjected to oppression based on her identity. Indeed, her anger toward the Bureau is primarily connected to their involvement with the attack on the Abnegation, not their systematic oppression of GDs.

Nita, here, succeeds in her analysis of the realities of the world around them where Tris does not: Nita correctly reasons that "[t]he Bureau values the experiments above GD lives. It's obvious" (Roth 269). Just as Tris previously has taken deadly action to secure her and her people's freedom and safety, Nita attempts to do just this by releasing the death serum in the Bureau, hoping that such a strike will precipitate a change that will free GDs from oppression immediately. Nita does not subscribe to the Bureau's pacifying, assimilationist belief in gradual, piecemeal changes that will advance GD rights theoretically but not practically. She identifies for Tobias (and the readers) some of the structural realities of oppression: "Genetically damaged people are technically—legally—equal to genetically pure people, but only on paper, so to speak. In reality they're poorer, more likely to be convicted of crimes, less likely to be hired for good jobs ... you name it, it's a problem, and has been since the Purity War, over a century ago" (243). Knowing that this kind of systematic oppression cannot be overthrown piecemeal without immediate relief for people who are actively being killed, Nita inscribes her commitment to change on her own body.

Racialized and dis/abled as Latina GD and, therefore, as a threateningly "exotic" woman, Nita gets a tattoo of shattering glass on her spine. She tells Tobias that she "got it because it suggests damage. It's ... sort of a joke" (Roth 194). The tattoo is, conceivably, also a reference to breaking open the dripping stone structure in the Bureau, whose glass lets out one drop of water at a time, slowly eroding the rock below, to symbolize the gradual, systemic change that the Bureau puts forth as necessary so that people will continue to tolerate mass-scale experiments on people. Defying this deadly idea with her body itself, Nita, through her tattoo and the last time readers see her, sitting in a wheelchair looking at the newly shattered stone structure, resists understanding herself as damaged while using precisely that idea to fight for change.

Tris, however, distances herself from Nita and all the potentially subversive politics and passions that she embodies. Tris saves GP David's life during Nita's attempted uprising by threatening to shoot him, and the narrative describes the tremendous amount of guilt she feels about that. She has difficulty coping with the fact that she pressed a gun to his head, and she writes, "Though I know that he had something to do with the attack simulation, and with all those deaths, I find it difficult to pair those actions with the man I see in front of me" (321). But of her decision to actually shoot Nita, however, Tris only says, "I feel strangely separate from her pain. I shot her. I had to. That's the end of it" (294). Readers and critics successfully argue that this disconnect—especially when considered alongside her mixed feelings about David, who killed her parents—is a whiteness-inflected lack of sympathy for a genetically impure woman of color (Chelsea). This point of view is bolstered by the fact that a key issue of *Insurgent* is Tris's inability to forgive herself for shooting her friend Will during the Erudite-engineered attack on Abnegation. Given Roth's descriptive writing style, which goes out of its way to identify POC as such (thereby positioning whiteness as the silent default position), it is safe to assume that Will is white. His death and Tris's shooting David, who is also presumably white, cause Tris to feel guilt in ways that shooting Nita simply doesn't.

Further, as a fan of the *Divergent* trilogy commented on a blog post about race and eugenics on Channel Chelsea's WordPress account,

> It ... bothered me how Tris's actions with the memory serum at the end of the book were excused, while Nita's were demonized, even though according to the morality set up in the story, what Tris did was much, much worse.
>
> I wanted to know more about Nita.... Her story parallels Tris's in so many ways, and I wish that this had been explored more. Instead, she was demonized in racist ways for taking action against her oppressors, and demonized in misogynistic ways for being pretty and talking to Tobias. And I am not here for that.

As this fan expresses, the lack of concern with Nita's character and the portrayal of her as less capable of effectively protecting fellow GDs than GPs are, especially compared with Tris's valorization, difficult to justify.

Dis/abling Memory

The narrative may erase Nita's personal memories, but the narrative also intentionally preserved her memories. That is to say, when Tris immersed the Bureau in an airborne memory serum, specifically programmed to alter Bureau leaders' memories regarding their belief in GP superiority, Nita and many other GD resistors were immunized against the serum. This means that the narrative has Nita remembering all the agony that the GPs inflicted on her through systemic oppression: however, the people that oppressed her have forgotten and are considered innocent of any wrongdoing by the government.

The narrative isn't interested in how Nita copes with this sudden reversal of roles—being surrounded by people who not only perpetuate her oppression but are now literally unaware that her oppression has existed—but it does consider how Tobias tries to cope with bearing the burden of remembering amidst so much privileged forgetting. Tobias, whom the Bureau labels as GD but whose genes are almost "healed" enough to make him pass as Divergent in Chicago, was also inoculated against the memory serum Tris released. Upon seeing David after Tris's death (David shot her while she was releasing the memory serum), Tobias is enraged, noting, "I feel like all my muscles and bones and nerves are on fire" (Roth 500). Even though David is "[h]unched and dazed, like all the others [GPs] who have lost their memories,"[5] Tobias tenses as though to attack him (500).

Although momentary, Tobias' anger is enormously significant: Tobias is told, both by another character and the narrative, to swallow his rage. He must accept that David, as his friend Cara tells him, "doesn't remember anything. The man you knew doesn't exist anymore; he's as good as dead. *That* man didn't kill [Tris]" (Roth 500). So David, through his forgetting, receives the privilege of still being a leader of the Bureau, and a forcibly forgiven leader at that. Tobias and other GDs must suppress their feelings and trauma responses—a form of affective oppression—in the face of such privileged forgetting.

Tobias has overwhelming feelings at seeing the former Bureau leader whose oppression of GDs both directly and indirectly killed Tris. These overpowering emotions are undoubtedly shared by Nita and the other GDs who, like Tobias, remember their oppression though their oppressors do not. The burden and the rage that it awakens emphasize the privilege of forgetting, begging the questions: Who is allowed to forget? Who is allowed to move on from pain without having to keep it inside, without being validated by the surrounding structures of society? Certainly, Tobias and the other GDs aren't.

While GPs who lost their memory are allowed the privilege of forgetting, GDs remember, reliving their fresh pains and traumas without validation from a society built on erasure. Tobias wants to become part of that society when he tries to inject himself with memory serum so that he can forget the pain of Tris's death.[6] Christina, however, convinces him not to, berating him for dishonoring Tris's sacrifice by trying to erase her. Christina assertively reminds him, "I know [Tris] wouldn't want you to erase her from your memory like she didn't even matter to you!" (Roth 506). This emotional scene is wrenching in the context of teenagers haunted by the specter of a murdered teenage loved one.

However, in the context of memory and forgetting, this exchange, which successfully convinces Tobias to honor Tris's memory by always remembering her, is quite disturbing: the narrative asserts that Tris is worth remembering and that her sacrifice must be valorized. But the narrative erases GD suffering. Tris's and Tobias's traumas, based on discrete, singular instances of death, pain, and fear, are considered more important than the traumas based on decades of continuous, unrelenting structural oppression against GDs. To keep society afloat, GDs who remember must not retaliate against GPs who have forgotten the horrible things they've done: GDs must, essentially, force themselves to constantly perform a forgetting of their own oppressions and traumas, pretending they have experienced no harm, while Tris—a noble GP—must be remembered.

This dual imposition of a violent forgetting and a violent forced remembering while performing forgetting mirrors the overall narrative erasure of race through its uncritical conflation with dis/ability. In Roth's dystopian Chicago, the erasure of race recalls the potential violence of forgetting and juxtaposes it jarringly against the violent pain of remembering. Tris's ability to remember her worst moments in vivid detail—the forced reliving of them—through her extreme PTSD (particularly prevalent in *Insurgent*) exists in strange disharmony against the memory loss she forced upon the GP Bureau members. Her dis/abling PTSD—for her, an extreme form of forced, visceral remembering—counters quite powerfully the forgetting that formed the basis of the Bureau's current power.

The idea that it might be desirable to hold onto one's bodily and/or mental difference exists in the narrative through Tobias. As Nita modeled for him, he learns to both claim and reject his "damage." While this represents a potentially radical politic of refusing to conform with the dominant societal desire to not be dis/abled, to not be racialized, because the ending of the trilogy depends upon systematically privileged people (GPs) simply forgetting their role as oppressors, the overall narrative challenges Nita's and Tobias's forms of remembering their oppression as "damaged" people. This physical erasure of an entire history of oppression mirrors the discourse created by eugenicists in the nineteenth- and twentieth-century United States: according to Nancy Ordover: "In constructing entire racialized categories of demonized others, eugenicists put forth an ideologically purified America—purged of past sins and guarded against future menace" (7). This purging of past sins in the hopes of guarding against "future menace" is literally the choice Roth makes as the basis for the new society that supposedly takes shape as the trilogy hastily concludes.

As *Allegiant* ends, the emotional conclusion for GD individuals might be to insist on keeping Uriah and Tris (significantly, both of whom are GPs) firmly in their memories, but the narrative frames the structural, systemic conclusion for society as a need to forget. Just as Chicago seems to simply have "forgotten" the structural violences of racism, GP individuals simply need to "forget" their prejudices against GDs. If they do so, the problems of anti-GD violence and systemic oppression will be self-resolving. This damaging erasure of structural violence is portrayed as necessary for a happy ending, one that Tris martyred herself for and, therefore, one that must be honored. This enacts the literal dis/abling of race: by erasing race as a category of analysis and a basis for structural oppression, Roth strips racism of its potency as a violently oppressive force that undoubtedly shaped the eugenics-based society she is writing about.

By prioritizing genetic difference as the central tenet of dis/ability in *Allegiant*, Tris's posttraumatic stress, which is the central focus of *Insurgent*, drops off significantly in *Allegiant*, subsumed by the last book's narrative structure. *Allegiant* alternates between Tris's and Tobias's points of view,[7] instead of Tris's narrating the entire book as she did in the series' first two books, so any extended trauma-induced experiences Tris has are inevitably deemphasized by the constant changes to Tobias's perspective. Accordingly, the book becomes more about his dis/ability than hers when Tobias learns that he is not Divergent but genetically damaged: his parts of the narrative become dominated by his fears as he tries to convince himself that he isn't damaged because of what medical scans of his blood say.

Ultimately, there is great potential to unpack the meaning of "damage" and unsettle the very definition of dis/ability. Indeed, Roth accomplishes this, at least somewhat, in *Allegiant*'s conclusion, where Tobias explains, "Life damages us, every one. We can't escape that damage. But now, I am also learning this: We can be mended. We mend each other" (526). By reclaiming the word that had been used to persecute others like him and ascribing it to everyone, Tobias rhetorically unsettles the power that medical science has over defining a person. It no longer matters whether the Bureau considered him GD or GP: if everyone is damaged, everyone is dis/abled, and, therefore, the terms lose their negative meaning. However, this conclusion can also be critiqued as an ironic form of erasure itself: everyone may, indeed, be damaged, but the state doesn't target everyone. Still, this conclusion leads into another potential subversion in the *Divergent* trilogy: the unsettling of race and dis/ability from inherent bodily traits.

Tobias was hunted as a Divergent in Chicago: when he arrived at the Bureau, however, he was revealed to be non-Divergent. He passed, in essence, as Divergent in Chicago, but he was considered genetically impure in the Bureau.

This stark contrast—which caused Tobias to question his identity—yields what is perhaps the *Divergent* series' only potential for subversion of racist ideology: by uncovering the social construction of racial and dis/ability formations, Tobias's identity changes based on his location demonstrate the ways that race and dis/ability are less about inherent bodily characteristics and more about the social power constructs that give differences meanings. As Kimberlé Crenshaw explains, "To say that a category such as race and gender is socially constructed is not to say that the category has no significance in our world. On the contrary, a large and continuing project for subordinated people … is thinking about the way in which power is clustered around certain categories and is exercised against others" (375). The different ways that power is clustered around certain categories differ vastly inside and outside the experiments: in Chicago, Divergence is hunted, but in the Bureau, Divergence is seen as genetically privileged. Through Tobias, the Divergent trilogy demonstrates both the real danger posed to people oppressed under artificially constructed categories and the power of governmental rhetoric in determining who is oppressed and how.

Along these lines, the Divergent series makes it clear that what is considered a "genetic impurity"—thus, who is considered racialized and dis/abled—depends on power structures that are themselves socially constructed and frequently changing. The trilogy then offers a destructive racial politic, erasing the violent implications of race from the futuristic world it portrays and valorizing whiteness as the ultimate marker of genetic purity at the expense of dis/abled women of color, but it also unintentionally offers a metaphorized conception of race and dis/ability, potentially unsettling the essentialist, racist, and ableist claims that racial and able-bodied superiority are biological facts rather than violent social constructions and power structures.

Notes

1. I use a slash in dis/ability to unsettle the notion that there is a discrete binary between disability and ability. As Minae Inahara states that "the binary categorical system that defines disability in opposition to an able-bodied norm" should be contested in favor of the idea "that the disabled body is a multiplicity or excess which undermines this able-bodied norm" (47).

2. In Roth's dystopian world, the US government is not the US government of today. Rather, *Divergent*'s Bureau of Genetic Welfare is a future manifestation of US government in that it represents a new government in the United States. However, it is separated from today's US government by several degrees of all-encompassing war and governmental restructuring. Because it claims to represent a future United States, it must grapple with, rather than erase, the ways that white supremacy are structured into the government. If that's no longer the case in the future, it's disingenuous to have this erasure occur without comment.

3. Essentialist understandings of identities such as race, dis/ability, sexuality, and gender assume that identities are "natural" rather than socially mediated, subscribed to an uncritical paradigm that only treats identity as immutable fact and assumes that people with dis/abilities all experience ableism the same way, regardless of race, sexuality, gender, specific dis/ability, class, and so on.

4. Prior to the coining of the term, however, white men raping Black women worked along with gynecological experiments, commonly performed without anesthesia on Black women during enslavement, revealing the country's acceptance that POC are less-than human and inherently dis/abled by their race (Washington 65). Similarly, the castration of Black men accused of raping white women was a common means of exercising reproductive control over enslaved peoples throughout the 1800s (Stubblefield 178).

5. People don't remain "hunched and dazed" forever after being subjected to memory loss: after "reeducation," they regain full functionality except of their deleted memories. The narrative positions the violence of erasing as less extreme than the violence of killing the Bureau leaders: significantly, both acts of violence are the only options discussed regarding overthrowing the Bureau. It is important to remember that the violence of erasing the Bureau leaders' memories doesn't negate the violence inflicted on GDs because of the relative GP privilege that comes with forgetting in this context.

6. Her death, despite its problematic representation, is widely accepted as wrenching for characters and readers alike.

7. Roth did this so the book could have a resolution beyond Tris's dying words: following Tris's death, Tobias narrates the last few chapters.

Works Cited

Chelsea. "Genetic Purity, Racism, and White Privilege in Veronica Roth's *Allegiant*." *Channel Chelsea.* 28 Oct 2013.https://channelchelsea.wordpress.com /2013/10/28/genetic-purity -racism-and-white-privilege-in-veronica-roths-allegiant/. Accessed 15 June 2015.

Cooper, Brittney. "In Defense of Black Rage: Michael Brown, Police, and the American Dream." *Salon.* 12 Aug. 2014. https://www.salon.com/2014/08/12/in_defense_of_ black _rage_michael_brown_police_and_the_american_dream/. Accessed 15 June 2015.

Couzelis, Mary J. "The Future Is Pale: Race in Contemporary Young Adult Dystopian Novels." *Contemporary Dystopian Fiction for Young Adults: Brave New Teenagers,* edited by Carrie Hintz, Balaka Basu, and Katherine R. Broad, Routledge, 2013, pp. 131–44.

Crenshaw, Kimberle. "Mapping the Margins: Intersectionality, Identity Politics, and Violence against Women of Color." *Stanford Law Review,* 1991, pp. 1241–99.

Erevelles, Nirmala, and Andrea Minear. "Unspeakable Offenses: Untangling Race and Disability in Discourses of Intersectionality." *Journal of Literary & Cultural Disability Studies,* vol. 4, no. 2, 2010, pp. 127–45.

Inahara, Minae. "This Body Which Is Not One: The Body, Femininity and Disability." *Body & Society,* vol. 15, no. 1, 2009, pp. 47–62.

Jackson, Sandra, and Julie E. Moody-Freeman, editors. *The Black Imagination, Science Fiction, Futurism and the Speculative.* Peter Lang, 2011.

Ordover, Nancy. *American Eugenics: Race, Queer Anatomy, and the Science of Nationalism.* University of Minnesota Press, 2003.

Roszak, Suzanne. "Coming of Age in a Divided City: Cultural Hybridity and Ethnic Injustice in Sandra Cisneros and Veronica Roth." *Children's Literature*, vol. 44, no. 1, 2016, pp. 61–77.

Roth, Veronica. *Allegiant*. HarperCollins, 2013.

Russell, Emily. *Reading Embodied Citizenship: Disability, Narrative, and the Body Politic*. Rutgers University Press, 2011.

Stubblefield, Anna. ""Beyond the Pale": Tainted Whiteness, Cognitive Disability, and Eugenic Sterilization." *Hypatia*, vol. 22, no. 2, 2007, pp. 162–81.

Washington, Harriet A. *Medical Apartheid: The Dark History of Medical Experimentation on Black Americans from Colonial Times to the Present*. Doubleday Books, 2006.

IV
RACIALIZED IDENTITIES

"Vine Head," "Snake Lady," "Swamp Witch"

Racialized Othering in Nnedi Okorafor's *Zahrah the Windseeker*

Joshua Yu Burnett

In 2004, the Nigerian American speculative fiction writer Nnedi Okorafor[1] published an essay entitled "Stephen King's Super-Duper Magical Negroes." Okorafor recounts her first encounter with the term "magical negro," as well as the term's significance: "a black character—usually depicted as wiser and spiritually deeper than the white protagonist—whose purpose in the plot was to help the protagonist get out of trouble...It is the subordination of a minority figure masked as the empowerment of one" ("Stephen King's Super-Duper Magical Negroes"). Okorafor shows how frequently King relies on the magical negro trope. While Okorafor argues King is not a racist, she does assert that King is guilty of perpetuating "the implication that black people are inferior and expendable, even when they have power to wield, and white people are superior and important, even when they have to rely on the Magical Negro" ("Stephen King's Super-Duper Magical Negroes"). While respectful, Okorafor's critique of King is pointed; she acknowledges him as an inspiration, yet she is unflinching in her well-justified critique of King's frequent reliance on racist tropes.

Okorafor's short-short story "The Magical Negro" was also published in 2004. Satirical and sarcastic in tone, the story begins by seemingly invoking the trope. Its seeming hero is a stock sword-and-sorcery figure named "Thor the Brave," whose whiteness is emphasized by the story's first sentence, which describes "his long blond hair blowing in the breeze" (91). Thor is preparing to make his hopeless final stand against a swarm of enemies. The enemies are also described in racialized terms, although in their case, it is their Blackness which is emphasized; they are described as "shadows," "savage beasts," and, finally, "horrible black things" from "the heart of darkness" (91). In a comic over-representation of the magical negro, a character called "the African" appears abruptly and, initially, seems to serve no function other than to teach Thor how to defeat his foes by using a magical amulet and telling him to "[l]ook deep within yourself. You have the power–you just haven't tapped into it" (92). The African will be slaughtered by the "horrible black things," directly sacrificing himself for Thor.

However, after the African is struck down, the story changes abruptly; he looks up and declares, "Yo, what the *fuck* is this bullshit...I ain't goin' down like this. Damn, *how* many *times*? *Always* the same shit!" (92–93). Okorafor's rhetorical purpose in invoking the trope becomes clear in this moment through the African's abrupt code switching from "proper" English, which articulates self-sacrifice and subordination to Thor's over-determined whiteness, to African American Vernacular English and profanity, which articulates a discourse of resistance, defiance, and rejection of "noble" Black subordination to white supremacy. The African's switch to vernacular, too, resists white supremacist tropes of Blackness; it empowers him. The African takes the master's language and subverts it so that it is both incomprehensible to and critical of whiteness. Following this shift, the African becomes illegible to Thor, who can only read Black bodies as a monstrous threat or a magical negro. Thor attempts to reinscribe the African's Blackness in terms of the trope of Black as threatening, asking himself, "Could it be...he had internalized the evil of the shadows. Could that be what turned his skin that horrible color? Blew out his lips?" (93). Using his magical abilities, the African throws Thor the Brave off a cliff. With Thor the Brave, as the prototypical figure of white (supremacist) fantasy, dead, the African speaks directly to the reader to deliver his—and Okorafor's—thesis:

> "Sheeeit," he drawled, looking directly at you, the reader. "All this bullshit you readin' is 'bout to change. The Magical Negro ain't gettin' his ass kicked 'round here no more."... [He] strolled into the forest to see if he could find him some Hobbits, castles, Rastas, dragons, juke joints, princesses, and shit. (94)

Since these early works, Okorafor has written speculative fiction for several age groups, including her debut novel *Zahrah the Windseeker* (2004), which was marketed to a middle-grades audience. The novel is in many ways distinct from much YA and middle-grades speculative and postapocalyptic fiction. Such genres have become incredibly popular in recent years, and many of the most popular novels, such as the *Hunger Games* trilogy, have earned praise for their use of strong female protagonists, but many of these books have also drawn criticism for their lack of ethnic and racial diversity, as well as for ignoring racism, sexism, and homophobia as potential themes. It is as if the apocalypses depicted in these novels have destroyed society, but somehow, magically, cured generations of persistent bigotry, misogyny, and structural inequality. While popular YA dystopian/science fiction novels frequently depict white girls and young women overcoming societal expectations and oppressions, they ignore the role whiteness plays in the protagonist's ability to resist. Okorafor's approach, however, is intersectional; she both recognizes the role racialization plays and the toll it takes, and she locates racialized otherness as a source of resistance and the overcoming of constricting social norms. Okorafor's work is valuable for this reason: she not only depicts Black and African girls in speculative settings, but she transforms their double marginalization into resistance and empowerment.

While Okorafor's work is often situated within the category of Afrofuturism, Okorafor herself has been critical of the term for a variety of reasons. Okorafor argues, "If we are going to use the word Afrofuturism, African writers from within Africa should be the majority when listing central examples," and she suggests that the term (which was, indeed, coined by a white American critic) has primarily been for American fiction and has largely excluded Africans (@ nnedi). Instead, she has asked that, if such a label must be applied to her work, it should be "Africanfuturist" ("How Africa inspires").

Criticism of the term "Afrofuturism" is not new, nor is criticism of categorizing speculative fiction written by Black writers together. For example, Samuel R. Delany dismisses African American science fiction as a genre "that exists largely by means of its having been named" (395). However, Okorafor's mission here is different; she appears to seek not to dismiss the categorization of Black speculative fiction, but to refashion that categorization so as to center the African continent, its stories, and its writers. While *Zahrah the Windseeker* predates Okorafor's grappling with the term "Afrofuturism" by over a decade, it does clarify the significance of the novel by identifying her central project—to, from her liminal position as an African who was born and lives in the US but is not African American, and as a self-identified African who nevertheless was not born or raised in Africa, create and facilitate the creation of a body of work that imagines African and Africa-centric futures.

In contrast to works such as *The Hunger Games*, *Zahrah the Windseeker* takes up a similar rhetorical, markedly intersectional, thrust to "The Magical Negro" and "Stephen King's Super-Duper Magical Negroes." When considered in dialogue with each other,[2] the short story and the novel serve to announce

Okorafor's mission statement within speculative fiction. Okorafor simultaneously critiques King's use of the magical negro trope, exposes the ubiquity of the trope within speculative fiction, and announces her own very different purpose, drawing both from the (very white) traditions of speculative fiction (hobbits, castles, dragons, and princesses) as well as from the cultural traditions of the global African diaspora (Rastas, juke joints, "and shit"). This style of repetition of tropes, disrupted by notable difference added to the repetition, with the collision between the repetition and the difference forming the basis of a critique of the thing being repeated, is characteristic of signifying identified by Henry Louis Gates Jr. as "the great trope of Afro-American discourse" (21).[3]

In so doing, Okorafor simultaneously positions herself both as a strong critic of speculative fiction's failings on matters of race and as a writer deeply committed to working within the genre. As such, she is one of several writers heeding Nalo Hopkinson's call to "take the meme of colonizing the natives and, from the experience of the colonizee, critique it, pervert it, fuck with it, with irony, with anger, with humor, and also, with love and respect for the genre of science fiction that makes it possible to think about new ways of doing things" (9). Indeed, this dynamic has defined Okorafor's career. Okorafor has consistently and unflinchingly examined issues such as racism and misogyny, both fueled by the privileged myopathy, which has long been prevalent within speculative fiction. Okorafor's mission to bring an intersectional lens to speculative fiction is not, despite the genre's lily-white reputation, entirely a new thing. African American writers Octavia E. Butler and Samuel R. Delany have shown readers that speculative fiction's racially problematic history belies its potential to analyze race, and race's intersections with gender and sexuality, beyond the limitations of the present's dominant ideologies. Okorafor similarly refigures YA/middle-grades speculative fiction, pointing it away towards far more interesting directions of counterhegemonic depictions of gendered and racialized otherness. From this unique perspective, Okorafor examines the intersections not only of multiple social groups within a society, but she also considers the experience of the outsider within the society itself. This perspective is clear in *Zahrah the Windseeker*, Okorafor's first novel. In the novel, Okorafor plays Hopkinson's trickster role, using and playing with the problematic and racist tropes common to speculative fiction as a means to both critique those tropes and to reclaim them as useful for marginalized writers and fans of the speculative genres.

Zarah the Windseeker is the first of Okorafor's several YA/middle-grades novels. It is set in the fantastical Ooni Kingdom, which might be described as an alternative Nigeria technologically developed but untouched by European colonialism and surrounded by tropical wilderness. While Ooni clearly draws on Nigeria's cultures, simply calling it a fantastical Nigeria would be reductive of the setting's complexities. Aside from the speculative factors, Ooni is distinct from Nigeria in that it has never suffered the trauma of colonialism, which has disrupted the real West African[4] culture, language, politics, and self-identity. However, while Ooni itself is never colonized, *Zahrah the Windseeker* is distinctly postcolonial in its thematic focus. This can be seen in several ways, particularly in the ways in which Okorafor reproduces several aspects of real-world racism.

The novel focuses on Zahrah, a fourteen-year-old Ooni girl, and her dangerous journey into the Forbidden Greeny Jungle. Few ever venture into the jungle because the Ooni are a conservative culture, and the jungle represents otherness and the unknown. Additionally, the Ooni falsely believe they are the only humans on their world; this insular viewpoint negates the potential importance of exploration beyond the kingdom's boundaries. However, Dari, Zahrah's best friend, rejects the Ooni's fear of the jungle and convinces her to travel with him into the borderlands. While in the borderlands with Zahrah, Dari is bitten by a deadly snake, which normally lives hundreds of miles deeper in the jungle. He falls into a deep coma, which will become permanent unless the cure—the yolk of an unfertilized elgort egg—is administered within a few weeks. The elgort is the jungle's most fearsome predator, making securing an egg practically impossible. Despite this, Zahrah ventures into the jungle alone, beats the odds, and saves her friend.

In one sense, Ooni has cultural but not racial diversity because all of its people are dark-skinned and share similar physical characteristics. However, Okorafor introduces racial difference as well. Madelaine Hron observes that Okorafor "turns to science-fiction to explore themes of doubles, racial discrimination, and the return to one's heritage" (39). Hron's insight here is key to understanding the intersectional work the novel does in presenting a sort of speculative racial diversity which both mirrors, distorts, and, in true signifying fashion, critiques real world discourses of racial diversity and conflict. For one thing, humans are not the only intelligent species in Ginen. When Zahrah travels into the Forbidden Greeny Jungle, she encounters several other intelligent species such as Greeny panthers and Greeny gorillas. Of course, panthers and gorillas are entirely different species than humans, so while the analogy of racial difference does not fit perfectly, this is essentially how they function within the novel. Indeed, in certain ways, these intelligent nonhuman species appear to comment on stereotypes of different racial groups in the real world. Most important are the Greeny gorillas, who are deeply intelligent and connected to the natural world yet reject technology to the point where they would rather risk destruction by an elgort attack than embrace technological development. This may be read as a comment on the myth of the noble savage and of the devastation of pretechnological cultures such as Native Americans and Australian Aboriginals by the more technologically and militarily advanced European "explorers" and settlers.

Here, Okorafor relies on the long-established generic trope of what Isiah Lavender calls "problematic representations of race as 'alien' others" (25). While this trope is problematic because it allows science fiction writers—very often white, middle class, and politically liberal—to represent a racialized otherness while maintaining the fantasy of a "colorblind" existence where race and racism have somehow vanished, and, indeed, people of color are often wholly absent. As Lavender explains, "External encounters with aliens symbolize the internal conflicts of a humanity unmarked, or perhaps scarred, by racial experience, our continual state of difference...the American obsession with race is often superimposed onto science fiction aliens" (25–26). Okorafor's use of the trope, however, is different. To begin with, her setting is an imaginary West Africa, as opposed to an imagined future United States. Additionally, and more significantly, forms of racialized difference, as I discuss below, are found within the human population of Ooni, rather than being limited to the more "alien" intelligent animals of the Forbidden Greeny Jungle.

The novel's most interesting form of racial difference can be found through the character of Zahrah herself. She is an oddity in the seemingly monoracial Ooni society as she is born a "dada girl." Dada children are born with dreadlocks and a living vine woven through each dreadlock, called "dadalocks." Aside from the very rare dada born, dreadlocks are unknown in Ooni. As such, dadalocks are a highly visible and stigmatized marker of racial difference and otherness, separating those, like Zahrah, who have them from the Ooni mainstream. Much as physical markers like phenotype or eye shape are used to signify racial difference in the real world, dadalocks signify racial difference for Zahrah.

Interestingly, the racialization that Zahrah experiences tracks closely with real world racialized responses to natural Black hair such as dreadlocks. Dadalocks, with their interlocking, living green vines, mark the dada as unclean, uncivilized, and linked to the jungle; the dada are, thus, "uncivilized." Zahrah is taunted by Ciwanke, her chief tormentor:

> Ciwanke...would gather many of [her] friends at least twice a week, track me down in the hallway, and lead a chant. "Vine head, vine head, how long will it grooo-oooow!" That day Ciwanke had laughed loudly after their little song and shouted, "Go live in the trees, since your hair grows like their leaves, all wild and dirty! Hee-hee!" (2)

This association of dada with dirtiness is consistent throughout the text. Prior to her journey into the Forbidden Greeny Jungle, Zahrah is taunted as a "'Vine head,' 'snake lady,' 'swamp witch,' and 'freak'" (3), all of which associate her dada identity, in derogatory fashion, with the jungle and in opposition to the "civilized" Ooni. In the northeastern region of Ooni, mirrors are a common cultural marker, yet due to her dadalocks, Zahrah finds it difficult and painful to even look at herself in a mirror (5), indicating a profound cultural alienation and sense of othering and rejection from the culture she is born into but remains unaccepted by. In this sense, Okorafor pushes against generic convention, racializing her protagonist rather than relegating such difference to the narrative's margins. The only other dada person Zahrah meets, Nsibidi,[5] also reinforces this association, telling Zahrah, "We're more connected to the trees and plants…We're born with memories of long ago" (35).

The real-world parallels here are striking. Natural Black hairstyles, particularly for women, are dismissed, using racially coded language, as unprofessional, dirty, and primitive. Indeed, Africanness generally is associated in the popular imagination with nature; despite Africa's fifty-four countries and 1.1 billion inhabitants, it is often depicted as a place devoid of humans (or at least "civilized" humans) and full of strange, wild, "exotic" animals (and, often, waiting for white "civilization" to colonize it). For example, in 2013, Prince William and Princess Catherine were expecting their first child, and they announced to the media that they were making an "African" themed nursery. Prince William spoke of his love of "Africa"; rather than specify a particular country, city, or location within Africa, he used the term to describe the world's second largest continent, eliding its cultural and ethnic diversity. Instead, he described the "bush" (Fisher) and discussed his concern for the continent's endangered animal species. Clearly, Africa was, as it so often is, depicted as wild and in need of "help" from beneficent white saviors; here, the Africa that needs external salvation is animal, not human. The interview occurred in August 2013, the same month a report showed that, in less than a year, the ongoing Central African Republic conflict had led to 200,000 internally displaced people and 20,000 refugees ("Central African Republic"), yet only endangered animal species are, apparently, worth Prince William mentioning. Thus, we see, again, that Zahrah's racialization as dada corresponds with real-world racializations of African people or "Africa" as a generic space within the Western colonialist imagination.

Interestingly, despite her bullying of Zahrah for her dreadlocks, Ciwanke herself wears a large Afro, itself a highly politically charged and racialized hairstyle. While this might seem to discredit the notion of dada as racialized within the novel's world, it in fact indicates how fluid and adaptive racialized stigma can be. Markers of race such as dreadlocks or Afros are at least partially arbitrary; while many Black people can grow such hairstyles naturally and many white people must go to great efforts to wear them, such hairstyles are not limited to Black-identified people. Dreadlocks, for example, are sometimes grown by South Asians, and both dreadlocks and Afros are common among Papua New Guineans, who are classified as Pacific Islander. In the Western imagination, however, dreadlocks remain exclusively associated with Blackness/Africanness. In an ostensibly monoracial culture since as Ooni, it is perfectly believable that one hairstyle that is racially marked in the real world (the Afro) can be seen as normative while another (dreadlocks) can be racialized.

In contrast with Zahrah's struggles, Nsibidi may superficially appear more at ease with her dada status. However, she too shows the effects of marginalization. Indeed, Nsibidi is more othered than Zahrah, having been raised in the wild far from "civilized" Ooni. At the novel's conclusion, Nsibidi reveals the secret of her mother's origin, that "she is from Earth" (306). In Ooni, Earth is a mythical land of rumor and fantastical tales such as "the mythical *Alice in Wonderearth* tales" (141). Thus, Nsibidi too feels the burden of dada racialization while living in Ooni. At some point prior to her appearance in the novel, Nsibidi shaved off her dadalocks, and hence forth, she keeps her head very closely shaved, which Zahrah finds unimaginable (35). Despite Zahrah's own ambivalence about dada identity, the revelation of Nsibidi's shaved dadalocks makes it clear that dadaness *is* central to Zahrah's sense of self-identity, whether or not she is always happy about that dadaness. Nsibidi initially refuses to tell Zahrah why she shaved her hair, and she finally says, simply, "I cut it because it grew too heavy to bear" (69). Given dadalocks' racialized status, we can read Nsibidi's shaving of her head as an attempt at passing as nondada. Again, Nsibidi's sense of fatigue from the burden of her visibly racialized identity mirrors real-world discourse. Researchers have coined the term "racial battle fatigue," defined as "the psychophysiological symptoms resulting from living in mundane extreme racist environments...[which] can become mentally, emotionally, and physically draining and/or lethal" (Smith, Yosso, and Solorzano 300). Nsibidi's "too heavy to bear" comment reflects just this sort of racial battle fatigue; she has tired of the micro- and macroaggressions she suffers in Ooni.

Nevertheless, the psychological effects of Nsibidi's marginalization remain clear. Zahrah first encounters Nsibidi in the Dark Market, a menacing subsection of Kirki's market where all manner of questionable and forbidden items are sold. The term "Dark Market" is itself interesting, as it, like the real-world term "black market," replicates the white supremacist association of darkness with threat, despite the fact that all of Ooni's people are dark skinned, and dark skin itself is not stigmatized in Ooni culture. In the Dark Market, Nsibidi works with intelligent baboons, called "idiok," who tell the future. Again, we see how dada are associated with the wild rather than the "civilized," yet the usual binary value of "civilized" over "wild" is subverted. Not only are the idiok intelligent, but they also possess abilities beyond those of humans. Nsibidi is the only person capable of reading their writing and, thus, deciphering their meaning (66). This inversion is a direct act of cultural resistance against the oppressive aspects of insular Ooni culture. After all, as Zahrah explains, "A large part of the culture in the northern Ooni Kingdom where I live is to look 'civilized'" (ix). "Civilized," for the northern Ooni, means stylish or fashionable, yet the choice of words—"civilized"—is not mistake in this context, being pitted against the wildness of the racialized and othered dada. As Zahrah journeys through the Forbidden Greeny Jungle and comes more in touch with her dada abilities, she begins to reject the northern Ooni preoccupation with appearing "civilized"; for example, she observes that her "habit of obsessing over [her] appearance started leaving [her]" (151). Once she returns from her journey, Zahrah completely rejects the northern Ooni notions of appearing "civilized": "I looked down at my tattered clothes. My hair and body needed a good washing...I was sure that I smelled strongly of sweat, mud, and leaves; the jungle. But I didn't care" (271). This moment shows us Zahrah moving beyond the burden of adherence to respectability politics, the notion that marginalized people must present themselves in perfect accordance with all societal norms to prevent their further marginalization. Instead, following everything she has been to, Zahrah adopts another model of response to marginalization: the rejection of the dominant group's externally imposed standards and the instance that the marginalized group has the right to live according to its own standards.

Interestingly, *Zahrah the Windseeker* does not necessarily show that stereotypes of dada are inaccurate but, instead, consistently inverts their value. Here, Okorafor follows the dictum of another Igbo writer, Chimamanda Ngozi Adichie, who observes "the problem with stereotypes is not that they are untrue, but that they are incomplete. They make one story become the only story" ("The Danger of the Single Story"). As previously discussed, many of the stereotypes of dada revolve around the perception that dada are connected to nature and that they possess mysterious magical powers. In both cases, these perceived differences are stigmatized; the connection to nature makes them "uncivilized," and the magical abilities render them threatening and strange. Both of these stereotypes are, in fact, proven correct for Zahrah. By leaving Ooni and venturing into the Forbidden Green Jungle, she achieves self-discovery; truly, she does possess a special connection to nature. What's more, she also learns that she has magical abilities. Before she enters the jungle, Zahrah discovers that she can float in the air.[6] She hears rumors that some dada are "Windseekers" who can fly, and, eventually, she learns that Nsibidi comes from a family of Windseekers. Still, before venturing into the jungle, and even for most of her journey, Zahrah remains tentative, unwilling to embrace her ability and uncertain if she can truly fly, as opposed to merely floating up and down in the air. It is only at the end of her journey, when she has taken the elgort egg she was seeking and is desperately fleeing for her life that Zahrah finally embraces her Windseeker ability. In accepting her position as a Windseeker, Zahrah ceases being passive regarding the racialized treatment she has received:

> I wheezed and could feel my legs ready to give way. Who was going to save me?...*I'm not born to die like this*. The thought echoed in my emptying mind. I'd been shy, introverted, lived my life up to the last few weeks cowering from the world. When people made fun of me, I would go home and hide in my room. I was born with a strange ability, and once again, I cowered from it. *But look at how I've survived in this place*, I thought...In that moment, I was sure... [A]s if I had always done it, I took to the sky. (260)

Strikingly, dada status eventually proves to be Zahrah's greatest strength. Without her ability to fly, Zahrah could not have survived; the elgort would have quickly overtaken her, and eaten her. Even if she somehow escaped the elgort's wrath, the entire journey would have been in vain; it took her about three weeks to find the egg, leaving just days to return before Dari's coma becomes permanent. While being dada has marginalized Zahrah, it also allows her to survive and resist. Indeed, the only reason Zahrah entered the jungle with Dari in the first place was because its isolation allowed her to practice flying in secret, away from prying Ooni eyes. Marginalization, though painful, enables Zahrah to look at both Ooni and the Forbidden Greeny Jungle from a perspective that is simultaneously that of an insider (she was raised in Ooni) and an outsider (she is marginalized in Ooni and is more willing than most Ooni to question social beliefs about the jungle as "forbidden" or evil). This new perspective is, of course, both literal and metaphorical: having found her courage, Zahrah metaphorically sees the jungle through new eyes, and she also quite literally sees the jungle in a new way, from "hundreds of feet in the air and bathed in moonlight" (261). The perspective of the marginalized and racialized other—the dada in Ooni, the African immigrant in the United States—is, therefore, privileged in Okorafor's work. Dari, as nondada, quickly falls prey to the jungle's dangers. He cannot even make it past the jungle's relatively innocuous outermost fringes without nearly dying. Zahrah, by contrast, is able, through her dada abilities, to move between the seemingly incompatible worlds of Ooni and the Forbidden Greeny Jungle.

Through Zahrah, Okorafor is, in one sense simply fulfilling a generic archetype of the journey of (self-)discovery through her protagonist's arc: the hero(ine) who begins the story timid and afraid but confronts his/her fears and emerges stronger than s/he had ever imagined possible. The elements of racialization she introduces complicate the seeming simplicity of this generic archetype, however. As we have seen, Zahrah's growing strength and confidence are tied to her embrace of her marginalized identity, which had previously appeared to be the very source of her initial timidity. Her strength is also tied to her partial rejection of Ooni culture, as seen in her indifference to her "uncivilized" appearance. At no point does Zahrah completely reject Ooni culture. Indeed, at the end of the story, Zahrah returns to Kirki, reveals the secret of her flight to her family (although she chooses to keep her Windseeker status from the rest of the community), and appears ready to reintegrate herself back into her village and the larger northern Ooni culture, albeit with a new inner strength. There is some suggestion that this arrangement may not last forever; Nsibidi tells Zahrah that "once a Windseeker learns to fly, he or she is plagued by wanderlust. Rarely do we stay where we were born and raised" (305). However, Zahrah, for her part, appears happy to be home. She has realized the oppressive aspects of Ooni culture and feels no compunction about critiquing them, but this does not lead her to leave or completely reject the culture she has grown up in. In this sense, Zahrah mirrors Okorafor herself, who critiques speculative fiction's blind spots yet refuses to abandon the genre or to reject it completely for its failings. Zahrah remains in Ooni, and Okorafor keeps writing—and critiquing—speculative fiction.

Interestingly, despite the many facets of dada and Windseeker identity that emerge in the novel—that they are socially stigmatized, that the otherness they mark is racialized, that the very marginalization can be a source of resistance—Zahrah and Dari first encounter the term "Windseeker" in an extremely unlikely source: an anthology of fashion articles from *Ooni Fashion Magazine*, which they find in Kirki's library and which appears to be the only book in the entire library that mentions humans who can fly. When they find the book, they discover what appears at first glance to be a photograph of a dada woman. However, they quickly realize that her dadalocks and vines are fake; they are "made of pliable plant byproduct. And look at the vines! They're pink!" (56). When they read the article, they find it is hyping "dadalock extensions" as the next big fashion trend:

> Few of us have ever seen a real person born with dadalocks...Most of them choose to lop off their strange locks in order to live a normal life. The ones who keep their hair are quiet people who somehow grow into wise men and

women, excelling in whatever career they choose. Or so legend says. But then again, another legend says that those born with dadalocks are rebels whose only cause is to make things go wrong. This year, anyone can take part in the myth and get the chic look of a wise (or strange) woman or man...Dada extensions are this year's hottest   look! Vines braided into the locks come in all colors, not just green! Many celebrities are even sporting the fab style in digi-movies and on netevision. (56–57)

For Zahrah and Dari, the article is significant because it introduces them to the term and concept of Windseeker, which explains the mysterious floating Zahrah has been experiencing. From a critical perspective, however, the brief passage offers interesting commentary on several levels. First, there is the exotification of the dada, marked as "strange" and in opposition to "a normal life." Elements of the noble savage and magical negro myths also come in, with these supposedly exotic dada described as "wise" and yet also potentially cursed. The passage also demonstrates a classic case of cultural appropriation, with the dominant element of society taking a part of the marginalized group's culture (here dadalocks), stripping it of its significance and regurgitating it as a banal fashion trend. Finally, the passage reveals the astonishingly persistent ability of capitalist society to transform and commodify markers of resistance. Dadalocks begin the novel as markers of Zahrah's othering, and by the end of the novel, they are a symbol of the strength and resistance her dada status has made possible. Either way, fashion designers see them as an easy way to make money. This recalls the early 1990s, when, following the release of Spike Lee's *Malcolm X* biopic, baseball caps featuring a bold "X" to honor the slain civil rights hero became a trend, "worn by everyone from social activists to fashion addicts" (Kissel), their very ubiquity stripping them of context and, thus, political meaning as a symbol of resistance.

If dadalocks are indeed a racial marker in Ooni, and dada identity is associated with magical abilities such as flying, we might reasonably ask if Okorafor is not then simply reinscribing the problematic generic cliché of displacing racial difference onto fantastic or alien others. For example, the Irish writer Eoin Colfer's popular *Artemis Fowl* (2001) features a human cast that is overwhelmingly racially white and culturally Western. The novel opens with a scene in Ho Chi Minh City, but the city is depicted in broad strokes and without culturally specific details, essentially serving as an "exotic" backdrop to get the attention of presumptively Western readers. The Ho Chi Minh City passage is brief, and the characters return to Europe. The whiteness and Westernness that characterize the remainder of the novel are quickly established. Against this white, Western background, Colfer projects racialized difference onto a plethora of fantastical creatures who live underground and avoid all contact with humanity. In fact, it is worth nothing that while the novel features a large number of different types of fantastical creatures, ranging from centaurs to trolls to leprechauns, *all* are Western in their cultural origin. If we ask, however, if Okorafor's depiction of the dada as racialized other is substantially different from Colfer's novel, the answer is clearly, yes. Okorafor's novel is meaningfully different. First, in *Artemis Fowl* (and other, similar novels; c.f. the *His Dark Materials* trilogy's witches, polar bears, etc.) race is essentialized. Species—including both humans and fantastical creatures—act the way they do because it is in their nature to do so. Trolls, for example, are brutal *because* they are trolls, and stupid brutality is the essential nature of the troll. In *Zarah the Windseeker*, by contrast, Zahrah is not depicted as being an outsider because of some dada essence; rather, she is an outsider because of the way "normal" Ooni project otherness upon her. In this sense, race is a social construct in Okorafor's world. Unlike being a troll or centaur (and thus fundamentally *not* human), being born with dreadlocks and vines is a basically meaningless social marker that is given social significance, much like dark skin's social significance in our real, racialized world.

While it is true that dada status is associated with magical abilities such as Windseeking, it is not this magical ability that creates Zahrah's othering and racialization; she is othered and racialized long before any magical powers manifest themselves. Okorafor's choice to associate dada racialization with magical ability can be read in a similar vein to #BlackGirlMagic and #BlackGirlsAreFromTheFuture,[7] two popular Twitter hashtags that essentially use speculative language—magic and the future—to argue that the double marginalization of Black women and girls give them a special insight into society, one which more privileged people lack. This is not to say that Okorafor is referencing either hashtag, since the novel came out several years before them. Rather, her novel anticipates a similar concept. Finally, it should be said that while her depiction of dada includes magical ability, Okorafor focuses on the marginalization of the dada within mainstream Ooni society. This depiction of racialization may seem curious given Ooni's roots in the cultures of Nigeria, which is, after all, multicultural and multilingual, but also a substantially monoracial society. However, this makes sense in terms of Okorafor's own positionality within Nigeria as a Nigerian American and also speaks to the persistence of racialization within society. Ooni, after all, is a place where colonialism has never occurred, and there is no hegemonic whiteness that defines itself in opposition to Blackness. However, the racializing and othering impulse persists—in this case, projected onto a racial marker (dreadlocks) that is, in the real world, deeply tied to Blackness. This tie to real-world Blackness may be meaningless to Zahrah and the novel's other characters, yet readers can recognize it as commentary on the powerful hold white supremacy has on our collective imagination: even in a never-colonized, all-Black society, racialization remains tied to Blackness. In all these ways, Okorafor's depiction far better reflects the way racialization *actually* operates in the real world, both ideologically and materially. Racialization in novels like *Artemis Fowl*, by contrast, is fantasy (in the pejorative sense).

By the end of *Zahrah the Windseeker*, Ooni appears to be undergoing a significant change due to the story of Zahrah's remarkable journey spreading through the kingdom. Soon after Zahrah's successful return with the elgort egg, scientists begin expeditions into the Forbidden Greeny Jungle for research purposes. When Zahrah and Dari go to the library to return the *Forbidden Greeny Jungle Field Guide* digibook, which Dari had been the first to check out in decades, they find the library has purchased five additional copies, "and all of them are checked out" (298). Clearly, due to Zahrah's bravery, some sort of social transformation is now underway, although it is not clear within the novel how profound or lasting that change will prove to be.

In Okorafor's next novel, *The Shadow Speaker*,[8] Ooni reappears, and the social transformation that began in *Zahrah the Windseeker* is apparent. While it's not clear precisely where *The Shadow Speaker* is set compared to *Zahrah the Windseeker*, it is in the first novel's near future; in *Zahrah the Windseeker*, Earth is a legend assumed by most to be false, while in *The Shadow Speaker*, passages between Earth and Ginen have opened, everyone is aware of Earth's reality, and the potential threat caused by Earth's technology has, indeed, become Ooni's number one political issue.

While the Ooni of *The Shadow Speaker* is far from utopic (it is ruled by a tyrannical chief who murders casually and is determined to make war with Earth), it shows a continuation of the transformation at which the ending of *Zahrah the Windseeker* hints. None of the prior Ooni paranoia about the Forbidden Greeny Jungle is apparent, although this could be influenced by the fact that, in *The Shadow Speaker*, Ooni is seen through the eyes of an Earth-born outsider. What is discernible, however, is that much of the stigma associated with being dada is gone, and Windseekers, like Earth, have become common knowledge. While Zahrah herself is not mentioned, we are told that most of Ginen's explorers are Windseekers. Sunrise, another Windseeker, is described as "the most known living explorer" (216). In the context of *Zahrah the Windseeker*, this description is remarkable for two reasons. First, because in the Ooni of the first novel, there were no living explorers at all before Zahrah. Second, in the first novel, Windseekers were mythic and extremely rare. If, in *The Shadow Speaker*, the world's explorers are Windseekers, and Sunrise is the most known of them, that implies both that Windseekers are well-known and accepted and that there are (at least) several of them who are known. Given the seemingly short time gap between the two novels, this is a remarkable social transformation that has been achieved in very little time. While this rapid transformation may not reflect real-world social change (where, after all, issues of race and racism remain foremost in the American public imagination decades after the passage of the Civil Rights Act of 1964, which itself came a century after the Emancipation Proclamation), it does reflect the audience's expectations for happy endings and a hopeful message, given that *Zahrah the Windseeker* was marketed to a middle-grades audience and *The Shadow Speaker* to a YA audience.

Since her early writings, such as "Stephen King's Super-Duper Magical Negroes," "The Magical Negro," and *Zahrah the Windseeker*, Okorafor has branched out as a writer, authoring both additional YA fiction such as *Akata Witch* (2011) and "Long Juju Man" (2009), and adult fiction such as *Who Fears Death* (2010) and *The Book of Phoenix* (2015). In doing so, she has continued the work she began in her early texts, both in terms of critiquing the limitations of white speculative fiction and in terms of developing her own African diasporic perspective on the speculative genre. Thus, just as those first three texts are best read in conversation with each other, so too should they, together, be read merely as the first stage of Okorafor's project as a writer, as opposed to some sort of definitive statement. Indeed, the aforementioned optimism about the possibilities of widespread social transformation is superseded by her later works, which are frequently far more pessimistic in these regards; in these works, change can and does happen, but it does so with great difficulty and sacrifice. For example, in Okorafor's novel *The Book of Phoenix* (2015), attempts at resistance to racialized oppression by the novel's protagonist, Phoenix Okore, perversely lead to decades if not centuries of oppression of Black Africans when her story is perversely twisted by her successors, who are so used to "understanding [their] ancestors as slaves" (230) that they willfully misrepresent Phoenix's condemnations of all humanity as condemnations of Black Africans alone.

While a reader of Okorafor's later works might be tempted to dismiss Ooni's rapid social transformation as evidence of youthful naiveté on the author's part, this is belied by her early critical acumen and sophistication as evidenced in "The Magical Negro" and "Stephen King's Super-Duper Magical Negroes." It may be, then, that this simply reflects the market demands that come along with the intended readership of *Zahrah the Windseeker* and *The Shadow Speaker*—middle grades and young adults. While Okorafor pushes boundaries of what might be deemed acceptable for these audiences—for example, *The Shadow Speaker*'s most striking scene features the protagonist's father being judiciously beheaded in front of her eyes—a sense of a happy ending and an optimistic portrayal of social change is understandable. With all of this in mind, *Zahrah the Windseeker* remains important in its subtle and insightful depiction of racialization and for its (unfortunately) still unusual use of West African culture and mythos in building a speculative world within YA literature.

Notes

1. In her early career, including the essay "Stephen King's Super-Duper Magical Negroes" and the novel *Zahrah the Windseeker*, Okorafor published under the name Nnedi Okorafor-Mbachu. Beginning with 2009's *Long Juju Man*, she began to publish as Nnedi Okorafor. For the purposes of this essay, I will simply refer to her as "Okorafor" as she has now been using that name professionally for several years. However, since the texts I am discussing are from early in her career, all citations will be to "Okorafor-Mbachu."

2. Okorafor references "The Magical Negro" in "Stephen King's Super-Duper Magical Negroes," referring to the African as a character who "gets a clue in the middle of things and decides to save himself and move on to things he wants to do instead of dying for a white stranger, who was supposedly the main character."

3. Given that we are discussing Okorafor here as an African Diasporic (as opposed to African American) writer, it should be noted that Gates also shows that signifying has its roots in West African as well as Diasporic African culture.

4. I use "West Africa" here rather than "Nigeria" because Nigeria itself is a colonial creation, cobbled together by British colonizers from several disparate cultures and regions; we cannot talk of a Nigeria that never suffered colonization because, without colonization, the very concept of "Nigeria" would not exist.

5. Nsibidi's name itself is a significant reference to West African culture. Nsibidi is a historical ideographic script found in West African cultures "compris[ing] nearly a thousand symbols that can be drawn in the air (as gestures), on the ground, on skin (as tattoos), on houses and on art forms, such as masks and textiles" ("Nsibidi").

6. Zahrah's discovery of this ability coincides with the onset of her first menses. In contrast with many cultures' traditional beliefs associating menstruation with uncleanliness and even sin, Okorafor connects menstruation with power and magic.

7. It is well documented that scholars and journalists—particularly ones who are white and/or male—have frequently appropriated concepts developed by Black women on social media for their own gain without properly acknowledging the Black women who actually originated and developed the concepts. As such, I want to acknowledge that #BlackGirlMagic was originated by CaShawn Thompson and #BlackGirlsAreFromTheFuture was originated by Renina Jarmon.

8. Unfortunately, due to conflicts with the publisher, *The Shadow Speaker* is currently the only of Okorafor's novels that is out of print.

Works Cited

Adichie, Chimamanda Ngozi. "The Danger of a Single Story | Chimamanda Ngozi Adichie TED Talks." *TED: Ideas Worth Spreading*, TED Talks, 7 October 2009, www.ted.com/talks/chimamanda_adichie_the_danger_of_a_single_story?language=en. Accessed 25 August 2015.

Cabell, Aphelia K. Rev. of *Zahrah the Windseeker* by Nnedi Okorafor-Mbachu. *Black Issues Book Review*, vol. 8, no. 1, 2006, p. 61.
"Central African Republic." *CrisisWatch Database*. International Crisis Group, 2016, www.crisis group.org/africa/central-africa/central-african-republic. Accessed 23 August 2015.
Colfer, Eoin. *Artemis Fowl*. Hyperion/Miramax Books, 2001.
Collins, Suzanne. *The Hunger Games*. Scholastic Press, 2008.
Fisher, Luchina. "Prince George's Nursery African-Themed." *ABC News*, 21 August 2013, abcnews .go.com/blogs/entertainment/2013/08/prince-georges-nursery-african-themed/. Accessed 23 August 2015.
Delany, Samuel R. "Racism and Science Fiction." *Dark Matter: A Century of Speculative Fiction from the African Diaspora*, edited by Sheree R. Thomas, Warner Books, 2000, pp. 383–97.
Gates, Henry Louis, Jr. *The Signifying Monkey*. Oxford University Press, 1988.
Hopkinson, Nalo. Introduction. *So Long Been Dreaming: Postcolonial Science Fiction & Fantasy*. Arsenal Pulp Press, 2004.
Hron, Madelaine. "Ora na-azu nwa: The Figure of the Child in Third-Generation Nigerian Novels." *Research in African Literatures*, vol. 39, no. 2, 2008, pp. 27–48.
Kissel, William. "THE X FACTOR: Caps with Malcolm X's initial are turning up everywhere. Are they political statements or just another way to look cool?" *Los Angeles Times*, 22 May 1992, articles.latimes.com/1992-05-22/news/vw-159_1_x-cap. Accessed 26 August 2015.
Lavender, Isiah, III. *Race in American Science Fiction*. Indiana University Press, 2011.
Mehan, Uppinder. "Introduction to Focus: The Other Sci-Fi." *American Book Review*, vol. 32, no. 2, 2011, p. 3. Web. Accessed 19 August 2015.
@nnedi (Nnedi Okorafor). "If we are going to use the word Afrofuturism." *Twitter*, 18 October 2017, 3:04 p.m., twitter.com/nnedi/status/920576323915014144?lang=en.
"Nsibidi." *Inscribing Meaning*. Smithsonian National Museum of African Art, 2014, africa. si.edu/exhibits/inscribing/knowing.html. Accessed 23 August 2015.
Okorafor, Nnedi. *The Book of Phoenix*. Daw Books, 2015.
Okorafor, Nnedi. "Please Stop Talking." *Facebook*, 20 September 2018, 8:34 a.m., www.facebook .com/nnedi/posts/10103947998895689.
Okorafor-Mbachu, Nnedi. "The Magical Negro." *Dark Matter: Reading the Bones*, edited by Sheree R. Thomas, Aspect, 2004, pp. 91–94.
Okorafor-Mbachu, Nnedi. *The Shadow Speaker*. New York: Hyperion, 2007.
Okorafor-Mbachu, Nnedi. "Stephen King's Super-Duper Magical Negroes." *Strange Horizons*, 25 October 2004, strangehorizons.com/non-fiction/articles/stephen-kings-super-duper-magical-negroes/. Accessed 18 August 2015.
Okorafor-Mbachu, Nnedi. *Zahrah the Windseeker*. Boston: Graphia, 2005.
Okorafor-Mbachu, Nnedi. "Fantasy Girls: An Interview with Nnedi Okorafor-Mbachu." *Bitch Magazine*, vol. 41, 2008, pp. 70–1. www.bitchmedia.org/issue/41. Accessed 19 August 2015.
Silverman, Karyn N. Rev. of *Zahrah the Windseeker* by Nnedi Okorafor-Mbachu. *School Library Journal*, vol. 51, no. 12, 2005, p. 151.
Smith, William A., Tara J. Yosso, and Daniel G. Solorzano. "Challenging Racial Battle Fatigue on Historically White Campuses: A Critical Race Examination of Race-related Stress." *Faculty of Color Teaching in Predominantly White Colleges and Universities*, edited by Christine A. Stanley, Anker Publishing Company, 2006, pp. 299–321.

Between "Castoff" and "Half-Man"
Pressuring Mixed-Race Identity in *The Drowned Cities*
Susan Tan

Paulo Bacigalupi is a notable example of a contemporary YA dystopian author whose works feature protagonists of color. While Bacigalupi's *Ship Breaker* and *Drowned Cities* have not attained the popularity of dystopian franchises such as *The Hunger Games*, his work has received marked attention, with *Ship Breaker* reaching number 15 on the *New York Times* bestseller list, awarded the Michael J. Printz Award, and noted as a National Book Award finalist.

Bacigalupi's texts feature multiracial casts of characters and are deeply invested in questions of identity. In fact, to successfully survive their dystopian worlds, his protagonists must confront and negotiate heritage. In *Ship Breaker*, protagonist Nailer struggles with identity through the lens of family behavior—he fears he will grow to resemble his violent, abusive father. In *Drowned Cities*, the half-Chinese, half-Drowned Cities (American) protagonist, Mahlia, also negotiates questions of family and legacy. However, Mahlia's negotiations are more complex: as she confronts familial abuse and trauma, she is simultaneously torn between the different facets of her racial and national identity, and she struggles with the resulting mixed and socially isolated identity of "castoff." As Mahlia returns to the Drowned Cities—her childhood home, the site of her father's abandonment and her mother's violent death—to save her friend Mouse from conscription into an army of child soldiers, she directly faces these questions of self and national and racial belonging. Given this focus on diversity in Bacigalupi's texts, particularly in *Drowned Cities*, Bacigalupi's work appears to stand as an example of YA dystopia's ability to powerfully address race.

However, even as *Drowned Cities* seems to assert the importance of racial diversity, questions emerge, as racial identity is aligned with posthuman identity, and Mahlia looks to Tool—a "half-man," created through a melding of human and animal DNA—as a model and solution for her own fragmented sense of self. In this chapter, I examine this representation of multiracial identity in Bacigalupi's YA work, focusing on *Drowned Cities* and drawing on Elaine Grahame's discussion of posthuman monstrosity as a means of identity articulation. First, I consider the layers and complexities surrounding race in the text, exploring how the multifaceted construction of identity presents exciting directions and possibilities for incorporating racial identity into the stakes of dystopian world-building. I analyze Tool, examining how the ontological questions he raises as a posthuman subject align with Mahlia's own violent experiences of selfhood and self as defined by community.

This reading of Mahlia's coming of age as inextricably linked with Tool's posthuman selfhood appears in Lars Schmeink's "Coming of Age and the Other: Critical Posthumanism in Paolo Bacigalupi's *Ship Breaker* and *Drowned Cities*." Examining how adolescent development in *Drowned Cities* and *Ship Breaker* is "influenced by social expectations and a stark genetic determinism," Schmeink explores how "At the heart of these decisions are issues of identity, community, and Otherness that Bacigalupi positions within contemporary discourses of posthumanism" (159). Schmeink then examines Tool as a figure of ultimate posthumanism, who operates "as a stand-in" who "reminds readers that in posthuman times, the human as a category is not exempt from the consequences of the anthropocene and that all life should be valued equally" (161).

Schmeink focuses mainly on Tool, and it is here that our arguments differ. Like Schmeink, I view Tool as a "reflective screen for issues of identity formation in the coming-of-age process of the adolescent" (161). However, while Schmeink discusses Mahlia's racial identity, he is concerned with the various components that make up her bodily "DNA"—her racial background, how her body is prized in the Drowned Cities' war economy, and other ways in which Mahlia is figured as a commodity. My reading focuses, however, on Mahlia and her perception of self and identity in relation to racial and national definition, as Mahlia's visions of herself as Chinese, Drowned Cities, and, sometimes, human are questioned throughout the narrative and ultimately reconciled only as Tool models a hybrid identity that Mahlia can emulate.

Ultimately, considering how Mahlia must "evolve," and how Tool pressures Mahlia's sense of self, I show that issues of ontological "wholeness" and spatial belonging are privileged over racial and cultural struggle. For both Mahlia and Tool, the acceptance of dystopian identity (in this case, an assertion and acceptance of a "Drowned Cities" identity) becomes paramount; as a result, racial issues are largely ignored. Exploring this silencing of racial issues, I examine the subtle ways that common dystopian tropes of human hybridity, posthumanism, and spatial belonging work to question and complicate real engagement with racial difference in Bacigalupi's text.

Right There on Your Face: Race and Castoff Identity

From the beginning of *Drowned Cities*, race is asserted as central to Mahlia's experience. Born to a Chinese father, part of a group of "peacekeeper" soldiers, sent to restore order in the Drowned Cities, Mahlia is immediately marked as "other" and enemy by the fact of her mixing, accused of being a "collaborator" because of her parentage (*Drowned Cities* 84). This otherness has high stakes. When the peacekeepers fled the Drowned Cities (the ruins of Washington, DC) as armies of child soldiers descended on the city, the families of peacekeepers, including Mahlia's mother, were summarily executed. Indeed, Mahlia is one of the few "castoff" children left, as she recounts watching her classmates die in a hail of gunfire. During these attacks, Mahlia was maimed by a group of child soldiers, who cut off her right hand. Mahlia survived because Mouse, a young, orphaned farm boy, saved her. Together, the two "war maggots," as orphans are labeled, find refuge with a pacifist physician, with whom Mahlia trains to be a doctor and fights the villagers' constant hostility and distrust (*Drowned Cities* 27).

An early conversation between Mahlia and a townswoman points to the many dynamics that shape Mahlia's castoff label and influence Mahlia's own attitude to her identity. Blaming Mahlia for the death of a young woman, whom Mahlia attempted to save, the townswoman remarks,

> "[S]he didn't need a useless crippled China girl for a nurse."
> Mahlia bristled. "I ain't Chinese."
> Amaya just looked at her. [...]
> "You got the blood right there on your face. China castoff, through and through." (*Drowned Cities* 37)

Here, we see the conflation of racial identity and national belonging, the same impulse that fuels accusations of Mahlia as "collaborator." Strikingly, however, Mahlia herself seems to conflate these two factors as well. When Dr. Mahfouz, who has taken Mahlia in, interrupts the rapidly escalating confrontation, Mahlia explains, "'She called me Chinese.' Mahfouz threw up his hands. 'You *are* Chinese! There's no shame in that!'" (*Drowned Cities* 38). However, Mahlia never accepts this label. For Mahlia, the assertion of a Drowned Cities identity and the rejection of Chinese national identity seem to demand a disavowal of ethnic and racial identity as well.

This rejection of Chineseness is all the more striking given the diversity of the rest of Mahlia's world and the presence of other Asian characters. It's made clear that to be Chinese, in itself, is not necessarily negative. When she meets another Asian boy, she reflects, "He could have been Chinese, but not like her. Not castoff. Some full-blooded patriot, born and raised in the Drowned Cities, instead of a half-breed like her" (*Drowned Cities* 298). Later, when she is told to cover her eyes with a cap to hide herself, she responds, "Other people got eyes like mine," and she is told, "Other people aren't you. Everything about you screams castoff. You're the right age, and you look too mixed. [...] You have no idea how much danger you put us all in" (*Drowned Cities* 313). To be Chinese is not necessarily at issue here: rather, to be biracial and Chinese is the crime. Age is an important component in the construction of castoff identity as well. We can assume that adults of mixed-race Asian identity, born before the arrival of Chinese peacekeepers, are safe from the soldiers who would "kill [Mahlia] on sight" (*Drowned Cities* 32). In a world where child soldiers wage systematic war on rival factions and civilians alike, young people similarly emerge as their prime targets.

This intersection of race, national affiliation, and age parallels Mahlia's own interior struggles with her family heritage. As the book continues, we learn that Mahlia's father instilled in her a strong sense of Drowned Cities inferiority. He viewed Drowned Cities residents as uncivilized, a community that "[fights] all the time, and blame[s] each other for being poor and broken, instead of standing tall" (*Drowned Cities* 61). In contrast, "the peacekeepers [are] tall and healthy," and Mahlia is taught that China has "culture. It was civilized." Mahlia takes pride in her identity as Chinese until she bites her father during a tantrum. He "slapped her then, and said she had too much Drowned Cities in her. 'No respect,' he said. 'Drowned Cities, through and through. Just like your mother. Animals'" (62).

This association of China with civilization and the Drowned Cities with barbarism permeates Mahlia's sense of self. She recounts "hid[ing] under her bed" following this incident and "bit[ing] herself for her stupidity," reciting "*[m]ei wenhau,*" [...] No culture." Young Mahlia "bit[es] herself again and again, driving the lesson home. But when she show[s] her father her bleeding hand, proving that she'd punished herself, he [...] only look[s] at her with more disappointment" (62). Mahlia internalizes her father's words to the point of self-harm, punishing herself for her perceived animality and, thus, enacting her perceived animality. Mahlia's childhood, then, was characterized by a sense of identity already tinged with associations of violence and war, framing the two sides of her racial and national identity in opposition. Mahlia believes that "she was the same as the people [her father] fought every day" (62), "[j]ust another one of the animals he'd found ungovernable" (*Drowned Cities* 63). Mahlia envisions the two sides of herself as engaged in constant war.

Mahlia's internalization of her father's labels has striking implications for her claims of Drowned Cities identity over Chinese identity. To fight for Drowned Cities belonging is also to lay claim to the violence and "no culture" of the Drowned Cities, a group "like animals," if not "less than animals," according to Mahlia's father (*Drowned Cities* 61). Indeed, Mahlia links her identity as Drowned Cities with violence and power, threatening, "[M]y old man might have been peacekeeper, but my mom was pure Drowned Cities. You want to war [...] I'm all in" (*Drowned Cities* 38).

This vision of Drowned Cities violence, however, is also wrapped up in questions of survival. Mahlia attributes her ability to survive to her Drowned Cities savagery. Equally, she equates her father's civilization with defeat, reflecting that her father had "been too damn civilized for the Drowned Cities [....] If [she] had been as civilized as the peacekeepers, she would have been dead ten times over" (*Drowned Cities* 63). At the same time, however, tensions emerge in Mahlia's vision of what it is to survive. For Mahlia, the violence that destroyed her domestic world is ordered by one clear authoritative voice. Well versed in the guns and weapons that could be heard perpetually firing over her childhood home, Mahlia remembers how "[h]er father had sat by the window [...] as gunfire echoed through the canals and he had named them all. '45, 30–06, AK-47, .22, QBZ-95, M-60, AA-19, AK-74, .50-caliber, 999.' Mahlia knew the many voices of war from her father's chant" (*Drowned Cities* 56). Violence is intimate, and it retains an association with both sides of Mahlia's identity—Peacekeeper and Drowned Cities.

As Mahlia allows her father's definitions to shape her sense of self, she similarly internalizes this narration of sound and destruction. As Mahlia's domestic world is destroyed by an invading army, she invokes her father's voice once more, recounting, "Later, when those guns were turned on her and she was belly-crawling out of hell, she'd known them, too: the chatter of the AKs and the bellowing of 12-gauges [...] Mahlia had whispered their names to herself as she'd tried not to be stupid and jump up like a rabbit in the open as bullets zinged all around. Trying to think like Sun Tzu and not make a fatal mistake" (*Drowned Cities* 56). Mahlia's internalization of her father's words helps her survive, even as it perpetuates a destructive vision of self and family. This tension is clear, particularly as she escapes. Mahlia draws upon her understanding of strategy—seen as "given" to her by her father—even as it means not "standing tall," a trait highly valued as civilized by Mahlia's father, in order to survive (*Drowned Cities* 61). Mahlia is caught within a dynamic that equips her to survive, all the while demanding that she "disappoint" her father's authoritative voice to survive. This tension seeps into Mahlia's vision of herself and her world. She represents her survival through her father's language: Drowned Cities' savagery cannot exist in peaceful balance with Chinese civilization. All the while, she hears this voice of civilization impose order on the sounds of indiscriminate slaughter.

Mahlia is profoundly caught up in cultural and social definitions. The rigid labels of her childhood—intimately tied to race and national identity—shape her and her initial sense of self. Mirroring the rigidity and self-hatred implied in her father's labels, Mahlia sees the world entirely through the imposed labels of her world. She is Drowned Cities, not Chinese; she is a castoff and a "maggot" (war orphan). Similarly, she sees the child soldiers she encounters as soulless, "killer[s] with footprints of blood behind [them]" (*Drowned Cities* 85). Enmeshed in the hierarchies of dystopia, Mahlia is caught up in "the tides of war" (*Drowned Cities* 313): the physical war that rages around her, the daily war she wages in asserting Drowned Cities identity over Chinese, or the internal war between two heritages that her father instilled within her.

Both Mahlia's sense of self and her actions are shaped by social currents. Mahlia's decisions are fueled by the desire to be seen as Drowned Cities, to assert her ability to fight, and to survive, as her status as maggot suggests. This focus on survival and belonging drives her initial choices. She saves Tool from infection so he will help her escape the Drowned Cities, she attacks a squad of child soldiers (a previously unthinkable action) in order to assist Tool, and she turns on the kind Dr. Mahfouz to achieve her goals.

However, her focus on survival is disrupted midway through the book. When Mouse is forced into a group of child soldiers, Mahlia decides to save him, an action that requires pursuit into the dangerous Drowned Cities. Her choice to prioritize another person over her own survival marks the first of many steps that Mahlia takes in order to finally escape the outside categorizations and forces that she sees as dictating her selfhood and choices. To fully escape the cycles of Drowned Cities violence, however, Mahlia must break free of these "tides," reconciling her fragmented visions of Chinese versus Drowned Cities and civilized versus uncivilized, and surmounting the language of "castoff" and "maggot." In short, Mahlia must come to terms with her heritage, as racial identity, national identity, and human identity are intertwined.

Mahlia finds a teacher and ally in Tool, the genetically modified soldier and "half-man," whom she enlists to help her reenter the Drowned Cities. While their arrangement is initially tenuous and born of self-interest, an intimacy slowly grows between them as Tool becomes an unlikely mentor. Indeed, many of the struggles Tool faces between his animal identity—and the valences of "savagery" it carries with it—and his human identity directly mirror the discourse that has defined Mahlia. Ultimately, Mahlia must adopt Tool's model of identity so that her own vision of self can evolve, with far-reaching implications for questions of race, nation, and self within the narrative. I will now turn to Tool, to explore how his animal-human hybridity articulates similar questions of identity and belonging, before returning to Mahlia and her evolving vision of self.

Creature, Monster, Tool: Posthuman Selfhood

First introduced in the novel *Ship Breaker*, Tool is a "half-man," a melding of human and animal DNA. Tool is a "DNA cocktail of killing—tiger and dog and hyena, and Fates knew what else. A perfect creature, designed from the blood up to hunt and war and kill" (*Drowned Cities* 6). Tool is continually described as a "creature" and "monster" (*Drowned Cities* 8), and his monstrosity centers around his hybrid human and animal composition. Tool's unnaturalness is eerily visible in his physicality; an observer notes that "[t]hough it [...] walked like a man, when it bared its teeth, tiger fangs showed, and when it pricked up its ears, a jackal's ears listened, and when it sniffed the air, a bloodhound's nose scented" (*Drowned Cities* 6).

This elision of boundaries between human and animal lies at the core of Tool's unsettling nature. In *Representations of the Post/Human*, Elaine Grahame writes that "[o]ne of the ways in particular in which the boundaries between humans and almost-humans have been asserted is through the discourse of 'monstrosity'" (12). For Grahame, "[m]onsters serve both to mark the fault-line but also, subversively, to signal the fragility of such boundaries. They are truly 'monstrous'—[...] in their simultaneous demonstrated and destabilization of the demarcations by which cultures have separated nature from artifice, human from non-human, normal from pathological" (12). Like Grahame's model, Tool's labeling as "half-man" and "dog face" (labels that I discuss in more depth later) showcases his presence as a destabilizing force. He is a reminder of the malleability of humanness and horrifying in his resemblance to human beings.

Tool's monster status, however, extends beyond his physical body and its reminder of human fragility. In *A Manifesto for Cyborgs*, Donna Haraway writes that the "cyborg is our ontology; it gives us our politics" (8). While Tool is not a cyborg per se—a creature which "fusing cybernetic device and biological organism" ultimately "violates the human/machine distinction" to "[challenge] the human-animal difference" and "[erase] the animate/inanimate distinction"—his posthuman animal-human hybridity operates to the same effect (Hayles 85). For Haraway, the cyborg stands as a "condensed image of both imagination and material reality, the two joined centers structuring any possibility of historical transformation" (8). As a "terrifying mix of science and war," Tool persists as a fascinating embodiment of this union: a product of a war-torn America, bred for war, yet capable of resisting his genetic coding (*Drowned Cities* 6). Drawing on Haraway and Grahame's models of monstrosity and the cyborg, Tool's constructed nature emerges as deeply tied to dystopian commentary, and Tool becomes central to the question of historical transformation and societal evolution. Tool is monstrous not simply in his physicality but also in his emergence as the one most suited to the realities of the new American landscape.

Tool's name is telling. In a section entitled "Tools, Bodies, and Environments," Grahame points out that tools and their physical implications have changed in the twenty-first century (4). Tools "such as the knife, the hammer, and the water-pot," "simple instruments of extension and containment," which were vital for human survival yet separate from human physicality, are now replaced by tools which demand that "the very boundaries between the human and the machinic is [sic] redrawn" (4). Thus, as performance artist Stelarc asserts, "[t]he contours of human bodies" change, and the skin, which "has been a boundary for the soul, for the self," is altered: the "'skin as a barrier is erased'" (as cited by Grahame 4[1]).

As an "augment," Tool embodies this vision, his name acknowledging that he stands as an evolution of the human tool. As a half-man, however, Tool troubles the boundaries of human physicality, this piercing of the skin, with its connotations for selfhood, seems to work both ways. Indeed, Tool's genetic coding should force him to relinquish his selfhood. Augments are meant to possess unwavering loyalty to the humans who command them. When their human commanders die, they are meant to die too, to lose all will to live. Tool, however, rejects this coding, living despite this commander's death. Rather than animality co-opting and warping human selfhood, Tool's hybridity has achieved the opposite effect, with Tool's individuality and capability for human logic and reasoning creating a new kind of hybrid creation.

While Tool rejects both the genetic coding that makes him a "tool" and his functions as a tool of war and humanity, he embraces his name, as well as some of the labels that mark him as nonhuman. Similarly, Tool accepts the labels "augment" or "half-man"; the only label he rejects is "dog-face." With these labels, Tool seems to acknowledge the many facets of himself: he embraces not only his hybridity and augmentation but also the tensions implicit in his name and what it signals about his birth. He rejects labels that cast him as an animal, reducing him to a singular component of his identity. Interestingly, his very rejection of certain terms highlights the unsettling human-animal balance that comprise him. When called "dog-face" by a ferry-man, Tool "growl[s] and bare[s] his tiger teeth. 'You may call me Tool, or half-man or augment, but if you think to call me dog-face again, I will tear open your chest, and eat your heart" (*Drowned Cities* 308). Here, Tool's very human articulation of labels and preference is underscored by his animal qualities: the bared tiger teeth, the threat to dismember and eat. Even further, Tool's delivery points to his ability to strategically deploy the animal parts of himself—Tool is very much in command of his physicality and the various animal traits that compose it. This command of his animality is striking too, as it furthers an otherwise "human" interaction: a conversation and negotiation. Even as Tool brings out his "tiger teeth" and threatens to consume the ferry-man, he evokes his animal violence for effective strategic purposes. Following Grahame's model, Tool's unsettling potential lies in the easy elision of categories of human and animal. His name, and the labels he chooses to assume, reflects his same tension and hybrid power.

At the Gates of Difference: Mahlia, Tool, and the Drowned Cities

In *Monster Theory: Reading Culture*, Jeffrey Jerome Cohen writes that monsters mark "the gate of difference" (7). Monsters are an "embodiment of the unknown yet also the keeper of the portal between the same and the other": their monstrosity demarcates boundaries even as it transgresses them (Grahame 52). As markers of boundaries, monsters are intimately tied to the social health of a society. Their presence signals some larger social ailment or failure, "prompt[ing] the question 'How could this have happened?'" (Grahame 52), or more specifically, how could society have allowed this to happen? Following Cohen's model, as Mahlia's sense of self becomes increasingly linked with Tool's, the idea of standing at "the gates of difference" emerges with increasing force for both Mahlia and Tool, as their senses of identity, self, and difference are pressured through the gaze and influence of the other (Grahame 52).

From their very first encounter, Mahlia finds that Tool disrupts her sense of herself as human. Caught in Tool's grasp, Mahlia is reduced to animal, recounting, "[s]he wasn't a person anymore. Just prey. […] Prey for other bigger, stronger animals" (*Drowned Cities* 77). While she and Tool rapidly move towards an alliance, Mahlia continues to find this question of predator and prey, animal and human, fascinating and unsettling. Her shock and terror stem from the destabilizing fact that Tool "just seem[s] too human [...] One minute [he] had been a beast; the next, a person" (*Drowned Cities* 72).

Immediately, a significant link between these two characters emerges, as one struggles with internalized visions of her own animality, and the other is actually made of composite animals. Tool unsettles Mahlia because he stands as a marker of difference—his very features blur, but also mark, the separation between animal and human. However, Tool also unsettles Mahlia, on a deeper level, as he reduces her to animal as well, turning her into "prey" on a larger, dystopian food chain. From their first meeting, then, Tool brings out the internalized vision of self that Mahlia has, to some degree, been carrying with her since her childhood. And, although Mahlia continually references her father's linking of Drowned Cities identity with animal identity, this is the first moment in the text where Mahlia situates herself as an animal. Tool's presence, then, pressures Mahlia's own status as marking the "gates of difference," simultaneously marking and transgressing an animal and human identity which deeply aligns with her vision of Chinese and Drowned Cities.

This sense of Mahlia's monstrosity, which in its ties to her parentage is inherently connected to questions of "[h]ow could this have happened?," is reinforced in Mahlia's social world, reflected in the demonization of castoffs (Grahame 52). In the town where she initially and precariously resides, Mahlia is seen as a purveyor of bad luck, and she is accused of "kill[ing] things [...] Everywhere she goes. Nothing but blood and death" (*Drowned Cities* 27). Mahlia is, in part, ostracized because of her experiences of violence and her link to a violent past. Interestingly, Mahlia seems partially aware of the dynamics surrounding her monstrosity early in the narrative, threatening one townswoman, "Maybe I cut you the same way the Army of God cut me. See how you do with just a lucky left. How'd you like that?" (*Drowned Cities* 38). Here, Mahlia acknowledges and uses her "monstrosity" to threaten and intimidate, recognizing that her very body—both her racial identity and her missing hand—reminds the townspeople of the precariousness of their peaceful lives. Her experiences mark the collapse of power and stability, the dissolution of the family unit, and the vulnerability of individual bodies in the face of armies. Mahlia stands as a reminder that all can, at any moment, be subject to the violence of child soldiers; her presence and the traumas she has experienced point to the easily shifting boundaries between peace and war as her existence is a reminder of the fragility of the Drowned Cities and its surrounding territories.

Thus, Mahlia becomes "monstrous" both in terms of her own internalized sense of self as human and animal and in her social signification. She implicitly acknowledges and embraces this vision of herself as "monster," a fact that, in turn, is caught up in the previously discussed ways that Mahlia sees herself defined by larger social tides as she internalizes discrete ideas of "Drowned Cities," "Chinese," "animal," "castoff," and "maggot." When she meets Tool, however, becoming "prey" and questioning his own human/animal identities, these ontological categories are, for the first time, troubled.

This internal destabilization quickly spirals outwards. As Mahlia and Tool return to the Drowned Cities, the opportunity to see another "monster" and to acknowledge the ontological questions his presence raises offers Mahlia a chance to reinterrogate her own social coding. Mahlia is initially uneasy with Tool because of his refusal to be one thing or another. Watching Tool eat, early on their journey, Mahlia reflects that "[w]atching something that looked so nearly like a human being feed like a beast—it wasn't natural, and it filled [her] with queasy dread" (*Drowned Cities* 176). As they approach the Drowned Cities, however, her compartmentalized vision of Tool as moving between either human or animal shifts subtly. Mahlia becomes "aware again of how many layers affected the creature. Part human, part dog, part tiger, part hyena ... pure predator" (*Drowned Cities* 312). This shift in language marks a subtle departure from earlier descriptions of boundary violation and their accompanying feelings of "dread." Rather than seeing Tool as a creature that moves uncontrollably between human and animal, Mahlia becomes aware of his "layers," and in their unity, she reflects that "as they [approach] the Drowned Cities, Tool seem[s] more and more alive. His huge frame seem[s] to pulse with the vitality of war. The hunger to hunt" (*Drowned Cities* 312).

The gradual shift in Mahlia's perception of Tool is brought to its climax as Mahlia, now a beaten and maimed prisoner of General Stern, the leader of the army that conscripted Mouse, watches as Stern tries to convince a captured Tool to join his cause. Offering Tool the chance to be his second in command, to fulfill his "function" as warrior and soldier, Stern hopes Tool will assist him in conquering the remnants of the United States, using Mahlia as his bartering tool. As Mahlia watches, she reflects that "[a]ll Tool's life, men like Stern had found a use for him. The half-man was, as his name implied, useful. Something men sought to wield, again and again" (*Drowned Cities* 396). This recognition of Tool and the issues that surround his posthuman status leads to a realization of her own. The survival-focused Mahlia realizes that "if men like Glenn Stern and the rest of the grown-ups in this room had a use for you, you could live a little while. But you were just a pawn. Her. Mouse. All those soldier boys who'd been hand-raised to shoot and knife and bleed out there in the Drowned Cities" (*Drowned Cities* 400).

As Mahlia sees how she herself is used as a tool, her vision of herself as merely swept along in outside cycles of violence and social labels falls away. Mahlia "thought that she'd been surviving. She thought that she'd been fighting for herself" (*Drowned Cities* 400–1). But in this moment, Mahlia realizes that her acts of survival have not been independent, active choices and that her assertions of identity have been similarly shaped and used by outside forces. "All she'd done," Mahlia reflects, "was to create more killing, and in the end it had all led to this moment, where they bargained with a demon of the Drowned Cities, not for their lives, but for their souls" (400–1).

This ontological shift is striking. As Tool's presence fulfills its posthuman, destabilizing function, General Stern's own monstrosity is made manifest. Together, they are "[t]wo monsters. Two killing creatures, bargaining and testing each other" (*Drowned Cities* 399). But only Stern, the human, is a "demon" (*Drowned Cities* 403). Whereas Tool is a "killing creature" because he was designed to be one, Stern has chosen to be one, and the evocation of the idea of the soul highlights his true monstrosity. Here, the soul—assumed to accompany humanness—is explicitly stripped from Stern, but not from Tool, despite his human-animal hybridity. Haraway's destabilization of boundaries is taken further, as it extends beyond physical disruption to question Stern's very status as "human" and to complicate assumptions of soul as comprising only human identity.

In keeping with this destabilization, Mahlia decides that she will no longer be a pawn in the cyclical violence of her world, concluding that she is "[d]one with the bargaining that always said that if she wanted to live, someone else had to die"; her resolution is also articulated through language of self and the body. Mahlia demands that Tool ask Stern "if he'll give me my fingers back [...] Long as he's making pretty promises, ask him if he's got my pinky somewhere. He gonna sew me back together?" (401).

Earlier in the book, Mahlia's missing hand served as a reminder of state violence and human fragility: it was a warning and threat that she herself used to intimidate the people around her. Now, she evokes her missing hand and fingers to signal her awareness of the impossibility of Stern's promise. Stern is not offering true survival; rather, he wants to conscript Tool and Mahlia back into their proper functions. Stern hopes that Mahlia and Tool will save themselves by waging war on his behalf, just as Stern's soldiers are children who are spared death if they agree "to shoot [...] and bleed out there in the Drowned Cities" (*Drowned Cities* 400). Pointing to her own bodily trauma, Mahlia identifies this offer for what it is—another form of violence using her body as an object of social definition and control, which will offer no ultimate survival or escape.

At this point in the book, the language of "maggot" and "castoff" disappears, and the labels and divisions which so ordered Mahlia's vision of herself and other people fall away. Faced with Ocho, the child soldier who rescues her from Stern, Mahlia suddenly sees him as more than a simple "soldier boy," recognizing "[s]ome part of whatever the sergeant had been before [...] The scared kid who'd been beaten and whipped and shoved around so long he'd almost lost every bit of his humanity. He was right there. A whole other person" (*Drowned Cities* 434).

Similarly, Mahlia's final escape from the Drowned Cities suggests a need for unification, and her escape aligns her—for one final moment—with Tool. Just as the Drowned Cities seem to summon a more cohesive vision of Tool, energizing him and his many layers, they are similarly linked to Mahlia and her own understanding of selfhood. Returning to her childhood home, the "tower of [her] memories" (*Drowned Cities* 340), Mahlia must finally lay to rest the vision of herself, in the fact of her racial mixing, as fragmented, and this shift is intimately tied with her sense of ownership over the city where she was born. As Mahlia returns to the Drowned Cities, she sees it with "a strange double vision," "memory and reality, superimposed" as the reality of the war-torn city stands in stark contrast with her memories of the city as a "place of play" with "[h]er school, her life with her mother and father, the collectors who came to buy antiques from her mother" (*Drowned Cities* 310–11). This schism is a relatively false one: Mahlia's childhood was far from happy, and her home was far from this "playful" space that she represents it to be, with war always hovering as a threat.

However, the juxtaposition between her two visions of the city is striking. Just as Tool's presence pressures and reveals the realities of war and cyclical violence, here, Mahlia's gaze reveals the reality of dystopian decline. Only Mahlia knows how the city has decayed, both in her ability to imagine the city preconquest and in her knowledge of American history. Indeed, wherever Mahlia looks in the Drowned Cities, she sees layers of history. Gazing on the ruins of the Capitol building, she reflects, "the place looked even worse than when she'd been here before, when her father had taken her to see the eagles and ancient sigils of a long-dead nation" (*Drowned Cities* 377). Here, Mahlia sees how the Cities have declined since her childhood, but she also sees the remnants of America. She alone recognizes the significance of the building and realizes that its actual power ended long ago—that this is simply a relic.

This language of death points again to the divisions that saturated Mahlia's childhood sense of the world. Reflecting his status as an outsider and his vision of Drowned Cities inhabitants as animals, Mahlia's father sees the remains of their civilization as "dead," reminders of their decline. And, reflecting his hatred towards Drowned Cities inhabitants, his interests in American history and his family are ultimately implied to be monetary: as a collector, her father saw his family as part and parcel of this collection and stored the money Mahlia's mother made in a bank in China. In contrast, even as Mahlia's mother was also interested in history as a means of making money, her emphasis lay on value, on teaching Mahlia the importance of "the stories behind" the remnants of America (*Drowned Cities* 260–61). Mahlia's mother was a "respected handler of antiquities" rather than a mercenary, and she taught Mahlia to "move . . . and blend . . . between two worlds," to "float the Drowned Cities" and "scavenge with the best," while simultaneously "mak[ing] foreign buyers look at her and take her seriously" (*Drowned Cities* 340).

As Mahlia makes her escape, leading Ocho and his soldiers to her mother's warehouse and using the artifacts there to buy their way to freedom, she uses both of her parents' legacies. Mahlia takes the soldiers to where "the warehouse lay waiting. Her mother's collection. Her father's hoarding. All of it still there [. . . .] Paintings and statuary and ancient books. The treasure trove of a dead nation" (*Drowned Cities* 427). Unlike Mahlia's earlier survival, represented to herself as made possible by her "uncivilized" Drowned Cities identity, even as it paradoxically was enmeshed in her association of her father with violence, this time, Mahlia unifies both sides of her heritage. Drawing on each parent's legacy and accepting the ugliness of her father's "hoarding" and betrayal, she takes their collections and, escorted by the former soldiers, goes to negotiate with the very "blood buyers"[2] whom her mother sold to. Unifying the lessons of both her mother and father, Mahlia escapes the Drowned Cities as a result of her once-rejected status as "castoff," a national and cultural mix.

Tool also finds resolution in a similar claiming of cohesive, Drowned Cities identity. Remaining behind as the city descends into chaos, Tool states, "The Drowned Cities may not be a place for you, but to me ... [t]his smells like home." Asserting his status as a "master" of war, Tool plans to unify the remnants of General Stern's army, whose "soldiers will need safe haven. They will hunger for a leader." Tool reflects, "I have fought on seven continents, but never for territory of my own [. . . .] Where you see terror, I see ... sanctuary" (*Drowned Cities* 428). As Tool lays claim to the Drowned Cities as his own, Mahlia "[f]or the first time" "[sees] him true: not a mix of creatures, but a singular whole, built entirely for war. Entirely at home" (*Drowned Cities* 429). Finally recognizing and coming to terms with Tool's hybridity, Mahlia's cohesive vision of Tool comes just moments before she makes her own escape. By confronting and, ultimately, mirroring Tool's status as posthuman "monster," Mahlia is offered the opportunity to see her identity as something unified, in contrast to the fragmented, rigid versions of identity proffered first by her father, then by her society, which pushed her to compartmentalize her Drowned Cities and Chinese selves.

However, as this resolution occurs, the issue of race—so painstakingly layered with questions of national belonging, family identity, and social status—is omitted from the conclusion of the narrative. It is the Drowned Cities identity that becomes the "answer" here, offering Tool a haven and Mahlia a means of escape as she draws upon history and her family's shared knowledge. Reflected in this elision, as Mahlia prepares to board a blood buyer's ship and to finally leave the Drowned Cities behind, she has one final crisis of self. Ocho, afraid and "touch[ing] his check and his brand," wonders if their saviors will really accept them, or if "they'll know what we did [...] They'll know what we are" (*Drowned Cities* 433). Mahlia "tr[ies] to tell him that everything [will] be okay. They [can] buy respect. They [can] go someplace where no one has even heard of the UPF or the Drowned Cities [...] They [can] disappear from everything that they'd been" (*Drowned Cities* 434). But she looks "down at her own hands, her missing right and the bandage on her left," and "wonder[s] the same thing herself. What good was anyone going to find in a doctor girl who only [has] four fingers?" (*Drowned Cities* 434).

As Mahlia looks at herself, she faces a new ontological question. No longer concerned with status as castoff or maggot, she—for one of the first times in the book—refers to herself as a "doctor," seeing herself as defined by what she hopes to be rather than by social categorization. However, even as Mahlia evokes that possibility, a new type of "difference" emerges—a difference tied to the experience of dystopian violence. Mahlia is missing one hand entirely and one finger on her remaining hand, she and the soldiers are branded on their cheeks, and as these wounds mark them as former soldiers and refugees, they suggest a new potential kind of "monstrosity." Now, it is their scars that will set them apart, that will remind those who live in safety outside of the Drowned Cities of the dystopian violence which rages across their precarious borders. It is dystopian identity, then, that emerges as the ultimate marker of "otherness," rather than any of the questions of race, racial mixing, and national identity, which so preoccupied the first half of Bacigalupi's narrative.

Conclusion: Racial Critique in Drowned Cities

At the end of *Drowned Cities*, Tool emerges as the ideal leader and master of the Drowned Cities. His rise, as he supersedes human ownership of the Drowned Cities, evokes N. Katherine Hayles's reflection that posthumanism carries with it a "terror," as "'[p]ost,' with its dual connotations of superseding the human and coming after it, hints that the days of 'the human' may be numbered" (283). Humanity, it is made clear, has no more power over the violence it has unleashed; dystopia demands not only new leaders but also new species.

What does it mean, then, that in this vision of dystopian critique and posthuman power, posthuman identity is also the key for a young mixed-race woman, struggling to escape entrapping visions of fragmented and warring selfhoods? Is this a progressive shift, an attempt to imagine a new world where multiple experiences of identity—be they national, racial, or cultural—are essential for continuation? Or is this a maneuver that merely "induce[s] fantasies about a future replete" with what Donna Haraway terms "'interracial' cyborgs," thus imagining Mahlia as an "exotic" articulation of narratives of human ontology in the face of posthuman creation (qtd. in Ifekwunigwe 2)?

I suspect that the answer lies somewhere in between. *Drowned Cities* is certainly not perfect. Even as it frames Mahlia as the central protagonist and positions her struggles with castoff identity as a central hurdle that she must surmount, the text's language of race is quite ambiguous. Mahlia never describes herself, and it's only through snippets of compared description, as she sees a man with "skin black like her mother's" (*Drowned Cities* 316), or when another character notes her "[d]ark skin and Chinese eyes" (*Drowned Cities* 334), that the fact that she is also Black is even acknowledged. This issue prevails on the cover of *The Drowned Cities*, where the dark, feminine eyes of a relatively light, if not white, face stare out. This whitewashing is even more egregious in the special edition of *Drowned Cities*, released by Subterranean Press, featuring a white-skinned, dark-haired Mahlia. While covers, of course, are not necessarily under an author's control, the fact that Mahlia's Blackness is so subtly described that it's close to hidden does seem to lend itself to this ultimate whitewashing.[3]

At the same time, however, even as *Drowned Cities* does not carry its racial narrative through—establishing the stakes of castoff identity only to silence them in the face of larger dystopian problems—the novel is notable for the critique it offers, firmly situating itself as a critical dystopia with its focus on legacy. As Mahlia looks on the Drowned Cities as the mausoleum of a dead nation and uses the relics of American history to purchase freedom, *The Drowned Cities* makes clear that the history and evils of the past cannot be escaped. There is no starting over—no rebirth from dystopia. Even the objects Mahlia uses to purchase freedom suggest this inescapability. Salvaging "old muskets" and "[u]niforms of blue and gray," Mahlia saves the remnants and relics of American objects of war (*Drowned Cities* 427), pointing to the violence which lurked, already, at the very heart of the American foundational myth. In Bacigalupi's world, dystopian America reaps the seeds it planted historically: from a heritage of war represented through sigils and relics to a history of globalism, colonialism, environmental degradation, factionalism, and religious fundamentalism, represented through the presence of child soldiers, warlords, blood buyers, and the rising tides slowly swallowing Washington, DC.

Bacigalupi's *Drowned Cities* is an ambitious, ambiguous, and imperfect text. Just as many critique *The Hunger Games* for its retreat into a heteronormative, domestic conclusion, so too perhaps can we approach Bacigalupi's narrative. As Tool pressures a new vision of identity and humanity for Mahlia—one that seems to offer powerful ways to reconcile questions of race, national identity, and heritage—these questions are raised but then relinquished. *The Drowned Cities* opens up exciting avenues for racial representation in YA dystopian literature, while ultimately failing to address the racial issues it so deftly brings to the fore. However, just as Tool and Mahlia stand as figures of disruption and difference, so too can we perhaps envision Bacigalupi's text. While not resolving its racial issues, it forcefully asserts their presence and disruption; in the process, it arguably unsettles readers' assumptions about these issues. Between castoff and half-man, unsettling questions of ontology, belonging, race, hybridity, and identity are raised. And these issues, once raised, linger, unsettle, and question, long after dystopian and American identity become the solution for the "monster" and "castoff" alike.

Notes

1. Here, Grahame cites an online interview with performance artist Stelarc by Paolo Atzori and Kirk Woolford. The full interview is available at *Ctheory*: http://www.ctheory.net/articles.aspx?id=71.

2. The "blood buyers" are traders from wealthier parts of the world and the remaining United States, who buy artifacts and relics from the Drowned Cities.

3. Portraying characters of color as white on YA book covers has been a persistent issue in YA and children's publishing. Notable examples include advanced reader copies of Justine Larbalestier's *Liar*, which featured a white model despite the fact that the protagonist is Black, and multiple editions of Ursula Le Guin's Earthsea Quartet, which feature white characters even as the book's protagonists are almost entirely people of color.

Works Cited

Bacigalupi, Paolo. *The Drowned Cities*. Little, Brown Books for Young Readers, 2012.
Bacigalupi, Paolo. *Ship Breaker*. Little, Brown Books for Young Readers, 2010.
Cohen, Jeffrey Jerome. *Monster Theory*. University of Minnesota Press, 1996.
Grahame, Elaine. *Representations of the Post/Human: Monsters, Aliens and Others in Popular Culture*. Rutgers University Press, 2002.
Haraway, Donna. "A Manifesto for Cyborgs: Science, Technology, and Socialist Feminism in the 1980s." *Feminism/Postmodernism*, edited by Linda J. Nicholson, Routledge, 1990, pp. 190–233.
Hayles, N. Katherine. *How We Became Posthuman*. University of Chicago Press, 1999.

Ifekwunigwe, Jayne O. "Introduction: Rethinking 'Mixed Race' Studies." *"Mixed Race" Studies: A Reader*, edited by Ifekwunigwe, Routledge, 2004, pp. 1–36.

Schmeink, Lars. "Coming of Age and the Other: Critical Posthumanism in Paolo Bacigalupi's *Ship Breaker* and *The Drowned Cities.*" *Posthumanism in Young Adult Fiction: Finding Humanity in a Posthuman World*, edited by Anita Tarr and Donna R. White, University Press of Mississippi, 2018, pp. 159–78.

Black Girl Magic
Bioethics and the Reinvention of the Trope of the Mad Scientist in Black YA Speculative Fiction
Esther L. Jones

Mainstream science and speculative fictions are rife with images of the "mad scientist." From as early as Mary Shelley's *Frankenstein*, which arguably serves as the prototype for the "the trope of the mad scientist," to writings in the contemporary era, images of various versions of the troubled Dr. Victor Frankenstein—isolated, obsessed with forbidden science, engaged in secret unspeakable acts that ultimately produce the most hideous of progeny or catastrophic violations of nature—abound in the popular imaginary. Even as more contemporary science fiction works move away from the depiction of the isolated scientist in pursuit of professional fame and groundbreaking glory, a number of questions remain as to what to make of such depictions. The mad scientist in the European tradition represents a collective psychic shift from the perception of doctors' presumably benevolent motives of helping and healing toward attention to the ways in which such power can devolve into malignant narcissism, resulting in unethical and corrupt practices motivated by ego, greed, and/or self-interest. Black women writers of YA and adult speculative fiction, however, offer alternative depictions of both "madness" and "the scientist." In this essay, I argue that Black women writers of speculative fiction explore representations of rage and "madness"[1] through development of young Black female protagonists in order to challenge dominant stereotypes of doctors/healers as white and male and to further reinvent the trope of the mad scientist from a Black feminist ethical perspective that I call Black Girl Magic bioethics. The figure of the young female warrior-witch in works by Nnedi Okorafor and

Tomi Adeyemi catalyze rage and madness into a transformational ethics of relationality that radically reimagines readers' notions of madness as well as our images of doctors and healers. Specifically, I consider the following questions: What constitutes "madness" for whom, and why? What are the contours that shape the ethical logic that guide humane interactions with "the mad?" In particular, what kind of ethics might enable us to act humanely towards the kinds of differences that have historically been the source for justifying social and political oppression in the arenas of health and medicine? Finally, what messages are communicated to YA readers with respect to how we view and treat the relationship between anger, rage, and mental illness, or "madness," in both mainstream figures and "alien" others?

In this essay, I apply a "health humanities" approach to understanding both the realities of the current crisis in adolescent and YA mental health as well as the fictive and metaphorical representations of YA protagonists' mental health issues in Black women writers' speculative fiction. My health humanities approach weaves together humanistic methodologies of literary analysis, historical analysis, and cultural studies to challenge and illuminate our understanding of mental health as experienced by young adults living within various iterations of disordered societies. Speculative fiction is uniquely situated to explore madness both literally and figuratively because of its capacity to challenge modes of knowledge construction as well as notions of who possesses the narrative authority to write socially accepted cultural scripts. Speculative fiction performs this function through literalized metaphor. For example, real-world discourse characterizing perceived cultural or physical difference as "other" translates to depictions of literal aliens from outer space in speculative fiction. Similarly, real-world medical discourse acknowledges that the brain is the most complex and least understood organ in the human body, while other discourses, such as philosophy, focus less on the materiality of the brain as an organ/object and more on the esoteric function of the mind. Speculative fiction often exploits this tension by exploring the ambiguity surrounding the brain/mind duality, the social scripts that define mental health and illness, and the cultural conditions that shape these sociocultural narratives. In other words, mental illness is defined and managed through sociocultural scripts. Representations of young adults in YA and adult speculative fiction by Black women writers can illuminate these scripts and engage young readers in thought experiments that help them to reconsider sociocultural narratives about mental illness.

The topic of rage and madness in YA speculative fiction is of primary import, given the dramatic rise in mental health issues in adolescents in the United States over the past fifteen to twenty years (Henriques). According to psychologist Gregg Henriques, there is significant data to suggest that the rates of mental health and distress in children, adolescents, and young adults have been on the rise since the 2000s. In the studies focusing on college students, the data indicates, "perhaps 10% were self-identified and seeking treatment in the 1980s, [whereas] now approximately 33% are" (Henriques). Furthermore, this rising trend is not specific to college students; rather, the trend reflects the experiences of this generation of young people as a whole. From 2006 to 2016, the suicide rate for adolescents and young adults increased at a rate of 50 percent; likewise, the National Institute for Mental Health has noted a near 50 percent increase in the number of diagnoses of major depressive disorder in adolescents (Henriques). These percentages suggest that, while help-seeking behaviors and diagnoses have increased alongside decreased stigma surrounding getting help, there has also been a real and substantial increase in actual levels of mental illness among young adults, particularly in the areas of anxiety, depression, and suicidal ideation (Henriques). These shifts in the mental health landscape cut across gender, class/socioeconomic status, race/ethnicity, and geographic location (Twenge 10). The social conditions of global warming, political instability, heightened intolerance, unsustainable personal and national debt, and so on create the conditions of a disordered society not unlike dystopian worlds so often featured in YASF and undoubtedly contribute to increased anxiety and depression for young adults. The "escapist" world of speculative fiction offers images of young people as active agents, frequently shaping more positive outcomes in chaotic worlds. Now, more than ever, we must explore the varied messages that young adults receive about mental health in a range of contexts, perhaps especially so in media historically regarded as "escapist," and consider the ways such depictions might creatively cultivate new habits of mind regarding YA agency, resourcefulness, and resiliency.

Complicating my analysis is the well-documented concern that much of mainstream YASF does not deal with ethnic characters in particularly complex ways—especially surrounding such a challenging topic as mental health. In her book *The Dark Fantastic: Race and the Imagination from Harry Potter to The Hunger Games,* Ebony Elizabeth Thomas calls attention to what she describes as the diversity crisis in children's and YA media, elaborating upon the problem of representation by mainstream (white) authors (1–4). Her analysis builds on work by Isiah Lavender, among other scholars, who explores the problematic "ethnoscapes" of mainstream science fiction. This essay, however, shifts focus to the ways in which Black writers of young adult and adult speculative fiction produce narratives of mental health featuring young adult Black protagonists that suggest alternate ways of seeing, understanding, and engaging mental health issues in young Black adults as a vulnerable population.

Three assumptions not commonly shared in the critical body of work on science fiction generally and YASF specifically undergird my argument. First, a sufficient body of science fiction writing by "ethnic" authors currently exists to begin to challenge the problematic representations of ethnic youths by mainstream (white) authors. Second, calling out and critiquing white authors' failed attempts at ethnic representation in mainstream (white) speculative fiction is a necessary, but insufficient, condition of remedying the problem of racist reifications of ethnic people in YASF. And finally, if YASF is a place where young adults learn how to understand difference and how to engage it—for good or for ill—then we, as both readers and scholars, must also attend to the ways in which the adults who write mainstream YASF themselves learn to think about race and racialization through the very genre in which they write. To this latter point, I argue that if there is to be a paradigm shift in ethnic and racial representation in YASF, it must begin with learning how to read both adult and YASF written by ethnic writers. Thus, I examine representations of Black female young adults in Black speculative fiction written for both YA and adult audiences by taking up the ways Black girls' rage is represented in the witch-warrior figure as a signification upon the Eurocentric "trope of the mad scientist." I then articulate the idea of Black Girl Magic bioethics—that is, a young, Black, female-centered ethics of relationality that functions as an important site for thinking through the rescripting of powerful sociocultural narratives of mental health and illness.

Tomi Adeyemi's *Children of Blood and Bone* opens in a girls' secret training dojo, which is disguised as a seamstress shop. There, the young protagonist, Zélie, is learning a fierce form of combat known as "the way of the staff" (Adeyemi 16). Within the novel's first few pages, readers learn that Zélie is a socially outcast *maji*, a class of magical people in an alternative Africa who once abused the great powers they possessed, now reduced to the pejorative slur "maggot" because of their distinctive white hair (6). In the first chapter, the text introduces Zélie's outcast status, her fierceness as a fighter, and her vulnerability to physical, social, and political abuse because of her social status as a *maji*. Having witnessed, as a child, the murder of her *maji* mother and having been subjected to the threat of rape in the novel's first few pages, Zélie appears to be a young woman full of anger and rage. In short, Zélie is "mad." The straight white hair and silver eyes that mark her as a *maji* serve as stigmatized physical markers of her difference and signal the potential of her latent magical abilities. Because she is easily identifiable as an outcast "other," Zélie must train to resist her oppressors using physical combat skill and ethical reasoning. "[T]he way of the staff" emblematizes what I have called elsewhere a Black feminist ethic of relationality: "It avoids rather than hurts, it hurts rather than maims, it maims rather than kills—the staff does not destroy" (Adeyemi 16). "The way of the staff" embraces the strength to fight but also the strength of restraint in that fight by adopting a code of ethics that "refuses to marginalize and mistreat others in the ways [Black women] have been mistreated" (Jones 4).

Similarly, Nnedi Okorafor's *Who Fears Death* features Onyesonwu, a young female protagonist whose difference as an *ewu* child—defined in the novel as someone who is the product of militarized rape of Okeke women by Nuru soldiers and, therefore, expected to be prone to violence—is physically marked by pale skin and lighter-colored hair in contrast to the brown-skinned, black-haired norm of the novel's futuristic African setting. Onyesonwu is introduced as she grieves for her dead stepfather, who was one of the only members of her community who treated her and her mother with dignity and respect in spite of the strong cultural scripts that stigmatize and marginalize *ewu* children and their mothers, who are products and survivors of rape, respectively. Intertwined with her grief is her rage at the society that has created the conditions that would take the goodness represented by her stepfather while allowing those who are violent and brutal to reign with impunity. Onyesonwu is known for her short temper and her impatience at being denied access to opportunities for self-actualization based on her gender and her *ewu* status, and it is in this scene that her burgeoning magical gifts as a sorcerer, which she has been working to control, erupt publicly. In this society, magic is known to exist, but is considered taboo and dangerous; therefore, exposure of her magical abilities to the community only furthered society's idea of her as outcast and dangerous.

Zélie's and Onyesonwu's anger, which ultimately transforms into rage, is an appropriate response to social injustice, bigotry, and oppression even as the societies in which they live attempt to circumscribe what constitutes socially acceptable responses to experiences of injustice, and they are both driven by a social justice imperative to end the oppression they and their loved ones experience. Unlike Victor Frankenstein, whose "madness" is driven by aspirations for personal fame and professional glory, Zélie and Onyesonwu's rage and "madness" are rooted in the protest against oppressive social codes and norms, aligning them more with the sensibilities of Frankenstein's "monstrous" creation than the creator. The excessive taxation and brutal oppression that *maji* endure are the result of a vengeful upending of the power hierarchy from a previous era when *maji* dominated society and oppressed nonmagic folk. The cyclical nature of reproducing hierarchy also reproduces systems of oppression, forever trading positions of dominance and suppression. Such patterns are difficult to end in the wake of vengeance politics. The outcast status of *ewu* children varies, however, according to their geographic location. The disfranchisement of *ewu* people intensifies in those towns nearest to the center of the conflict between the Nuru and Okeke. Merely shut out of societal norms and customs related to marriage and childbearing in her hometown, Onyesonwu learns on her journey to end the fighting that *ewu* are treated far worse in other towns. In fact, many are forced into prostitution and enslaved.

Both Zélie and Onyesonwu undergo a spiritual "awakening" and a series of initiations before they can access the full potential of their magical powers, which will help them to end the violence in their societies. It is important to note that, while belief in "magic" and spirits constitutes a form of insanity or madness in the "real world" according to a Western worldview—making it a signal feature of fantasy in mainstream speculative fiction—belief in the spirit world and inexplicable magical phenomena in African epistemology is for many Africans part of their everyday reality. Hence, in African-based speculative fiction, the fantastical elements have less to do with the existence of a spirit world and magic and more with futuristic or alternate settings that upend mainstream assumptions of normativity (such as colonial beauty standards that equate white skin and hair with attractiveness and status) and, in turn, center African culture as richly innovative, technologically complex, and future oriented from a distinctly African perspective. Such world creation is what distinguishes Black and African speculation from magical realism, which tends to be more firmly rooted in contemporaneous or historical mimetic reality. In this way, reading African speculative fiction can shed light on the ways in which mental illness, madness, insanity, and all other stigmatizing labels for cognitive and/or epistemological difference might be socially constructed. The stories we tell about what constitutes mental health and mental illness change over time, and the stories change according to societal norms and contexts as well.

Strikingly, the literary speculations on Black female rage and mental illness or "madness" echo real-world issues surrounding Black women's mental health. One example is the story of Henrietta Lacks and her family. Henrietta Lacks was a Black woman from Baltimore who died in 1951 from cervical cancer (Skloot 3). Her cells were harvested, cultured, and used to generate the first immortal cell culture for medical research resulting in the HeLa cell line, which has been used to develop drugs for everything from influenza to Parkinson's disease (Skloot 4). Lacks's cells, however, were collected without her or her family's knowledge or consent, and doctors continued to test members of her family without their proper understanding of the purpose for continued testing of the family's biospecimens (Skloot 6). In the book describing Lacks and her family's experiences, Lacks's daughter Deborah is depicted as experiencing significant anxiety and mental distress over the way in which her mother's body was used for science. She describes the profound effect the revelation had on her mental and physical health:

> I always thought it was strange: if our mother cells done so much for medicine, how come her family can't afford to see no doctors? Don't make no sense. People got rich off my mother without us even knowing about them taking her cells, now we don't get a dime. *I used to get so mad about that to where it made me sick and I had to take pills.* But I don't got it in me no more to fight. I just want to know who my mother was. (Skloot 9; emphasis mine)

Deborah's question in this passage, posed with what Martin Luther King Jr. would have called "ungrammatical profundity" (Rieder 185), recognizes the paradox of many American Blacks' relationship with medicine when she remarks upon the contribution of her mother's cells to medicine and her family's struggle to access basic health care. Her query further evokes concerns central to all Black people about the unethical treatment Blacks have historically experienced at the hands of the medical establishment. Her experience highlights how, historically, Black people have been used as test subjects to advance science for everyone, while at the same time, agents of the medical establishment invoke charges of inherent racial defect to limit the social policies that might extend the benefits of medical science to Black persons. More important to this analysis, however, is how Deborah's stress and anxiety are central: she identifies her anger and rage at systemic racism and injustice in the medical system as the source of her physical illness. Indeed, at various points in the text, Rebecca Skloot describes Deborah as swinging between mania and depression, paranoia and hopefulness, rage and peace despite the cocktail of medications that she used in an attempt to manage her mental and physical health. These observations reveal the ways in which racism impacts mental health and physiological illness. In short, the Lacks family's poverty, their knowledge of medical malfeasance, and their recognition of injustice all combine to produce the anger, anxiety, and subsequent hypertension that Deborah describes as the primary social determinant of her poor mental and physical health. Further, the situation highlights the role of medical malfeasance as the source of generational trauma that actually contributes to, if not creates, poor mental health from one generation to the next. For this reason, it is difficult to separate the effects of medical malfeasance based on social/racial position and the subsequent trauma that is inflicted on Black adults from the impact it has on Black young adults. This is why it is crucial to think about depictions of young adults in both YA and adult speculative fiction; it offers an opportunity to map the intersection of multiple vulnerabilities around race, gender, and age in societies that are designed to diminish Black survival.

The culturally devalued position of poverty and perceived ignorance of the Lacks family maps onto the ways in which Deborah's understanding of spirituality is also diminished, relating to the previous discussion of the reality of spirits in African-based worldviews. Deborah's belief that her mother's "spirit" lives on through the HeLa cell culture and possesses the capacity to exact material vengeance in the real world is presented with near-dismissive neutrality in the text. Read in relation to the descriptions of anxiety, anger, depression, and the other episodes underscoring the profound mental and emotional effect of science and society's abuse, from Deborah's perspective, of her mother and her family, Skloot's narrative walks a fine line to avoid overtly stating that Deborah is mentally ill by allowing the audience to interpret the behavioral "evidence" for themselves. If read according to mainstream Western medicalized standards, Deborah's belief in the world of spirit and her mother's continued influence on the material world—in the spirit and in the flesh—is evidence of mental illness. When read according to African-based epistemes, the belief in spirits does not constitute a legitimate data point for labeling someone mentally ill. This is not to dismiss the anxiety and stress that Deborah clearly exhibits, however; rather, it is to suggest that the constellation of factors contributing to mental illness must be more carefully parsed to understand how the societal conditions (in this instance, racism, classism, and poverty) and narratization of worldviews (Euro centered versus African centered) interact to produce varied understandings of mental illness as well as approaches to treating mental illness. Parsing these distinctions may, in turn, enable us to behave more ethically across perceived differences.

While it is true that Skloot's *The Immortal Life of Henrietta Lacks* has raised considerable insight into myriad bioethical issues surrounding informed consent, vulnerable populations, and the intersections of race, culture, poverty and heath care access and equity, the ethical breaches specifically around the treatment of the Lacks family continues. Since the publication of Skloot's book, it would seem that the medical establishment as a whole would embrace the positive potential for the publication of the Lacks family story to generate better, more informed ethical behavior given the newly highlighted conversations around the use of the HeLa cell line. Surely, the text would have helped us to learn our ethical lessons.

However, in 2013, scientists at the European Molecular Biology Laboratory mapped the full genome of the HeLa cells and published it online, without the family's knowledge or consent (Landry 1213). The scientists responsible justified their decision to do so with the disingenuous claim that "we cannot infer anything about Henrietta Lacks' genome, or about her descendants, from the data generated in this study." Other experts, however, took to Twitter to debunk the claim for the lie that it was (Skloot, "The Immortal Life of Henrietta Lacks, the Sequel"). This breach constitutes ethical violations related to privacy and consent, and the ways in which, despite the presumably heightened awareness of ethical problems specifically related to the HeLa line, scientists continue to gamble with the lives of this family (Callaway 132). So the guiding questions that emerge in the speculative fiction of Adeyemi and Okorafor converge with real-world issues in a seemingly immortal cycle: Despite the altruistic aims of medicine, why are some bodies treated unethically and inequitably? And what kind of ethical framework must be constructed if we are to relate humanely across perceived differences, especially as they relate to anger, which evolves to rage in the light of ongoing abuse, and ultimately results in the potential for madness and mental illness? The "madness" of Zélie, Onyesonwu, and Deborah stems from a righteous indignation at social injustice. In the works of Adeyemi and Okorafor, readers are invited to imagine a different destiny for someone like Deborah. The capacity to simultaneously develop and manage the rage at injustice productively becomes the source of Zélie and Onyesonwu's transformational Black Girl Magic in a version of agency that is too often denied Black girls and women in ordinary reality, and that certainly seemed to be routinely denied Deborah and the Lacks family.

In Adeyemi and Okorafor's texts, Black Girl Magic becomes the metaphor for an ethics of relationality. Zélie and Onyesonwu embody the defining terms of the popular concept defined on urbandictionary.com as "the art of pure, unadulterated dopeness that every Black woman exudes, which beholds not only her internal and external beauty but demonstrates the glory of God the Creator." In these texts and in everyday realities, Black girls are perceived by most societies' norms of physical beauty as unattractive, yet they embrace their physical difference as an accentuating adornment. Zélie and Onywesonwu's "big" hair is a focal point for this difference; their hair, in its natural state, functions as a site of visibility and resistance in the length and fullness of it that they flaunt rather than hide as their crowning "glory." Unapologetic about being born this way, Zélie and Onyesonwu express the ways in which the everyday reality of the politics of Black women's natural hair is claimed as a source of both stigmatizing difference by others and of conscious pride by Black women. It is because of this persecution of their difference based in part on seemingly frivolous physical markers that the internal grit and determination to create a more just society—the internal beauty articulated in the definition above—emerges to shape their external beauty as expressed in their ethics of relationality. Their magical powers are awakened through a series of rituals that enable them to channel their rage at society's unjustified oppression into powerful efforts to end the cycles of dominance and oppression from generation to generation.

The awakening of Zélie's and Onyesonwu's magical abilities is accompanied by physical combat training. This duality of magical abilities and physical training pairs the necessity for preparing for basic, everyday survival while at the same time seeking out ways to most powerfully wield gifts that come from within, or their "magic." These dualities call for a balancing of opposites that animates the potential for the so-called subjugated to become saviors. They realize that as sorcerers or witches, the most effective healer is also the most effective killer, and they cultivate the art of restraint in striking that balance. Resourcefulness and resilience are also hallmarks of these witches who are also warriors. As they develop their magical skills, defined as the process of becoming the bricoleur—one who uses whatever is available to do what one must do—YA readers can begin to think about "magic" as a metaphor for resourcefulness and resilience. Ironically, however, it is this mode of knowledge production that is summarily dismissed as "madness" when Western values, perspectives, and interpretations dominate the critical literature.

To that end, I argue that it is to the field of the health humanities, and the subfield of literature and medicine specifically, that we can turn to explore the ways in which literary analytical approaches illuminate and interrogate modes of knowledge construction about mental health and illness in the layered social and ethical dimensions of medicine, science, and society. Everyone must become more adept at cultivating the capacity to radically reimagine what we think we know and how we know it. A special burden to cultivate these habits of mind lies with those who wield the power of life and death in their hands as medical practitioners, but also those who seek to write creatively and speculatively about YA ethnic others.

Ultimately, these ruminations on the role of speculative fiction in shaping how to ethically relate to alien others has led me to a singular, pointed insight, and it is this: the failure to act ethically is, ultimately, a failure of the imagination. A failure of the imagination leads to a range of spectacular ethical failures like that experienced by the Lacks family. This historical example exemplifies a host of failures: the failure to imagine the potentially negative consequences and outcomes of unfettered biological and/or technological experimentation; the failure to face the evidence of our past and, in turn, the failure to imagine the possibility that the worst of human behavior and the conditions that produce such unethical action could and likely will rise again; the failure to imagine others in ways that move us outside of our own received and often richly cultivated biases; the failure to imagine the possibility of ourselves as the unethical monsters whose patterns of belief—especially as they inform practice—must be unmade.

Thus, I offer a conceptualization of YASF and its relationship to the fields of literature and medicine, narrative medicine, and more specifically bioethics. Speculative fiction represents a group of literatures characterized by their concern for the possibilities and social implications of scientific, technological, and social change; as such, it provides a dramatic mirror for bioethics (Rabkin 138). This is especially important in the realm of YASF. Bioethics in YASF provides a lens that enables us to interrogate our naturalized assumptions about our social patterns and behaviors, how we construct difference generally and mental health issues specifically, and the development of ethical codes to deal with those differences. At its best, speculative fiction raises genuinely complex questions that force the reader to reflect on personal and societal values as well as to thoughtfully consider the possible consequences of current courses of action or inaction. And as Rabkin suggests, "If we cannot adjust our ethics through a change in our own customs, our behaviors, our relations with our group, our habits, we can adjust our ethics through enlarging our habits of mind" (148).

Black women writers have long been aware of the complex nexus of personal health, larger societal problems, and the challenge of locating the kind of medical care that attends to their needs as whole persons, rendering them vulnerable subjects in many instances. Similarly, young people are vulnerable subjects in the medical arena as well, as they lack the autonomy to make decisions about their own medical care without the guidance of parents or guardians. Black women writers of YA and adult speculative fiction, however, routinely affirm the agency of historically vulnerable subjects, including young adults and people of color. These authors center perspectives of Black women and young adults and their experiences of mental health and illness, articulating methods of survival while forging an alternative ethics of relationality that refuses to marginalize and mistreat others in the way they have been treated. These writers employ methods of extrapolation and cognitive estrangement in their use of the speculative to identify historical patterns, amplify contemporary social and political problems, and envision futures in which alternate approaches to justice may be imagined. In such aspects, YASF overlaps with medical ethics, which is ultimately about achieving a form of social justice at the foundational level of health and well-being.

In focusing on the contributions of Black women writers of speculative fiction to the field of speculative fiction, medicine, and bioethics, specifically, I argue that speculative works by Black women go beyond cataloguing the historical wrongs done to them and other vulnerable populations or exploring and reifying a victimized positionality. Rather, they engage in the speculative project as means of acknowledging sources of agency, authority, and actualization that function to effectively write themselves and their progeny into futures that historical and contemporaneous instances of medical malfeasance would seemingly deny them—in other words, they imbue the project of speculative theorizations of ethical practice with Black Girl Magic.

In some of these texts by Black women speculative fiction writers, the capacity to familiarize the strange and to mystify the familiar—a process articulated in science fiction theory as cognitive estrangement—has proven generative in radically imagining new ethical relations across perceived difference. Historical and contemporary empirical realities function as sources from which Black women speculative fiction writers draw in order to extrapolate alternate and/or future worlds. As Octavia Butler suggests, speculative fiction is an apt genre for this kind of theoretical work because of the freedom and flexibility it offers to explore sociological and technological problems (Harrison 4), as well as the relationship between technological and medical breakthroughs and their impact on "the sociological aspects of our future lives" (Harrison 8). By attending to the sociology of human relations in imagined types of difference, many of these writers challenge us to consider the limitations and the malleability of ethical standards and behaviors. Thus, Black YA and adult speculative fictions feature worlds populated with images of Black young adults in times and spaces that fundamentally challenge our habituated patterns of thinking—that is, our social and cultural scripts—about race, gender, sex, and mental health. Through speculative fiction, these novelists write a future of health justice by rewriting old yet persistent cultural and social scripts that undercut the authority of Black women and girls as healing agents in their personal lives as well as that of their communities.

Black women's speculative fictions contribute to bioethics through narrative methodologies in three significant ways. First, they engage in the project of humanizing others who exemplify embodied difference, or "alien" otherness, by fleshing out the complexities of multiplicity and intersectionality in the formation of individual and collective identities. Second, they challenge traditional narratives of authority and discourse legitimation, roles historically denied young people as well as Blacks. Finally, they develop alternative ethics derived specifically from denigrated African religious traditions that have historically been characterized as "mad" from a Western standpoint. All of these strategies work together to enable readers to engage in cultivating the habits of mind necessary to imagine the possibility of ethical actions across alienate difference.

In the realm of Black women's YA and adult speculative fiction, the concerns with contemporary biomedical and ethical issues generate a challenge to the source of narrative authority. While not necessarily pitting Western biomedicine against traditional medicine, the authors invariably call out the societal structures that create the cultural context of raced, gendered, and classed experiences of health disparity and unethical treatment. As such, practices of implementing socially scripted narratives of belonging become critical touch points for the protagonists' efforts to rewrite those scripts and, in the demonstration of those efforts, force us to define and redefine notions of madness and the monstrous other.

In *Who Fears Death*, Onyesonwu's rage transforms the strong cultural scripts that define her as an *ewu* girl born as a product of militarized rape and forced impregnation. Because they are conceived in violence, *ewu* children are expected to grow up to be violent people. Indeed, Onyesonwu is full of rage as she reaches maturity and begins to understand her socially outcast status. The violence of militarized rape, however, depends on the strong social scripts that define women as literal and figurative culture bearers. The responsibility for preserving communal health falls disproportionately on their shoulders. Intransigently embedded in this portrayed society's power structure and culture, any failure to perform prescribed gender roles results in a denigrated outcast status, suggesting that individual healing can only occur when certain traditional beliefs and cultural scripts about Black girls' difference are transformed by cultural forces.

In *Children of Blood and Bone*, Zélie must pursue a number of artifacts that are purported to bring the suppressed magic of the *maji* back; vulnerability and marginality are central to her experience as a young adult and raises the stakes for the restoration of lost power so central to her quest. Her journey promises to illuminate the violently outlawed truth of the death of magic in Orisha's history as a nation. The ruling family's narrative of the death of magic perpetuates the ongoing oppression of *maji*, not because of who they are, but because of the potential of what they might become. Zélie's efforts to restore magic reveal the lies and deception of the reigning family. In this instance, cultural transformation lies not in rewriting ancient myths and falsehood but in restoring historical truth.

For both Onyesonwu and Zélie, their minoritized, liminal status as young girls of an outcast class enables a critique of the dominant culture's problematic belief systems that delimit their capacity for survival. Further, their vulnerability status is intimately linked with the highly disordered societies in which they live. This insight holds not only for the protagonists developed by Nigerian American authors Adeyemi and Okarafor, but also for other young female protagonists penned by Black women writers. Ti-Jeanne of Nalo Hopkinson's *Brown Girl in the Ring* is a third-generation Caribbean Canadian young single mother whose community is being exploited by Rudy, a dangerous drug lord whose reign is enabled by a negligent and absentee government. In Octavia Butler's *Parable of the Sower* series, protagonist Lauren Olamina lives with hyperempathy syndrome, a psychological delusional disorder that causes her to feel the pain she believes others are experiencing. This condition heightens to a disability status in the novel's dangerous postapocalyptic environment, where violence and torture, death and disease are rampant. As such, Lauren is highly invested in the ethical thoughts, beliefs, and behaviors of the desperate masses. Each text I have considered here articulates, in turn, the interplay between the vulnerability of youth, dis/ability status, and Blackness and larger societal sickness to challenge the issue of narrative authority. In the case of *Who Fears Death* and the *Parable* series, narrative authority is represented by controlling traditional religious documents that inculcate widespread problematic beliefs and practices. How these controlling narratives operate in the world is a fundamental issue, and the protagonists engage in the rewriting of such narratives as a starting point for devising a new ethics of relationality based on intersectionality, interdependency, and invitational co-creation.

Hopkinson, Butler, Okorafor, and Adeyemi, in varying ways, propose rewriting of grand narratives and controlling cultural scripts and stereotypes that call to account the sicknesses within societal systems that produce and reproduce individual and/or group illness, mental health, and disability. In this way, they reimagine bioethics and institute a cultural bioethics of relationality that is radical in its capacity to imagine the unmaking of racism, sexism, heterosexism, ableism, classism, and bigotry of all kinds. They poignantly highlight the context in which survival strategies and newly conceived ethical practices might be born, but not without the necessary process of critical reflection and interrogation of our own presumed innocence that countless ethical codes and statements of principles have tried to shore up, usually after our more monstrous tendencies have held sway in turning a blind eye to ethical breaches, and which all too often continue to fail too many of society's most vulnerable members. We need the alienating distance of speculative fiction and the glorious potentiality of Black Girl Magic to see and radically reimagine—with fresh eyes—ourselves, our societies, the complexities of our ethical failings, and our obligations to rethink mental health to create a new ethics in new ways. The capacity to achieve a future culture of health equity—only ensured by the force of our collective convictions and commitment to act humanely across all perceived difference—depends on it.

Note

1. I place quotations around "madness" and "mad" to emphasize that what constitutes madness and what it means to be mad are socially contingent and culturally scripted. Thus, being seen as "mad" is dependent on an individual's gender, race, class, location, and the time period in which they live, among other things.

Works Cited

Adeyemi, Tomi. *Children of Blood and Bone*. Henry Holt and Company, 2018.

"Black Girl Magic." *Urbandictonary.com*, 5 Oct. 2016, https://www.urbandictionary.com/define.php?term=Black+girl+magic, Accessed 25 Oct. 2019.

Butler, Octavia. *Parable of the Sower*. Four Walls Eight Windows, 1993.

Callaway, Ewen. "Deal Done over HeLa Cell Line: Family of Henrietta Lacks Agrees to Release of Genomic Data." *Nature 500*, 8 August 2013, pp. 132–33.

Harrison, Rosalie G. "Sci-Fi Visions: An Interview with Octavia Butler." *Conversations with Octavia Butler*, edited by Consuela Francis, University Press of Mississippi, 2010, pp. 3–10.

Henriques, Gregg. "The College Student Mental Health Crisis (Update): What's behind the Rise in Reported Problems." *Psychology Today*, 18 Nov. 2018, https://www.psychologytoday.com/ca/blog/theory-knowledge/201811/the-college-student-mental-health-crisis-update, Accessed 4 Nov. 2019.

Hopkinson, Nalo. *Brown Girl in the Ring*. Warner Publishing, 2018.

Jones, Esther L. *Medicine and Ethics in Black Women's Speculative Fictions*. Palgrave MacMillan, 2016.

Landry, J. J. "Genomic and Transcriptomic Landscape of a HeLa Cell Line." *G3: Genes,Genomes, Genetics*, vol. 3, no. 8, 2013, pp. 1213–24.

Okorafor, Nnedi. *Who Fears Death*. DAW Books Inc, 2010.

Rabkin, Eric. "Science Fiction and Bioethical Knowledge." *Bioethics and Biolaw through Literature*, edited by Daniela Carpi and Klaus Stierstofer, Walter de Gruyter Publishing, 2011, pp. 137–48.

Rieder, Jonathan. *Gospel of Freedom: Martin Luther King, Jr.'s Letter from Birmingham Jail and the Struggle that Changed a Nation*. Bloomsbury, 2013.

Shelley, Mary. *Frankenstein*. Norton, 2012.

Skloot, Rebecca. *The Immortal Life of Henrietta Lacks*. Broadway Books, 2010.

Skloot, Rebecca. "Opinion: The Immortal Life of Henrietta Lacks, the Sequel." *The New York Times*, 23 March 2013, https://www.nytimes.com/2013/03/24/opinion/sunday/the-immortal-life-of-henrietta-lacks-the-sequel.html, Accessed 19 November 2019.

Thomas, Ebony Elizabeth. *The Dark Fantastic: Race and the Imagination from Harry Potter to the Hunger Games*. New York University Press, 2019.

Twenge, Jean M. *iGen: Why Today's Super-Connected Kids Are Growing Up Less Rebellious, More Tolerant, Less Happy—and Completely Unprepared for Adulthood—and What That Means for the Rest of Us*. Atria Books, 2018.

Fore-fronting Race and Law
Ambelin Kwaymullina's *The Interrogation of Ashala Wolf* and Challenging the Expectations for Idealized Young Adult Heroines

Zara Rix

The politically transformative work performed by a YA text relies heavily on its publishing context. Of this, Palyku author Ambelin Kwaymullina's *The Interrogation of Ashala Wolf* (published in 2012 in Australia) is a particularly acute example. Penned by a prominent Indigenous Australian author and published alongside educational materials like study guides, discussion questions, and tips for classroom use, Kwaymullina's novel demonstrates how YA texts can serve sharp political purposes. *The Interrogation of Ashala Wolf* is the first novel in Kwaymullina's Tribe series (2012–2015) and partakes in three genres: YA literature, dystopian/utopian fiction, and Indigenous Futurism. Within the first novel of her Tribe series, the interplay of Australian law with the rights, representation, and history of Australia's Indigenous peoples combines to question of the type of citizenship the novel's youthful readers are expected to possess. Without a working knowledge of the genre of Indigenous Futurism or an understanding of Australia's political landscape, a reader misses the novel's potential to open larger questions regarding citizenship in a contemporary nation-state.

Indigenous Futurist works employ science fiction and fantasy to confront issues facing an Indigenous author's community and the political realities within which the author lives. Scholar Gerald Taiaiake Alfred (Kahnawá:ke Mohawk) argues that works of Indigenous Futurism allow Native artists and writers to simultaneously "'engage colonial power in the spirit of a struggle for survival'...[and to] 'look at traditions in a critical way, not trying to take them down, but to test them and to make sure they're still strong'" (qtd. in Dillon, "Imagining" 3). When writers employ Indigenous Futurism, critic Grace L. Dillon (Anishinaabe) argues, they "reveal Native presence" in a way that joins Native intellectualism and theory with Indigenous scientific literacies, "western techno-cultural science," and the material realities and possibilities revealed by Skin thinking ("Imagining" 2).[1] Significantly, the joining of these bodies of knowledge reconfigures speculative genres to include Indigenous patterns of knowledge. Thus, works of Indigenous Futurism reveal "that Indigenous science is not just complementary to a perceived western enlightenment but is indeed integral to a refined twenty-first-century sensibility" (*Imagining* 3). This wedding of Indigenous and Western ideologies, and the accompanying insistence that the two must live and work together in order to thrive, finds a ready home in YA literature, a genre known for its political engagement and social critiques.

Within *The Interrogation of Ashala Wolf*, Kwaymullina uses the genre of YA dystopian fiction to engage Australian law and encourage her readers to become citizens knowledgeable of their nation's history with its Indigenous peoples. In peritextual materials, she explicitly frames her readers as members of a world-wide community subject to international law. Kwaymullina's writings suggest a world in which Indigenous worldviews are affirmed and, perhaps unsurprisingly considering Kwaymullina is a lawyer, the novel emphasizes Indigenous understandings of law. To paraphrase Dillon's understanding of Indigenous science, Kwaymullina enlists the social, cultural, and political systems of her own people group, the Palyku of the Pilbara region of Western Australia, in a discourse that asks readers to understand Indigenous law not merely as a complement to a perceived Western enlightenment, but also as part of a necessary debate regarding the future of civic nations like Australia.[2] She insists that understanding Indigenous systems of law is integral to Australia's future despite the significant challenges Indigenous sovereignty poses for the nation-state. By merging this discussion with YA literature, she provides Australian youths with an Indigenous perspective on the conversation.

Significantly, Kwaymullina's joining of Indigenous Futurism with the YA genre restructures some of the powerful underlying expectations of works written for adolescents. Ideas surrounding adolescence are deeply entangled with colonial legacies, including recapitulation theory. As Nancy Lesko explains in *Act Your Age!: A Cultural Construction of Adolescence* (2001), recapitulation theory paralleled the stages of a human being's development with the "'ancestral progress of the human race'" (Ernst Haeckel, qtd. in Lesky 32). The theory provided a scientific basis for likening tribal groups to childhood and for likening the responsible, middle-class, voting adult male with a republican government, which was perceived as the evolutionary pinnacle of statehood (Lesko 32). In basing a future version of our world on understandings of law derived from the Palyku people group, Kwaymullina's work directly and indirectly acknowledges these colonial ideologies and insists upon their untruth. She therefore creates space to imagine different ideological and political futures for both young Australian citizens and YA literature.

In this essay, I begin by outlining a larger discussion surrounding the combined genres of utopia/dystopia and YA literature before examining citizenship within those arenas, focusing on the increased demands that neoliberal citizenship places on young women and Indigenous peoples. I then examine *The Interrogation of Ashala Wolf* as an intervention into the discourse surrounding Australian citizenship and ask how those of us invested in reading, teaching, and distributing YA may best understand the hope of real political change that may be found within Indigenous futurist YA.

Utopian Disruptions and the YA Novel, Its Heroines, and the Challenges of Citizenship

The fields of utopian/dystopian writing and YA literature share a desire to engage in social transformation. One of the foundational concepts of utopian and dystopian works is that they reflect the anxieties of their time of writing, operating along a continuum that reflects the social changes desired by the author or cultural milieu of their production.

Like utopian and dystopian writing, YA literature emphasizes idealism and the desire to foster awareness and action among citizens. Utopian and dystopian works intended for young adults have burgeoned in popularity in the decades since the inception of YA literature in the mid-twentieth century, and definitions of both genres assume that adolescent readers are discontented with their current world. In fact, scholars understand utopia and dystopia's entrenchment in YA literature as an extension of adolescent readers' frustrations with the adult world, particularly regarding societal power. In *Utopian and Dystopian Writing for Children and Young Adults* (2003), Carrie Hintz and Elaine Ostry demonstrate that utopian and dystopian works intended for adolescents focus upon the sociopolitical apparatus of the teenage characters' worlds: "[T]he system behind the utopia or dystopia is analyzed for the reader, and its components enumerated," so that the teenaged protagonist "comes to recognize the faults and weaknesses of his or her society, and rebels against it" (9). This collapsing of readers and teenaged protagonists—despite their vastly differing social circumstances—occurs because, Hintz and Ostry argue, "dystopia can act as a powerful metaphor for adolescence" (9). For them, personal and social awakenings occur during adolescence, causing adolescents to face questions that are central in both society and the YA genre, such as "the proper limits of freedom" and the costs of conforming to society or rebelling against it (10). Luckily, within most YA dystopia/utopias, "the adolescent knows best," so adolescent characters embody hope (10). The adolescent who survives and overcomes a dystopian world thereby becomes a cornerstone of society, a goal that the adolescent reader is expected to share.

Following the large boom of dystopian YA novels in the early twenty-first century, scholarship on the topic focused largely on the female YA protagonist, one who can be represented as an "ideal" citizen. Several of the most visible examples of the genre shared not only a dystopian setting but also a passionate young woman attempting to change her world. However, as Sara K. Day, Miranda A. Green-Barteet, and Amy L. Montz argue in *Female Rebellion in Young Adult Dystopian Fiction* (2014), the contours of the female protagonists' citizenship vary.

Before directly engaging Kwaymullina's *The Interrogation of Ashala Wolf*, a work that is both YA fiction and Indigenous Futurism, I consider two key aspects of YA female protagonists. First is Anita Harris's qualification on the changing definition of "citizenship" for youth, and particularly for young women, in the twenty-first century. This bears particular relevance as Ashala Wolf, Kwaymullina's young female protagonist, descends from a tribe of Australia's first peoples, and due to a history of invasion and colonialism, citizenship for Indigenous Australians does not comfortably fit into broader discussions of citizenship within a nation-state. The second aspect returns to a question of genre: most contemporary scholarship focuses on mainstream YA utopian or dystopian texts produced in the United States or Great Britain. While *The Interrogation of Ashala Wolf* may be discussed alongside other internationally-published YA texts, it bears distinct differences to them. Both of these points must be considered in order to examine the alternative to neoliberal citizenship proffered by the character of Ashala Wolf.

As Harris notes in *Future Girl: Young Women in the Twenty-first Century* (2004), young women are coded as ideal citizens. Twenty-first-century citizenship is based upon the political and economic ideologies of the neoliberal marketplace. Under this rubric, citizenship becomes a matter of individual responsibilities rather than state-ensured rights. Particularly for adolescents, citizenship involves "responsibilities rather than rights, managed forms of participation, and consumption" (63). Therefore, young citizens must individually assume responsibility for their social and economic rights as rights "will not be granted to them simply on reaching the age of majority" (68). Citizenship within a neoliberal nation-state is thus imagined as a protracted subjecthood that can only be surmounted once an individual achieves economic independence from family and state or, more explicitly, once one "secure[s] employment" (66). For Harris, necessitating financial independence results in a political irony in which youth are considered fully developed citizens only when they no longer call upon the state to secure their social rights (71). In this context, the bind of national expectations placed upon young people becomes particularly impossible for Indigenous populations who have suffered state-sponsored dispossession and genocide.

Central to a nation-state such as Australia is the belief that all state citizens are equal and ought to partake equally in citizenship, yet a liberal view of citizenship within settler nations suffers serious challenges from ongoing histories of invasion. In *Sovereign Subjects: Indigenous Sovereignty Matters* (2007), Aileen Moreton-Robinson (Goenpul) argues that within Australia, legal and political decisions affecting Indigenous communities are not designed to promote Indigenous sovereignty but rather to increase these communities' economic dependence on the nation-state (4). This conflict stems from the radically opposed understandings of "sovereignty" held by the Australian state and Australia's Indigenous peoples, the Aborigines and Torres Strait Islanders. As Moreton-Robinson explains, Indigenous Australian sovereignty "is embodied, it is ontological (our being) and epistemological (our way of knowing)" (2). Because Indigenous sovereignty and Indigenous social systems and systems of governance are held in and by Indigenous bodies, they cannot equate to systems imposed by the liberal nation-state. Rather, for Australian Aboriginals and Torres Strait Islanders, sovereignty derives from a web of relationships that form the foundation of Indigenous societies, from the "intersubstantiation of ancestral beings, humans and land" (2).[3] Governance models based upon social contracts, borders, and even a concept of rights simply do not fit within Indigenous frameworks of sovereignty, and this dissonance is exacerbated by the demands of neoliberal citizenship.

As both Harris and Moreton-Robinson demonstrate, young adults and Indigenous peoples find common ground in that they are similarly denied full citizenship by neoliberal states. For young adults, citizenship divorced from an age of discretion (or, to employ *Bildungsroman* themology, education) classifies those unable to secure employment as childlike subjects. Those who are not economically independent are the responsibilities of their individual families, not the state. The logic in the case of youth is that "for the state to maintain the social rights of citizenship would be to interfere with the free market and provide a disincentive to youth to become self-disciplined"

(Harris 67). For Indigenous peoples, neoliberalism's focus on individually succeeding in the marketplace interprets "the impoverished conditions under which Indigenous people live [as] a product of dysfunctional cultural traditions and social pathology" rather than long-standing policies created by the state (Moreton-Robinson 6).

Within the contradictions of this system, young women occupy a unique position. Harris argues that in the neoliberal arena of the free market, young women are simultaneously commodified and held up as the hope for the future: they are viewed as youths who are capable of achieving secure economic futures without the help of the state, they are prime consumers within the market, and they often serve as national symbols (63). However, Harris observes that the reality of young women's lives is far more complex. While contemporary realities allow some young women greater access to some educational, employment, and civic opportunities, the reconceptualization of citizenship over the past forty years has alienated others (63). The dividing line breaks according to social class and race. A young woman within a remote, impoverished Aboriginal community is not idealized as a future citizen; centuries of displacement, genocide of Native populations, and targeted disenfranchisement leave most Indigenous peoples unable to achieve the economic security necessary to be considered socially and economically productive neoliberal citizens. The cultural discourse that blurs lines of class and race in order to idealize young women as future citizens continues within many YA dystopian novels published at the beginning of the twenty-first century.[4]

Changing these narratives and their underlying ideologies remains key to the work of Indigenous Futurism. As a genre, Indigenous Futurism insists upon thinking outside of the usual patterns of European-based ideologies. It explicitly identifies the historic and present injustices inflicted by those ideologies while simultaneously acknowledging the presence, history, and validity of Indigenous knowledge and Indigenous community structures, including political bodies that are not nation-states. The genre enables a more multifaceted examination of Western and Indigenous knowledges and sharpens the critiques undertaken by utopian/dystopian works by providing a more comprehensive range of human anxieties and desires.

The Interrogation of Ashala Wolf and an Indigenously Defined Citizenship

Within Australian literature, the widespread attention to indigeneity in children's and YA texts stems from the late twentieth-century surge of Indigenous publishing and the high-profile and hotly contested Native Title cases and policies of the 1990s, which determined that Indigenous peoples held precolonial rights to land ownership. In the 1992 *Mabo* case, Australia's High Court ruled that Native Title rights existed within the state's common law and that previous denials of these rights during Australia's colonial history were baseless. While the wording of the ruling acknowledged Native Title to only "some" lands and waters, and while Aboriginal people bore the burden of proving continuous significant connection to their lands, the decision was still significant in Australian history as it overturned *terra nullius*, the legal policy under which Australia was settled.[5] In *Apocalypse in Australian Fiction and Film: A Critical Study* (2011), Roslyn Weaver contends that the 1990s formed a turning point in the politically responsive field of YA literature. After the 1990s, YA became "preoccupied with questions of legitimacy... interrogat[ing] the notions of home and belonging in a post-apocalyptic Australian setting, particularly in the context of imperialism and Indigeneity" (113).

While white Australia struggled with questions of legitimacy, the increasing prominence of Indigenous publishing houses and an increase in published Indigenous authors meant that literature became a space within which Indigenous voices could be heard. Catriona Mills argues that during the 2000s, the increased publication of YA fiction by Indigenous publishing houses allowed the genre to become an avenue through which Australia's Indigenous people could participate in the national conversation rather than simply be the object of it (7). She identifies the 2012 publication of *The Interrogation of Ashala Wolf* as making Ambelin Kwaymullina "the dominant figure among [Australia's] Indigenous young adult and fantasy writers" (8), and since then Kwaymullina has actively used her position to advocate for diversity in YA books and bring Indigenous worldviews into the mainstream of Australian publishing.

Kwaymullina's turn to writing YA serves as an extension of the decolonizing work she performs as a picture book author and professor at the University of Western Australia's Law School. As a writer and an educator, Kwaymullina engages in political and cultural discussions regarding Aboriginal reconciliation, policies, and cultural representations, and her nonfiction describes Aboriginal peoples' beliefs and connection to the land as well as commentary upon proposed changes to legislation.

The Interrogation of Ashala Wolf and the peritextual contexts surrounding its publication directly engage Australian national discourse regarding Indigenous beliefs and the position of Indigenous people within the state. Kwaymullina overtly declares both the significance of Indigenous rights within Australia and her desire to reach an adolescent audience. Her 2013 speech as guest of honor at the Australian National Science Fiction Convention connected the two:

quoting Larissa Behrendt (Eualeyai and Kamillaroi), Kwaymullina declared that "Indigenous people are the benchmark against which Australian society should be judged, because '[t]he way to measure the effectiveness and fairness of our laws is to test them against the way in which they work for the poor, the marginalized and the culturally distinct'" (156). For Kwaymullina, "The most important are those who are the most powerless, the most vulnerable, the most disadvantaged. That will often be the very people who I write for—the children and the teenagers of this planet" (156).

While her speech's association of Indigenous communities, children, and teenagers suggests that Kwaymullina thinks of Indigenous youth as she writes, I would also stress that in writing for "the children and teenagers of this planet" and publishing the Tribe series through one of Australia's largest publishing houses, Walker Books, Kwaymullina consciously wrote for all Australian youth. As Graham J. Murphy contends, writing the Tribe series allowed Kwaymullina to serve as a "cultural broker" of Indigenous scientific literacies (191); it allowed her to fight "against the infantilizing of Indigenous worldviews as quaint or primitive anachronisms" and insist upon "Indigenous worldviews as important and equally compelling ways of understanding and shaping the universe" (192). Being a cultural broker also enables Kwaymullina to speak to those teenagers who will become the privileged, culturally dominant citizens of the coming generation, those who may never otherwise hear an Indigenous perspective on their state. By employing Indigenous Futurism's ability to "reveal Native presence" and ideologies (Dillon 2), Kwaymullina demonstrates disjunctions within Australian concepts of citizenship, reveals Palyku understandings of law, places the two together, and encourages all Australian teens to engage in the work of holding their government accountable to respecting human rights.

The Interrogation of Ashala Wolf centers on concepts of citizenship: in it, Ashala, her tribe members, and Citizens from the local region dismantle Detention Center 3, a holding place for illegal individuals whose citizenship has been nullified. The novel is set three hundred years after "humanity's abuse of the environment ... made the life-sustaining systems of the earth collapse" (6). At the end of this period, a single land mass emerged from the shifting tectonic plates. The protocols governing human society in Ashala's time are based upon a "Letter to Those Who Survive." Laws now exist to preserve "the inherent Balance between all life, and the only way to preserve it is to live in harmony with ourselves, with one another, and with the earth" (22). Some people possess special abilities to control wind or fire or, like Ashala, to alter the laws of physics while in a dreamlike state. However, after a catastrophic event early in humanity's renewed history, the governing authorities believe that those with abilities are outside of the Balance. The humans of the world are therefore split into three categories: Citizens; Illegals, whose special abilities cause them to be considered dangerous; and Exempts, those with abilities considered benign. As Illegals are believed to be a threat to the Balance, they are restrained within detention centers.

At twelve, when she was supposed to be detained due to her ability, Ashala escaped her home city and took refuge in the Firstwood, an ancient place where life first resurged on the planet. The Firstwood is alive and aware of the experiences of its inhabitants; it remembers humanity's abuse and planetary destruction. Ashala, whom readers learn is a descendent of those who were once Aborigines, promises the Firstwood that she will defend it with her life. In return, the Firstwood protects her and other refugee children and teenagers who join her "tribe." On the fringes of the Firstwood, however, stands Detention Center 3. Implacable in his determination to contain Illegals, Neville Rose, the center's chief administrator, plans to destroy the Firstwood and detain the tribe of young Illegals.

The novel begins in *medias res*, with sixteen-year-old Ashala apparently betrayed and detained in Detention Center 3. Flashbacks revealed through Rose's interrogation of Ashala comprise the beginning of the novel. Later, readers discover that Ashala and the Tribe's other leaders planned her capture as a way for Ashala to infiltrate the center, discover the true treatment of Illegals, and ascertain the truth regarding the rumors of Rose's illegal actions. False memories, implanted by a fellow leader, prevent Ashala from revealing the Tribe's plan while she is interrogated.

During Ashala's time in the detention center, two significant events shake the reader's understandings of citizenship. First is the revelation that the novel's futurist universe is entirely Palyku in its understandings and in the way it ought to operate. This framing of the world enables Kwaymullina to immerse her readers in a Palyku worldview, demonstrating its variance from the colonial concepts that established Australia as a state that is fundamentally opposed to the legal systems of its Indigenous people. The second event is Ashala and her allies' discovery of the extent of Rose's illegal activities. Within the novel, this discovery precipitates a communitywide search for truth and allows Kwaymullina to suggest ways in which her readers may take social action in their own world.

In *The Interrogation of Ashala Wolf*, Kwaymullina explicitly introduces a Palyku understanding of the world when Ashala meets the Serpent after an almost fatal attack. The attack causes Ashala to slip into an in-between reality where she questions whether she's dead or dreaming. This state of consciousness breaks through Ashala's false memories, and while in this other reality, Ashala meets a great Serpent who identifies himself as the ancestor of the

Firstwood and Ashala's "many-times grandfather, one of the creators of your people" (111). He is, in fact, one of the creation spirits who spun new life into being after the planet's destruction. This meeting reframes Ashala's, and the readers,' understanding of her world.

For non-Indigenous YA readers, Ashala's meeting with Grandfather, the Serpent, allows Kwaymullina to demonstrate a Palyku understanding of the world, and Kwaymullina cautions against defining her as a writer of speculative fiction as she insists that the Palyku beliefs illustrated in her novel aren't fiction. She calls herself "one of many Indigenous speculative fiction writers in the world," implying that the label should be used cautiously as "Eurocentric genre categories are difficult to apply to works that were not created out of a Eurocentric worldview, because the very notion of what is speculative and what is not relies on assumptions about the real" (Continuum 154, 155). In his analysis of the Tribe series, Graham J. Murphy argues that Kwaymullina employs Palyku understandings of Country[6] to explain Indigenous concepts of the interconnected web of existence, immersing her non-Indigenous readers in a different worldview. By portraying how the interconnected web of existence works, however, Kwaymullina also reveals a Palyku understanding of law.

In "Learning to read the signs: law in an Indigenous reality" (2010), Kwaymullina and her coauthor, Blaze Kwaymullina, demonstrate that the underlying difficulty in coming to "a true reconciliation of peoples and laws" in Australia is a fundamental divide between "Western" thought and practice and the integrated expression of Aboriginal practices and laws. They thus acknowledge that their perspective derives from the Palyku people of the Pilbara region, the people to whom they belong, and they explain that multiple Aboriginal perspectives exist. The perspectives vary depending upon "the specific Aboriginal country from which we each come, the people to whom each of us belong, and our individual and collective experiences of colonialism" (196). They nonetheless demonstrate the distinctions between their understandings of law and those accepted within Western thought, using the term "Western" as shorthand for Enlightenment-derived ideologies imposed during the colonization of the Australian state.

As Kwaymullina and Kwaymullina describe, the vastly different understanding of time and space within a Palyku worldview renders law inseparable from other Palyku beliefs; it cannot be treated as a discrete field of study. Within Palyku reality, "knowledge is both constructed and transmitted around the idea of balancing relationships between all things in the universe" (196). Rather than being a body of regulations to adjudicate practices within human society, Aboriginal law is intimately connected with the concepts of Country and Dreaming, words that have no exact parallel within Western ideologies.[7]

Kwaymullina and Kwaymullina explain that law, Country, and Dreaming are living, breathing parts of Aboriginal society, which include all of existence. "Country is the source of all creation," nourishment, and guidance, and thus, it sustains "a web of relationships" between all life, including the consciousness and life which Western ideology would reckon as "inanimate" or as "empty space," such as stones or an area of ground or water ("Learning" 197; *Heartsick* 10). The Dreaming began when "the Ancestors—who themselves came in many forms, and who went back into country—gave law to *all* life, not just life in human forms," and set in place the "complex ongoing happening that Aboriginal peoples engage with through songs, dance, ceremony, art and story" ("Learning" 202, 199). Quoting the Yanyuwa elder Mussolini Harvey, the authors explain, "All things in country have law, they have ceremony and song, and they have people who are related to them" (202). This means that all life follows customs prescribed by the ancestors, who are still present in Country, and that the Dreaming—the patterns of relationship between individual places and life forms—ensures that each is cared for in an appropriate way to sustain Country.[8] Here, law is the living enactment of the Dreaming, practiced by the people, places, and other forms of life inhabiting Country. Governance maintains that system of relationships. As Ambelin Kwaymullina explains in "Country and Healing: An Indigenous Perspective on Therapeutic Jurisprudence" (2007),

> Everyone has a place in this system, and by knowing this place, people know their rights and responsibilities—to provide another with food, to care for a specific story or site, to punish a wrongdoer. And the rights and responsibilities that one person has with regard to another depend on their respective places in the system. It is not the right or responsibility that defines the relationship, it is the relationship that defines the right or responsibility. (2)

The Interrogation of Ashala Wolf articulates a system of governance that prioritizes "the Balance," a concept taken from Kwaymullina's understanding of Aboriginal worldviews. However, even within this balance, she creates a context in which the need, importance, and good of each place and creature is still not completely understood, resulting in conflict over the right to citizenship. As Murphy argues, part of Kwaymullina's larger purpose in the Tribe series is to illustrate how Ashala Wolf understands and establishes an increasingly Palyku system of governance. He shows how, even within the series' first novel, Ashala's "profound kinship with Country" comes both from her Indigenous bloodline and from the fact that she "*listens* to the spirits of the living world around her" (183–84). Thus, she and her tribe are protected by the Firstwood due to her promise that "we won't eat any of the animals or cut down any trees or do anything else you don't like" (*Ashala* 177). The lack of anthropocentricity in her relationship with the Firstwood is revealed as she explains to it that "I won't hurt you or anyone else because I think you don't count as much as me" (*Ashala* 179). As Kwaymullina reimagines a system of law modeled around Palyku-based beliefs, she demonstrates that within such a system, citizenship based upon incomplete, anthropocentric documents will become unnecessary, as all citizens will treat each other with respect and honor.

Until such time as a perfectly balanced, Palyku-based government may be established, however, Kwaymullina also demonstrates how Australian readers may engage the imperfect government of their own time. The textual basis for this comes at the end of the novel, as Citizens in Ashala's world realize the extent of Neville Rose's illegal abuses of the earth and the detainees in Detention Center 3.

Significantly, Kwaymullina depicts the governance of Ashala's world as initially having been based on Palyku understanding; it became corrupted when the Citizenship Accords divided humans into distinct categories, causing a divisive chasm between humans, animals, Ancestors, and the earth. The two main considerations of a Palyku style of governance—one, which emphasizes the Balance, and the other, wherein such emphasis is unnecessary as it becomes an intrinsic part of lived experience—are depicted in Kwaymullina's description of the Cities, their Citizens, and the Firstwood and Illegals who take refuge there. Most Citizens live in collections of towns based around "Cities." The description of these communities bears similarities to Kwaymullina and Kwaymullina's discussion of the location-specific nature of law within Country. They argue that "law flows from the living hearts of Aboriginal countries" and, thus, is location-specific to differing tribes and ecosystems. These legal systems hold commonalities since "law did not develop incrementally and haphazardly, with every nation independently and in isolation producing its own rules," but rather the Ancestors gave specific "ways of living in country" to "all life" along the coasts or in the grasslands, deserts, or forested areas (202). Similarly, in *The Interrogation of Ashala Wolf*, humans live in cities named for their locations. The Gull City towns, from where Ashala hails, include "Eldergull, Aspergull, Halligull, Stonygull," while the Spinifex City towns echo the names of coastal conifers like "Junifex" (87). Elected representatives manage the daily governing of the Cities while the Council of Primes oversees all the cities and establishes accords regarding what has "to be done, or *not* done, in order to maintain the Balance" (93–94). Ashala begins her infiltration of Detention Center 3 recognizing that "most Citizens" believe that "locking Illegals like me away was a good thing, or at least a necessary thing," and she thinks that even Neville Rose's determination to contain Illegals is based on his desire to protect the Balance, rendering the "sweet," "grandfatherly" man more mistaken or mad than actively cruel (2, 31). However, after Ashala's meeting with the Serpent, she recognizes Rose as evil: his imprisonment and torture of Illegals and his mining of the earth's resources stem from a ruthless zest for power (132–33).

In creating a world where Palyku understandings of Balance form the unstated truths believed by all humans, Kwaymullina depicts a future Australia in which Western ideologies are not the basis of the state. Significantly, this places controversial contemporary issues such as mineral extraction outside the realm of debate. After all, Rose appalls the Citizens of his world by mining, which is deemed one of the acts so destructive to the Balance that it is forbidden by the Cities' Accords. In reality, mining is a leading cause of land disputes between Aboriginal peoples and the Australian government; the implication is that despite the imperfect governing system of Ashala's world, even they recognize that treating the earth as a commodity for the convenience of a select group of humans is reprehensible. Readers would have to purposefully oppose the logic of Kwaymullina's world to advocate mining.

Nonetheless, the concept of a state-like governing body exists within the novel, offering readers a means through which they may draw parallels with their own situation as citizens, and the ending of Kwaymullina's novel demonstrates the collective accountability citizens should demand within their civic contexts. From the beginning of the narrative and Ashala's imprisonment with the Detention Center, Kwaymullina's story references social movements that question the justness of the Citizenship Accords. The names of these groups are reminiscent of politically active human rights groups within our own contemporary world. Within Kwaymullina's novel, the "Friends of Detainees" are described as "a growing reform movement, a loose alliance of groups and individuals who were pushing to have the Citizenship Accords dismantled altogether" and who have succeeded in creating an independent Inspectorate to assess Detention Center conditions for Illegals (12, 67). An interrogation of the very system separating humans into Citizens, Illegals, and Exempts is emphasized as the Friends of Detainees write "the Question"—"Does a person with an ability belong to the Balance?"—in red paint across the front of the Bureau of Citizenship offices and by wearing "Question" pins (12, 303). By the novel's conclusion, when Neville Rose's illegal activities are revealed, a "Citizens' Occupation" occurs at Detention Center 3. Ashala happily recounts that "It wasn't only reformer types, either"; many Citizens who "had never even asked the Question" came to aid the Inspectorate in "opening every container, unlocking every door, and meticulously recording everything they found" so that "there was no chance of anyone in the government being able to conceal what had gone on in Detention Center 3 (390–91).

While *The Interrogation of Ashala Wolf* demonstrates numerous unnamed Citizens actively interrogating their government in the name of justice and transparency, peritextual materials published by Kwaymullina and others underscore parallels between the circumstances of the novel and Australia's political realities. In a 2015[9] article written for the Walker Books' "Education Resource Booklet" for her series, Kwaymullina explains that she based the Citizenship Accords upon the Western Australian Natives (Citizenship Rights) Act of 1944, which gave Aboriginal people a "limited set" of rights including, as Kwaymullina explains, the right for Aboriginal people carrying citizenship papers to move around the state of Western Australia (4). She describes for young readers how many Aboriginal people sardonically referred to their papers as "dog tags"; that Aborigines with citizenship received some relief from "racially based controls that only applied to them in the first place because they were Aboriginal"; and that free movement is important because one cannot find work if one cannot travel (4). Kwaymullina additionally explains how her family's experiences as members of the Stolen Generations, Indigenous children who were forcibly separated from their families by various government policies instituted between 1910 and 1970, informed her creation of the Detention Centers (4).

Australian reviews of the novel recognized the political relevance of Kwaymullina's work. A review from *Reading Time* shows that through the detention centers, the book also addresses "modern-day refugee issues" (Quealy-Gainer 35). Likewise, Walker Books' "Education Resource Booklet" includes "Classroom Ideas." These offer connections between textual themes and key curriculum goals such as understanding "Violent or Non-Violent Participation in Rebellion or Dissent," "Indigenous Cultural Influences and Beliefs," and the "Treatment of, and Detention of Refugees" (Sheahan-Bright 6). Within this "Education Resource Booklet," author Robyn Sheahan-Bright suggests class discussion points that revolve around the concept of citizenship in and out of the novel: "Ashala's world defines 'citizenship' according to whether or not someone has an ability. How does Australia define what it is to be a citizen? What is the definition of a refugee, and how are refugees created?" She provides links to resources from the Department of Immigration and Border Protection and the Australian Human Rights Commission, "Face the Facts: Asylum Seekers and Refugees," and further suggests that students compare contemporary Australian groups advocating on behalf of refugees with the "proliferation of groups in Ashala's world" that ask the Question and advocate on behalf of detainees (9).[9] Sheahan-Bright's questions frame Kwaymullina's novel within larger discussions of human rights and Indigeneity. Doing so situates Australia within a larger context of international law and underscores a challenge to the integrity of a nation-state even based on the liberal formulation of representation.

Citizenship within Australia is a vexed concept. As Bain Attwood and Andrew Markus argue in *The 1967 Referendum: Race, Power and the Australian Constitution* (2007), "The Australian Constitution, unlike the famous American one, makes no reference to citizenship. It is simply not that kind of constitution. It is instead a compact designed by rulers to meet the needs of government and capital, and so it is concerned with the parliament and its powers, the executive and the judiciary, the states, and finance and trade" (vi). In 1999, a referendum failed to change the Australian Constitution, and while the government has acknowledged the need for Aboriginal people to have "special rights, including Indigenous rights" since the early 1970s, the implementation of these rights has been steadily lacking, despite the examples of other "comparable nations," like Canada, which created provisions within a constitutional or legislative bill of rights (84–85). Despite the High Court formally acknowledging Native Title claims during the *Mabo* cases, Attwood and Markus explain that incorporating Indigenous rights into the fabric of Australian civic life becomes a complicated issue. In Australia, Indigenous rights differ from those governing the rest of the population. The nature of a democratic, liberal nation-state means that Indigenous rights are "much more difficult for states to accommodate" as their basis "is both permanent and collective in nature rather than temporary or individual" and "the calls for land rights, but more especially the recognition of sovereignty, pushes democracies to their intellectual limits" (76). By foregrounding questions of Indigeneity in the novel's textual and peritextual contexts, Kwaymullina, Sheahan-Bright, and Walker Books prompt YA readers to engage these intellectual limits. Australian readers as young as fourteen (the lower end of the book's recommended reader age) are encouraged to confront complex questions regarding the nature and workings of their state.

One of the further implications of the international sources suggested for study by students and teachers in Sheahan-Bright's "Classroom Ideas," then, is that in framing Indigenous rights through a larger lens of human rights, both Kwaymullina and Sheahan-Bright encourage young Australians to understand themselves as citizens of a larger global community. Kwaymullina's essay within the "Education Resource Booklet" produced by Walker Books points students towards sources such as "The United Nations Permanent Forum on Indigenous Issues and the United Nations Permanent Forum on Indigenous Peoples, Who Are Indigenous Peoples?" (Factsheet 5). Similarly, both her essay and Sheahan-Bright's questions encourage students to research human-rights-based sources released by the Australian government, such as "The Australian Human Rights Commission Bringing Them Home Education Module" (5, 9). These sources refer students to one of the major conundrums they and their fellow citizens currently face: what relative weight ought to be given to the Australian Constitution as opposed to international Human Rights treaties? Scholars document the conflicts faced by Indigenous Australians caught between international and domestic law; by introducing young readers into these conversations, Kwaymullina's books and their peritextual materials encourage readers to become further engaged in these political discussions. This, as Kwaymullina declares elsewhere, is the point of creating space for Indigenous and other marginalized people to speak: "[W]hen different perspectives are listened to respectfully and with understanding, we generate possibilities that did not exist before. ... We are so ingenious, we human beings. What marvels might we create if we could only be informed by other worldviews without subsuming them" (Continuum 157)?

The Interrogation of Ashala Wolf proposes that these marvels may include a reimagined state created by Indigenous Australians and adolescent readers. Yet this proposal does not rest solely on the work of the Kwaymullina's novel. The challenge to engage in the work of truly reimagining a state, and the prerequisite questioning of a citizen's state, society, and self, comes through the multiple avenues of discourse employed by Kwaymullina and her publishers and their deep investment in portraying a world based on Palyku beliefs and human rights. Because Kwaymullina and Robyn Sheahan-Bright, the well-established scholar and educator whom Walker Books hired to create classroom materials for the Tribe series, explain Indigenous beliefs, history, and understandings of law alongside the fictional text, Kwaymullina's challenge to the Australian nation-state can be readily recognized by readers. Facilitating that recognition, then, becomes the true invitation offered by Kwaymullina's radical text to those of us invested in the distribution and teaching of works that may change the world.

Notes

1. The terms "Skin thinking" or "thinking in skin" were originally coined by Joy Harjo (Mvskoke), but the terms have accrued multiple meanings via scholars such as Robert Warrior (Osage), Tol Foster (Anglo-Creek), and Lisa Brooks (Abenaki). "Skin thinking" emphasizes a reader's specific embodiment, "fusing our bodies with our intellects connected to material realities," expanding beyond the individual to their larger communities (Dillon 243). It additionally emphasizes reading while consciously maintaining "the richness and awareness of the specific tribal frameworks relationally within an intertribal setting," attending to the "interactions and negotiations" amongst Indigenous nations that are revealed in Native literature (243–44).

In her author's note, Kwaymullina states that the ideologies underlying *The Interrogation of Ashala Wolf* draw primarily from the Palyku people to whom she belongs. However, her other published works reveal a vast knowledge of Native intellectualism and her own commitment to Skin thinking.

2. Although Kwaymullina uses "the social, cultural, and political systems" of the Palyku to achieve her aims, I acknowledge that I explain these ideas using distinctly Western terminology, a distinction that I discuss later in the essay.

3. Following the description of Indigenous sovereignty quoted here, Moreton-Robinson continues to explain that she and her colleagues within the volume "do not purport to provide the quintessential definition of Indigenous sovereignty" (2). Given the diversity of Aboriginal and Torres Strait Islander communities, this would be impossible. As Indigenous peoples, however, the communities are often grouped together in state, national, and international law.

4. See Mary J. Couzelis's excellent example of this in "The Future Is Pale: Race in Contemporary Young Adult Dystopian Novels."

5. Unlike in Aotearoa (New Zealand), the United States, and Canada, Australia never had treaties with its Indigenous peoples, partially because the legal policy of *terra nullius* deemed the land was unsettled and free for the claiming. The *Mabo* case I refer to was, in fact, the second of two cases led by Eddie Mabo, David Passi, and James Rice, all of the Mer Islands in the Torres Straits. Both cases were brought against the State of Queensland and sought to establish the legality of recognizing traditional land claims by Indigenous peoples.

6. Here, as elsewhere in my text, I capitalize the word "Country" when describing the concept rooted in Aboriginal ideology although Kwaymullina varies between capitalizing and not capitalizing the word in various publications.

7. See Murphy for a detailed analysis of Country within Kwaymullina's Tribe series. See James for an analysis of Kwaymullina's use of Country and the Indigenous Futurist movement.

8. Kwaymullina and Kwaymullina explain:
> In the legal field, the colonial inability to conceive of Aboriginal legal systems as equal to those of the West is reflected in the persistent description of Aboriginal legal systems as comprising "custom" or "customary law." Such terms are inevitably burdened by historical constructions of Indigenous societies as inferior and lacking in "real" law. ... Aboriginal creation stories tell that law was given by the same Ancestors who made the world and continue to live within it, and that the purpose of the gift of law was to show all life how to sustain country. In this context, Aboriginal statements that "something is to be done because the Ancestors did so" ... It is possible that a scholar employing a Western perspective might disagree with Aboriginal views on the nature of creation, but what is important is that Aboriginal systems are based on this view being true. (198)

9. For an idea of the prominence of refugees and asylum seekers within Australian national awareness, see Ben Hightower's "Refugees, Limbo and the Australian Media" (2014). For a more complex discussion of Australian detention's "legal black hole where security decisions are immune from scrutiny" (685), see Ben Saul's "Dark Justice: Australia's Indefinite Detention of Refugees on Security Grounds under International Human Rights Law" (2015).

Works Cited

Attwood, Bain, and Andrew Markus. *The 1967 Referendum: Race, Power and the Australian Constitution*. 2nd ed., Aboriginal Studies Press, 2007.

Basu, Balaka, Katherine R. Broad, and Carrie Hintz, editors. Introduction. *Contemporary Dystopian Fiction for Young Adults*. Edited by Balaka Basu, Balaka, Katherine R. Broad, and Carrie Hintz, Routledge, 2013, pp. 1–15.

Bradford, Clare. *New World Orders in Contemporary Children's Literature: Utopian Transformations*. Palgrave-Macmillan, 2008.

Buchan, Bruce. *Empire of Political Thought: Indigenous Australians and the Language of Colonial Government*. Pickering & Chatto, 2008.

Couzelis, Mary J. "The Future Is Pale: Race in Contemporary Young Adult Dystopian Novels." *Contemporary Dystopian Fiction for Young Adults*. Edited by Balaka Basu, Katherine R. Broad, and Carrie Hintz, Routledge, 2013, pp. 131–44.

Day, Sara K., Miranda A. Green-Barteet, and Amy L. Montz, editors. Introduction. *Female Rebellion in Young Adult Dystopian Fiction*. Edited by Day, Green-Barteet, and Montz, Ashgate, 2014, pp. 1–14.

Dillon, Grace L. "Imagining Indigenous Futurisms." *Walking the Clouds: An Anthology of Indigenous Science Fiction*. Edited by Grace L. Dillon. Arizona University Press, 2012, pp. 1–12.

Falk, Phillip, and Gary Martin. "Misconstruing Indigenous sovereignty: Maintaining the fabric of Australian law." *Sovereign Subjects: Indigenous Sovereignty Matters*. Edited by Aileen Moreton-Robinson, Allen & Unwin, 2007, pp. 33–46.

Harris, Anita. *Future Girl: Young Women in the Twenty-first Century*. Routledge, 2004.

Hayes, Summer. Review of *The Interrogation of Ashala Wolf*, by Ambelin Kwaymullina. *Booklist*, vol. 110, no. 16, 2014, p. 49.

Hayn, Judith A., editor. *Teaching Young Adult Literature: Integrating, Implementing, and Re-Imagining the Common Core*. Rowman & Littlefield, 2016.

Hightower, Ben. "Refugees, Limbo and the Australian Media." *International Journal for the Semiotics of Law-Revue Internationale De SéMiotique Juridique*, vol. 28, no. 2, 2015, pp. 335–58.

Hintz, Carrie, and Elaine Ostry. Introduction. *Utopian and Dystopian Writing for Children and Young Adults*. Edited by Carrie Hintz and Elaine Ostry. Routledge, 2003, pp. 1–20.

James, Lynette. "Children of Change, Not Doom: Indigenous Futurist Heroines in YA." *Extrapolation*, vol. 57, nos. 1–2, 2016, pp. 151–76. DOI: http://dx.doi.org/10.3828/extr.2016.9.

Kwaymullina, Ambelin. Ambelin Kwaymullina, Writer & Illustrator. Ambelin Kwaymullina, 2013–2015, http://www.ambelin-kwaymullina.com.au/#!/.

Kwaymullina, Ambelin. Continuum X/53rd Australian National Science Fiction Convention. InterContinental Melbourne The Rialto, 8 Jun. 2014, Guest of Honor Speech, *Andromeda Spaceways: InFlight Magazine*, no. 61, 5 Jun. 2015, pp. 153–58.

Kwaymullina, Ambelin. "Country and Healing: An Indigenous Perspective on Therapeutic Jurisprudence." *Transforming Legal Processes in Court and Beyond: 3rd International Conference on Therapeutic Jurisprudence*. Edited by Greg Reinhardt and Andrew Cannon, Australian Institute of Judicial Administration, 2007, pp. 1–8.

Kwaymullina, Ambelin. "The Cultural and Historical Background to The Tribe Series: An essay from the author." *The Tribe*, Ambelin Kwaymullina: Education Resource Booklet, Walker Books Australia, 2015, pp. 4–5, http://classroom.walkerbooks.com.au/home/wp-content/uploads/2015/07/The_Tribe_Education-Booklet_LR.pdf.

Kwaymullina, Ambelin. Introduction. *Heartsick for Country: Stories of Love, Spirit and Creation*. Edited by Sally Morgan, Fremantle Press, 2008, pp. 6–20.

Kwaymullina, Ambelin. *The Interrogation of Ashala Wolf*. 2012. First U. S. edition Candlewick Press, 2014.

Kwaymullina, Ambelin, and Blaze Kwaymullina. "Learning to Read the Signs: Law in an Indigenous Reality." *Journal of Australian Studies*, vol. 34, no. 2, 2010, pp. 195–208.

Lesko, Nancy. *Act Your Age!: A Cultural Construction of Adolescence*. Psychology Press, 2001.

Mills, Catriona. "Minority Identity and Counter-Discourse: Indigenous Australian and Muslim-Australian Authors in the Young Adult Fiction Market." *TEXT: Journal of Writing and Writing Courses*, no. 32, Oct. 2015, pp. 1–15.

Moreton-Robinson, Aileen. Introduction. *Sovereign Subjects: Indigenous Sovereignty Matters*. Edited by Aileen Moreton-Robinson, Allen & Unwin, 2007, pp. 1–11.

Murphy, Graham J. "For Love of Country: Apocalyptic Survivance in Ambelin Kwaymullina's Tribe Series." *Extrapolation*, vol. 57, no. 1–2, pp. 177–96.

Quealy-Gainer, Kate. Review of *The Interrogation of Ashala Wolf* by Ambelin Kwaymullina. *Bulletin of the Center for Children's Books*, vol. 67, no. 8, 2014, pp. 412.

Quigley, Dawn. "Silenced: Voices Taken from American Indian Characters in Children's Literature." *American Indian Quarterly*, vol. 40, no. 4, 2016, pp. 364–78.

Saul, Ben. "Dark Justice: Australia's Indefinite Detention of Refugees on Security Grounds under International Human Rights Law." *Melbourne Journal of International Law*, vol. 13, no. 2, 2012, pp. 685–731.

Sheahan-Bright, Robyn. "Red, Yellow, and Black: Australian Indigenous Publishing for Young People." *Bookbird: A Journal of International Children's Literature*, vol. 49, no. 3, 2011, pp. 1–17.

Sheahan-Bright, Robyn. *The Tribe*, Ambelin Kwaymullina: Education Resource Booklet. Walker Books Australia, n.d., http://classroom.walkerbooks.com.au/home/wp-content/uploads/2015/07/The_Tribe_Education-Booklet_LR.pdf.

Trites, Roberta Seelinger. *Disturbing the Universe: Power and Repression in Young Adult Literature*. Iowa University Press, 2000.

Weaver, Roslyn. *Apocalypse in Australian Fiction and Film: A Critical Study*. McFarland & Company, Inc., 2011.

Contributors

Malin Alkestrand is an assistant professor in comparative literature at Linnæus University. In her dissertation *Magiska möjligheter: Harry Potter, Artemis Fowl och Cirkeln i skolans värdegrundsarbete* [Magical possibilities: Teaching values in schools with Harry Potter, Artemis Fowl and the Circle] (2016), Alkestrand, explores how fantasy literature can be used to discuss and problematize democracy, human rights, and multiculturalism in schools. Her current project focuses on the relationship of power between adults and adolescents in Anglophone and Swedish YA dystopias.

Joshua Yu Burnett teaches English at Tallahassee Community College. His work focuses on Black speculative fiction. His current work examines Afrofuturism in contemporary African American music. His work has appeared in *African American Review*, *Gender Forum*, *Mosaic*, and *Research in African Literatures*.

Sean P. Connors is an associate professor of English education at the University of Arkansas. His scholarship and teaching focus on the application of diverse critical perspectives to YA literature. He is the editor of *The Politics of Panem: Challenging Genres*, a collection of critical essays about the *Hunger Games* trilogy.

Jill Coste is a doctoral candidate at the University of Florida, where she is specializing in children's and YA literature. Her current research focuses on different forms of feminist resistance and social justice in YA fairy-tale retellings. Her work has appeared in *Girlhood Studies* and the edited collections *Neil Gaiman: Critical Insights* (Salem Press, 2016) and *Beyond the Blockbusters: Themes and Trends in Contemporary Young Adult Fiction* (University of Mississippi Press, 2020).

Meghan Gilbert-Hickey is an assistant professor of English at Guttman Community College, a part of the City University of New York. Her recent and forthcoming publications focus on intersectionality in contemporary YA fiction and other popular culture venues. She has recently edited a special issue of *South Central Review* on the #MeToo movement and is currently working on a book about intersectional motherhood in YA speculative fiction.

Miranda A. Green-Barteet is an associate professor at the University of Western Ontario. She is the coeditor of both *Female Rebellion in Young Adult Dystopian Fiction* (Ashgate, 2014) and *Reconsidering Laura Ingalls Wilder: Little House and Beyond* (University Press of Mississippi, 2019). Her work has appeared in *Girlhood Studies*, *Canadian Review of American Studies*, *South Central Review*, and *The Lion and the Unicorn*.

Sierra Hale received a master of arts in English—children's literature from Kansas State University. She is currently a senior library information specialist at the University of Missouri-Kansas City.

Kathryn Strong Hansen is a senior lecturer at Chalmers University of Technology in Gothenburg, Sweden. Her research interests range from issues of gender and representation in YA fiction to the ways that fiction can benefit higher education pedagogy in the teaching of science and technology.

Elizabeth Ho is assistant professor in the School of English at the University of Hong Kong. She serves as consultant editor of *Neo-Victorian Studies* and coeditor of *Thatcher & After: Margaret Thatcher's Afterlife in Contemporary Culture* (Palgrave, 2010). She is the author of *Neo-Victorianism and the Memory of Empire* (Continuum/Bloomsbury 2012). Her latest book, *Map-able,* examines how cultural texts collaborate with maps to interrogate claims to space and enable political agency.

Esther L. Jones currently serves as associate provost and dean of the faculty at Clark University in Worcester, MA. She is also associate professor of English and the E. Franklin Frazier Chair of African American Literature, Theory, and Culture. Her research specializations include race and gender in the medical humanities, literature and medicine, speculative fiction, and Black diasporic women's literature.

Sarah Olutola is a graduate of the English and Cultural Studies Department at McMaster University. She is the 2018–19 Gordon F. Henderson Postdoctoral

Fellow and a member of Ottawa University's Human Rights Research and Education Centre. She has edited special issues and published in *Safundi*, *Popular Music and Society*, and *Atlantis: Critical Studies in Gender, Culture and Social Justice*. She also writes and publishes children's fiction.

Alex Polish is the author of two YA fantasy novels, *Lunav* and *Lost Boy, Found Boy*. They've taught theater and English in the CUNY system, and in 2019, they got their PhD in English from the CUNY Graduate Center, where they studied the racialization of mental health in YA writing spaces (and a lot of lesbian fan fiction). They're currently a lifestyle news writer for Bustle.com and a contributor to Barbend.com. They live with their wife and fantasize about having multiple puppies.

Zara Rix holds a PhD in English from the University of Connecticut and works with brave, inventive, and passionate young adults in the Massachusetts Public Schools.

Susan Tan received her PhD from the University of Cambridge in critical approaches to children's literature. She is currently an assistant professor at the University of Massachusetts Boston.

Roberta Seelinger Trites holds the rank of distinguished professor of English at Illinois State University, where she has taught since 1991. She is the author, among other works, of *Waking Sleeping Beauty: Feminist Voices in Children's Literature* (1997); *Disturbing the Universe: Power and Repression in Adolescent Literature* (2000); *Twain, Alcott, and the Birth of the Adolescent Reform Novel* (2007); *Literary Conceptualizations of Growth: Metaphors and Cognition in Adolescent Literature*; and *Twenty-First-Century Feminisms in Children's and Adolescent Literature* (2018).

Index

Aboriginal Law, 243, 246–48, 251, 253n3, 253n8
Abron, Dawn, 3
Adeyemi, Tomi, 223, 225–26, 230, 234–35
Afrofuturism, 189
Alexander, Michelle, 144n3
Alfred, Gerald Taiaiake, 237
Alkestrand, Malin, 93
Allegiant (2013), 167–82
Allegory, as diversity, 8; in *Of Beast and Beauty* and *The Lunar Chronicles*, 54–69
Allen, Amanda K., 28
Artemis Fowl (2001): diversity in, 35–41, 198–200; sexuality in, 36, 39–41, 44, 48–49
Artemis Fowl: The Arctic Incident (2002), 37
Artemis Fowl: The Atlantis Complex (2010), 37, 41, 46
Artemis Fowl: The Eternity Code (2003), 35, 39, 43, 46, 47
Artemis Fowl: The Last Guardian (2012), 38
Artemis Fowl: The Lost Colony (2006), 40, 42–43, 46, 49
Artemis Fowl: The Opal Deception (2005), 37, 38
Ask and the Answer, The (2010), 132, 138
Attwood, Bain, 251
Australia, literature, 9, 237–52
Aveyard, Victoria, 15

Bacchilega, Cristina, 55, 57, 69
Bacigalupi, Paulo, 204–6
Basu, Balaka, 56
Batra, Anupa, 37, 38

"Beauty and the Beast," 58, 60–61
bildungsroman, 28, 241
bioethics, 81, 222–35
biopolitics, 75, 76; in *Cinder*, 81; and Foucault, 80; in *Orleans*, 82, 84
black girl magic, 199; defined, 230; in works by Nnedi Okorafor and Tomi Adeyemi, 222–35
Blackness: in *Chaos Walking*, 135–36; and hair, 194–99; in *The Magical Negro*, 188
Black Space: Imagining Race in Science Fiction Film (2008), 22, 23, 25
blood, as racial marker: in *Clockwork Angel*, 153; in *Orleans*, 78–83; in *The Red Queen*, 15–29
Blood Rain series (2014–2017), 94–108
bodies, 144n4; black, 33n5, 66, 188; cyborg, 77, 113; female, 39; male, 40, 42; racialized, 18, 19, 27, 29, 46, 136
Bornstein, Kate, 44
Bradford, Clare, 56, 81, 83, 84
Brekhus, Wayne, 144n4
Broad, Katherine R., 56
Brooks, Lisa, 252n1
Breu, Christopher, 80
Brown, Nancy, 150
Burnett, Joshua Yu, 18, 187
Butler, Judith, 39, 40, 48
Butler, Octavia, 233, 234

Cart, Michael, 15
Carter, Prudence, 28

Chaos Walking trilogy (2010): colorblindness in, 135–38, 144n3; settler colonialism in, 8, 131–34; violence in, 137–38, 139, 141–43
Children of Blood and Bone (2018), 225, 234
Cinder (2012), 59, 64–68, 75–79, 114–24; biopolitics in, 81–82
Cinderella narrative, 24–32, 64–68, 77
City of Bones (2013), 160, 162n4
Clare, Cassandra, 147, 162n4
Clayton, Dhonielle, 91
Clockwork Angel (2010), 147–55
Clockwork Prince (2011), 147–58
Clockwork Princess (2013), 147, 155–59
Cohen, Jeffrey Jerome, 60, 65, 212
Cole, Susan Guettel, 38
Colfer, Eoin, 35, 198–99
Collins, Patricia Hill, 55–56, 94–97, 103
Collins, Suzanne, 75, 81, 84
colonialism, 17–23, 58; settler in *Chaos Walking*, 8, 131–34, 139–44
colorblindness, 5–10, 192; in *Chaos Walking*, 135–38, 144n3; in *Divergent*, 165–70; in *The Lunar Chronicles*, 111–13, 121–25, 126n6
Connors, Sean P., 75
Contemporary Dystopian Fiction for Young Adults: Brave New Teenagers, 56
Cooper, Brittney, 176–77
Coste, Jill, 54
Couzelis, Mary J., 4–5, 92, 144n2, 171, 253n4
Crary, Alice, 87, 88
Crazy QuiltEdi, 3
Crenshaw, Kimberle, 95, 182
Cress (2014), 67, 68, 125n2
cyborg, 210–11; *Cinder* as, 64–68, 77–81, 126n4; in *The Lunar Chronicles*, 111–25

Dark Fantastic: Race and the Imagination from Harry Potter to the Hunger Games, The (2019), 58, 219
Dark Fantastic: Race and the Imagination in Children's and YA Books, Media, and Fan Cultures, The (blog), 3, 10
Day, Sara K., 10n2, 161n1, 240
DeGraw, Sharon, 111, 122–23
Delany, Samuel R., 44, 122, 123, 125n1, 189, 190
Dickens, Charles, 161
Dillon, Grace L., 238, 244, 252n1

disability, 9, 38, 39, 65, 235
Divergent series (2011–2013): colorblindness in, 165–70; dis/ability in, 165–82, 182n1, 183n3; rebellion in, 165–66
Diversity, 191, 204–7; allegorical, 54–70; in *Artemis Fowl*, 35–41; lack of, 3–4, 10, 33n1, 189, 224
Dorr, Lisa Lindquist, 137
Driskill, Qwo-Li, 143
Drowned Cities, The (2012), 204
Du Bois, W. E. B., 86, 116
Dyer, Richard, 47, 65, 66, 108n5
dystopias, 15–32, 54–69, 75–91, 131, 138–40, 144n2, 204–20; defined, 108n1; in *The Interrogation of Ashala Wolf*, 237–42; rebellion in, 93; in Swedish, 93–108

Elam, Michele, 162n5
Eleria trilogy (2014–16), 101–8; rebellion in, 95, 105–7
elf, as race, 35, 36, 46, 47
Elias, Sean, 96
Erevelles, Nirmala, 167
ethnicity, 35, 75, 76, 83, 90, 91, 94, 95, 96, 98, 102, 103, 104; in *Cinder*, 117, 123; in *Clockwork Angel*, 150, 155, 159
Ethnoscape, 112–13, 224; in *Cinder*, 119–23; in *The Giver*, 112
eugenics, 165–81; and whiteness, 169

fairy: magic, 49; as race in *Artemis Fowl*, 36, 37, 41, 44–47, 51
fairy tales, 54, 55–58, 64, 68, 69; in dystopias, 54–69
fantasy, 6, 16, 23, 36, 50, 55, 91, 138, 237
Feagin, Joe, 96
female protagonists, 111, 144, 222; in the *Blood Rain* series, 96; in *Cinder*, 114; in *The Hunger Games*, 78, 93, 189; in *The Interrogation of Ashala Wolf*, 240; in *Legend*, 78; in *Orleans*, 78; in *The Red Queen*, 15; in *Who Fears Death*, 226
Female Rebellion in Young Adult Dystopian Fiction, 240
Finley, Chris, 143
Foster, Tol, 252n1
Foucault, Michel, 33n6, 80, 149, 161n2

Frankenberg, Ruth, 144n3
Frankenstein, 222, 226

Gallagher, Charles A., 124
Gallardo C., Ximena, 111, 119
Gates, Henry Louis, Jr., 190
gender: non-normativity, 35–49; queerness, 39–44, 48–51
Gilbert-Hickey, Meghan, 131
Gill, R. B., 6
Gilley, Brian Joseph, 143
Gilton, Donna L., 121–22
girlhood, 76, 149
Giver, The (1993), 93, 112–13, 124
globalization, 75–87, 151
Grahame, Elaine, 205, 210–13, 220n1
Green-Barteet, Miranda A., 10n2, 138, 144n2, 240
Griswold, Jerry, 61
Guerra, Stephanie, 81

hair, 46, 109n7, 197, 199, 230; as racial marker, 192–94
Hale, Sierra, 111
Hamilton, Steve, 5
Haraway, Donna, 210–11, 219
Harjo, Joy, 252n1
Harris, Anita, 240–42
Harvey, David, 76, 83
Harvey, Jennifer, 135
Hayles, N. Katherine, 211, 218
Heilman, Ann, 148
Heinlein, Robert A., 6
Henriques, Gregg, 223–24
heteronormativity, 143; in *Artemis Fowl*, 39–41, 43, 51
Hidalgo, Alexandra, 153
Highwater, Ben, 253n9
Hintz, Carrie, 10n2, 56, 108n1, 239–40
Ho, Elizabeth, 147
Hopkinson, Nalo, 190, 234, 235
Hron, Madelaine, 191
Hubinette, Tobias, 94, 96, 108
Hunger Games, The (2008), 78–84, 144n2, 162n3, 189, 220

identity, 183n3; gender, in *Artemis Fowl*, 37, 41, 43, 48, 51; in *Cinder*, 65, 68, 126n4; Eurasian, 147–61; indigenous, 140, 143; mixed-race, in *The Drowned Cities*, 204–19; in *Zahrah the Windseeker*, 193–94, 198
Immortal Life of Henrietta Lacks, The (2010), 229
Inahara, Minae, 182
indigeneity, stereotypes of, 131, 140, 144n7
Indigenous Futurism, 9, 237–44, 253n7
Indigenous rights, 251
Indigenous sovereignty, 141, 238, 241, 253n3
Infernal Devices series (2010–2013), 147–61
Interrogation of Ashala Wolf, The (2012): as dystopian fiction, 237, 238; and Indigenous Futurism, 9, 237–44, 253n7
intersectionality, 96, 102, 131–32, 189–91; defined, 95

Jarmon, Renina, 202n7
Jay, Stacey, 54
Jenkins, Christine A., 15
Jim Crow, 66, 70n3, 84, 144n3
Johnson, Dianne, 46
Jones, D. Marvin, 115
Jones, Esther L., 222

Keenan, Celia, 50
Kennedy, Tonya Ann, 5
King, Stephen, 187–201
Knife of Never Letting Go, The (2010), 132, 138, 142
Koshy, Susan, 22, 154
Kwaymullina, Ambelin, 237, 243–44
Kwaymullina, Blaze, 246

Lacks, Deborah, 227–30
Lacks, Henrietta, 227–31
Larbalestier, Justine, 220n3
Lavender, Isiah, 44–45, 112–14, 119, 122, 125n1, 192, 224
Legend (2013), 78–90
Little Mermaid, 58
Little Red Riding Hood, 58
Le Guin, Ursula, 220n3
Lesko, Nancy, 238, 239
liminality, 36, 60, 68, 100, 189, 234
Litwack, Leon F., 136
Llewellyn, Mark, 148

Louie, Kam, 158
Lowry, Lois, 93, 112–13, 124
Lu, Marie, 78, 84
Lunar Chronicles series (2017–): allegory, as diversity, 54, 64–69; color-blindness in, 111–13, 121–25, 126n6; cyborg as racialized metaphor in, 111–25, 138–39; Lunars as racialized others in, 65–66, 77, 114
Lundstrom, Catrin, 94, 96, 108

magic: black girl, 199; defined, 230; fairy, 49; in works by Nnedi Okorafor and Tomi Adeyemi, 222–35
Magical Negro, The (2004), 187, 202n1; blackness in, 188
Mallan, Kerry, 56
March of Progress (1965), 19–21, 33n3
Marez, Curtis, 133, 139, 140
marginalization, 15, 44, 55, 189, 195
Markus, Andrew, 251
masculinity: Asian, 147–61; non-normative in *Artemis Fowl*, 36–42, 45, 47, 48, 49
McCallum, Robyn, 56
McGregor, Gaile, 144n7
McHale, Brian, 148
mental health, in YASF, 223–24, 227–29
Meyer, Marissa, 55, 58–59, 64–69, 77, 84, 111–38
Mills, Catriona, 243
Minear, Andrea, 167
Mitchell, Jennifer, 64, 126n4
Molin, Paulette F., 144n7
monster, 60, 61–62, 65, 212; in *The Drowned Cities*, 210, 213–15
Monsters of Men (2010), 132–43
Monstrous, the, in *Of Beast and Beauty*, 55, 59–63
Montz, Amy L., 10n2, 240
Moreton-Robinson, Aileen, 241–42, 253n3
Morgensen, Scott Lauria, 140, 143
Morris, Christine, 140
Mulvey, Laura, 28
Murphy, Graham J., 244, 246, 247, 253n7

Nama, Adilifu, 22, 23, 25
neoliberalism, 8, 17, 75–91
neo-Victorianism, 148–49, 151–52, 155–61, 161n2

Ness, Patrick, 131
Newton-Francis, Michelle, 5
New World Orders in Contemporary Children's Literature: Utopian Transformations, 56
noble savage, 140, 144n7, 192, 198

Of Beast and Beauty (2013), allegory, as diversity, 54–64
Okorafor, Nnedi, 187, 202n3
Okorafor-Mbachu, Nnedi, 202n1
Olutola, Sarah, 15
Omi, Michael, 94
Ordover, Nancy, 167, 169, 175, 180
Orleans (2014): biopolitics in, 82; blood in, 78–83
Ostry, Elaine, 239–40
otherness, 6, 205–6, 225; in *Cinder*, 65–69; of racialized bodies, 18–20, 27, 29; in *Zahrah the Windseeker*, 189–92, 197–99
Owen, Christopher, 96, 102
Oziewicz, Marek, 6, 57

Painter, Nell Irvin, 5
Palyku: culture, 238, 239, 244; worldview, 245–49, 252, 253n1
Parable of the Sower series (1993), 234, 235
Paton, William Agnew, 33n5
Pinder, Sherrow O., 5
Polish, Alex, 165
Pomerantz, Shauna, 76–77
Pon, Cindy, 91
postapocalypse, 56, 75, 235
Poznanski, Ursula, 94
Pullman, Philip, 149

queerness: in *Artemis Fowl*, 39–44; in *Cinder*, 64, 126n4; in vampires, 48–49

Raby, Rebecca, 76–77
race, 123, 151, 152, 161, 162n5; cyborg as metaphor for mixed, 114, 118; and diversity, 35–41, 54–70, 204–7; in *The Drowned Cities*, 204–19; mixed, 24; oppression of, 15–32, 93–108, 118–23, 124–25, 166–81, 201
racism, 44–45, 58, 66, 85–89, 93–116, 131–51, 165–77, 181, 189–92, 228; defined, 94; tropes, 18, 45, 187–201; and white privilege,

46–51, 65–66, 86–89, 94–101, 107–8, 113–14, 154–55
rebellion, 15, 16, 24; in the *Divergent* series, 165–66, 172–73; in the *Eleria* trilogy, 95, 105–7; in *The Red Queen*, 24–27, 32; in YA dystopias, 93
Red Queen, The (2015): blood, as racial marker, 15–29; rebellion in, 24–27, 32; representations of race in, 17–18
representations of race, 4, 114, 122, 162n5, 192, 220, 225; in *The Red Queen*, 17–18
Rifkin, Mark, 139, 140, 205
Rix, Zara, 237
Road to Homo Sapiens, The (1965), 19–21, 33n3
Robertson, Roland, 83
Robinson Crusoe, 33n2
Roszak, Suzanne, 168
Roth, Veronica, 165
Russell, Emily, 170

Said, Edward, 18, 19, 33n2, 95, 97, 103, 104
Saul, Ben, 253n9
Sawers, Naarah, 80, 81
Scarlet (2013), 68, 125n2
Schieble, Melissa, 57
Schmeink, Lars, 205
science fiction, 18, 22, 44–45, 93, 111–14, 120, 122–25, 189–92, 222–25; and YASF by black women, 3–10
Seelinger Trites, Roberta, 75, 93, 100
settler colonialism, in *Chaos Walking*, 8, 131–34, 139–44
sexuality, in *Artemis Fowl*, 36, 39–41, 44, 48–49
Shadow Speaker, The (2007), 200–201, 202n8
Sheahan-Bright, Robyn, 250–52
Sheehan, Anna, 54
Sheller, Mimi, 19, 33n5
Shimizu, Celine Parrenas, 152, 158
Ship Breaker (2010), 204–5, 210
Skloot, Rebecca, 227–29
slavery, 22, 24, 46, 119, 133, 138–39, 140
Smith, Sherri L., 75
Smith, William A., 194
Solorzano, Daniel G., 194
speculative fiction, 6, 189–90, 197–201, 222–28, 232–35; black women's, 189, 222–23, 232–33

St. Clair, Nancy, 150
Stephens, John, 56
Stewart, Susan Louise, 112, 124
Strong Hansen, Kathryn, 35
Stubblefield, Anna, 167, 169, 183n4
Subject of Race in American Science Fiction, The, 111, 122–23, 126
Sullivan, Shannon, 133–34, 142, 144n3

Tan, Susan, 204
Teng, Emma Jinhua, 151
Thomas, Ebony Elizabeth, 3, 6, 10, 58, 224
Thompson, Cashawn, 202n7
Tolkien, J. R. R., 50
Tolliver, Stephanie, 10
Trimble, Sarah, 85
tropes, 18, 187–201; changeling, 30; mad scientist, 222; magical negro, 187, 190; nerd girl, 78; race as alien other, 192, 198–99

Uglies series (2005–2007), 93

vampire, Artemis Fowl as, 47–49
Veracini, Lorenzo, 140
violence, racialized, 23; in *Chaos Walking*, 137–38, 139, 141–43

Wahl, Mats, 94
War of the Worlds, The, 19
Warrior, Robert, 252n1
Waugh, Linda R., 144n4
Weaver, Roslyn, 243
Weinkauf, Mary, 140
Wells, H. G., 19
Westerfeld, Scott, 93, 94
whiteness, 22–24, 32; in *Artemis Fowl*, 35–36, 45–51; in fairy tales and dystopias, 54–57, 66, 94, 96, 138; in the Infernal Devices trilogy, 147–61, 162n3, 165–69
white privilege, 46–51, 65–66, 86–89, 94–101, 107–8, 113–14, 154–55, 162n3; defined, 94
whitewashing: in *Allegiant*, 168; in *Chaos Walking*, 131–33; in children's literature, 123; in *The Drowned Cities*, 219; in *Infernal Devices*, 151, 159–61, 162n4; in *Lunar Chronicles*, 138–39
Who Fears Death (2010), 226, 234–35

Winant, Howard, 94
Winter (2015), 68, 70n4, 125n2, 126n6

Yosso, Tara J., 194
Young, Adrian Valdez, 151
Young, Helen, 46, 50, 138
young adult literature, 3–10, 15–16, 32, 54, 57, 81, 237–40; dystopias in, 15–32, 54–69, 75–91, 94
young adult speculative fiction (YASF), lack of diversity in, 3–4, 10, 33n1, 189, 224
Yu Burnett, Joshua, 187

Zahrah the Windseeker (2004), 18, 187; otherness in, 189–92, 197–99
Zallinger, Rudolph Franz, 19–21
Zamora, Lois Parkinson, 16, 24
Zipes, Jack, 57

www.ingramcontent.com/pod-product-compliance
Lightning Source LLC
Chambersburg PA
CBHW030613230426
43661CB00053B/1967